CROSS-CULTURAL TOPICS IN PSYCHOLOGY

CROSS-CULTURAL TOPICS IN PSYCHOLOGY

2nd Edition

Edited by LEONORE LOEB ADLER
and UWE P. GIELEN

Foreword by Florence L. Denmark

PRAEGER

Westport, Connecticut
London

Library of Congress Cataloging-in-Publication Data

Cross-cultural topics in psychology / edited by Leonore Loeb Adler and Uwe P. Gielen ;
foreword by Florence L. Denmark.
    p. cm.
    Includes bibliographical references and index.
    ISBN 0–275–96972–X (alk. paper)—ISBN 0–275–96973–8 (pbk. : alk. paper)
    1. Ethnopsychology. 2. Psychology. I. Adler, Leonore Loeb. II. Gielen, Uwe P.
GN502.C77 2001
155.8—dc21   00–032379

British Library Cataloguing in Publication Data is available.

Library of Congress Catalog Card Number: 00–032379
ISBN: 0–275–96972–X
     0–275–96973–8 (pbk)

First published in 2001

Praeger Publishers, 88 Post Road West, Westport, CT 06881
An imprint of Greenwood Publishing Group, Inc.
www.praeger.com

Printed in the United States of America

The paper used in this book complies with the
Permanent Paper Standard issued by the National
Information Standards Organization (Z39.48–1984).

10 9 8 7 6 5 4 3 2 1

This book is dedicated to our siblings, to Margo, Ute, Dina, and Anka, who always supported our ideas and activities with candor.

With great sincerity,
Leonore and Uwe

Contents

Foreword

Florence L. Denmark

Psychology is a science that seeks to explain the fundamental questions regarding human thought and behavior. This is a broad and far-reaching goal. The majority of human psychological research today is focused solely on the thought and behavior patterns of Americans. While this research is meaningful, it certainly does not provide an adequate explanation for all human thoughts and behaviors. Restricting the scope of research to the population in the United States of America inherently limits the capability of the results to provide universal explanations. This consequence is a tremendous detriment to the discipline and highlights the overwhelming need to expand the breadth of research to include individuals from other countries across the globe.

Psychologists have long debated whether human behavior is caused by nature, the genetic makeup of individuals, or by nurture—the environment in which individuals are reared. Culture is one of the most pervasive elements of a person's nurture because it represents the overarching principles that shape a society, which will in turn influence upbringing. The study of cross-cultural psychology may play a critical role in resolving specific issues within the nature-nurture debate. Reminiscent of a controlled experiment, individuals living in different countries share the same basic biological composition, but differ in respect to the environmental influences impinging on them. Investigating precisely how their behavior is different is thus a function of cultural difference. We can see more clearly the areas of behavior in which nurture is dominant.

Thus, cross-cultural psychology provides a glimpse of both similarities and differences in human nature. Research is guided by a search for the universal explanations underlying behavior, and one common goal is to synthesize findings into a single cohesive theory. However, as is often the case, thorough examinations of human behavior often point to areas of difference, and it is equally important to draw conclusions based on these distinctions. Cross-cultural psychology draws its theoretical strengths from working within this framework of similarities and differences.

The importance of cross-cultural psychology can be demonstrated more clearly by drawing an analogy to a basic area in psychological research—the controlled laboratory experiment. When psychologists undertake a systematic study of human behavior, they must choose a sample of participants for examination. In most instances, the researchers are seeking broad explanations for human behaviors that are generalizable and can be applied beyond the laboratory setting to a variety of people. Thus, it is imperative that this sample population include a diversity of individuals. If an experiment utilized African American males ages 18 to 25 as participants, then the subsequent conclusions would pertain to this very specific segment of the population only. Indisputably, the results of this study cannot be applied to males from other age brackets, males from other ethnic groups, or females. This consequence is not inherently problematic; perhaps the researcher's endeavors were carefully directed toward this select group. However, if the researcher is attempting to construct a broad theory of human behavior, then a larger, more diverse sample is required. It logically flows from this example that it is impossible to obtain a complete understanding of human behavior by narrowing perspective to include individuals from only one cultural background.

Incorporating cultural diversity into psychological experiments is only one area in which cross-cultural studies can expand knowledge. Of equal importance is the need to examine the ideas and theories that originate in countries outside of the United States. Psychologists do not reside solely within the confines of Western culture; they are a breed of professionals who inhabit all corners of the world. Anyone who attends an international psychology conference realizes that valuable contributions to research and practice are derived from individuals residing in countries besides the United States. In fact, one of the main reasons to organize conferences is precisely reflective of this relationship. These meetings provide an appropriate setting to convene people from all over the world to compare and contrast their thoughts and beliefs. In a similar fashion, this volume of *Cross-Cultural Topics in Psychology* assembles varied perspectives and explores the many applications of cultural studies on traditional psychological theory. Just as each conference participant contributes insights gained through personal research and experience, each chapter of this book is infused with insights that are gleaned from cross-cultural comparisons. The science of psychology benefits tremendously from this exchange of information and would be incomplete in its absence. Underlying this collection is the belief that we must not be so narrow-minded as to lose sight of the significance of cultural relativism and of the power of diversity to enrich psychological theory and practice. The publication of this volume is a significant achievement toward the goal of widespread dissemination of a psychology that is sensitive to multiculturalism.

I am extremely pleased to introduce the second edition of *Cross-Cultural Topics in Psychology*, a highly valuable resource and an important contribution to the ever-expanding field of psychology. Leonore Loeb Adler and Uwe P. Gielen have compiled a text of unparalleled scope, drawing from both traditional topics in the discipline of psychology and from areas inextricably linked to multiculturalism. Some chapters provide a thorough reexamination of fundamental psychological subjects, such as personality, development, and psychopathology, by infusing them with a cross-cultural perspective. Other chapters consider topics that naturally lend themselves to inspection through cross-cultural lenses, such as immigration and multinational enterprises. These editors are renowned for their expertise in cross-cultural psychology, and in this volume they have assembled an insightful collection of psychological theories that are sensitive to cultural relativity. A quick review of current literature will reveal the dearth of textbooks on multicultural psychology, and consequently, it is impossible to overstate the necessity for a resource of this kind.

I must also highlight the overwhelming need to introduce cultural studies into the academic discipline of psychology. Specifically, it is important to expose psychology students at both the undergraduate and graduate levels to a global perspective so that they may gain an appreciation for the influence of culture and not be blinded by the American viewpoint that currently dominates their curriculum. The lack of cross-cultural course offerings is certainly a void in any complete education in psychology. Further, I enthusiastically recommend this second volume of *Cross-Cultural Topics in Psychology* as an excellent learning tool to perfectly complement any instruction in psychology.

Finally, understanding other cultures can allow us to better appreciate global concerns, ensuring us to work in unison toward solutions of international problems. The contributions of psychology from other nations can also accrue to a deeper and broader-based understanding of ourselves. As experts in human behavior, psychologists can influence other disciplines and serve as leaders in the academic arena, adopting a wider worldview that is beneficial to all.

I

History and Methods
of Cross-Cultural Studies

1

Introduction to Cross-Cultural Psychology

David Yau-Fai Ho and Madalina Wu

Cross-cultural psychology has a long past, but only a short history. Psychologists have had a long-standing interest in the impact of cultures on individuals. For instance, how do child-rearing practices influence personality formation in various cultures? Do speakers of different languages have different patterns of thought, as claimed by the Whorfian hypothesis? Is the Oedipal complex universal? As an organized intellectual discipline, however, cross-cultural psychology is no more than two or three decades old. A developmental milestone was the establishment of the International Association for Cross-Cultural Psychology in 1972, when its inaugural meeting was held in Hong Kong.

Today, cross-cultural psychology is firmly established as a psychological science. Yet most students of psychology probably complete their studies, even at the graduate level, without coming into formal contact with cross-cultural psychology. More seriously, many psychologists still regard it as peripheral to the concerns of mainstream psychology. The reason is that psychology has always aspired to be a universal science, to be achieved through the study of individuals, without reference to cultural contexts. It aims to discover "objective," universal psychological principles. Ideally, these principles, like those in physics, should be invariant through time and space. For instance, the principles of conditioning apply at any time, at any place—and, it might be added, to dogs and humans alike. There is, presumably, nothing "cross-cultural" about conditioning or other psychological "facts," such as maturation and individual differences. The same assumptions of regularity or lawfulness governing behavior would apply regardless of historical and cultural context. True enough, people behave differently in different cultures, but that is of central concern to cultural anthropology, not psychology.

Our contention is that no serious psychologist can remain indifferent to and ignorant of cross-cultural psychology. Psychology is distinct from the physical sciences in that the agent of investigation is also the object being investigated: It is the study of human beings by human beings. It studies not only human behavior but also conceptions about human behavior, including our own—that is, the question of how psychological knowledge, including that about the self, is generated. Culture enters into the generation of psychological knowledge because of its pervasive influence on both behavior and conceptions of behavior. As we shall see, cross-cultural psychology is much more than the intellectual luxury of studying people's oddities in exotic cultures. It challenges mainstream psychology to a self-examination and to make good its claim of being a universal science.

CROSS-CULTURAL PSYCHOLOGY DEFINED

Cross-cultural psychology is the scientific study of human behavior and mental processes, including both their variability and invariance, under diverse cultural conditions. Its primary aims are to investigate (a) systematic relations between behavioral variables and ethnic-cultural variables, and (b) generalizations of psychological principles.

This definition embodies a number of important notions. First, cross-cultural psychology is a science, by virtue of the scientific principles and methods it employs. We may go as far as to say that cross-cultural psychology owes its gain in stature largely to its methodological contributions to psychological science.

Second, unlike cultural anthropology, cross-cultural psychology is not primarily concerned with the comparative study of cultures per se, that is, the enduring characteristics that mark a culture apart from other cultures. It is still focused on the individual and thus retains its identity as a psychological science. The units of comparison are not modal or normative patterns at the collective or population level but are the psychological functioning of individuals across cultures. However, it insists on adopting a perspective of crucial significance: The individual is not regarded as an abstract entity to be studied without reference to culture; accordingly, the unit of analysis is now the individual-in-a-cultural-context.

Third, as in general psychology, included in the scope of investigation are both observable behavior and mental processes that cannot be directly observed but must be inferred from behavioral or physiological observations. Animal behavior is excluded, presumably because culture is unique to humans. More important, the scope of investigation is explicitly enlarged to include, ideally, the total range of human behavior and mental processes under all known cultural conditions. Virtually nothing about life's secrets in diverse cultures is left untouched—not even unusual behavior under extreme cultural conditions. The enlarged range of observations forms the foundation for attaining the two stated aims.

Fourth, by definition, a comparative framework is always operative. Both differences and similarities in psychological and social functioning across ethnic-cultural boundaries are studied. Strictly speaking, however, cross-ethnic and cross-national comparisons do not qualify as cross-cultural research, unless relevant cultural variables have been included.

Comparison is thus the hallmark of cross-cultural psychology. It should be noted, though, that all scientific investigation entails comparison. The significance of a phenomenon can be gauged only against a background of patterns, regularities, or uniformities established after prolonged observation. Cross-cultural psychology goes to an extreme in delineating conditions under which legitimate, systematic comparisons across cultures can be made. It pays special attention to questions of comparability of samples and equivalence of measures used in different cultural contexts. Probably it is in answering these questions that its methodological contributions will be most strongly felt.

THE STRENGTHS AND PROMISES OF
CROSS-CULTURAL PSYCHOLOGY

Cross-cultural research is far more ambitious than merely cataloging behavioral differences across ethnic-cultural groups. The scope of investigation is enlarged, giving substance to the claim that psychology is a universal science of human behavior. We are compelled to recognize the inadequacy of basing our knowledge on research conducted within only one culture or under a limited range of cultural conditions. We are thus challenged to examine the completeness of psychology as a body of knowledge about human beings. Ideally, the scope of investigation should be panhuman— that is, inclusive of the entire range of human behavior under all known cultural conditions.

Obvious advantages follow from conducting research in diverse cultural conditions. The range of cultural variables is increased, especially if extreme or unusual cultural environments are included. The likely result would be a corresponding increase in the range of observed behaviors. Consequently, we lay a more solid empirical foundation upon which theories may be constructed.

Let us consider, for instance, the advantage of increasing the range of cultural variables in estimating the heritability of the intelligence quotient (IQ)—a research problem that continues to be hotly debated. Heritability is a statistical concept derived from genetics. A coefficient of heritability, which ranges from 0.00 to 1.00, tells us the percentage of variance accounted for by genetic factors. Many investigators have put the value of the heritability coefficient for human ability or achievement around .80, which is quite high. But is this a fair estimate? Research on the heritability of the IQ has been plagued by a host of methodological problems. Here we shall consider only one: the sampling of populations. Most of the research has been conducted in Euro-American societies. Suppose we extend the sampling to the entire universe of populations, including those living under Stone Age conditions. (This requires the construction of IQ tests that have panhuman applicability—in actuality, far from being achieved.) The range of environmental variables would be immensely increased. Consequently, in all likelihood, a much lower heritability coefficient would be obtained. The point is that a finding about heritability is applicable only to the population where the study is made. Furthermore, if the environmental characteristics of the population change over time, it is applicable only to the generation studied. In sum, the finding is subject to both spatial and temporal limitations.

We can also test the generality of psychological laws or principles. For example, are Piaget's stages of intellectual development invariant across cultures? And Kohlberg's stages of moral development? The degree of generality may be assessed by their range of applicability, that is, by delineating the cultural conditions under which they remain valid or become invalid. Suppose we have a principle stating that there is a specific pattern of relations among several variables. We find that the pattern of relations is highly similar across the cultures studied. It would be reasonable to conclude that the principle tested has a high degree of generality.

Panhuman variability and invariance in psychological functioning can be established with confidence only when observations have been made under a sufficiently wide range of cultural conditions. Principles presumed to have panhuman validity, that is, invariance across all known cultural conditions, are universal generalizations. They are especially significant because the quest for universal principles has been a long-standing aim of psychological science. Cross-cultural psychology participates in this quest by helping to distinguish universal concepts from emic impostors. In practice, however, panhuman validity is difficult to demonstrate. What is required is that no major exception is found in a sizable number of diverse cultures investigated.

Another promise of cross-cultural research stems from its inclusion of and emphasis given to ethnic-cultural variables, in addition to the usual variables of psychological functioning. Investigating systematic relations between these two classes of variables is now brought into the research agenda. These relations may be causal or merely correlational. If causal relations are entailed, usually psychological variables are regarded as the effects (or dependent variables), and cultural variables as the causes (or independent variables). The reason is that, traditionally, behavioral scientists are interested in how culture shapes psychological functioning. However, there is no intrinsic reason why this has to be so. A fertile area of investigation attracts the attention

of psychologists and cultural anthropologists alike: How does the psychological and social functioning of individuals collectively affect cultural processes and translate into cultural change? Boyer (1994), for example, has
explored the relation between cognitive constraints and the recurrence of
certain features of religious representations across a wide range of cultures.

If our research agenda were successfully followed, cross-cultural psychology would attain the status of a mature science. The promise is no less than
a coherent body of knowledge about behavior-culture interactions involving
both individual and collective phenomena. These interactions are of unsur-
passed significance in behavioral science because they tell the story of how
human character and culture create each other. If culture is defined as that
part of the environment created by human beings, then we create environments that, in turn, make us human. In short, human beings are both the
creators and the products of culture.

ANALYTIC CONCEPTS USED IN CROSS-CULTURAL PSYCHOLOGY

Cross-cultural psychologists have introduced three important terms that
serve as analytic concepts: *emics, etics,* and *theorics.* Emics are culture-specific
concepts; they apply in a particular culture, and no a priori claim is made
that they apply in another. The emic approach aims to describe and interpret
behavior in terms that are meaningful to members of a particular culture.
Etics are culture-invariant concepts or universals; or, if not entirely universal, they apply to more than one culture—many more. They may be used
to analyze emic phenomena. The etic approach aims to make valid cross-
cultural comparisons and is characterized by the discovery of true universals
in different cultures. Etics that are assumed, but have not been demonstrated, to be true universals have been called imposed etics (Berry, 1969,
p. 124) or pseudoetics (Triandis, Malpass, & Davidson, 1972, p. 6). Such
etics are said to be usually only Euro-American emics indiscriminately, even
ethnocentrically, imposed on the interpretation of behavior in other cultures. A true etic, in contrast, is empirically and theoretically derived from
the common features of a phenomenon under investigation in different cultures. Berry (1969, p. 124) called this a derived etic. At an even higher level
of analysis, general principles are formulated to explain or account for systematic variation as well as invariance in human behavior across cultures.
Naroll (1971a) proposed that the term *theorics* be applied to this level of
analysis. Berry (1980, p. 13) defined theorics as "theoretical concepts employed by social scientists to interpret and account for emic variation and
etic constancies."

An example may be used to illustrate the meanings of emics and etics.
The term *face,* which is Chinese in origin, may be cited as an example of
emics. An emic approach would investigate face behavior in Chinese society,

as perceived by Chinese people. It may be argued, however, that the concept of face has universal applicability. In terms of the emic-etic distinction, we would say that the emic conceptualization of what constitutes face and the rules governing face behavior may vary considerably across cultures; however, inasmuch as the concern for face is culturally invariant, the concept of face is an etic. The reader may also find it a challenging intellectual exercise to think of some examples of theorics. It may be observed that the term *theorics* is itself a theoric. More interesting is to note that the term *emics* is not an emic, and the term *etics* is not an etic; both are indeed theorics, abstract constructs used to interpret and explain culture-specific and universal phenomena, respectively.

The emic and the etic approaches may be combined in cross-cultural research. An example is the study of cross-cultural similarities and differences in conceptions of human nature by Oerter, Oerter, Agostiani, Kim, and Wibowo (1996). Methodologically, it has been proposed that the combined emic-etic approach consists of three stages of inquiry: "Initially, the researcher identifies an etic construct that appears to have universal status. Secondly, emic ways of measuring this construct are developed and validated. Finally, the *emically defined* construct can be used in making cross-cultural comparisons" (Davidson, Jaccard, Triandis, Morales, & Díaz-Guerrero, 1976, p. 2, italics added). An objection may be raised, however. In itself, to begin by identifying an etic construct calls for an ethnocentric or, more precisely, a culturocentric judgment. It would be better to begin with no presuppositions about universals; instead, universals are to be discovered. Emics pertaining to a domain of behavior from different cultures are first gathered and examined; among these, emics that appear to be similar across cultures suggest the existence of a universal.

An approach without presuppositions has been described by Ho (1988, pp. 56–62). It appears to be well suited to the emic level of investigation, particularly during the initial stages. One begins with no preconceptions, no hypotheses, and no claim to any foreknowledge. One does not even entertain notions of the procedures to be followed, what one is searching for, or even the goals to be reached. There is only a global, undifferentiated notion of the subject matter to be investigated, which is subject to change as one proceeds. In fact, one does not even presume to know what questions should be asked, let alone the answers; that is, one admits not only that one does not know but also that one does not know what one needs to know. One proceeds, that is, as if one were in a state of total ignorance. With such an intellectual attitude, the researcher attends to the phenomena as they appear, without interpretation, as a starting point. The raw data consist of what people say and do, as well as the labels and conceptual schemes they use to interpret behavior. The researcher is then guided by the data obtained to discover what concepts need to be clarified, what the relevant variables are, and what measures can be suitably used. Further investigations, leading to reformulations, may be necessary before arriving at a formal research plan.

A cross-cultural psychology that relies solely or primarily on Euro-American concepts cannot be expected to achieve its stated aims. Unfortunately, however, a perusal of the literature reveals a paucity of theorizing with the use of concepts that are non-Western in origin. We would argue that cultures should be treated not only as targets of investigation but also as sources of intellectual nourishment. Concepts from each culture may be regarded as potentially useful, both as emics for interpreting behavior native to that culture and as alien concepts for interpreting behavior in another. We need to hold no prejudice against alien concepts as necessarily ethnocentric. On the contrary, borrowing alien concepts is in the spirit of cultural cross-fertilization and may result in a creative synthesis of native and alien ideas. Enriquez (1993), for example, advocates using the cross-indigenous method that calls for a multilanguage-multiculture approach. In the same spirit, Ho (1988, pp. 62–64) argues that the richness of Asian concepts (e.g., face), pregnant with psychological and sociological meanings, may be more fully exploited to provide fresh ammunition for innovation in the behavioral sciences.

CONCEPTUAL AND METHODOLOGICAL ISSUES

Using the concept of culture as an explanatory construct is full of intellectual traps. We shall attempt to answer three broad questions. First, how can the concept of culture be used to explain psychological phenomena in a meaningful way? Second, how can the units of culture be defined, and what are the difficulties involved? Third, how can cultural variables be measured?

Culture as an Explanatory Construct

How do we interpret empirically established differences in behavior between cultural groups? There is a temptation to explain, all too readily, the group differences on the basis of cultural differences. It would be wise to resist this temptation and to reflect on the intellectual traps of invoking the concept of culture as an explanatory construct. To begin with, very often cross-cultural or cross-ethnic differences decrease or even disappear when socioeconomic class is controlled. For example, Cashmore and Goodnow (1986) found that differences in parental values between Anglo-Australian and Italian parents in Australia decreased when indicators of socioeconomic status were taken into account. Lambert (1987) reported a similar finding in a study of child-rearing values in ten countries. Now suppose we systematically control for other potentially relevant factors, such as age, sex, and

intelligence as well. Differences that survive elimination may then be attributed to cultural differences. In effect, culture is treated as a residual variable.
It explains the yet unexplained portion of the between-group variance. But
has it now become a wastepaper-basket construct—a victim of having been
invoked to explain too much?

In its crudest form, a simplistic yet overinclusive cultural explanation reduces to: People in Culture A behave differently from people in Culture B,
because Culture A is different from Culture B. For example, if Chinese are
found to be more authoritarian than Americans, it is because Chinese culture
is presumed to be more authoritarian than American culture. But what has
been explained? A fuller explanation would trace the difference in authoritarianism, a personality variable, to differences in socialization; in turn, differences in socialization could be traced to specific differences in cultural
values, which must then be identified. Available evidence suggests that, in
Chinese culture, attitudes toward filial piety may indeed be linked to psychological attributes such as authoritarian moralism and cognitive conser-
vatism (Ho, 1996). The Confucian ethic of filial piety is, of course, markedly
different from the corresponding American ethic governing intergenera-
tional relationships.

Thus, to revitalize explanatory potency of the culture concept, we need
to go beyond global explanations. A more satisfactory account of cultural
effects requires conceptual linkages between culture and psychological functioning. We need to identify specific features of culture that can explain
cross-cultural variances as well as constancies (Segall, 1984). One example
of this type of approach is to focus on specific cultural practices (e.g., who
sleeps with whom within the family) in studying the cultural environment
that shapes child development (Shweder, Jensen, & Goldstein, 1995). The
concept of internalization is relevant here. It deals with the crucial question:
How do cultural influences originally external to the individual transform
into psychological forces operating within the individual? We need to gain
a knowledge of how cultural differences translate into differences in the
individual's psychological experience. In turn, the causal links between individual experience and personality formation—a classic psychological problem—will have to be investigated.

The Boundary Problem in Unit Definition

The term *cross-cultural* itself predisposes us to think in spatial terms: cultural groups located in different countries or geographical settings. But attempts to delineate boundaries between groups have proved to be anything
but simple (Ho, 1995). Regrettably, the literature of cross-cultural research
is replete with studies that classify individuals arbitrarily according to the
national, ethnic, or racial group to which they belong. Common practice is,
however, a poor guide to sound research. National or ethnic group mem-

bership does not necessarily correspond to cultural group membership. Multicultural or multiethnic groups may live in the same country, and some ethnic groups living in different countries share the same culture; also, cultural or subcultural diversity may be found within ethnic groups, and different ethnic groups may share elements of the same culture. Cross-cultural studies are, therefore, not to be confused with cross-national or cross-ethnic studies. Yet the comparative nature of cross-cultural research demands that we deal with the problem of defining what constitutes a unit of culture.

issue

In attempting to define such a unit, we confront the boundary problem. A cultural group is supposed to refer to a group of individuals who share a common culture. But what is "common," and what marks a culture apart from other cultures? It is misleading to speak of, for instance, the Indian culture as if it were a single monolithic entity, when in fact India is so rich in ethnic, linguistic, and religious diversity. This brings us to the question of how cultural boundaries may be delineated. Time, place, and language are obviously three differentiating factors of basic importance. In anthropology, Naroll (1970) employs the concept of *cultunit*, which encompasses "people who are domestic speakers of a common district dialect language and who belong either to the same state or the same contact group" (p. 248). The double-language boundary method is proposed to establish language boundaries (Naroll, 1971b). Instead of trying to establish one boundary between two language communities, we proceed in two directions: from language A to language B, and from language B to language A. If a boundary is established in both directions, that is, if mutual unintelligibility is indeed found, we may treat the two language communities as two cultunits.

For cross-cultural research, classification based on well-defined cultural units is an improvement over that based on national or ethnic group membership. That is, however, merely a first step. Accelerated changes in the modern world compel us to take cognizance of the dynamic nature of culture. The temporal dimension has now assumed added importance in the boundary problem. Unfortunately, cross-cultural researchers have paid more attention to synchronic studies (i.e., those of a process at one point in time) than to diachronic studies (i.e., those of a process as it changes over time). Typically, culture is treated as a static variable, as if it were frozen in time (Ho, 1995). Members of the same cultural group are lumped together, regardless of age or generational differences. This practice runs into serious difficulties when a culture is undergoing rapid changes.

In addition, when cultures come into contact with each other, often in conflict, acculturation results. This is a process—which may be bidirectional—whereby members of a cultural group learn and assume the behavior patterns of another cultural group to which they have been exposed. It may also lead to biculturalism or even multiculturalism, in which individuals are exposed and enculturated to more than one culture. These phenomena have not received the attention they deserve, but they do pose intellectual challenges to cross-cultural psychology. For instance, does it make sense at all to speak of cultural boundaries within the bicultural or multicultural mind?

Toward the Multidimensional Measurement of Cultural Variables

Classification is only one of the many steps of scientific inquiry; and the definition of cultural units, even if satisfactorily achieved, is only a step toward mature cross-cultural research. Unfortunately, in too many research studies, culture is still treated as a nominal variable: That is, individuals are assigned into groups on the basis of their cultural group membership. Observed group differences in behavior are then explained by reference to cultural differences between the assigned groups. Note that the behavioral differences are obtained empirical results, but the cultural differences are presumed on the basis of a prior knowledge of the cultures compared.

An approach that reduces culture to the status of a nominal variable is inherently limited. First, categorical assignment presumes that each subject belongs to one, and only one, cultural unit. This presumption is untenable in the case of bicultural or multicultural individuals. Second, subcultural variations arising from potent factors such as age, sex, and socioeconomic class are ignored. More fundamentally, within-group individual differences in enculturation, and hence in the extent to which culture is internalized, cannot be dealt with. Cultural differences are thus reduced to differences in kind, not in degree. Third, culture is treated as a unidimensional variable; the multidimensional nature of cultural processes (e.g., language acquisition, socialization, and cultural cognition) is not addressed.

As social psychologists know, the group to which an individual belongs is not necessarily the same as the reference group with which the individual identifies. Cultural group membership per se, it should be pointed out, is not a psychological variable, but internalized culture, cultural identification, and cultural orientation are—just as age, sex, and socioeconomic class are not, in themselves, psychological variables, but psychological maturity, gender, and class identification are. Internalized culture may be defined as the cultural influences operating within the individual that shape (not determine) personality formation and various aspects of psychological functioning (Ho, 1995). The concept of cultural identification acknowledges that individuals may differ in the extent to which they identify with the cultural traditions of their group. It enables us to appreciate how there may be more similarity among members of comparable socioeconomic statuses across groups than among members of different socioeconomic statuses within the same group. And the concept of cultural orientation reaffirms a measure of autonomy in one's preference for various cultural patterns, perhaps even in articulating one's own transcultural value system. These concepts liberate us from the rigidity of looking at people solely in terms of their cultural group membership.

A great deal more work will have to be done to develop multidimensional, quantitative measures of cultural variables. Three main classes of cultural variables are of special interest to cross-cultural psychology: (1) *exposure*, the quality and quantity of how an individual is actually exposed to the external culture (e.g., child-rearing practices); (2) *enculturation*, the process of how an individual learns from, adapts to, and is influenced by the culture to which he or she is exposed, and (3) *internalized culture*, a consequence of enculturation. Note that exposure refers to cultural processes external to the individual, in itself without reference to psychological functioning. In contrast, enculturation and internalized culture pertain at once to both external culture and internal psychological functioning, thus serving as conceptual links between these two domains.

The psychological approach to the study of cultural processes, it is now clear, differs from the anthropological. Psychologists certainly need to be better informed of the work of cultural anthropologists. They are also equipped to make a distinctive contribution in their own right. The psychological conception of culture is not the culture external to the individual but the cultural internalized as a result of enculturation within the individual. Introducing the concept of internalized culture opens the door to a new territory of thought. Interest is now focused on how culture is experienced and internalized by the individual. Thus the psychological conception gives full recognition to individual differences in cultural processes. Given their penchant for measurement, psychologists are in a position to show how such processes can be measured, a necessary step for gaining fuller psychological knowledge.

NOTE

The authors gratefully acknowledge the financial support they received from the Committee on Research and Conference Grants, University of Hong Kong, in the revision of this chapter.

2

Cross-Cultural Psychology in Historical Perspective

John D. Hogan and Bradley D. Sussner

Cross-cultural psychology is a relatively new discipline, but one whose time has come. Some of the most basic issues in scientific psychology have a limited empirical backbone without a knowledge of behavioral differences across cultures (e.g., the nature-nurture controversy). Even widely accepted theories of development, most of which purport to have universal explanatory power (e.g., the theories of Jean Piaget and Lawrence Kohlberg) remain unfinished until their validity is confirmed through cross-cultural observations. Cross-cultural psychology reminds us that "The scientist, no less than the most unsophisticated layperson who knows only his or her own society, becomes prey to ethnocentric judgments" (Segall, 1979, pp. 22–23).

Cross-cultural research provides the opportunity to explore psychological issues that otherwise would be difficult to explore. How do important variables manifest themselves when their contexts are different? How universal are "universal" laws of psychology? What can be learned from "natural" experiments that cannot be reproduced in the laboratory? (Triandis, Malpass, & Davidson, 1973).

These are not easy questions for the traditional experimental psychologist. In fact, they are almost impossible to answer by the old methods. The conventionally trained psychologist is raised in a tradition that places the laboratory at the core of science and touts the most exquisite controls as a goal. The new experimental psychologist must be willing to go beyond these historical emphases and adapt to broader, often less controlled, techniques.

To psychology's credit, it has shown a willingness to respond to the challenge, although its response has been tardy and far from unanimous. Now, it is possible to ask less naive questions of the data, and the importance of these questions has not gone unnoticed. The amount of cross-cultural research published in recent decades has become massive (Adler, 1977; Brislin, 1993). Klineberg (quoted in Segall, 1979, p. v) says that now "the significant material would fill a fair-sized library, with contributions by psychologists from many different countries." But how did cross-cultural psychology reach this point?

THE BEGINNINGS

Jahoda (1977) and Klineberg (1980), in two surveys of cross-cultural psychology, describe the development of the discipline, with sources selected from ancient times through the mid-1970s. Klineberg, in particular, notes that many of the earliest writings display an interest in cross-cultural issues. This is true for a variety of fields, from history to art and philosophy, regardless of the label under which the writings were produced.

At its most basic level, cross-cultural research had its inception when one group, with certain folkways and language, began to observe another group, with somewhat different characteristics. When the observations became part of a record, usually with a view to promoting the superiority of one of the groups, the history of cross-cultural psychology began. There are many early examples.

For instance, Hecataeus of Miletus, a Greek historian who lived between 600 B.C. and 500 B.C., is reported to have written two books in which he described the inhabitants of Europe and Asia (Price-Williams, 1975). During the fifth century B.C., Herodotus wrote extensively about the differences between Greek and Egyptian culture (Baldry, 1965). Tacitus, the Roman historian who lived during the first century A.D., wrote about the differences between the behavior of the Germanic tribes and the citizens of Rome (Barnouw, 1963).

Many of the first examples of work in this area were attempts to explain the origins and evolution of cultural differences. For instance, Thucydides, the Greek historian who lived during the fifth century B.C., attempted to explain the evolution of cultural differences by hypothesizing that during earlier generations all cultures possessed essentially the same characteristics. He suggested that the observable differences that developed between groups of people were largely superficial (Jahoda, 1993). Around this same time period, Hippocrates surmised that any differences in the character of various cultures were the result of differences in climate or the institutions that exist in each society. Posidonius, a Syrian who lived in Greece during the first century B.C., cited the same causes for the differences in the physical characteristics and moral character of people throughout the world (Baldry, 1965). He suggested that the unchecked impulsive character of the Nordics could be subdued by a southward migration to a warmer climate. Explanations for cultural differences were extended to the heavens by Ptolemaeus, an astronomer, mathematician, and geographer who lived in Egypt during the second century A.D. He argued that differences in the mental and cultural states of people of various cultures were due to astronomical forces, a view that had a profound influence on cross-cultural thinking for generations (Jahoda, 1993).

Much of the early work in cross-cultural issues, however, was judgmental as well as descriptive. For instance, in the fifth century B.C., the Greek playwright Euripides portrayed foreigners as lacking in morals and personal restraint. Aristotle, who lived during the fourth century B.C., extended previous claims of Greek superiority by citing the incomparable contributions of populations living around the border of the Mediterranean Sea (Klineberg, 1980). The Tunisian scholar Ibn Khaldun (1332–1406) is often cited for his conclusion, based on a survey, regarding the superiority of his own people. These ancient claims of superiority found later expression in the belief that certain groups were less developed than others, but possessed the capability to advance in the direction of modern civilization.

Despite all these early observations, it should be noted that a history of remarks aimed at group differences does not constitute a field of study. The remarks remain largely random comments until organized in some systematic way. This systematization occurred only in recent times as scholars attempted to document more fully the range of human behavior across cultures.

In addition, it should be remembered that psychology itself did not emerge as a separate area of scientific study until the latter part of the nineteenth century, when it found its first clear expression in Germany. Some have argued that it was during that same period, also in Germany, that the first formal glimmerings of cross-cultural psychology (as a subdiscipline of social psychology) were seen.

THE EMERGING DISCIPLINE

Segall (1979) states unequivocally that the roots of social psychology lie in the nineteenth century, nourished mostly in Germany by such works as J. F. Herbart's *Lehrbuch zur Psychologie* (1816). Herbart argued that the individual could be understood only in a social context and that psychology must embrace the methods of science to pursue the systematic description of ethnic groups.

In 1860, the publication of a journal began that embodied a number of Herbart's ideas: *Zeitschrift fur Völkerpsychologie und Sprachwissenschaft* (Journal of Folk Psychology and Language Science). The journal, a scholarly work, was founded and edited by Lazarus and Steinthal and was published for thirty years. The journal had a broad range of articles, which included group behavior, the psychology of culture, comparative studies, and a special emphasis on language.

Another German, Wilhelm Wundt, best remembered as the founder of experimental psychology, devoted many years to writing about customs, myths, and the relationship between a language and its people. Wundt published his *Völkerpsychologie* (Folk Psychology) in a series of ten volumes over a period of 20 years (1900–1920). As Adler (1989) has pointed out, these volumes do not constitute a cross-cultural treatise, as is sometimes believed, nor is their title properly translated into English as "Folk Psychology." It was concerned instead with a broad range of issues including language, art, myths, and morals. Perhaps its greatest contribution was to recognize the two sides of the "new" psychology—the social as well as the experimental. Nonetheless, Adler describes the work as Wundt's "mega-contribution to the discipline." Herbart and Wundt's contributions to social psychology are now rarely mentioned, except in a historical context.

Whereas anthropologists and sociologists seemed willing to look to the findings of psychology, many psychologists remained oblivious to data outside their limited subfields. Consequently, the earliest experiments in cross-cultural psychology were, for the most part, conducted not by psychologists but by anthropologists using psychological techniques. Because of the difference in their background, the data gathering techniques and interpretation of these workers often differed from that of the traditional psychologist. For example, many of the early anthropological/psychological researchers questioned the emphasis on objective methods and the quantification of data, considering such procedures to be of doubtful utility. Although it is clear that many events anticipated the development of cross-cultural psychology as a part of social psychology, and that several choices could be made in identifying its formal introduction, "most psychologists now date the beginning of social psychology from 1908. That year saw the almost simultaneous publication of two textbooks with 'social psychology' in their titles, one by the psychologist William McDougall (1908) and the other by the sociologist E. A. Ross (1908)" (Segall, 1979, p. 29).

The first textbook in social psychology to be written from a comparative, cross-cultural approach was *Social Psychology*, by Otto Klineberg, and it did not appear until several decades later (Klineberg, 1940). Using examples from various cultures around the world, Klineberg highlighted the diversity of human behavior and encouraged others to question any claim regarding the universality of psychological concepts. In addition, Klineberg criticized the concept of biological determinism that had been used to support the belief in the inferiority of non-Western peoples (Segall, Dasen, Berry, & Poortinga, 1990).

FRENCH AND BRITISH INFLUENCES

René Descartes (1596–1650) reiterated the suggestions of Hippocrates and others through his belief in the mechanistic view of humankind. Although he acknowledged that certain basic concepts, such as perfection, unity, infinity, and the geometrical axioms, were common to all people, he suggested that differences in character across cultures were the result of environmental influences (Jahoda, 1993). In fact, he argued that any child reared from infancy until adulthood would develop the character common to the people of that society regardless of the racial stock of the child's ancestors.

Outside of the work of Descartes, cross-cultural differences were largely ignored by Europeans prior to the eighteenth century. During this time, a number of scholars proposed that a study of "primitive peoples" from remote areas of the globe could help foster a clearer understanding of social development from "savagery" to "civilization" (Segall et al., 1990). These discussions fostered a growing interest in obtaining accurate information about non-Europeans through expeditions to foreign lands that would remove the ambiguity that resulted from centuries of speculation.

Constantin François Volney (1757–1820) argued that direct contact with non-Western peoples was essential in the pursuit of a better understanding of cultural differences (Jahoda, 1993). Volney met with people of various cultures in the Middle East and concluded that psychological characteristics were the result of variation in religion and government.

This new interest in hands-on investigation led to the establishment in the late 1700s of the *Société des Observateurs de l'Homme* of which Volney was a member. This organization, composed of philosophers, naturalists, and physicians, was concerned with the scientific study of humankind and emphasized direct observation rather than unfounded suppositions. The *Société* promoted European expeditions to foreign lands in an effort to pursue commercial, political, and scientific goals around the world.

One such expedition that occurred in the early part of the nineteenth century included the measurement of the physical strength of a sample of Tasmanian natives. This survey, which was inspired by Dégerando, a founder of the *Société*, was cited by Jahoda (1982) as "probably the first cross-cultural study employing physiological instrumentation."

The inspiration of scholars from many countries affected the direction that cross-cultural psychology was to take—sometimes by omission. For example, French sociologists of the nineteenth century were often more concerned with identifying the factors that shaped human behavior within Western cultures than they were with the influence of cross-cultural differences.

Several important works gave the discipline a focus that lasted until the mid-twentieth century. Émile Durkheim's (1897) *Le Suicide* emphasized the harmful effects of society. Durkheim believed that individual behavior was under the control of society. He maintained a sociologically oriented perspective that did not clearly distinguish between culture and social structure. *The Crowd* by Gustave Le Bon (1895) emphasized the notion of a group mind whereas *The Laws of Imitation* by Gustave Tarde (1903) highlighted abnormal aspects of social psychology. Because the influence of the French was greater than that of the British and Germans, the result was to retard development of a more normative, culturally oriented, social psychology (Segall, 1979, p. 31). One exception, however, was the contribution of Lucien Lévy-Bruhl who argued against the universality of human cognitions. He felt that the thought processes of "primitives" were inherently different from those of Europeans living in the early years of the twentieth century (Berry, Poortinga, Segall, & Dasen, 1992).

Perhaps the first British scholar to comment on the origin of cross-cultural differences was John Locke (1632–1704). Building on his belief that people are born as "blank slates," Locke, like Descartes before him, argued that cultural differences are exclusively caused by variations in the environment into which people are born. He felt that anyone, regardless of race, would mirror the common characteristics of the culture into which they were born (Jahoda, 1993).

Although the influence of environment continued to be cited as the common cause of individual difference in the eighteenth century, some scholars used environmental factors as evidence for the superiority of one culture over another. For instance, in his essay "Of National Character," David Hume (1711–1776) suggested that the cultures that exist beyond the Arctic Circle and within the Tropical Zone are inferior to those that can be found in the Temperate Zones of the earth (Hume, 1742/1894 as cited in Jahoda, 1993).

Among the later British contributors to the field of cross-cultural psychology, the work of William H. R. Rivers (1864–1922) is particularly noteworthy. In 1899, while teaching at Cambridge, Rivers was persuaded to participate in an expedition to the Torres Straits, an area located between New Guinea and Australia. Organized by Alfred C. Haddon, an anthropologist, the expedition also included C. S. Myers, William McDougall, and C. G. Seligman, each of whom later attained a level of celebrity in his own right, although not all connected to anthropology. McDougall, in particular, later promoted ideas directly at odds with a cultural interpretation of behavior. But it was Rivers's work on intelligence and sensory acuity among "primitive people" (Rivers, 1901) that has been called "the first modern empirical cross-cultural psychological study" (Jahoda, 1982, p. 19). Rivers's work was instrumental in dispelling two previously held cultural myths. The first was that non-Western people, assumed to be less intelligent than the "civilized" people of the West, would be more likely to be fooled by visual illusions. The second myth to be disproved was that non-Western people would be more sensitive to sensory input than people from Western nations.

Much of Rivers's subsequent writing reinforced the view that training in psychology was essential to success as a field anthropologist. One of his most visible students, A. R. Radcliffe-Brown (1881–1955), supported this position early on but later came to repudiate it. Instead, he adopted Durkheim's view and focused on the search for general laws of society.

Another great British contributor to early cross-cultural psychology was Bronislaw Malinowski (1884–1942). Born in Poland and educated in Cracow, he received a Ph.D. in physics and mathematics, became enthralled with J. G. Frazer's *The Golden Bough* (1890), and subsequently found himself studying experimental psychology under Wundt at Leipzig. Later Malinowski traveled to London where, through the efforts of Seligman of Torres Straits' fame, he was able to obtain support for fieldwork in New Guinea. A second trip to the Trobriand Islands near New Guinea followed. When World War I broke out, Malinowski stayed put, which resulted in a longer stay and a greater immersion in the culture than he had originally intended. Much of Malinowski's later work found its beginnings in this second trip, including his attack on the universality of Sigmund Freud's Oedipus complex. Malinowski's fieldwork was invaluable to the evolution of modern cross-cultural anthropology because previous efforts in the field had been largely based on anecdotal evidence. Throughout his career, Malinowski continued to emphasize psychological processes, although his focus often had a group emphasis to it.

Another British contributor who was sensitive to cross-cultural issues before his time was R.A.C. Oliver. He argued for the inclusion of indigenous elements in intelligence test items in order to reflect the true intelligence of non-Western people more effectively. Oliver mirrored the modern criticism of intelligence tests, which states that the assessment of intelligence is often hampered by differences in language that exist between the test designer and the test taker (Oliver, 1934). In a landmark study using the Seashore Test for Musical Abilities, Oliver (1932) found West African students scored higher than American students on a variety of measures. The West African students, however, scored lower on tests of timbre and tonal memory, the only two measures that correlated with intelligence. Oliver suggested that this difference was probably due to the fact that the West African students had difficulty understanding the instructions rather than being due to any significant difference in the true intelligence of the two groups (Berry et al., 1992).

The early work on methodology in cross-cultural research also owes a debt to Great Britain. John W. M. Whiting (quoted by Price-Williams, 1979) identified the first cross-cultural methodological paper as that by Edward Tylor in 1889, given at the Royal Anthropological Institute of Great Britain. The first application of the cross-cultural method in testing a hypothesis, according to Whiting (also quoted by Price-Williams, 1979), was a paper on alcohol and anxiety by Horton (1943).

FRANZ BOAS AND THE U.S. INFLUENCE

German-born Franz Boas (1858–1942) moved to the United States early in his career and came to dominate American anthropology. Throughout his career, he retained an active interest in the psychological aspects of anthropology, challenging many of the positions psychologists took as a matter of course. Klineberg (1980, p. 36) called this a breakthrough in the relations between psychology and anthropology. The students of Boas, who included Edward Sapir, Ruth Benedict, and Margaret Mead, continued his general approach. Boas is "regarded as the founder of what became known as 'psychological anthropology', which flourished in America at a time when Radcliffe-Brown's influence in Britain had led to coolness and skepticism regarding the contribution of psychology" (Jahoda, 1982, p. 27). Boas asked that cultures be understood in their own right, not as a rung in a hierarchical ladder of evolution, nor as a genetically inferior cluster, but simply as a qualitatively varied entity.

The students of Boas began to apply his principles to a great many areas. Sapir became well known for his work in language, particularly regarding the way in which language affected perceptions within a culture. This work was carried on by his illustrious student Benjamin Whorf. Sapir also studied the relationship between anthropology and psychiatry. Benedict focused on culturally derived notions of abnormality and, later, on studies of national character. Mead had the most direct impact on psychology. She began by attacking theoretical concepts of G. Stanley Hall as they related to adolescent development, showing them to be of questionable validity when applied to other cultures. Later, she performed a similar function for several other cherished psychological concepts.

Another significant contribution was made by William Graham Sumner, a sociologist at Yale University. Contrary to the German concept of *Volksgeist*, Graham argued that culture is not biologically transmitted. He argued that the characteristic traits of a people are the result of a society's efforts to satisfy basic needs. These traits serve to regulate the daily activities of subsequent generations and develop into the social character of the society (Segall et al., 1990).

Donald Campbell (1961) made a valuable methodological contribution to the field of cross-cultural psychology when he suggested that any theory that is believed to be universal should be empirically tested in cultures other than the one in which it was developed. His argument, which was later revised with Raoul Naroll in 1972, was in response to the long-standing controversy that developed following Malinowski's (1927) criticisms of the belief in the universality of the Oedipus complex.

THE INFLUENCE OF CARL G. JUNG

Despite the increasing criticism of the belief in the universality of human behavior, Carl G. Jung, the noted Swiss psychoanalyst, traveled extensively in the 1920s in an attempt to identify the commonalities that exist in the unconscious of both modern Europeans and "primitives" from all parts of the globe (Jacobi, 1973). Jung traveled to North Africa in 1921, spent several months with the Pueblo Indians of Arizona and New Mexico in 1924 and 1925, and visited the people of Mt. Elgon in Kenya in 1926. In addition, he studied Chinese philosophy to identify parallels in the psyche across cultures that would support his belief in the "collective unconscious." Jung determined that people of all cultures possess similar "archetypes" or symbolic tendencies that find expression in art, literature, and dreams. Jung's influence on mainstream cross-cultural psychology, however, remains quite limited.

OTHER NATIONAL INFLUENCES

Although the influence of Western Europe and the United States on the history and evolution of cross-cultural psychology has been great, the contributions of other nations should be noted. A survey of articles published in the *Journal of Cross-Cultural Psychology* from 1970–1979 revealed that 52 countries were represented, 28 of which were outside of Europe and the United States (Lonner, 1980). Some countries have been contributing for many years; others, no less important, have found a voice more recently.

For example, in New Zealand at the end of World War II, Ivan Sutherland and Ernest Beaglehole began to develop a distinct "New Zealand psychology," combining anthropological and psychological approaches. James Ritchie, a student of Beaglehole, investigated the Rakau Maoris, the study of which "must surely be one of the first empirical studies of an indigenous tribal group made from a psychological viewpoint" (Shouksmith, quoted in Sexton & Hogan, 1992). Lise Bird (1991) has studied gender roles in New Zealand and Aotearoa, and Corey Muse (1991) has written about culture in Western Samoa.

Other countries view themselves as natural laboratories for cross-cultural research and have produced books and articles to demonstrate that viewpoint. Among these countries have been Hong Kong, a place where Eastern and Western cultures intersect and are surrounded by political uncertainty; Israel, with its mixture of immigrants from different regions and cultures; Canada, a country of two distinct languages and customs; Australia, with its contrast of white Australians and Aborigines; and the United States, which has long been a so-called melting pot of ethnic and cultural diversity. Other countries, such as Iran, Egypt, Papua New Guinea, and Taiwan, have also made similar claims to uniqueness.

All of this should serve as a reminder. Although it is true that the literature in cross-cultural research is dominated "by individuals from relatively affluent, Western, predominantly English-speaking countries" (Lonner, 1980), the significant contribution of other countries cannot be denied.

THREE POPULAR AREAS OF RESEARCH:
DEVIANCE, PERCEPTION, AND PERSONALITY

Cross-cultural researchers have shown a tendency to focus on a limited number of areas. A discussion of three of the more popular areas follows.

Psychopathology and Deviance

Cross-cultural psychology has been concerned with conceptions of deviant behavior virtually from its beginnings, a tradition that Marsella (1979) has traced to the writings of the eighteenth-century philosopher Jean Jacques Rousseau. Rousseau's conception of humankind as naturally good (along with the corollary that institutions are responsible for making humanity "bad") is cited as evidence that Rousseau was among the first to consider "the role of cultural factors in the etiology of mental disorders" (Marsella, 1979, p. 234).

During the nineteenth century, physicians interested in social reform commented on "the price we pay for civilization," suggesting that modern patterns of social organization were associated with an increase in mental disorders (Marsella, 1979). More refined attempts to explore the role of cultural factors in mental disorders began to appear in the early twentieth century. For example, Emil Kraepelin, the leading psychiatrist of his day, noted cultural differences in the expression and frequency of mental disorders among various populations in Indonesia in 1904. Reports on "culture-specific disorders" such as *latah* (Van Brero, 1895), *mali mali* (Musgrave & Sison, 1910), and *Arctic hysteria* (Brill, 1913) were published, as was research on the existence of "Western" disorders in non-Western cultures (e.g., Cleland, 1928).

Marsella (1979) notes that the first epidemiological studies of mental disorders in various cultural groups began to appear in the 1930s and 1940s, with estimates of the rates of mental disorders in countries such as Germany (e.g., Brugger, 1931) and Japan (e.g., Akimoto, Sunazaki, Okada, & Hanashiro, 1942).

The concept of normalcy itself became another major issue when it was argued that what was abnormal in one culture could be viewed as normal in another (e.g., Benedict, 1934). The next 40 years witnessed the emergence of research focused on the role of cultural variables in the etiology and the expression and the treatment of mental disorders (e.g., Carothers, 1948; Yap, 1951; Leighton, Lambo, Hughes, Leighton, Murphy, & Macklin, 1963; Kleinman, 1977). Several journals concerned with the cross-cultural study of mental illness have also appeared, including the *International Journal of Social Psychiatry, International Mental Health Research Newsletter, Transcultural Psychiatric Research, Culture, Medicine and Psychiatry*, and *Social Science and Medicine*. More about psychopathology and mental health issues may be found in the two chapters by J. Draguns and H. Lefley included in this volume.

Perception

Studies of perception in relation to cultural factors have been of particular importance in the history of cross-cultural psychology also. The literature in this area is vast; only a few of the more pertinent studies are mentioned here. A more comprehensive review can be found in Deregowski (1980).

Perhaps the first discussion of cross-cultural differences in perception can be found in the work of the British politician William Gladstone (Berry et al., 1992). Citing the absence of words for brown and blue in the poetry of Homer, Gladstone (1858) hypothesized that the ancient Greeks possessed a limited ability to differentiate among colors when compared to Western Europeans of his day.

The first empirical investigation of perception was performed by H. Magnus (1880) who sought to establish the range of color vision of "uncivilized peoples" and the words they used for various colors by collecting data from foreign residents of a number of different countries (Berry et al., 1992). Contrary to his expectations, Magnus found that people of different cultures possessed a similar range of color vision. The number of words for various colors were found to differ between cultures. The languages of many foreign cultures were found to lack words for colors with a short wavelength (green, blue, violet). Magnus hypothesized that these colors were less common in non-Western cultures, which helped to explain the lack of names for certain colors.

Cross-cultural studies of perception became more common at the turn of the century. Early efforts included anecdotal reports of differences in perception of orientation among Malawi housemaids (Laws, 1886), more sophisticated reports on visual and auditory acuity (Rivers, 1901), and other reports on the perception of geometric illusions, color, and form among the subjects of the Torres Straits expedition (Deregowski, 1980). The same expedition included a study of time perception (Myers, 1903) and an investigation of cutaneous sensation (McDougall, 1903).

Other notable pieces of research in this area have included investigations of perceptual constancy (e.g., Beveridge, 1935; Thouless, 1933), the influence of visual cues (Beveridge, 1940), closure (e.g., Michael, 1953), binocular disparity (e.g., Bagby, 1957), pictorial perception (Hudson, 1960), and retinal pigmentation (e.g., Silver & Pollack, 1967). More recent efforts include cross-cultural responses to the Ponzo Illusion (Kilbride & Leibowitz, 1975, 1977, & 1982; Brislin & Keating, 1976), perception of spatial relationships (Nicholson & Seddon, 1977), and factors influencing orientation errors (Jahoda, 1977).

Personality

The origins of cross-cultural personality research have been traced to descriptions of "primitive peoples" found in the writing of pre-Enlightenment European explorers, traders, and missionaries. Speculation about the psychological attributes of the "savage" were used to justify European dominance over native peoples (Bock, 1988). During the nineteenth century, Social Darwinism fostered the notion that differences between European and non-European cultures reflected evolutionary processes. White Europeans were considered superior; nonwhites were "ranked according to their resemblance to white Europeans and their physical differences were related to levels of cultural development" (Bock, 1980, p. 9).

The birth of anthropology during this period saw a departure from racist interpretations of intercultural differences, although many early anthropologists continued to think of culture in terms of progressive levels of development, and people at a given level were thought to share similar psychological features. Lewis H. Morgan, one of the pioneers of this movement, associated specific psychological development with each level in a series of progressive cultural evolutionary stages. Another scholar, Sir Edward Tylor, argued that human thinking became progressively more rational as cultures evolved from simple to more complex forms (Bock, 1988).

Franz Boas asserted that primitives and civilized people did not have fundamentally different ways of thinking; he rejected the idea that racial and cultural differences reflected different evolutionary stages. Edward Sapir, influenced by Gestalt psychology, emphasized cultural and behavioral patterns of organization and suggested that a given personality organization or "configuration of experience" is a microcosm of its "official" culture. Benedict and Mead also became known as "configurationists," that is, they attempted to associate "cultural elements with aspects of personality" (Bock, 1980, p. 80).

The 1930s and 1940s witnessed further developments, including a new approach based on the concepts of basic personality structure and modal personality, which can be seen in the works of Kardiner, Ralph Linton, and Cora DuBois. Cross-cultural researchers began using projective tests such as the Rorschach during this period, a tactic that remained popular through the 1950s. For example, DuBois used the Rorschach as a means of studying the modal personality of the Alorese in the Dutch East Indies. Other researchers employed the Thematic Apperception Test in combination with the Rorschach (e.g., Gladwin & Sarason, 1953). This period also saw the emergence of "national character" studies (e.g., Benedict, 1946), which used the methods of basic and modal personality studies (Díaz-Guerrero, 1977; Bock, 1988; Díaz-Guerrero, 1995—see also his chapter in this book).

Later work in personality has included research by Aronoff (1967) who compared the needs and major personality characteristics of different Caribbean nations. Lynn (1971) compared anxiety and hostility levels in 16 industrialized countries. Guthrie and Bennett (1971) applied multivariate statistical techniques to identify a culture's "implicit personality theory," which is the way a specific culture organizes various personality traits. Carment (1974) found that locus of control was interrelated with the cultural mores of Indian and Canadian societies. Kohlberg's (1969) research in moral development prompted a number of researchers in recent years to investigate the universality of moral stages (Edwards, 1981, Gielen, 1996;

Snarey, 1985; see Gielen and Markoulis's chapter in this volume). Thus cross-cultural research in personality has proved to be invaluable in identifying the similarities that exist between people, but also in recognizing the great diversity and uniqueness that exists among the cultures of the world. Some of the recent research in this area is reviewed in R. Díaz-Guerrero's chapter contained in this volume.

Other areas of extensive cross-cultural investigation have included psychological testing, memory, cognitive style (Ahmed, 1989); field independence (Witkin, 1975); emotion, authoritarianism, attitudes (Graubert & Adler, 1982; Adler, Denmark, & Ahmed, 1991); developmental issues (Adler, 1977, 1982, 1989); and competence.

MODERN DEVELOPMENTS

Although many social psychologists continue to look exclusively within their own cultures for their source of inspiration and study, some prominent exceptions have arisen. One outstanding case was the emergence of an extraordinary group of interdisciplinary researchers at the Institute of Human Relations at Yale University during the 1930s and 1940s. Strongly empirical, and using Hullian learning theory as their major theoretical emphasis, they produced a number of classic contributions. Among these was the establishment of the Human Relations Areas Files, which permitted the exploration of a number of cross-cultural hypotheses. For instance, from these files was to emerge the classic Whiting and Child book (1953) describing child-rearing practices across cultures and the effect of these practices on adult personality.

Although there were few textbooks in social psychology that stressed the effects of culture, even into the 1950s, there is one exception worth noting—that by Kluckhohn and Murray (1953). "It was built around a simple premise: 'Every man is in certain respects like all other men, like some other men, like no other man' (p. 53). With these words Kluckhohn and Murray expressed the need for a social psychology that encompassed anthropology, sociology, and psychology" (Segall, 1979, p. 33).

Another major development is the institutionalization of cross-cultural psychology. What began as a movement highlighted by the work of isolated individuals has become a global movement with an increasing degree of organization and cooperation. Scholarly journals devoted to cross-cultural psychology such as the *International Journal of Psychology* (1966), the *Journal of Cross-Cultural Psychology* (1970), and *World Psychology* (1995) have been valuable sources of information for students and scholars across the globe. The multivolume handbooks of cross-cultural psychology by Triandis et al. (1980) and Berry, Poortinga, and Pandey (1997) also helped to establish cross-cultural psychology as a distinct discipline. Researchers from around the world have come together to form international organizations for the promotion of the field. These have included the International Association of Cross-Cultural Psychology founded in Hong Kong in 1972 and the Association pour la Recherche Interculturelle (ARIC) founded in 1984.

Interest in cross-cultural psychology has continued to grow in recent years, nurtured in part by a world made smaller by mass communication and rapid transportation. A multicultural movement has spread throughout the United States, Canada, Australia, and Western Europe whose main purpose is to correct the ethnocentric errors of the past. Although significant inroads have been made in promoting the importance of a cross-cultural viewpoint, there is much work that still needs to be done. It seems fair to conclude that the "missionary goals of cross-cultural psychology have been attained, even though all Western psychologists may not have been converted" (Doob, 1980, p. 70). With these goals attained, the field of cross-cultural psychology finally entered the mainstream of the discipline of psychology.

3

Research Methods for Studies in the Field

Harold Takooshian, Nihar R. Mrinal, and
Uma Singhal Mrinal

"It's your human environment that makes climate." Few modern psychologists would challenge this simple maxim from essayist Mark Twain (1835–1910), emphasizing the importance of culture. In fact, virtually all psychologists today would likely go further and agree on two added points: (1) Human culture is a potent force that shapes not only our outer behavior but also our innermost identity. (2) As fish ignore water, psychology research for too long has overlooked this potent force, whether for lack of knowledge or lack of energy.

To what extent must we behavioral researchers adapt our methods when working cross-culturally? This chapter offers a concise overview of this question, in four parts: first, the context of the question; second, an overview of general methods of research and sampling; third, issues in cross-cultural research; and fourth, a conclusion.

THE CONTEXT OF CROSS-CULTURAL RESEARCH

Without question, the growth of cross-cultural research has accelerated apace these past 20 years, to the point where "the amount of cross-cultural research published in recent years is massive" (Hogan & Sussner, this volume). Cultural diversity, at one time overlooked, is now becoming essential within general psychology (Feldman, 1997), sociology (Ferrante, 1992), and social psychology (Moghaddam, 1998; Moghaddam, Taylor, & Wright, 1992; Peplau & Taylor, 1997). Still, the picture is mixed. The past 20 years have made us more certain about the importance of recognizing cultural factors in our research but less certain about how best to achieve this (Adler, 1993). For example, the long-awaited second edition of the *Handbook of*

Cross-Cultural Psychology (Berry, Poortinga, Pandey, Dasen, Saraswathi, Segall, & Kagitçibasi, 1997) now features a new notion of "cultural psychology" absent from the *Handbook*'s monumental first edition a generation earlier (Triandis, Lambert, Berry, Brislin, Draguns, Lonner, & Heron, 1980). Today, in fact, we might discern a three-point continuum ranging from (1) traditional "universal" psychology to (2) cross-cultural psychology, to (3) cultural psychology.

The middle position in this continuum is "cross-cultural psychology," as defined by Ho (this volume)—an attempt to use standardized methods to study individuals across cultures. As noted by the editor of the journal *World Psychology*, "Both within and across cultures, psychologists need to search for unity in the midst of diversity, while exploring diversity within unity" (Gielen, 1995, p. vii). In contrast, the newer "cultural psychology has grown out of dissatisfaction with cross-cultural psychology" (Greenfield, 1997, p. 306) and sees it as possible to study the individual only within a specific culture; attempts at comparison across cultures are misdirected, since "culture and behavior, and culture and mind are viewed as indistinguishable" (Greenfield, 1997, p. 306). One cultural psychologist enunciates the "seven flaws of cross-cultural psychology" (Boesch, in Berry et al., 1997, p. 57) compared to culture-specific "indigenous psychologies." The other extreme of the three-point continuum is the traditional "universal" psychology, which seeks immutable laws of behavior that are true not only across cultures but even across species. Indeed, an estimated 20 million animals are studied by researchers in the United States each year (Mukerjee, 1997), likely far more than human subjects, based on the premise that social as well as physiological processes transcend species. In his 1995 address to the International Council of Psychologists, Hans Eysenck voiced this view, that the psychologist's role is to identify "concepts, theories, and measuring instruments which are as universal as possible; otherwise our empirical findings will remain incapable of generalization beyond the narrow confines of a particular nation or state" (1995, p. 26). In this universalist view, the value of cross-cultural psychology is to help science determine which of its laws are indeed universal across cultures.

In short, the cultural psychologist accentuates cultural differences, the universal psychologist minimizes them, and the cross-cultural psychologist in the middle balances these extreme views. The focus of this chapter is cross-cultural psychology and its methods.

GENERAL METHODS OF RESEARCH AND SAMPLING

From the outset, any discussion of cross-cultural research methods should distinguish theory from practice. In theory, the basic philosophy of science underlying all social research is invariant, transcending specific cultures (Kerlinger, 1986, pp. 3–41, 279–343). Table 3.1 lists eight general methods used by social researchers worldwide, regardless of culture, with each having

Table 3.1
General Methods of Research

1. Experiment—Lab: The researcher creates a situation in a highly controlled setting and predicts the resulting behavior.

2. Experiment—Field: The researcher creates a situation in an uncontrolled setting and predicts the resulting behavior.

3. Observation-Objective: The researcher passively, objectively observes ongoing behavior. (Behavior mapping) (Structured observation)

4. Observation-Subjective: The researcher passively, subjectively observes ongoing behavior. (Participant observation) (Clinical observation) (Unstructured observation) (Qualitative research)

5. Survey: The researcher asks individuals to self-report their own behavior or attitudes. (Questionnaire, interview, scale, test)

6. Archival: The researcher reanalyzes existing data, such as Census, police, health, nativity, morbidity, mortality, usually to test a theory. (Secondary analysis) (Content analysis) (Meta-analysis)

7. Norm violation: The researcher violates some unwritten social rule (norm) to see how the system readjusts itself. (Ethnomethodology) (Candid Camera)

8. Case study: In-depth analysis of one or a few specific cases.

its own set of proper procedures. In practice, however, the general methods typically need to be adapted to specific cultures where, for example, the same survey or experimental situation in one culture has a different meaning within another (Bond, 1989; Segall, Dasen, Berry, & Poortinga, 1990; Peplau & Taylor, 1997). This duality of theory and practice was expressed quite forcefully by Donald T. Campbell in his 1975 presidential address to the American Psychological Association, where he went so far as to chastize the scientific study of individual behavior as misdirected, unless psychologists pay greater attention to progress within parallel behavioral sciences—anthropology (culture), sociology (social structure), biology (genetics and evolution). He felt that to ignore the truths revealed by these other disciplines is to produce a distorted picture of one's behavior and mentality—this, even while psychologists continue to use their proven, standardized techniques from their century-old arsenal of research methods. Fortunately, psychologists have a wide array of research methods from which to choose (as listed in Table 3.1) and a growing knowledge of how to adapt these general methods to specific cultures.

Experimentation

Experimentation is the backbone of research in psychology, its most commonly used method (Aronson, Ellsworth, Carlsmith, & Gonzales, 1990). It has a few defining features. The experimenter creates or manipulates an independent variable (IV) to observe its effect on the dependent variable (DV) in order to establish a causal relation between the two. Moreover, the experimenter strives for total control of the situation—including random selection and assignment of subjects to test groups and elimination or monitoring of any unwanted, extraneous variables (EV). In double-blind experiments, neither researcher nor subject are aware of the specific hypothesis or the group being tested. Aronson et al. (1990) offer a detailed volume-length guide to general principles of experimentation. Experiments come in at least a few forms: laboratory, field, and quasi-experiments.

Laboratory experiments are done in a controlled setting—if not a laboratory, at least some classroom or other space over which the research has control of the environment (e.g., access, sound, lighting, temperature).

Field experiments occur outside of a controlled space—streets, parks, workplaces—manipulating the IV in a more "natural" setting. Whereas laboratory experiments are deliberately artificial, field experiments gain in realism what they sacrifice in control. Moreover, field subjects typically do not know they are being studied, so their behavior is more free of the "demand characteristics" commonly found in a laboratory (Barber, 1976). Bickman and Henchy's (1973) *Beyond the Laboratory* offers models of field experimentation, including cross-cultural work.

Quasi-experiments are a particular type of field experiment. *Quasi* means "almost"—a design halfway between true experiment and correlational study. In a school, for instance, the researcher often cannot randomly select or assign pupils to treatment groups, so self-selection reduces the potency of any findings; one is not sure whether the obtained difference is due to treatment variation or to selection differences. Cook and Campbell's (1979) book *Quasi-Experimentation* is the classic that offers creative techniques to enhance our inferential powers in quasi-experimental designs.

Content analyses of U.S. social psychology journals (like Higbee, Lott, & Graves, 1976) typically find that fully 80 percent of all articles findings are based on laboratory experimentation, only 3 percent on field experiments, and the remaining 17 percent or so on all other methods combined. Sadly, some 83 percent of published social psychology experiments draw on the convenient but "narrow data base" of U.S. college sophomores taking a psychology class (Sears, 1986). In his brilliant, if little-known book *Pitfalls in Human Research*, T. X. Barber (1976) identifies 10 points that are especially relevant for cross-cultural research, where seemingly "tight" experiments actually allow unseen errors to creep in.

Overall, experimentation is a pivotal technique in cross-cultural comparison because of its precision (Sechrest, 1970). Note, for example, that our behavior can be viewed in three very different ways: as a product of our internal dispositions (genes, bicohemicals, personality traits), our situational context (physical and social environment), or the interaction of these two (dispositions within situations). These three factors can be experimentally separated for testing. For example, to see the effect of some specific reward on people in culture A and culture B, subjects in both cultures can be assigned to two different praise or reward conditions making a 2 X 2 between-subjects factorial design (two cultures X two rewards). The main effects of A and of B can be studied separately while the A X B result is the interaction effect. Thus, experimental method can replicate identical situations across cultures to directly compare not only the what but the why of cultural differences. Such is the case with Stanley Milgram's (1961) doctoral dissertation comparing the "texture" of conformity in Norway versus France, as well as his noted obedience experiments, which have now been replicated in at least eight countries (Blass, in press). As the French naturalist Georges Cuvier (1769–1832) noted, "The observer listens to nature, but the experimenter can question her, and force her to reveal her secrets."

Observation

In observational studies, the researcher passively observes ongoing behavior in a natural setting. Unlike the experimenter, the observer does not create the situation; the subjects are self-selected and normally do not know they are being studied. Thus, observation offers total realism in place of the total artificiality of the experiment (Kerlinger, 1986, pp. 347–363). This is necessary when systematic manipulation of an IV is simply beyond the control of the researcher or when ethics prohibit its manipulation (as in morbidity studies). Here, a relationship between two or more variables is tested by monitoring both; if change in one (the predictor) correlates with another (the criterion), a link between them is posited.

Observation is typically "unobtrusive" because it studies subjects' behavior without their knowledge, thereby reducing the "reactive" biases inherent in experiments and surveys (Longabaugh, 1980). In experiments, for instance, people "react" when they know they are being studied, thus distorting their natural behaviors (Bochner, 1986). In surveys, too, people often act differently when asked their opinion publicly (Sechrest, 1975), giving "socially desirable" answers if not other distorted replies based on their own particular "response style"—ingratiating, acquiescent, suspicious, hostile. Such sources of error haunt obtrusive methods.

There are at least a few different types of observational research. In *objective observation*, the researcher is objective and detached from his or her objects of study, for example, counting the frequency of a certain behavior in such a way that any other observer would count the same result. For example, Marc and Helen Bornstein (1976) studied "the pace of life" in 15 cities within 6 nations by simply using a stopwatch to measure how fast pedestrians walked 50 feet. In *subjective observation*, the researcher is also detached from his or her subject of study but is highly subjective, for example, using his or her "gut" impressions to better understand the why as well as the what of subjects' behavior. A pioneer of this subjective approach is the Tavistock Institute in London, in which clinical observers apply the psychoanalytic concepts of individual pathology to better understand problems within industrial and other "neurotic" organizations.

Participant observation is a form of subjective observation in which the researcher is immersed within the subject of study (Berry, 1969), for example, becoming a member of a street crowd in order to study crowd behavior. Though unusual in psychology, it certainly is a favored method within cultural anthropology (Bernard, 1994). Participant observation has been used in three types of research: process research, theory generating research, and case studies. Here the process means what happens over a period of time, whereas outcome research describes the end point or result. When we have little knowledge of the process, process research is useful. Participant observation is also used to verify theory. Case study has been used to study language development in babies, personality disorder, and community reactions to disaster. A key method in psychoanalysis, the case study may involve a single person or group of persons, animals, organizations, or events.

Participant observation has been criticized on various grounds. The emotions of the participant observer may color the data. An observer of another race easily attracts the attention of the target group and thus must be prepared for questions like "Who are you?" and "What are you doing here?" In such research it is wise to have distribution copies explaining your role and your plans, and ensure the participants of your safeguards to maintain confidentiality. The researcher should decide whether the emphasis will be qualitative or quantitative (counting variables). Finally, the researcher should design units of observation in terms of time, space, people, and events (Munroe & Munroe, 1971).

Ethology emerged from zoology as the systematic observation of the behavior of organisms and how this contributes to the preservation of the species. For example, the ethologist may film and then analyze the actions of newborns—their grasping reflex, search for the nipple, facial expressions, other fixed action patterns, and releasers. Another example common in cross-cultural work is analysis of gestures and greetings—some culture-specific, others more universal (Morris, 1967). Eibl-Eibesfeldt (1989) offers a magisterial survey of cross-cultural research in the tradition of ethology, much of it conducted in non-Western cultures.

Ecological psychology is a specific form of systematic observation pioneered by Roger Barker (1963, 1968). Here behavior is best viewed as the result of interaction between the individual and his or her environment. Similarly, Edward Hall's pioneering research on proxemics studied how personal space varies across cultures, with four "distances" common between two speakers: intimate, personal, social, and public (Hall, 1959, 1966; Little, 1965). Whiting and Whiting (1978) studied socialization of children simultaneously in six different societies. Though Hall and the Whitings do not use the term *ecological psychology*, their anthropological techniques exemplify the same approach to ecological psychology and behavioral mapping enunciated in Roger Barker's copious writings.

Surveys

While experiments and observations test overt behavior, surveys are well-suited to assess intangibles—one's attitudes, beliefs, expectations, values (Fowler, 1993; Kerlinger, 1986, pp. 377–388). Surveys measure what people say about themselves. They may be in the form of written questionnaires or oral interviews and often incorporate scales or tests.

Questionnaires. The questionnaire, or written survey, should be as brief as possible (one page is ideal) and normally consists of three parts in this order: introduction, body, biodata. The introduction offers the title of the survey, its general purpose (but not specific hypotheses), its sponsor, directions for completion, the anonymity of responses, warm thanks, and possibly an address or phone number that an interested respondent might contact for further information. A succinct example follows:

WOMEN'S OPINION SURVEY. How do women around the world feel about the feminist movement? We are researchers from the United Nations who would appreciate your frank opinions on the 20 statements below. For each item, circle whether you Agree (A), Disagree (D), or have No opinion (N). This survey is anonymous. Thank you.

The body of the questionnaire is its self-report attitude or behavior questions, in the form of open-end questions allowing write-in or, more commonly, closed-end questions from which the subject must choose between preset choices. Finally, biodata questions follow the body, so as not to influence the prior answers, and record the possibly relevant profile of the respondent—age, education, gender, occupation, race or cultural group, income, religion, and so forth. Questionnaires may be completed in person, through the mail, or electronically via the Internet or by fax.

Interviews. The interview, or oral survey, has been defined as "a conversation with a purpose." It may be unstructured, semistructured, or structured—depending on the degree of advance preparation to preset the order and wording of each question (Schultz & Schultz, 1994, pp. 90–97). The extremely structured interview schedule is an oral questionnaire, while the extremely unstructured interview is a stream-of-consciousness conversation. "A critical qualification of the successful interviewer is sensitivity in identifying clues in the interviewee's behavior . . . [that] . . . lead to further probing" (Anastasi & Urbina, 1997, p. 465). Personal features of the interviewer,

such as age, sex, race, dress, color, background, accent, may affect the interview situation and should be minimized (Converse & Schuman, 1974).
Interviews might be in person or over the phone. The group interview, or
focus group, has become highly popular in industry and marketing (Stewart
& Shamdasani, 1990), convenes 8 to 12 people for a semistructured group
interview of 90 minutes or more, and is focused on some specific topic.
Focus groups are powerful in revealing hidden feelings not accessible by
other methods, and international corporations have found them useful in
cross-national testing to quickly identify consumer sentiments prior to a
more costly systematic survey.

   Scales. When several items in a questionnaire or interview can be combined into a single number, this becomes a scale—an approach common in
psychology, since it invites in all the powers of statistics. Scales might assess
general personality traits, specific attitudes, abilities, or behaviors. Scales can
be assessed for validity and reliability to check their structure across cultures.
One rich source of attitude scales awaiting cross-cultural adaptation is Robinson, Shaver, and Wrightsman's (1991) collection of more than 100 original, public-domain instruments, most of them tested for reliability and
validity on an array of topics—subjective well-being, self-esteem, shyness,
depression, loneliness, alienation, trust, locus of control, authoritarianism,
sex roles, and values. Scales come in many possible formats (Judd, Smith,
& Kidder, 1991; Kerlinger, 1986, pp. 449–467), including Thurstone
equal-appearing intervals (Likert, 1932), social distance (Bogardus, 1925),
Guttman forced-choice (Rotter, 1966), adjective checklists and semantic
differential (Osgood, Suci, & Tannenbaum, 1957). Moreover, some scale
formats seem especially suited for cross-cultural use, for example, figure-
placement task (Adler & Graubert, 1976; Graubert & Adler, 1982); visual
attitude scales like Bem's 1974 Androgyny Scale or Watts and Free's "Ladder of Life" (in Lindsey, 1975); Smiling faces (Butzin & Anderson, 1973);
"Own Categories" technique (Sherif & Sherif, 1969); and Sociogram.

   Tests. Some scales are available in the form of marketed tests, which their
publishers have already checked for reliability, validity, and standardization
in one or more cultures (Conoley & Impara, 1995). Though almost all
major tests are Euro-American in origin, an increasing number have been
translated or otherwise adapted for cross-national use. Some rich source-
books for finding valid, reliable, standardized tests are *Tests* (Keyser &
Sweetland, 1991), Anastasi and Urbina's (1997) classic textbook *Psychological Testing* (available in many languages), *The Twelfth Mental Measurements
Yearbook* (Conoley & Impara, 1995), and the journal *Educational and Psychological Measurement.*

Archival

Archival research, or secondary analysis, has the researcher reanalyzing
existing data originally collected by others, usually to test some theory.

These others are often agencies of government (census, police, housing, health-care, urban planners) or the United Nations (UNESCO, UNICEF, *Demographic Yearbooks*, World Health Organization). Meta-analysis is the combination and reanalysis of data collected by other behavioral researchers. Content analysis is the reanalysis of existing nonnumerical information, such as speeches, song lyrics, fables, advertisements, or any sort of visual or textual information. Though archival research is more common among economists or sociologists scanning aggregate data, it is increasingly used to address psychological questions (Elder, Pavalko, & Clipp, 1994), for example, Robert Mitchell's (1971) cross-cultural studies of the psychological effect of crowding checked for correlations between data on housing (population density) and law enforcement (crime) in Hong Kong and elsewhere, and Jonathan Freedman's (1975) analyses of urban neighborhoods in the United States. Compared with primary analysis (all methods in which researchers collect their own data), secondary analysis can be much more convenient, yet fraught with more pitfalls when the researcher is less intimate with the definitions and procedures of data collected by others.

Norm Violation

The method of norm violation, or ethnomethodology, was first developed by sociologists for intracultural research (Garfinkel, 1964) and readily embraced by some psychologists who saw it as a unique path to understanding individual behavior (Maas & Toivanen, 1978; Milgram & Sabini, 1979). "Symbolic interactionist" sociologists see virtually all human behavior as governed by unwritten, informal, yet powerful rules (i.e., norms) shared within each culture, so the best way to understand social behavior is to simply identify and then violate one of these rules to see how the social system readjusts itself. For example, how will a rider sitting in a crowded subway in New York or Tokyo react if someone simply asks them the rare question "Can I have your seat so I can sit down?" (Milgram, Sabini, & Silver, 1992). Will a pedestrian shake the outstretched hand of a smiling stranger? The answers invariably contain surprises. Those familiar with "Candid Camera" know the prankish quality of this sort of research, which produces imaginative situations in real-life settings to catch people offguard. ("When it's least expected, you're elected, you're the star today; smile, you're on Candid Camera!"—Funt, 1971.) Though the norm violator and experimenter are both "active" researchers who create their situations, the cutting difference between these two methods is that norm violation is uncontrolled exploratory research with no expectations in advance, while experimentation must be a highly controlled test of a hypothesis. In the example above, once we hypothesize that strangers will more likely surrender their subway seat to a woman than a man, then our norm violation becomes a field experiment. Oddly, ethnomethodology is a highly suited, if underused, method to study behavior cross-culturally. What unexpected insights await discovery when we replicate the same unusual behavior across cultures and then note how groups respond in a similar or different manner. Yet this method is totally absent from even the most thorough tomes on cross-cultural methods (Lonner & Berry, 1986; Berry et al., 1997). As one psychologist noted, "A kind of attempt to understand some of the implicit, unspoken bases of social life, it started in that part of the university campus called sociology, but it's essentially very sociopsychological in its application, and yet it has not been fused yet with the tradition of experimental social psychology" (Milgram, 1980).

Case Study

The case study method is an in-depth analysis of one or a few specific cases, in the hope of shedding light on others. It is based on the sage insight of psychologist Carl Rogers that "our most private thoughts are our most universal." The case may be an individual person, group, or even culture. This method has a long history in medicine, learning theory, and clinical psychology, long predating the turn-of-the-century publications by Freud, Jung, Adler, Pavlov, Watson, Skinner, or Piaget. In cross-cultural psychology, as in other fields, the case study is best seen as a propaedeutic method to segue into other forms of inquiry.

Multimethod Research

One study may combine several diverse methods to understand human behavior—a valuable if unusual approach in cross-cultural research. For example, McClelland and Winter (1969) correlated cross-cultural TAT test scores on nAch (need for achievement) with aggregate data on the gross national product across countries. In a field experiment by Takooshian (1979), a lost child asked 200 pedestrians for help in 20 neighborhoods within New York City and found that pedestrians in neighborhoods high in reported child abuse were less helpful to the child on the street ($r = -.54$). Going beyond this, Robert Levine (1989) used several methods (observation, experimentation, medical data) to compare 36 U.S. cities and confirm a correlation between the per-city rate of coronary heart disease with citizens' speed of walking, talking, working, and wearing of wristwatches (time urgency). Such multimethod studies help us better understand the why as well as the what of behavioral variations across cultures.

Sampling

Cross-cultural comparison requires representative and equivalent samples across cultures lest the results be misleading or ambiguous. This requires a sampling frame—some definition of each full population (Henry, 1990).

Probability Sampling. Probability sampling is essential if the results of the sample are to be generalized to a larger population. The assumption of many statistical tests is that the data have been collected according to the rules of probability. There are a few types of probability sampling, including simple, stratified, and stage. In a *simple random sample*, each unit or individual has an equal chance of being selected from the entire population. To get a sample of 100 from a population of 5,000, we selected every "nth," or fiftieth individual. It is routine here to use a random-numbers table, or some computer-generated source of random numbers to select the 100. In a *stratified random sample*, the population is divided into strata, or subparts, such as men or women, juniors or seniors. For this, a list of each stratum is required and every nth case is sampled, moving from one stratum to another. Thus the same proportion of the sample is obtained as it existed in the population. *Stage sampling*, or area sampling, is used when the investigator is working with a large population. First, the areas on the basis of nation, state, or region are selected. Second, blocks are selected within the areas. Finally, housing units may be selected. For example, in a survey of school children, first districts, then schools, then classrooms, and finally individual children are selected. At each stage selection is random.

Nonprobability Sampling. When it is not possible to produce a sampling frame of the population, nonprobability (nonrepresentative) sampling may be necessary (Sechrest, 1970). This sacrifices generalizability of the results for convenience of recruiting available subjects. In cross-cultural research, particularly in anthropology, such nonrandom samples are common because of various factors such as limited budget, time pressure, pilot studies, or as pretesting prior to larger studies. There are many types of nonprobability samples. In *convenience sampling*, the researcher recruits the most convenient "warm bodies" prepared to cooperate, such as people in a school, bus or train station, park, office or factory. In *purposive sampling* (or judgmental, selective, or deliberate sampling), subjects are selected to meet the preset criteria of the investigation. In *quota sampling*, the researcher wants to be sure that he or she has included some minimum number of persons from preset subgroups, such as specific age or sex, but unlike stratified probability sampling, a sample frame is not used for quota samples. Subgroups are identified, an arbitrary size per subgroup is set, and the first individuals to fill the quota are selected. In *cluster sampling*, particularly for large-scale surveys, adjacent units or clusters may be selected, such as three adjoining housing units in a large housing complex. In *snowball sampling*, the researcher selects a few subjects who possess the desired qualities, then uses these to ask the names of other people who have the same qualities. For example, left-handed people may suggest left-handed friends to enlarge the sample. *Expert choice sampling* is similar to judgmental sampling except that an expert selects the sample based on personal expertise with the group.

Cross-cultural sampling. Sampling across cultures raises at least four methodological issues, three detailed by Lonner and Berry (1986) and one by Hunter and Schmidt (1990). The first issue is selection of cultures. How should we choose our specific cultures to be compared? This requires prior knowledge of the cultures. Detailed information about world cultures can be accessed easily in the manuals of the Human Relation Area Files (HRAF). *The Outline of Cultural Material* (Murdock, 1971) consists of 700 subject categories under 79 major sections. *The Outline of World Culture* (Murdock, 1975) classifies them into eight major geographical regions: Asia, Europe, Africa, Middle East, North America, Oceania, Russia, South America. Ember and Ember's 1988 manual covers 350 societies indexed by 700 topics. The anthropological survey of India is a prime source on India's tribes and its people. Frazier and Glascock's chapter (Chapter 8, this volume) on aging in cross-cultural perspective discusses how the difference in selection strategies by psychologists, anthropologists, and sociologists has influenced their conclusions about the nature of aging in different types of societies.

The second issue is community selection. The selection of a Primary Sampling Unit (PSU) should also be based on judgment. It is culture in miniature form. Various key criteria should be considered, like size, type, characteristics, representativeness, replicability, age, and sex. At least three problems complicate the selection of PSU (Lonner & Berry, 1986). First is the continuous variation in culture and language over broad geographical areas. The Tharus, for example, are spread from Nainital in India to Janakpur in Nepal and are divided into three subgroups: Rana, Dangora, and Katharia (Singhal & Mrinal, 1991). Ranas think themselves superior to most. The Gonds are also spread throughout India and nothing is common except the generic name. The second difficulty in sampling is nomadism—the members may not be static at one place. Third, there may be ethnic variation within the basic cultural groups. It is suggested that a single community should be assumed as representative of the culture as a whole, and whenever there are differences due to ethinicity, acculturation, religion, or language, the different groups may be selected.

The third issue is selection of individuals. A sample should be representative as well as equivalent. In cross-cultural research, getting this kind of sample is difficult. Osgood, May, and Miron (1975) note that the relationship between these two is opposite—if efforts are made to increase representativeness, equivalence drops, and vice versa. In India, a representative sample requires proportionate numbers of many castes, religions, and languages. It will also have many illiterates. This sample would hardly have an equivalence with the representative sample of any other country. Indian college students have higher equivalence with the students of other countries, but certainly they are less representative. In fact the sampling strategy should entirely depend on the purpose of research. Osgood favored maximization of equivalence and preferred subjects who can read, are homogeneous, and are accessible—hence average high school adolescents. The representative sample in cross-cultural research is inappropriate except in particular circumstances, like opinion polls or some sort of national or community survey. Judgment is needed since, sadly, "many cross-cultural studies tend to ignore sampling differences . . . [so] the results are confounded by sampling differences, [and] it is difficult to provide an unambiguous interpretation" (van de Vijver & Leung, 1997a, p. 264).

The final issue is sample size. Small-sample research is far more likely to yield misleading results. In their extensive review of some 500 test validation studies across 12,000 jobs in several hundred organizations, meta-analysts Hunter and Schmidt (1990) found some 90 percent uniformity across studies, with the 10 percent of exceptions tending to be small-sample studies. There was a negative correlation between sample size and uniformity among studies, implying that, for methodological reasons, the smaller a sample, the more idiosyncratic its findings. Since this trend may well apply to cross-cultural as well as cross-organizational research, it creates a greater onus on researchers to either avoid small-sample research that may produce exceptional results or else take such studies' findings as tentative. Sadly, the complete absence of the terms *meta-analysis* or *validity generalization* from the indexes of recent cross-cultural texts (Triandis, 1994; Berry et al., 1997; van de Vijver & Leung, 1997a, 1997b) indicates these growing statistical techniques have hardly been applied yet to cross-cultural work.

CROSS-CULTURAL ISSUES

How can we best adapt our general research methods to study specific cultures and avoid misleading results? A number of issues face cross-cultural researchers.

Translation

Accurate comparison of two or more cultures requires not only equivalence in sampling (as stated above) but also equivalence in materials. For example, the alternate forms of a multilingual test must be identical in order for our findings to tap genuine cultural differences rather than simple language variations.

For a researcher developing a new test for cross-cultural comparison, Brislin (1986) provides guidelines for preparing easy-to-translate materials. They recommend using brief items with one dominant idea per sentence and active rather than passive voice (which is clearer to understand). Not to confuse the translator and the respondent, they suggest repetition of nouns only, not pronouns. Avoid metaphors and colloquialisms, because they may not have equivalents in the target language. Avoid subjunctives like could, should, would. The key idea should be followed by an additive sentence, because some respondents in the target culture may require more information. Avoid prepositions and adverbs indicating "where" and "when," such as upper, lower, beyond, frequent, and by, since they may not have adequate equivalents in the target language. Avoid possessive forms, because the target language may not have a clear understanding of the concept of ownership. Avoid words indicating vagueness, like probably, perhaps, maybe, and so forth. Avoid two different verbs in a single sentence. Finally, use words most familiar to the translators.

In translating a new or existing instrument, back-translation and centering is essential. A team of bilinguals is required. Bilingual A translates items from the source language (say, English) to the target language (say, Hindi); bilingual B then translates it back into the original language, English, blindly. This process of decentering (since no language is the center of attention) is repeated for a round or two.

English   Hindi   English   Hindi   English
Bilingual   Bilingual   Bilingual   Bilingual
A   B   C   D

After some rounds, the original English version and last back-translated English version are compared. Any discrepancy is an indication of the fact that the concept is not fit for translation. After discussion, this discrepancy may be removed. When adapting major personality tests, like the MMPI and CPI, emphasis should be on general intent more than word-for-word content. Finally, the results obtained with the translated material should be subjected to multivariate analysis of translated material using standard techniques to check reliability and validity (Anastasi & Urbina, 1997, pp. 84–139). For instance, Guzewicz and Takooshian (1992) adapted a standardized 36-item American scale to assess Japanese attitudes toward homeless people in Tokyo; they found an immediate alternate-form reliability of $r = +.97$ among 40 bilingual Japanese-Americans and a delayed (two-week) alternate-form, reliability of $r = +.74$ among 40 students in a Tokyo English school—suitable for a meaningful cross-cultural comparison. The International Test Commission has published its "Guidelines for adapting educational and psychological tests," including 22 specific points to consider in cross-national testing (Hambleton, 1994).

Cross-Cultural Testing

If a psychological test is defined as "an objective, standardized measure of a sample of behavior" (Anastasi & Urbina, 1997, p. 4), we know that such tests have been used in many parts of the world (including ancient China and Greece) for some 2,500 years (Bowman, 1989). Also well known are the problems of tests in the cross-cultural assessment of personality

(Guthrie & Lonner, 1986), of ability (Lonner & Berry, 1986, pp. 206–230), and of psychopathology (Draguns, this volume).

Personality. Cross-cultural assessment of personality faces at least four challenges (Guthrie & Lonner, 1986). First, there is no single theory of personality that can be generalized across cultures. Instead, there are the widely differing analytic theories of Freud, Jung, Erikson, Sullivan; the learning theories of Dollard, Miller, Skinner; and the humanistic theories of Rogers and Maslow. All these theories have a Western orientation that may be inappropriate for non-Western cultures. Second, broad and sweeping terms like "modal personality" or "national character" of one culture have proved unsatisfactory, since all cultures have a wide range of personalities. Third, there is no substitute for a detailed knowledge of the cultures under investigation. Library or brief "airport" visits are inadequate (Campbell, 1964; Guthrie, Jackson, Astilla, & Elwood, 1983). Fourth, cross-national samples may not be ideal, for example, college students, urbanites, or other volunteers who have become quite familiar with various tests and scales; they understand the five-, seven-, or nine-point scales while in fact their compatriots may not understand beyond the extremes of good and bad. Still, some researchers favor college student samples as a safe choice because of their ease of comparison cross-nationally (Sechrest, Fay, Zaidi, & Florez, 1973).

Ability. Most of the hundreds of cognitive ability tests available today are culture-specific and would be biased if used cross-culturally. Still, many so-called "culture-fair," nonverbal tests of intelligence and aptitude have been available since the 1920s (Keyser & Sweetland, 1991), for example, the Beta II, the Science Research Associates (SRA) Nonverbal Form, SRA Pictorial Reasoning Test, Raven's Standard Progressive Matrices and Advanced Progressive Matrices, Cattell's Culture-Fair Intelligence Tests and the D-48 or D-70 Dominoes Tests. Two cautions belong here. As Anastasi and Urbina (1997) note, being nonverbal does not make a test culture-fair; indeed, bias may enter at many stages of the research process—test design, administration, interpretation, and use. Second, culture-fair tests seem to have only "moderate" reliabilities and validities compared with more traditional, culture-specific tests (Takooshian, 1985).

Psychopathology. The *Diagnostic and Statistical Manual of Mental Disorders* (DSM-IV of the American Psychiatric Association, 1994) is the official source of definitions of psychopathology in the United States, yet this manual makes no claim to be culture-free; indeed it is heavily imbued with political and social judgments specific to American culture. Kleinman's (1991) review finds all but four *DSM* categories fell short of universality across cultures. In *Culture and Mental Disorders*, anthropologist Ralph Linton (1956) notes: "The test of relative normalcy is the extent to which the individual's experience has given him a personality conforming to the basic personality of his society." This cultural relativism among anthropologists is based on three types of evidence: (1) Normal behavior in one society may be considered abnormal in the other. Zuni Indians regard as abnormal white Americans' normally expected initiative and drive. (2) Some disorders are widespread only in specific cultures, like *Amok, Koro,* or *Latah* among the Malaysians, and *Dhat Syndrome* in India (Khubalkur, Gupta, & Jain, 1986). (3) Culture can also shape symptomology (Gurland & Zubin, 1982). With depression, for example, a North American patient may experience hopelessness, helplessness, guilt, suicidal ideation, feelings of worthlessness and loss of interest in various activities, and loss of ability to experience pleasure; yet a depressed Nigerian has heaviness or heat in the head, burning sensation in the body, crawling sensation in the head or the legs, and the feeling that the belly is bloated with water (Ebigno, 1982). Thus a depression scale developed in one culture may be invalid in another. Researchers should develop their own test—a time-consuming process—or else use some other methods like observation to assess psychopathology (Sartorius, Shapiro, & Jablensky, 1974). This is further discussed in Juris Draguns' chapter (this volume).

Emic/Etic

Since the terms *emic* and *etic* were coined in 1967, it has been common to distinguish these two approaches to culture (Triandis, 1994). Emic is culture-specific, referring to concepts and behaviors that are unique within a culture. Etic is cross-cultural, referring to concepts and ideas than can span cultures. Such distinction about cultures actually seems to echo a similar, long-standing distinction about individuals—the idiographic versus nomothetic approaches to personality (Allport, 1937). The nomothetic approach looks for uniformities of personality or behavior that link individuals, while the idiographic approach looks in depth into what makes each individual unique. Just as idiographic and emic research tends to be more qualitative, nomothetic and etic research lends itself to quantitative research. Let us not forget that these two approaches, though vastly different, are not in opposition but complement each other in our more complete understanding of individual and cross-cultural psychology.

Validity Generalization

Following the passage of the U.S. Civil Rights Act of 1964, industrial-organizational (I-O) psychologists in the United States were charged with taking a closer look at the predictive validity of their selection tests of ability and personality to determine whether they were equally predictive of all subgroups of U.S. workers based on gender, race, ethnicity, age, and disability. This also raised the question of how much tests varied in validity from one organization to another, thus requiring "local validation." At first, I-O psychologists may have seen such emphasis on moderator variables as extra effort, though most soon actually welcomed this new emphasis as a way to fine-tune their methods. As it turns out, 30 years of meta-analysis have found high validity generalization (or VG): "A test valid in one company will be valid in other companies. A test valid for one ethnic group will be valid for other ethnic groups" (Schultz & Schultz, 1994, p. 116). Moreover, several studies by meta-analysts like John Hunter and Frank Schmidt (1990) find that the few exceptional findings tend to be associated with limitations of those specific studies, such as small or irregular samples. Though the findings of several decades of cross-cultural research might lead us to expect that variations between nations will be much greater than variation between industrial organizations, we must, as scientists, also recognize this is really an empirical question. Though the terms *meta-analysis* and *VG* currently are absent from all key volumes on cross-cultural psychology, it is only a matter of time before meta-analysts begin probing this issue. For example, McCrae and Costa (1997) tested the popular five-factor model of personality with 7,134 people in six nations (Germany, Portugal, Israel, China, Korea, Japan) and found a rotated factor structure highly similar to U.S. respondents. They conclude, "Because the samples studied represented highly diverse cultures with languages from five distinct language families, these data strongly suggest that personality trait structure is universal" (p. 509).

Globalization

Historically, one clear impediment to cross-cultural psychology has been the high concentration of psychologists in a single nation—the United States. What can be done to make psychology more global? Our world of 5.7 billion people (Wright, 1997) contains some 500,000 psychologists (Rosenzweig, 1992). North America contains one of every 20 of the world's people (5 percent) but 12 of every 20 psychologists (60 percent). With such imbalance, North America can hardly help but dominate world psychology in every way—its books, journals, publishers, theories, researchers, and even subjects. In recent years, North America's own psychologists have occasionally chastized themselves as being "isolationist" (Sexton & Misiak, 1984), "self-absorbed" (Rosenzweig, 1984), or even "xenophobic" (Sexton, 1984) and have suggested ways to make psychology more global, increasing the impact of non-American colleagues. We might note three points here: (1) An analysis of the ten most-cited researchers in U.S. textbooks finds this list: Sigmund Freud, Jean Piaget, B. F. Skinner, Albert Bandura, Erik Erikson, Carl Rogers, Ivan Pavlov, Stanley Schachter, Neal Miller, and Abraham Maslow (Knapp, 1985). Clearly, three of these top ten are non-Americans from three different nations—an Austrian psychiatrist, a Swiss developmentalist, and a Russian physiologist. (2) Some North American journals, like the *Journal of Social Psychology*, give explicit preference to research using non-American samples, and others, like *World Psychology*, explicitly solicit a balance of American and non-American authors and editors (Gielen, 1995, vii). (3) The American Psychological Association's Committee on International Relations in Psychology, formed in 1944, is increasingly active in developing new ways to globalize psychology, and APA voted to form a new Division 52 for International Psychology in 1997 (Fowler, 1997). Other organizations, like the International Council of Psychologists, promote cross-national research collaboration (Adler, 1994), and hundreds of American foundations now fund international psychology programs (Foundations Center, 1996).

Compare psychology here with medicine. Western medicine would be incomplete without cross-national research. Over the years, for instance, allopathic physicians have found that the French suffer fewer heart attacks because their cholesterol-laden diet is mediated by flavinoids in their red wine; the incidence of specific diseases across countries can be linked to national variations in diet, for example, legumes, rice, red meat, and that Western medicine can learn from studying other cultures' herbs, shamans, and *chee* (acupuncture and Chinese medicine) (Adler & Mukherjee, 1995). Western medicine's treatment of its patients would be far less adequate if it were not for cross-cultural research yet, at the same time, this Western medicine—in the form of missionary hospitals and other outreaches—has been of life-saving value to millions of non-Western patients. We might well hope that as psychology globalizes, it continues to be a valuable field enriched by its globalization.

CONCLUSION

Like A.P.A. President Donald Campbell, psychologists increasingly seem to recognize that psychology must take cultural diversity into account in order to produce a veridical understanding of human behavior. It is becoming standard for introductory psychology textbooks in the 1990s that "Every chapter includes a section called Exploring Diversity . . . [to] highlight the way in which psychology informs (and is informed by) issues relating to the increasing multiculturalism of our global society" (Feldman, 1997, xxii-xxiii). To the extent that cross-cultural research will become more common in psychology's future, it is important for both the natural and social scientists among us to adapt our methods for the work ahead.

4

Language and Communication

John Beatty

Communication generally means the sending of a message in such a way
that a receiver understands the message transmitted by a sender. Those acts
in which information is communicated are rather complex. When a communicative act is broken down into its constituent parts, each part can be
seen as a variable, which, if altered, in some way changes the nature of the
message being sent. The following parts or variables can be isolated: a
sender, a message, a code in which the message is sent; the medium through
which the code is sent; the context in which it is sent; and a receiver. Each
of these constitutes a variable in the communicative act. By changing the
variable, the nature of the message is altered in some way.

Consider the following statement made by a police officer to a driver of
a stopped car: "Let me see your license and registration." In this example,
the variables are filled in the following way:

sender	the police officer
receiver	the driver
message	the request for specific materials
code	language (in this case specifically English)
medium	speech
context	official, at a car stop

Changes in any of the variables may alter the nature of the message. If
the sender is not in fact a police officer but a civilian, the request can be
handled quite differently than if the sender is actually the police.

If the driver of the car is the chauffeur for the limousine being driven in a cavalcade with the president of the United States riding in the back seat, such a request is likely to meet minimally with the police officer being suspended.

One suspects that the police officer might be sent to psychological services for help if instead of speaking English, the officer spoke in Croatian, or if instead of speaking, the officer approached the car and attempted to transmit the message in a different code, say through gesture in pantomime. Even simply shifting the medium and writing the request would likely be seen as strange.

In a different context, a police officer making such a request of the president while touring the Capitol would definitely be seen as bizarre.

This is not to say that any or all of these might not happen, but one would need to construct a highly specific context that would allow the other variable to be considered rational. If a police officer suspected that the driver of the presidential limousine were an impostor and an agent of a foreign government, then the question coming in a language other than English is reasonable.

Such situations, where contexts are generally seen as out of the norm, are often called "marked." They require the construction of some situation before the are seen as acceptable.

PARTICIPANTS IN COMMUNICATION

Various cultures define different possibilities for the variables. Senders occur in all communicative acts. They may vary as to age, sex, position, occupation, and so on. The implications of having or being a specific sender clearly can alter the message.

In English, when Mr. John Smith meets Ms. Jane Doe, there are a number of possible ways they can address each another. Even the decision as to which one speaks first can be significant. The Japanese book *Kojiki* contains an episode in which the sex of the person speaking first is crucial!

(a) Good morning Mr. Smith.
    Good morning Ms. Doe.

(b) Good morning John
    Good morning Ms. Doe.

(c) Good morning John.
    Good morning Jane.

In the first example, one might conclude that the speakers are formal or distant but relatively equal in status. In the second example, Ms. Doe has status over John, and in the third example, the speakers appear more equal and informal or close.

In Japanese, formality and distance are not linked in such a way. One can be formal and close, formal and distant, informal and close, informal and distant. Immediately it is apparent that the categories used in analyzing the English situation are not quite comparable to the ones we would need in Japanese where, in fact, far more possibilities exist.

Many titles are possible in Japanese: -san; -sama; -kun; -chan, and so on. Each of these can be suffixed to a person's name regardless of sex—Japanese does not distinguish Mr. from Miss, Mrs. or Ms. In addition, Japanese can affix these titles to either the family name or the given name, as well as to occupational titles. Hence one can say to someone, male or female, with the family name of Watanabe "Watanabe-san," "Watanabe-sama," "Watanabe-kun," or "Watanabe-chan." If the person's given name is Hajime, one can also use "Hajime-san" or "Hajime-sama." In addition, all these titles can be affixed to occupations as well. The Japanese word for fish store is *sakanaya* (*sakana*: "fish"; *ya*: "store"). The person operating such a store can be referred to or addressed as *sakanaya-san*, meaning "Ms. Fishmonger," "Mrs. Fishmonger," "Miss Fishmonger," or "Mr. Fishmonger."

These various titles do not reflect formal versus informal or equal or skewed status distinctions the same way English does.

Similarly, various cultures will define various statuses and contexts differently. Any attempt to assume that a category that exists in one society will exist in another is dangerous.

CODES

Codes occur in many forms. The most common (and most studied) is language, but others, such as gesture, touch, smell, distance, and actions, are exploited regularly by people in all cultures. The following are indications of the kinds of codes and the variables contained within them (after Beatty and Takahashi, 1994).

Body Language, Gesture, and Posture

Body language deals largely with the human body as it is used for communication. Different parts of the body can be used to carry different symbolic meanings. Hair is one of the more common. Hair length and style can send messages about age, gender, political position, and so on.

The use of body position and movement for communicative purposes is also part of this variable. The way the body is held and moves can convey a good deal of meaning. One has only to look at Greta Garbo in *Camille*, when she is told that she must give up her lover. At first she fights the idea, but then, with her back to the camera, she accepts this. Her whole body sags, and the audience knows immediately she has made that decision.

Gestures, in which are included generally body movements as well as facial expressions, use movement of parts of the body to convey meaning. Shaking the head for yes or no, or shrugging the shoulders ("I don't know" or "I'm not sure") are well known in Western society. Some societies reverse the meaning of nodding and shaking the head.

Gesture and body language have been particularly irksome to work with since no really good notation system is available. The international phonetics alphabet, which allows linguists to transcribe and define virtually any sound in any language, has no real equivalent in any of the other variable areas. Even effort-stress notation or labonotation in dance do not come close. Most dancers feel these are mnemonic devices rather than real transcription systems.

Cross culturally different body positions and movement can vary enormously. Despite this, it is possible to classify communicative movements into five types (Ekman, 1980). These are:

1. Emblems: those associated with clear meaning, like the circle made with the thumb and index finger in America with the other three fingers extended meaning "OK." Morris's book *Gestures* (1979) deals basically with emblems. The peculiar stance taken by members of the Japanese underworld and secret handshakes of particular organizations are examples. The most complex variables in this category are the sign languages used by deaf mutes or American Indians of the Great Plains.

2. Illustrator: the movements made mostly by hands and arms, which are imitative or which show some attribute like size, shape, or speed. Somewhat akin to this are the illustrators that are deictic and point toward objects (their relative position is an attribute). Cultural variation is possible here as well. The Japanese tend to point to their own noses to indicate "I," while Americans generally point at their chests.

3. Body manipulator: the touching of one's own body or object for no practical purpose. Examples of body manipulators are fidgeting or touching one's clothing. These are held by Ekman as being nonintentional. This class of acts is not associated with a specific meaning, but people tend to attribute them to certain psychological states, such as nervousness, boredom, or anxiety, or to personalities.

4. Regulator: largely movements of the eye and the surrounding tissues, which can vary the eye's appearance. Thus frowning, squinting, and eye movement itself are examples. These Ekman calls regulators because he feels they are involved with regulating the communicative interaction. Even here, cross-cultural variation can occur. The eyebrow flick, commonly associated with recognition, is not universal but is conspicuously absent in Japan (although eyebrow movement in and of itself is sufficiently important that even the traditional Japanese *bunraku* puppets have moveable eyebrows).

5. Facial expression: an expression of external state through the musculature of the face. Ekman demonstrates that, as far as the most fundamental emotions (happiness, sadness, anger, disgust, surprise, and fear) are concerned, there is a good deal of universality with little cultural variability. However, there seem to be culture-specific rules to interpret the more subtle aspects of emotional expression.

Touching (Haptics)

Montagu (1971) has indicated a psychobiological foundation for touching and has noted the importance of tender loving care. There are a number of case histories of the importance of touch in children, who have literally died from a lack of it. Symbolically, touching is used in all cultures whether it be handshaking, kissing, or some other form of body contact.

The variables in this area involve which parts of the body can be touched and with what intensity. Whether one touches softly, slaps, or hits, for example, varies the message dramatically. The range of message in this area is limited, however. Touching seems generally to define or reconfirm the social and emotional relationships between the participants.

Distance and Space (Proxemics)

There seems to be some evidence that overcrowding leads to stress, and so physical distance and space are intimately related to psychobiological variables

E. Hall (1966) has established four ranges of physical distance that occur between people: intimate, personal, social, and public. Each of these distances serves a particular function, but significantly, the actual distances that define these ranges seem to vary from culture to culture. What Americans regard as personal distance is regarded in parts of Latin America as public, hence Latin Americans tend to stand closer together when talking than is comfortable to Americans.

Physical space can also be used symbolically to indicate social distance, status, role, rank, and so on. Consider such problems as occur in trying to create a seating arrangement at a banquet.

Dress and Body Alteration

The human body can itself be altered or decorated. The ways in which material objects are attached onto the body or the way the body itself is manipulated can all signal various kinds of meaning. Clothing and accessories require some sort of purchase, and the accessibility of these objects becomes important. The possession of material objects leads to so-called "status symbols," which send a good deal of meaning to people in a given culture.

The body itself may be temporarily or permanently altered. Humans alter the appearance of their own bodies by applying objects to them in order to enhance their communicative values. Body paint and makeup are good examples of temporary changes made to the body. Within American culture, the various degrees and levels of makeup, for example, change between people of different social statuses and in different contexts.

Tattooing, scarring, and piercing represent more permanent change. The mutilation of the body constitutes the most dramatic form of communication in this area. In some societies, knocking out a tooth, circumcision, or clitorectomy may be used as markers showing that the person has achieved a certain status in that culture.

Actions

The idea that actions carry meanings is hardly new. "Actions speak louder than words" is an old saying in English. Acts usually involve a "sender" doing something that carries meaning with it. The act may be something like bringing a gift to someone with whom the person is having dinner. The act of gift giving carries with it significant meaning.

Similarly, the way people conceive of time and sociability may all have an effect on the way they act. Whether people show up on time or late, whether they hold several different conversations with several people at once, all of these things send messages. The context in which gifts are presented and the size and nature of the gift vary from culture to culture and have to be considered as part of the communicative process in any culture.

LANGUAGE

Language seems to be the code *par excellence* for specific communication. It is the most commonly used and the most studied form of communication.

It is not uncommon to make several distinctions in dealing with language. The first of these is the difference between language and speech. Saussure (1959) (using the terms *langue* and *parole*) indicated that speech is what people actually say—the language being the rules for what they say. This distinction is later echoed in Chomsky's (1965) concept of competence (language) versus performance (speech). When talking, people frequently make errors. They backtrack, change their minds in the middle of a sentence, and in the process the sentence loses its grammaticality. People can often recognize grammatical errors in sentences, and in normal speech they may either go back and correct them or let them slide.

A second distinction is between Language (written with a capital L and not pluralized) as a generalized or universal category and language(s), the specific forms found in different societies. All human societies have Language, but the language they have varies. This distinction between the universal and the specific has important ramifications, which are discussed later in this chapter.

The Nature of Language: Phonology, Morphology and Syntax

Most linguists recognize that languages are made of contrasting units of sound called phonemes. Phonemes are the significant contrastive units in speech. No speaker makes exactly the same sound each time (as sound spectrograms show), but rather makes sounds that fall within acceptable and generally predictable ranges. Sapir (1933) recognized that it was the phoneme, not the actual sound, that had psychological reality for the speakers of a language.

Phonemes merely mark contrasts. They have no meaning. The sounds /p/, /i/, and /g/ are simply sounds in English and have no meaning of their own. When meaning is added, the resulting structure is called a morpheme: generally, the smallest unit of sound with meaning. While the separate sounds of *pig* are meaningless, when taken together, they have the meaning they do for English speakers. This feature is known as "duality of patterning" and is thought by many to be unique to language (Hockett 1960).

The last level of analysis is syntax—the organization of words into phrases and sentences. Morphology (the study of morphemes and their arrangement into words) and syntax taken together is called grammar.

These three areas are generally known as "descriptive" or "structural" linguistics. In addition, linguists have been interested in another area, that of historical or comparative linguistics, which examines language change and the relationships between language. A third division of linguistics involves the relationship between language and three other areas: social organization (sociolinguistics), culture (ethnolinguistics), and psychology (psycholinguistics). This last area generally deals in the areas of cognition, where it has ties to ethnolinguistics, and language acquisition.

Cognition

When working within a given culture and language, it is possible to come to some understanding of cultural categories through the language. The relationship between language and cultural categories is one which has been investigated for many years. Its most popularly discussed formulation is known as the Sapir-Whorf hypothesis (Whorf in Carroll, 1956).

An insurance investigator named Benjamin Lee Whorf postulated that certain kinds of accidents were caused by a lack of understanding of certain linguistic forms, which then affected their behavior. The idea that "inflammable" was ambiguous and could be analyzed to mean "not flammable" or "able to inflame" led to the idea that language determined thought and structured reality.

The hypothesis is itself far more complex and holds that grammatical relationships cause people to perceive the world differently. This idea is discussed by Whorf in several places and the formulation of strict causation seems to vary from place to place.

Most linguists feel at this point that the Sapir-Whorf hypothesis is basically incorrect (see Hudson, 1980), at least in most instances, and that language reflects cultural categories more than being causal. Popular writing has recently "discovered" the Sapir-Whorf hypothesis and has moved it into the foreground. Many groups have felt that by legislating the alteration of linguistic categories, the categories themselves will change. The classic example has been the move to change words like *chairman* into *chairperson*. The argument here is that by completely supporting the most extreme form of the Sapir-Whorf hypotheses, a change in the language will cause a change in the behavior and culture. Bendix (1979) has succinctly argued against this, claiming that the ability to change the terminology does not cause change, but the ability to cause the linguistic change to happen is an example of growing political power.

Although there are many problems with the Sapir-Whorf hypothesis, it is still possible for outsiders to gain entrance to the culture through the language. Even if the language may not cause the cultural categories to appear, they may well be markers of the existence of at least some categories. Hence understanding the language may require some analysis of its culture.

Many anthropologists have felt that by examining the language one can get a glimpse of the underlying categories reflected in the language. In these cases, a "folk taxonomy" structure is sought, and the researcher is able to use terms in the language to show a kind of inclusion of terms in some semantic categories. In the same way that biologists would classify living things into different taxons (e.g., humans are primates, which are mammals, which are vertebrates, which are animals), language may allow for the classification of activities as seen by people in different cultures.

Classic examples of this kind of approach can be seen in Spradley's study of tramps (1968, 1970, 1971) and bars (Spradley and Mann, 1975), where an attempt is made to show how the linguistic categories reflect an underlying conceptualization of the world (see also, for method, Spradley, 1979, 1980).

Spradley is able to discuss, for example, "ways to make a jug" (i.e., ways to get an alcoholic beverage). These can be shown as:

    Ways to make a jug
        making a run
        making the V.A.
        bumming
        making a frisco circle
        panhandling
        bumming
    cutting in on a jub

In this example, "making a run," "making the V.A.," "bumming," and "cutting in on a jug" are subdivisions of "ways to make a jug" in the same way that birds, reptiles, mammals, and fish are kinds of vertebrates. "Making a frisco circle," "panhandling," and "bumming" are kinds of "bumming" in the same way that cats, dogs, people, and monkeys are kinds of mammals.

The area in which most work has been done is known as *componential analysis*, which involves the analysis of the morphemes of a language to expose the component parts of the semantic systems. Much of the early work in this area was done in the area of kinship, and the significance of this kind of analysis has been hotly contested (Burling, 1964; Wallace, 1965; for criticism of several analytical methods see Beatty, 1980). The basic idea, though, is that the semantics of different languages reveal underlying categories for each culture.

Universals versus Specifics

One of the more formidable tasks in researching the relationship between language and culture, however, has been the question of how much of what is known is universal or culture-specific.

In terms of language acquisition, a major area of research for many linguists has been the way in which people develop linguistic competence. It has been discovered that in any culture, children learn their native languages at about the same speed. No language seems easier or more difficult than any other. The actual order in which various aspects of language are acquired has received significant attention (Jakobson, 1968). The way in which children acquire significant sounds (phonemes), the specifics of learning regular and irregular verbs, syntactic constructions, and semantics are still under study and will undoubtedly be studied for many years to come. There seems to be considerable universality in certain aspects of language acquisition. Jakobson reports, for example, that children learn front consonants before they learn back consonants, and fricatives are acquired only after homorganic stops.

Another area of importance in universals in linguistics is understanding just what patterns may be common to all languages, or which seem to be linked. For example, no language seems to have more nasals (/m/, /n/, etc.) than it has stops (/p/, /t/, /k/). It also appears that, by and large, SVO languages, in which the word order is Subject Verb Object (e.g., in English "The man sees the woman"), put relative clauses after the word they modify (i.e., "The man, who is standing on the corner, sees the woman"—literally "man [topic] woman [object] sees"), while those languages that tend toward SOV (e.g., in Japanese "otoko wa onna wo mimasu"), tend to put the relative clause before the word it modifies ("kado de tatte iru otoko wa onna wo mimasu"—literally "corner on standing is man [topic] woman [object] sees").

Of particular interest in this area has been the study of Creoles. Creoles in different parts of the world share certain similarities that are difficult to explain by claiming a common ancestor for all of them, since many are "hybrids" of different languages.

Lounsbury's (1964) formal analysis argues that certain universal characteristics can be found in all kin terms that allow for the analysis of kinship systems. For Lounsbury, one need only define eight basic or "primitive kin types" (mother, father, brother, sister, son, daughter, husband and wife). When different sets of rules are added to these kin, all the various kin types will be produced. Hence some radically different kinship systems may vary solely on the basis of a missing rule or two.

In a similar vein, Berlin and Kay (1969) have argued that although a variety of cultures have different numbers of terms for colors, the focus of the colors and the order in which new color terms are added is basically constant.

Adler (1992) has shown that in experimental and laboratory situations, certain schema regarding the distancing of different classes of people (i.e., blood relatives) remain the same cross-culturally.

The work on universals has been significant in raising questions about why such universals exist. Whether scientists opt for a genetic basis for universal behaviors, or whether they are seen as species-typical rather than species-specific (Aronson, Tobach, Rosenblatt, Lehrman, 1972) has been the focus of much debate in the area. The question of the biological foundation of language and culture is likely to persist for quite some time.

CULTURE AND CULTURES

Anthropologists often make use of the concepts of "Culture" and "cultures" as being related but somewhat different. Culture (like "Language") is generally written with a capital letter and cannot be pluralized. By this, anthropologists refer to something that is universal and, to many, uniquely human. Language, similarly, implies something that occurs in all human societies and, again, to many, is uniquely human. These same two words, when written with small letters ("language" and "culture") and that may also occur as pluralized nouns ("languages" and "cultures"), tend to refer to specific examples rather than the universal concepts.

These concepts are analytically important, since it is possible to have variation in something while still maintaining that there is enough similarity to refer to the different varieties as being "the same." Hence people may speak different languages, but they all have "Language." People may have many different "cultures," but all people have "Culture."

The fact that there are different languages and cultures makes for problems in communication. The fact that they are reasonably similar allows for at least some degree of translation between them. Each culture has its own set of rules and values, which cause all kinds of events to have a variety of meanings. Cultural variation in values leads to even greater problems. Although these are not normally seen as part of the communication system, it is imperative that they be considered when looking at communication. Both Uriel Weinreich and Kenneth Pike were instrumental in drawing attention to the idea that knowledge of one particular system may cause problems when dealing with a second system. This was called "interference." It is most clearly seen when a person learns a second language and makes errors in that language based on their knowledge of their first language. For example, a person whose native language is English, may make errors when learning a second language. For example, English speakers often have difficulty pronouncing the German "ch" [x] in words such as *ich, mich, sich,* or *richtig.* The sound [x] is missing in most English dialects. English speakers tend to produce either a "k" [k] as "ch" [x] or "sh" [s]. The sound [x] is a velar spirant and, hence, made in the same position as [k], which is a velar stop. On the other hand, [x] is a spirant as is [s], but [s] is alveolar.

Similarly, English speakers tend to use English word order in German. German requires that if the subject clause of the sentence is not initial, then it must follow the verb. English does not have such a rule. Hence, in German as in English, it would be "Ich sah ihn." [I saw him.] But unlike English it would be "Gestern sah ich ihn." [Yesterday saw I him.] English speakers often produce the "non-German" "Gestern ich sah ihn." [Yesterday I saw him.] There has been "interference" with the German word order based on the speaker's knowledge of English.

Similarly, mistaken interpretations of events can even be made by a member or two members of the same culture. When the two people are members of different cultures, the chances of misinterpretation escalate. These kinds of errors are a bit more complex.

Earlier, it was pointed out that statuses such as "teacher," may exist in different cultures, but different cultures define that role in diverse ways. In the same way, the roles of women and men are likely to be defined in a variety of ways in different cultures. In order to understand a communicative act, it is necessary to take into consideration the dimension of the statuses of the participants in the act. In and of themselves, they might not be seen as aspects of communication, but they clearly affect the interpretation of the speech act.

Additionally, the values, judgments, and interests of the various cultures need to be considered. These will have an effect on the way various speech acts will be interpreted. For example, Margaret Locke, in a lecture at the City University of New York, has drawn our attention to the fact that although Japanese seem relatively unconcerned about the question of abortion, they do not feel comfortable with heart transplants, which is just the opposite in the United States, where pro- and antiabortionists war with one another, and heart transplants are taken as normal.

When such differences are considered, a number of problems arise dealing with what might be called "cultural presuppositions." How a given culture structures the attitudes and feelings of its members will have an impact on how communication operates. While it is clear that people in a given culture may have widely differing opinions, the differences between the way Japanese and Americans deal with topics such as abortion and heart transplants clearly reflect cultural variation, not individual variation.

When one looks at examinations given to foreign students to test their grasp of the English language, it becomes clear that many of these variables have not been recognized or have been ignored.

One university regularly tests incoming students for their understanding of English by asking them to write an essay on the position they hold on a specific topic. Recently students have been asked to take stands on such issues as abortion and gays in the military.

Consider some of the difficulties. First of all, the topic may be of absolutely no interest to the students, and, hence, they have given little thought to the matter and have not paid any attention to the standard rhetoric, which must, perforce, be discussed in the essay.

Writing versus pronunciation (English "he" and "she") is different. Japanese /h/ is pronounced [x] before /i/ and in some cases [s]. /s/ is pronounced [s] before /i/ hence in some dialects "he" (/hi/ is [si]) and "she" (/si/ is [si]) fall together.

WHAT IS ACCEPTABLE TALK?

Consider cultural factors—stylistic devices especially now that we are multicultural happy and want to preserve the very differences that we are trying to eradicate! (Foreign students are supposed to learn American culture—whatever that is, and worse who is teaching it to them?)

Adding to the complexity is the question of evaluators' ability to grade such a paper objectively, since they themselves are biased by the answer. Despite protests from several of the people who graded such papers that they were in fact objective, it was instructive to hear them discussing papers on religion. "I couldn't believe that anyone took such beliefs seriously." If this is the attitude of the marker, one suspects things are not so objective as they are held to be.

Students who have no idea who the people are who grade the test may feel discomfort at not knowing the social status of the individual and also at not being able to see the responses. In some cultures, argumentation is not as crucial as it is in America. Probably no American would deny the idea that, even in America, one sometimes drops an argument in favor of keeping the other person as a friend. Heated arguments can easily cause friends to be lost, and if holding on to the friendship is more important, the discussion is best dropped.

In testing methods the drill may or may not be significant. In cultural teaching methods, what do students see as being important? If drill is important then not having something drilled may mark it as unimportant.

In each of these cases, specific cultural differences result in a variety of problems. Just what is being communicated and how it is being communicated are locked into a complex set of symbolics, which are culturally determined. It is impossible to understand many of the linguistic utterances without knowledge of the system in which they occur. To some degree, this has become the major premise of postmodern theory, which tries, at least in part, to examine the nature of dialogue in societies.

CROSS-CULTURAL VERSUS INTERCULTURAL PROBLEMS

For most researchers working in this area, cross-cultural studies are comparative and involve the analysis of data in different cultures with an eye toward comparing the similarities and differences that occur between cultures. In a sense, one can examine the variables used by each culture in communication through verbal and nonverbal means.

Intercultural studies deal with the problems that arise when people from one culture attempt to communicate with people from another. In this area, the variables used by people from different cultures are often not the same and hence the potential for confusion and misunderstanding increase enormously.

Language and communication can be seen as two areas of human behavior that vary dramatically from culture to culture. None the less, there is a certain kind of similarity postulated by some linguists, psychologists, and anthropologists that, at the core of all this variation, there is something universal. Without this basic core, translation from one language to another would be virtually impossible. In effect, by careful analysis of cross-cultural communication, it becomes possible to understand how individuals are able to communicate interculturally. All human languages and cultures seem to share a certain amount of commonality. Specific languages and cultures are variations on this common core allowing for all cultures to be simultaneously unique yet the same.

II

Developmental Aspects of
Cross-Cultural Psychology

5

Child and Adolescent Development:
Cross-Cultural Perspectives

Harry W. Gardiner

Nearly two decades ago, T. Schwartz, an anthropologist, writing about the acquisition of culture, declared that "anthropologists had ignored children in culture while developmental psychologists had ignored culture in children" (1981, p. 4). Five years later, Gustav Jahoda, a well-known European psychologist and early contributor to the developing discipline of cross-cultural psychology, was more optimistic and pointed out that cross-cultural studies of human development were on the rise (Jahoda, 1986). Studies comparing the content in recently published developmental books with those of only a few years ago reveal that the inclusion of cross-cultural topics and findings has grown tremendously (Best & Ruther, 1994; Gardiner, 1996).

Much of this recent interest in the cross-cultural approach is the result of efforts to view human development within its cultural context. Early contributors to this rapidly evolving view include Urie Bronfenbrenner and his ecological systems approach (1979, 1986, 1989, 1993), Charles Super and Sara Harkness with their concept of the developmental niche (1986), and John Berry's original studies of cultural ecology and cognitive style (1976).

The merging of culture and human development is particularly well represented in a number of contemporary books including *Lives Across Cultures: Cross-Cultural Human Development* (Gardiner, Mutter, & Kosmitzki, 1998), *Family and Human Development Across Cultures* (Kagitçibasi, 1996), *Parents' Cultural Belief Systems* (Harkness & Super, 1996), *Cultural Psychology* (Cole, 1996), *Cross-Cultural Roots of Minority Child Development* (Greenfield & Cocking, 1994), and the four volume *Handbook of Parenting* (Bornstein, 1995b). In addition, there is the recently revised three-volume *Handbook of Cross-Cultural Psychology* (1997), edited by John Berry and others, containing material relevant to the study of cross-cultural development along with chapters on the role of cross-cultural theory and methodology. Finally, for a historical perspective, one should look at such classics as Urie Bronfenbrenner's *Two Worlds of Childhood: U.S. and U.S.S.R.* (1970) and the series of volumes on *Six Cultures* by Whiting (1963), Whiting and Whiting (1975), and Whiting and Edwards (1988).

INTRODUCTION

As with the earlier version of this chapter (Gardiner, 1994), any effort to include more than a small portion of the cross-cultural findings related to child and adolescent development is impossible. Therefore, the discussion that follows is necessarily subjective and representative of only a few areas of current interest. This chapter has been significantly revised since its first appearance, and readers, therefore, are referred to the earlier book by Adler and Gielen (1994) for a discussion of original topics (e.g., parent-child interaction, Piagetian theory, and mathematical achievement).

SOCIALIZATION

The first step in successfully explaining cultural differences in human development requires an understanding of the crucial process of *socialization* or the process by which an individual becomes a member of a particular culture and takes on its values, beliefs, and other behaviors in order to function within it. Chamberlain and Patterson (1995) clearly describe the complexity and reciprocal nature of this process when they state that "In a very real sense . . . socialization . . . is something that emerges from thousands of exchanges between the child and family members spread out over a period of many years. During these exchanges, the child is altering the behavior of the parent at the same time that the parent is presumably 'socializing' the child. It is this mutuality of effects that makes it very difficult to analyze cause and effect relations" (p. 211–212).

Adding to this difficulty is the fact that many modern societies are characterized by contradictory value and belief systems as well as by competing systems. This contrasts dramatically with the earlier period when the term *socialization* was first introduced by social learning theorists and cultural anthropologists who thought in terms of relatively unitary value and belief systems and who believed learning was based on reinforcement, imitation, and similar concepts. This raises a number of interesting (but often perplexing) questions, such as "Which of these systems (if any) does a child or adolescent adopt?" and "Why does a child adopt one system rather than another?"

Answering these questions is not easy for several reasons. First (and an important point to keep in mind throughout this discussion) is that frequently there is more variability in specific behaviors *within* cultures than between or among them. Second, attempts to understand behavior from a more traditional straight forward socialization viewpoint, not taking into account subtle individual differences or examining the full range of influential others within one's environment, is severely limiting.

Of significant assistance in overcoming these limitations is the concept of the developmental niche (Harkness & Super, 1995, 1996; Super & Harkness, 1986) providing a framework for understanding how various components of one's culture affect developmental and socialization processes. Briefly, these components consist of (1) the physical and social settings of daily life, such as one's family; (2) the culturally determined customs of child care and childrearing, such as sibling interactions; and (3) the psychology of the caretakers or characteristics of a child's parents, for example, belief systems and developmental expectations. Super and Harkness (1994) succinctly sum up their approach when they state, "At the center of the developmental niche, therefore, is a particular child, of a certain age and sex, with certain temperamental and psychological dispositions. By virtue of these and other characteristics, this child will inhabit a different cultural 'world' than the worlds inhabited by other members of his family—and further, the child's world will also change as the child grows and changes" (pp. 96–97).

As Maccoby (1992) has noted, contemporary approaches to socialization are placing greater emphasis on the interactive exchanges between parents and children and, compared with earlier explanations, are becoming more complex and multidimensional. Socialization theories are also undergoing significant revision as theorists and researchers recognize their cultural limitations (Edwards, 1996). For far too long, theorists have been victims of their own socialization in promoting what Kagitçibasi (1996) has called "an indigenous psychology of the Western world." For an interesting glimpse into the ecological world of Japanese families and the way in which they socialize their children, see the work of Hendry (1993).

Infancy

When a newborn arrives into the world, independent of its particular culture, it has a number of basic needs requiring immediate attention. How these needs are met and the manner in which they are socialized vary considerably across cultures and often among ethnic groups within a single society (Gardiner, Mutter, & Kosmitzki, 1998).

When and how parents attend to their infant's basic needs, the extent to which they allow them to explore their environment, how nurturing or restrictive they are, and which behaviors they value and socialize are strongly influenced by culture from the first hours following birth. In the words of Bornstein (1995a), "With the birth of a baby, a parent's life is forever changed. The pattern that those changes assume, in turn, shapes the experiences of infants and, with time, the people they become. Parent and infant chart the course together. Infancy is a starting point of life for both infant and parent" (p. 30). A major contribution to our understanding of the origins, expressions, and consequences of the cultural belief systems held by parents can be found in the recent work of Harkness and Super (1996).

Sleep. All infants require sleep, but as the psychological, anthropological, and pediatric literature reveals, there are considerable variations in cultural sleeping arrangements (Morelli, Rogoff, Oppenheim, & Goldsmith, 1992; Super & Harkness, 1996; Super, Harkness, & Blom, 1997; Wolf, Lozoff, Latz, & Pauladetto, 1996). According to Harkness and Super (1995), the way sleep is organized, including where and with whom, is a particularly interesting aspect of culture because, although it is a private rather than public behavior, it is highly structured by different societies. For example, in an early study of Kipsigis farming families in rural Kenya, the authors reported that, after the birth of a younger child, the next youngest child still sleeps with its mother and other siblings but its position changes from the front of the mother to her back. This change, accompanied by an end to breast-feeding and back carrying, represents a "fundamental shift in the child's physical and social settings of life" (Harkness & Super, 1995, p. 227).

It should be noted that the practice of *cosleeping* just described is indigenous to most of the world's cultures. The expectation that children should sleep in their own beds, in their own rooms, away from parents is seldom seen outside the United States and other parts of North America (Barry & Paxson, 1971; McKenna, 1993). As Super and Harkness point out, for infants to be able to sleep through the night without some contact or involvement with parents may be "pushing the limits of infant's adaptability" (1982, p. 52). This is only one example of how cultural, as well as individual and familial, differences play a major role in the socialization and expression of specific behaviors. To learn more about how sleep management is related to cultural differences in independence and dependence, see work by Caudill and Plath (1966), Gardiner, Mutter, and Kosmitzki (1998), Morelli et al. (1992), Wolf et al. (1996), and others.

Feeding. When awake, infants are activity engaged in another socialized activity strongly influenced by cultural values, customs, context, and parental beliefs—*feeding*. Infants everywhere are in need of adequate nutrition if they are to grow and develop into healthy children and adults. Early nutritional deficiencies can have long-range effects as noted in recent studies reporting a link between inadequate nutrition in infancy and cognitive functioning in adolescence (Pollitt et al., 1993) and relationships between maternal beliefs about infant feeding and childrens' nutritional levels during the first year (Engle, Zeitlin, Medrano, & Garcia, 1996). In this regard, no issue has probably received greater attention than that of breast-feeding versus bottle feeding. For an excellent overview of this topic see the book by Virginia Colin (1996).

Crying. While all infants (and many children) cry, this behavior does not always have the same meaning nor is it responded to in the same way in all cultures. Crying is an infant's earliest form of communication and the way it lets others know that it is hungry, not feeling well, has a wet diaper, wants attention, or would like its older sibling to stop annoying it. By crying, infants are bringing their parents and others into their world and socializing them into understanding their feelings when there is no other way to express them.

Childhood

In a discussion of the parenting of toddlers, Edwards (1996) has outlined the developmental tasks she believes children are confronted with during their second and third years. As with our earlier comments on infancy, Edwards states that "Although socialization processes in the field of toddler development are by no means fully understood . . . bidirectional, multicausational, and transactional models have become the goal" (p. 59). Due to space limitations, we will focus on only two behaviors subject to socialization during this period: aggression and formal versus informal learning. For an in-depth discussion of other important topics, see Gardiner, Mutter, & Kosmitzki (1998).

Aggression. The many ways in which feelings and actions associated with hostility and aggression are socialized and expressed by children are highly dependent on differences in gender and culture. In most cultures, boys generally exhibit more aggression than do girls, particularly after the ages of two and three (Legault & Strayer, 1990). There is a strong possibility this may be related to an increased awareness of one's gender role and the rules society has for the expression of such behavior. For example, Wylie (1974) notes that while French parents discourage physical aggression, they permit verbal aggression (e.g., insults) as a socially accepted way to deal with anger. Bourguignon (1979) supports this view by indicating that adults tend to model this behavior and may themselves "on occasion make a great public show of anger in words and threats, but physical fighting is said to be rare" (p. 2).

There are certainly considerable cross-cultural differences in the amount of aggressiveness various societies will tolerate. For example, one could draw a line and place the least aggressive cultures on one end and the most aggressive on the other. Among the former would be the Mbuti Pygmies of Zaire (Turnbull, 1965), certain Zapotec communities in Mexico (Fry, 1992), the Zuni Pueblo Indians of New Mexico (Fromm, 1977), and the Ladakhi, a Tibetan society in northwest India (Gielen, 1994, 1995; Gielen

& Chirico-Rosenberg, 1993). The latter would most certainly include the Yanomamö from the Amazon region of Brazil and Venezuela, often described as the "most fierce and violent people in the world." According to Chagnon (1983), the first anthropologist to report on Yanomamö society, aggressiveness is the major determinant of status for males within this cultural group and learning aggressive behavior starts early. The Semai of central Malaya, on the other hand, are known for their timidity and are raised to be nonviolent by parents who rarely, if ever, express aggressive behavior (Dentan, 1968; Ember & Ember, 1993).

We would be remiss if we did not mention the findings of the Six Cultures Study (Whiting, 1963; Whiting & Edwards, 1988; Whiting & Whiting, 1975), which examined aggression (along with a wide range of other behaviors) among three- to eleven-year-old children in India, Japan, Kenya, Mexico, the Philippines, and the United States. For example, it was reported that while American parents were fairly tolerant of displays of aggression against other children, Mexican parents tended to be the most punitive, perhaps due, in part, to a higher level of interdependence within extended Mexican families, resulting in more adult supervision and greater management of children's behavior. In terms of American parents' greater tolerance of peer-directed aggression, Moghaddam and his colleagues (1993) quote one mother as saying, "If he can't get along with one child, he can always play with someone else" (p. 126). As they point out, this view suggests that relationships are a matter of choice and can be changed at any time and, "Given this element of choice and impermanence, it is less consequential to be aggressive against those around you" (p. 126). Again, we observe the multiple effects of cultural and individual differences as influences on behavior. By considering this topic (and others) from a cross-cultural and developmental perspective, the richness and diversity of human behavior is more clearly seen.

Any readers interested in looking further at aggression within a cross-cultural framework are directed to Segall, Dasen, Berry, and Poortinga (1990), who conclude their presentation on a positive note by stating that "Because the evidence reviewed in this chapter does not support the view that it is inevitable that male adolescents will aggress, there is hope that the pervasive amount of aggression that presently characterizes the world may be reduced, but only if we become more knowledgeable about the experiential factors, rooted in culture, that presently encourage so many people to aggress" (p. 285). We can only hope that they are right.

Formal versus Informal Learning. Children in nonindustrialized societies are primarily socialized in informal settings, for example, within the family or among peers and siblings, and their experiences are an integral part of daily activities. *Informal learning* does not follow a defined curriculum and is usually acquired through a process of observation and imitation. As Cushner has indicated, "The responsibility for learning falls mainly on the learner, making it rather personal, with extended family members often playing a critical role in the act of instruction . . . change, discontinuity, and innovation are highly valued" (1990, p. 100). An example is the learning of hunting and fishing skills by young boys in many tribal societies in South America or Africa who observe and imitate adult males in their culture. In the same way, girls learn cooking and childcare techniques, not in school, but by helping their mothers, aunts, and other women.

In many other countries, children are taught important cultural skills as part of their society's formal education system. In this case, *formal learning* is "set apart from the context of everyday life and is typically carried out in the institution we know as school . . . (and is characterized by) . . . an explicit and highly structured curriculum . . . (where) . . . material is learned from a book that may or may not be useful at a later time" (Cushner, 1990, p. 100). A thoughtful presentation on the failures of formal schooling, in what Kagitçibasi (1996) calls the Majority World, can be found in studies conducted in Zambia (Serpell, 1993).

In the earlier version of this chapter, Gardiner (1994) summarized some of the evidence on formal versus informal learning and the socialization of mathematical skills. The focus was on the argument that American school children fell far behind children of other nations in math achievement, particularly Japan and China. For example, in a study of parents' beliefs, cultural values, and children's math achievement, it was reported that Chinese parents more often set higher standards for their children and work closer with them on homework assignments than do American parents (Chen & Uttal, 1988). Similar findings were found in a cross-cultural study comparing performance among Thai and American students (Gardiner & Gardiner, 1991). At that time, it was stated that "cross-cultural evidence strongly suggests that an informal learning style, like that found in Asian cultures, focused on building interest, is a more effective way to teach children a variety of skills, including math" (Gardiner, 1994, p. 71). Aptekar (1989, 1994) provides support for this view from his intriguing studies among Brazil's "Mennios de Rua" and Colombia's "Gamines" or "Chupagruesos"—street children, many of whom barely survive by selling vegetables and fruits on street corners. Although the majority of these children dropped out of school by the age of ten (before learning good math skills), they carry out dozens of informal, error-free, math transactions daily with customers. However, when presented with formal, written, math problems requiring similar calculations of change, most cannot do them without making frequent mistakes. For these children, their school is the street and it is here they have been socialized and learned the functional math skills that allow them to survive and successfully live out their lives in the street cultures of their societies.

A number of other studies linking socialization and the development of mathematical skills in a variety of cultural settings are available. Of particular interest is one study by Wassmann and Dasen (1994) focusing on the presence of an elaborate numbering system among the Yupno of Papua New Guinea, but the lack of importance attributed to counting in everyday activities. While older Yupno men can perform mathematical calculations using the traditional and informally taught Yupno system and younger children can solve problems using algorithms learned in formal school settings, there are young men who are unable to solve any problems because, due to sociohistorical change within their culture, they lack the necessary skills—old or new.

Adolescence

From a cultural contextual perspective, adolescence is seen as a developmental stage in some, but by no means all, cultures (Burbank, 1988; Hollos & Leis, 1989). According to Cole and Cole (1996), a great deal depends on whether or not "young people reach biological maturity before they have acquired the knowledge and skills needed to ensure cultural reproduction" (p. 629). For example, there are some young adolescents (ages 12 and up) in North America with children of their own who, lacking education or a job, are unable to provide for their children or for themselves. By contrast, there are the !Kung San, living in the Kalahari Desert, where children, even before reaching the years of adolescence, have been socialized to gather plants or hunt animals as part of their nomadic life. They, like their North American peers, are biologically capable of having children but already know their niche in their society and have the skills to support themselves and a family, if necessary (Draper & Cashdan, 1988). Much of this learning is influenced by the presence or absence of rites of passage—a topic to which we now turn our attention.

Rites of Passage. In many cultures, the transition from childhood to adolescence is marked by a ritual or public ceremony known as a *rite of passage.* These "coming of age" experiences vary significantly from one culture to another but, according to Schlegel and Barry (1991), are found in most nonindustrialized societies where nearly 80 percent of girls and 70 percent of boys go through some form of initiation.

According to Delaney (1995), rites of passage consist of several characteristics including separation from one's society for a period of time, instruction from one's elders, transition from one developmental stage to another (e.g., child to adult), and an acknowledgment of one's changed status within the community.

These rituals frequently can be harsh and painful. For example, in eastern Africa, Kaguru boys, 10 to 12 years of age, are led into the bush by male members of the community, stripped of all clothing, ritually circumcised, and taught adult sexual practices. They then return to their village, are honored at a large feast, receive new names, and are expected to become responsible adult members of their society (Beidelman, 1971). Passage for a

Kaguru girl is not as extensive and occurs when she experiences first menstruation and is taught the ways of womanhood by her grandmother or older women in the tribe. She is fortunate in escaping the very painful and widespread practice of female circumcision already experienced by as many as 114 million women in 28 countries in Africa, India, the Middle East, and Southeast Asia (Armstrong, 1991; Kelso, 1994).

In North America and many other industrialized Western societies, the transition from adolescence to adulthood is not marked by such clearly defined rituals but instead by a rather lengthy period of ambiguity, which may last, in some cases, as long as ten years (from about age 12 to the early 20s). In part, this ambiguity results from different definitions of adulthood and varying ages at which individuals assume adult responsibilities (e.g., working and driving a car at age 16, voting and serving in the military at age 18, and legally drinking alcohol at age 21). In addition, parents and others often disagree on when one is "grown up." The marker of adulthood for some is high school or college graduation. For others, it is marriage or the first job. Many would say there are no true rites of passage in industrialized societies and, if there ever were, they have disappeared (Elkind, 1984), except among certain ethnic groups within the larger society who may practice such ceremonies as the Bar or Bas Mitzvah for Jewish boys and girls. Particularly interesting, in this regard, is the Vision Quest, an experience found among many of the more than 500 culturally diverse Native American tribes in North America (Delaney, 1995). Suzuki and Knudtson (1992) state that for adolescent Dakota Indian boys, "the personal vision quest was a mandatory rite of passage to manhood and environmental consciousness. During this solitary sojourn into the mountains, a boy spent several days naked, vulnerable, and fasting as he awaited the arrival of animal-spirit allies who might help him to develop and actualize his understanding of the spiritual and ecological unity of nature. . . . Traditionally, during ceremonial preparations for the boy's departure, an elder filled a sacred pipe with tobacco, gestured to the cardinal points of the cosmos, and offered a prayer for the boy's successful journey and for new levels of insight into Dakota duties to nature" (p. 212).

For more information on rites of passage and the role they play in adolescent socialization, readers are referred to Delaney (1995) and Loughery (1995).

COGNITION

In the 1994 version of this chapter, considerable attention was given to the cognitive developmental theory of Jean Piaget. This included an assessment of cross-cultural findings related to each of his stages along with some of the contributions being made by neo-Piagetians. Some of these researchers were showing an interest in issues Piaget either ignored or to which he gave only superficial attention, while others were disproving some of his basic theoretical positions, providing fresh support for them, or generating ideas for new positions. Rather than go over this material once again, readers are referred to the earlier chapter for information on this topic (Gardiner, 1994).

In the section that follows, we have chosen to present some of the ideas of the Soviet psychologist Lev Vygotsky who, more than 60 years ago, put forth a contextualist's approach to the study of cognitive development. While the majority of mainstream Western developmental theories tradi- tionally have viewed individuals outside their physical and social surround- ings, Vygotsky was among the first to propose an approach that took into account social, cultural, and historical factors. With contemporary interest in looking at human development and behavior within the cultural context in which it takes place, Vygotsky's theory has begun to attract increased attention. Its importance has been recognized by Kagitçibasi (1996), who recently stated that, "This important body of thinking and research has brought in a corrective to traditional work in mainstream developmental psychology that was oblivious of culture. It has also helped to create a rec- ognition of the 'indigenous' cognitive competence of people (children and adults alike) who were too readily labeled as lacking in competence because they did not perform well on standard psychometric tests . . . or school- related activities. Finally, it has contributed to a better understanding of the interactive nature of the learning process" (pp. 39–40).

Vygotsky's Sociocultural Theory of Development

According to Piaget, cognitive development was primarily an individual achievement, in large measure directed and shaped by the environment. He said little about the possible influence of the social context in learning, a view challenged by Vygotsky, who suggested that development is the result of interaction between cultural and historical factors (Vygotsky, 1978). For Vygotsky, the key to successful development was in matching childrens' demands with the requirements of their culture. His theory (Kozulin, 1990) consists of three major components: the role played by culture, the use of language (social, egocentric, and inner speech), and the child's *zone of prox- imal development* (ZPD), which refers to the difference between what children can achieve independently and what their potential level of devel- opment might be if given help or guidance. This concept of a ZPD em- bodies Vygotsky's view that children's cognitive abilities are significantly influenced by social factors and that mentoring or guidance by others strengthens their growth (Steward, 1994).

While many have praised Vygotsky's work for its originality and useful- ness, like the pioneering ideas of Piaget, it has its critics. Some argue that the zone of proximal development is vague and cannot be adequately measured (Paris & Cross, 1988), while others believe portions of the theory have been lost or misunderstood in translation and are, therefore, confusing and incomplete (Nicolopoulou, 1993). Berry and his colleagues (1992) suggest there are also difficulties in transferring learning from one task to another unless similarities occur in the specifics of the task. At the same time, however, other researchers report successful transfer of everyday math skills and formal reasoning practices (Carraher, Schliemann, & Carraher, 1988; Nunes, Schliemann, & Carraher, 1993).

As a result of present day interest in contextual approaches, this author believes Vygotsky's theory will receive increased attention from developmentalists as well as cross-cultural researchers as we move into the twenty-first century.

Some Cultural Variations in Cognition

Over the past three decades, researchers in many cultures have not only made extensive use of Piaget's theory and given increased attention to Vygotsky's theory but, at the same time, have subjected each to careful scrutiny. The result is that the cross-cultural literature, particularly in the case of Piaget, is immense and could not be given anything approaching the full attention it deserves here. There are, however, several excellent reviews for those interested in taking a closer look and include work by Rogoff and Chavajay (1995), Dasen (1994), Segall, Dasen, Berry, and Poortinga (1990), and D'Andrade (1990).

Although we will attempt to follow the same format as in other sections of this chapter (infancy, childhood, and adolescence), the task is made more difficult here because Vygotsky, unlike Piaget, did not present his theory in terms of stages or periods but rather as a continuous process of interaction between individuals and the sociocultural factors that affect their behavior at any given time. Since Vygotsky's theory has not been subjected to as much investigation as has the theory of Piaget, there is the added problem of having less cross-cultural research on which to draw. With these points in mind, let us look at some of the available evidence.

Infancy

An example of Vygotsky's contextualist research during the sensorimotor period can be seen in the work of Bornstein and his colleagues (Bornstein, Toda, Azuma, Tamis-LeMonda, & Ogino, 1990; Bornstein, Tal, & Tamis-LeMonda, 1991; Bornstein & Tamis-LeMonda, 1989). Infant cognition was studied through observations of interactions between infants and their Japanese or American mothers. Findings revealed that American mothers responded more favorably to their infants' requests when the infants were playing with physical objects whereas Japanese mothers were more responsive when they and their infants were engaged in play. In addition, maternal responsiveness appeared to be positively correlated with IQ scores of Japanese children when about two-and-a-half-years of age and to scores of American children at four years. Infants in both cultures were equally likely to engage in goal-directed behavior and showed early signs of object permanence at five months. This example clearly supports Vygotsky's claim that culture plays an active role in directing cognitive activity, even in infancy.

Further support comes from a recent study of parent-child play interactions in which the researchers (Uzgiris & Raeff, 1995) found that the variety of activities involved in play (e.g., talking, touching, and interacting) helped children to learn skills that enabled them to be active participants in later cultural interactions.

Childhood

Another of Vygotsky's contentions was that cultural influence, mental processes, and language are dynamic processes that occur simultaneously (Wertsch & Tulviste, 1994). He further believed that the continuous interaction between language and thought, embedded in a particular cultural context, results in dialogue between individuals, especially a mother and her child. It is this social interaction that Vygotsky said helps shape the quality of mental abilities at various ages across the lifespan (Philip & Kelly, 1992). With this theoretical perspective in mind, Vygotsky coined the expression "Talking to Learn." By this he meant that as children verbally interact with others, they internalize language and then use it to organize their thoughts (Vygotsky, 1978). In short, as children interact with their parents, they become socialized into a specific set of cultural beliefs and values (Greenfield & Cocking, 1994).

In turn, while passing through Vygotsky's zone of proximal development and becoming enculturated into a way of life, children are also acquiring specific cognitive skills. An effective method for achieving this is *scaffolding* or the temporary guidance and support provided a child by parents or others in the course of problem solving. These individuals observe the child's behavior, determine how much help is needed to complete a task or activity, and provide whatever is necessary. As the activity continues, they became increasingly sensitive to the child's needs and this results in the child doing better on later tasks (Pratt, Kerig, Cowan & Cowan, 1988).

In recent years, Vygotsky's theory has been receiving increased attention. Clearly, there is a need for additional research, and we predict that once cross-cultural investigators begin to do more contextual research and become aware of how well Vygotsky's sociocultural theory complements Bronfenbrenner's ecological systems theory, a variety of interesting and significant studies will begin to appear (Gardiner, Mutter, & Kosmitzki, 1998).

PERSONALITY

One's personality does not appear all at once. Some characteristics, set in motion by genetics, can certainly be observed shortly after birth (e.g., activity level, emotional disposition, and alertness to the environment). Others characteristics, such as attitudes, values, interests, and patterns of behavior, will develop slowly as a result of one's interactions with parents, peers, teachers, and culture. One point is clear—while there may be similarities, no two people will be exactly alike, not even identical twins. The beginnings of personality can be found in temperament.

Infancy

Individual differences in *temperament*—a person's typical pattern of responding to environmental events—are often observed shortly after birth. For example, while some newborns and infants are irritable and cry frequently, others are calm and quiet. In many cases, these differences come to play a central role in one's development and may reliably predict adult personality (Buss & Plomin, 1984), although others have sometimes reported surprising results (Kagan, 1994).

Temperament and "Goodness of Fit." How temperament, development, and culture relate to each other is often explained in terms of *goodness of fit*—the quality of the match between a child's temperament and the demands of his or her immediate environment. This concept was first introduced by Thomas and Chess (1977) in an elaborate longitudinal study of children's temperament based on interviews with and observations of middle-class families of European background living in New York City. Three temperament types emerged from the study: (1) the *easy child* characterized by a good mood, regular sleeping and eating cycles, and general calmness; (2) the *difficult child* characterized by a negative mood, slow adaptation to and withdrawal from new experiences and people, irregular sleep and feeding patterns, and high emotional intensity; and (3) the *slow-to-warm-up child* who showed few intense reactions, positive or negative, and tended to be mild and low in activity level. According to Thomas and Chess, it is not the individual child's temperament alone that is related to future maladjustment but, rather, the match or mismatch of the child's temperament with the environment that predicts problematic behavior.

A follow-up study conducted among Puerto Rican families in New York City provided further confirmation for the goodness-of-fit concept while also sounding a note of caution. For example, early "difficult" temperament was not always predictive of poor adjustment and behavioral difficulties in later childhood (Korn & Gannon, 1983). The researchers point out that in these families characteristics that were originally classified as "difficult" were not perceived as necessarily problematic and, therefore, did not disrupt family life or result in negative reactions toward a child. These and other studies provide convincing evidence that culture is a critical determinant of the "goodness of fit" between an individual child and his or her environment.

This concept received further attention in a series of studies conducted among infants living in various parts of Kenya (DeVries, 1994; DeVries & Sameroff, 1984). Finally, Meijer, Super, and Harkness (1997) have recently attempted to further clarify the nature of "goodness of fit" and find a systematic relationship between maternal judgments of "difficult" and specific dimensions of child behavior. In a comparative study involving Dutch and American mothers, the researchers reported that parents in the two different cultural settings systematically interpreted the causes of this behavior differently. For example, American parents were more likely to view difficulty as inherent in a child, while Dutch parents were more likely to view it as resulting from environmental factors. As this example clearly demonstrates, behavior and the interpretation of it are strongly influenced by one's culture, ecological setting, and specific developmental niche.

Childhood

Are there cross-cultural differences in children's temperament? If so, what effects do they have on one's behavior during childhood? A number of studies have attempted to answer this question and will be briefly presented as examples in the section below.

Malaysian Children. Banks (1989) conducted a study with parents of infants and preschool children in a Malay village near the capital city of Kuala Lumpur using interviews based on translated versions of Carey's Infant Temperament Questionnaire (Carey, 1970) and Thomas and Chess's Parent and Teacher Questionnaire (Thomas & Chess, 1977). When comparisons were made with American infants in Carey's (1970) study, differences emerged on four temperament dimensions. Specifically, Malay parents described their children as less eager to approach new experiences, less adaptable, less regular in their daily patterns, and as having a lower threshold for responses to stimuli.

These differences, according to Banks, can be explained by cultural variations in parental values and in childrearing approaches. For example, she indicates that children in Malaysia tend to have a lower threshold in responding to stimuli because their parents actively encourage them to be aware of such sensations as changes in temperature, pain, light, orders, and sounds, especially if these produce discomfort. Malaysian children learn to immediately tell their parents or caretaker when a diaper needs to be changed even if it means interrupting their play. For a parent to delay a diaper change would be seen by others as very neglectful.

Malaysian children's lower adaptability to new situations, compared with American children, may also be the result of differences in parents' cultural belief systems. For example, as pointed out earlier, a child who is slow to adapt to new situations, based on American values, is considered difficult and fussy because the expectation is that parents know what is best for their child and the child adapts to parents' wishes. On the other hand, parents in the Malaysian culture are expected to consider all situational factors and, to a far greater degree than in American culture, pay respect to a child's wishes and decisions. Finally, since Malaysian children rarely encounter situations in which very much adaptability is expected, their adaptability is generally lower.

Japanese Children. Shwalb, Shwalb, and Shoji (1994) have taken a different approach to the identification of infant temperament in Japan. Rather than simply translating existing temperament measures into Japanese, they developed the Japanese Temperament Questionnaire and asked more than 450 mothers to describe their infants' temperament when one, three, and six months of age. As a result, they suggested that Japanese infant temperament could be described along nine dimensions, which tended to be fairly consistent during the first six months of life. These included: (1) ease or difficulty of care, (2) intensity of emotions or reactions, (3) sociability or social responsiveness, (4) motoric activity, (5) stability or gentleness, (6) willfulness, (7) reactivity to change or cautiousness, (8) sensitivity to physical contact, and (9) indulgence or dependency.

In analyzing the results, Shwalb, Shwalb, and Shoji caution that even though the broad dimensions seem to be very similar across cultures, the content of the statements that comprise the dimensions may differ considerably and are worthy of further cross-cultural study.

Adolescence

Personality development during adolescence is particularly interesting from a cross-cultural perspective. Most nonindustrialized societies have clear social markers that define the time at which a young person is considered mature enough to assume adult responsibilities (voting in elections) and adult privileges (driving a car or consuming alcohol). In most industrialized cultures, adolescence typically lasts several years longer than it does in most nonindustrialized cultures. According to Kett (1977), adolescents in nonindustrialized societies assume adult responsibilities at a much earlier age than in industrialized cultures because they are unable to afford the luxury of being "nonproductive" and spending time in "self-discovery." For an interesting look at "coming-of-age" experiences in 22 cultures spread throughout the world, see John Loughery's *Into the Widening World* (1995).

Development of Individual Identity. It is during the adolescent years that many young people find themselves dealing with one of the most important developmental tasks—the establishment of an *identity* separate and distinct from others. Simply stated, the adolescent is trying to answer the question *"Who am I?"* It's a puzzle with an answer not always easy to find and involves pieces supplied by many of those within one's environment including family and friends, members of peer groups, teachers, and others.

Psychologist Erik Erikson (1963) is usually given credit for providing the first thorough analysis of identity development. Although cross-cultural findings suggest an element of universality in identity development, the precise process by which individuals achieve their identity is ultimately determined by contextual factors existing within each individual's unique cultural setting. Of particular importance are the developmental changes, physical and psychological, experienced during this period of transition from childhood to adulthood. Marcia (1980) considers attainment of physical and sexual maturity to be a necessary condition for the performance of adult roles and later developmental tasks. The task is made even more challenging in that individuals must take into account their view of themselves along with the views of others and of society. As suggested earlier, it is this sociocultural element that helps to explain, in large part, cultural differences in adolescent identity.

Even though we may agree that establishment of identity is critical to one's development, empirical findings of cross-cultural similarities or differences are surprisingly scarce. Only a limited number of studies have specifically looked at adolescents' identity development in terms of sociocultural influences. These include work by Mead (1970), Keniston (1965), and Stiles, de Silva, and Gibbons (1996). Considering this lack of information, two studies will serve as examples of this type of research.

The first study focused on identity formation within a collective context, specifically an Israeli kibbutz. Using extensive interviewing procedures, Wiseman and Lieblich (1992) revealed that adolescents living here were especially concerned with issues of autonomy. They reported having problems integrating their individual identity with the norms of the collective, which emphasized conformity, communal rules and control, and close relationships. A major challenge for these adolescents was finding ways to assert their individuality while, at the same time, conforming to the adult world of the collective. For them, this was a unique problem and one not shared by peers living in urban areas (Sharabany & Wiseman, 1993).

The second study examined identity conflicts in two cultural groups, Israeli Jews and Israeli Arabs, living in close proximity within the same society. Tzuriel (1992) set out to discover if adolescents exposed to multiple (and sometimes conflicting) norms and expectations experience greater identity conflict than adolescents in less ambiguous settings. Israeli Arabs, who represent a relatively small minority in Israel, grow up experiencing elements of their traditional culture as well as of the Jewish majority culture. Under these conditions, would they have a more negative view of themselves or express more confusion about their identity? Among the six identity factors examined, Arabs scored higher on three and lower on the other three, re-sulting in no significant difference between the two groups on total identity score. Specifically, Arab adolescents expressed greater self-confidence, a stronger sense of ideological and vocational commitment, and more genu-ineness. Jewish adolescents reported greater feelings of alienation and un-happiness with their physical appearance and behavior. At the same time, they also recognized that others valued them and their abilities.

Overall, findings suggested that Jewish adolescents experienced greater difficulty in their identity development than did Arab young people. In ex-plaining the results, Tzuriel speculates that the ambiguous setting of Israeli Arabs may, in fact, facilitate increased identity exploration and self-awareness in relation to identity issues and may have a more positive influence than one might expect. With successful resolution of the identity crisis, most adolescents go on to achieve an identity with which they are comfortable and adjust their future behavior accordingly.

EPILOGUE

At the beginning of this chapter we made note of the welcome increase in developmental studies providing comparative data using cross-cultural theories and methodology. Unfortunately, within the limits of this chapter, it has been possible only to whet the reader's appetite by putting a few hors d'oeuvers on the table in the areas of socialization, cognition, and person-ality. If possible, we would place before you some other courses including cultural similarities and differences in physical growth and development, is-sues of sex and gender, social behavior, variations in family contexts, health concerns, and many more. For the latest findings in all of these areas, in-cluding a chronological-within-topics approach that covers subject matter from infancy through later adulthood, readers are referred to the recently published *Lives across Cultures: Cross-Cultural Human Development* by Gar-diner, Mutter, and Kosmitzki (1998). Several of these topics are also dis-cussed (from different perspectives) in Volume 2 of the second edition of the *Handbook of Cross-Cultural Psychology: Basic Processes and Human De-velopment* (1997).

6

Preference for Principled Moral Reasoning: A Developmental and Cross-Cultural Perspective

Uwe P. Gielen and Diomedes C. Markoulis

To follow the *Dao* and not the ruler,
To follow justice and not the father,
This is the great conduct of man.

Xunzi (ca. 310–230 B.C.E.)

The study of moral reasoning and moral judgment constitutes a central concern of social psychology since moral reasoning provides the norms that regulate social interaction. Earlier theorists in social psychology and anthropology tended to equate morality with conformity to cultural norms. They assumed that the moral development of children and adolescents depends upon the internalization of culturally variable norms through a process of social reinforcement, imitation of culturally structured behavior, and identification with authority figures such as parents. Learning theorists, cultural anthropologists, and psychoanalysts agreed that moral norms are culturally relative and learned in nonrational ways (Brown, 1965). More recently, cultural anthropologists and psychologists such as Shweder and J. Miller have also emphasized that the moral reasoning of individuals is structured by and embedded in culturally shaped and culturally variable systems of moral meaning (e.g., Shweder, Mahapatra, & Miller, 1990).

During the last few decades, the cognitive-developmental theorists Kohlberg (1984), Lind (1986), and Rest (1979) have suggested an alternative vision of what morality is about, how it develops, and how it should be studied. They have emphasized the universal aspects of reasoning about moral problems involving issues of justice. Because they have made quite specific, if controversial, predictions about the nature of moral reasoning, and because they have developed a variety of challenging research methods, their approaches have in recent years dominated the cross-cultural study of moral reasoning. Using their theoretical and methodological frameworks, empirical studies of moral reasoning have attempted to find out whether moral reasoning in a wide variety of societies develops in a structured, stage-like manner.

More than 100 studies have investigated whether development follows a universal trajectory, beginning with a preconventional level of moral reasoning focused on the pragmatic consequences of one's actions, to a conventional level focusing on internalized conventional moral conceptions and expectations, and ending with a principled level emphasizing universalizable conceptions of justice, human solidarity, and dignity. Most cross-cultural studies on moral reasoning have validated the existence and developmental properties of the preconventional and conventional levels of moral reasoning, but the cross-cultural evidence for the postconventional, principled forms of moral reasoning has been weaker (Boyes & Walker, 1988; Eckensberger, 1993; Eckensberger & Zimba, 1997; Edwards, 1981, 1986; Gielen, 1991, 1996; Moon, 1986; Snarey, 1985; Snarey & Kelko, 1991). Indeed, critics of the cognitive-developmental approach have argued that Kohlberg's and Rest's stages of moral reasoning, and above all the principled stages, include fundamental Western, male, and social-class biases (Dien, 1982; Gilligan, 1982; Simpson, 1974; Vine, 1986). In the critics' view, Kohlberg's emphasis on moral autonomy as the endpoint of development reflects an ideological, male-oriented preoccupation with the modern Western themes of autonomy and individualism, thus making his theory ethnocentric and sexist in nature.

This chapter focuses on a series of published and unpublished cross-cultural studies, which taken together suggest that principled forms of moral reasoning are recognized and preferred in a considerable variety of Western and East Asian societies. Specifically, the chapter reviews cross-cultural studies employing Rest's Defining Issues Test (DIT), a test that aims at measuring a person's preference hierarchy for moral arguments. After introducing a number of theoretical and methodological issues pertaining to the DIT, the chapter reviews fifteen studies that are based on the DIT.

It is argued that contrary to the views of critics, the sequence of preconventional, conventional, and principled forms of moral reasoning does not embody a Western and male-oriented ideology of "cold justice," but an evolving, gender-neutral search for more sophisticated and morally valid forms of social cooperation. The claim is made that the results of the studies under review provide support for a multicultural conception of morality while throwing into doubt the more extreme forms of cultural and ethical relativism. In addition, it is demonstrated that a principled emphasis on moral autonomy and "human-heartedness" (*jen* or *rén*) can already be seen in the golden age of Chinese philosophy some 2,500 years ago and also in various forms in some other cultures of the time.

THE QUESTION OF CULTURAL AND
ETHICAL RELATIVISM

Cultural relativists emphasize that basic moral values and behaviors differ radically from society to society and, within a society, from one cultural group to the next. For the relativist, morality is a concept relative to culture, referring to those values, attitudes, beliefs, and behavior patterns that are prescribed in a given society (Herskovits, 1948). Relativists argue that a belief in universal or universalizable moral conceptions is inherently ethnocentric in nature and frequently reflects a deplorable Western form of "moral imperialism." Ethnocentrism is said to lead to scientific misjudgment and to the morally illicit imposition of the values of one's own society upon the equally valid but different values of another society. In this criticism, cultural relativism—the factual statement that morality *does* vary across societies—is joined to and confused with, ethical relativism—the normative statement that one *should not* judge other societies by the standards of one's own society. Various versions of relativism pervade modern social science in the form of social learning theory in psychology, Marxism in political economics, "culturology" in anthropology (Hatch, 1983), and various postmodern interpretations of the pervasiveness of cultural differences and the uniqueness of ethnic, gender, and other identities. Relativism constitutes the reigning ideology in much of cross-cultural psychology as well.

In contrast to these widely accepted relativistic positions, Kohlberg (1981, 1984) has proposed that moral reasoning everywhere follows a sequence of stages that culminates in principled forms of moral reasoning. In his view, the later stages are not only psychologically more advanced but also represent more comprehensive and purer forms of justice. Consequently, his approach to the study of moral reasoning contains two fundamental claims: (1) The scientific or empirical claim that moral conceptions everywhere evolve from less differentiated toward more differentiated stages of reasoning and (2) the ethical or normative claim that from a philosophical point of view the higher stages are superior to the lower stages. The first claim must be investigated empirically, while the second claim must be redeemed philosophically. The two claims are separate but intertwined in nature because the empirical and cross-cultural study of moral reasoning can lead us to a more lucid understanding of our own ethical presuppositions.

Kohlberg opposes both cultural relativism and ethical relativism. He claims that cultural relativism is factually incorrect since reasoning about problems of justice does develop in similar ways in both Western and non-Western cultures. In addition, he opposes ethical relativism as being inherently contradictory and thus philosophically unsound: If moral ideas reflect nothing more than internalized cultural norms, are not the theories of the relativists themselves culture-bound and thus devoid of any general validity? Do not the relativists derive prescriptive-normative judgments ("should statements") from descriptive statements ("is statements"), thereby committing the fundamental logical error identified by philosophers as the "naturalistic fallacy"? These criticisms of the relativistic position have never been satisfactorily answered since they point to basic logical and philosophical flaws inherent in the various forms of moral relativism. In addition, cultural relativism is typically based on some form of *cultural reductionism*: Persons are seen as prisoners of their culture unable to transcend it or to seriously question its basic assumptions since their very perceptions and thoughts are already prefigured by the culture they have internalized.

Historical considerations suggest that cultural-ethical relativism develops when rapid social changes in a given society lead to *anomie*, that is, a state of normlessness. Persons lose the conviction that the conventional values, norms, and beliefs of their society possess general validity. Alienation, pronounced individualism, and social disorganization are frequent responses to such a situation. This already occurred in the later stages of classical Greek civilization when the Sophists introduced history's first version of cultural-moral relativism. It may also be seen in many present-day Western societies. Individuals are thrown back onto themselves but will, under favorable circumstances, develop their own moral principles. It may be said that the development of generally valid moral principles constitutes the "cure" for the "disease" of moral relativism. Implied in this statement is the assumption that moral development proceeds from the preconventional level, to the conventional level, to a transitional stage incorporating relativistic ideas, to the postconventional-principled level (Gielen, 1986). Kohlberg (1984) and Rest (1979, 1986b) assume that this progression can be captured by their theory of successive stages of moral reasoning.

STAGES OF MORAL REASONING

Kohlberg (1984) and Rest (1979, 1983, 1986b) have proposed that thinking about interpersonal conflict situations develops in a systematic way. Six stages of moral thinking are assumed to be identifiable in all situations where persons have conflicting moral claims. Each stage of moral reasoning represents a separate and coherent theory of justice attempting to balance the conflicting claims. The six stages as conceptualized by Rest (1983) are depicted in Table 6.1

When inspecting Table 6.1, it is important to keep several considerations in mind: (1) The stages are concerned with *justifications* that moral actors give for their actions. Persons in all cultures may be asked why they should, or should not, help, steal, lie, kill, or support another person in a specific situation of conflict. It is the answers to such why questions that are of crucial importance for Rest's theoretical scheme. (2) Rest's emphasis is on the *structure* or *form* of the justifications rather than the specific and culturally variable *content* of the moral decision-making process. (3) Each stage

Table 6.1
Stages of Moral Development According to Rest

Coordination of Expectations about Actions (How Rules Are Known and Shared)	Schemes of Balancing Interests (How Equilibrium Is Achieved)	Central Concept for Determining Moral Rights and Responsibilities
Stage 1 The caretaker makes known certain demands on the child's behavior.	The child does not share in making rules but understands that obedience will bring freedom from punishment.	The morality of obedience: "Do what you're told."
Stage 2 Although each person is understood to have his own interests, an exchange of favors might be mutually decided.	If each party sees something to gain in an exchange, then both want to reciprocate.	The morality of instrumental egoism and simple exchange: "Let's make a deal."
Stage 3 Through reciprocal role taking, individuals attain a mutual understanding about each other and the ongoing pattern of interactions.	Friendship relationships establish a stabilized and enduring scheme of cooperation. Each party anticipates the feelings, needs, and wants of the other and acts in the other's welfare.	The morality of interpersonal concordance: "Be considerate, nice, and kind, and you'll get along with people."
Stage 4 All members of society know what is expected of them through public institutionalized law.	Unless a society-wide system of cooperation is established and stabilized, no individual can really make plans. Each person should follow the law and do his particular job, anticipating that other people will also fulfill their responsibilities.	The morality of law and duty to the social order: "Everyone in society is obligated and protected by the law."

Table 6.1 (*continued*)

Coordination of Expectations about Actions (How Rules Are Known and Shared)	Schemes of Balancing Interests (How Equilibrium Is Achieved)	Central Concept for Determining Moral Rights and Responsibilities
Stage 5 Formal procedures are institutionalized for making laws, which one anticipates rational people would accept.	Law-making procedures are devised so that they reflect the general will of the people, at the same time insuring certain basic rights to all. With each person having a say in the decision process, each will see that his interests are maximized while at the same time having a basis for making claims on other people.	The morality of societal consensus: "You are obligated by whatever arrangements are agreed to by due process procedures."
Stage 6 The logical requirements of nonarbitrary cooperation among rational, equal, and impartial people are taken as ideal criteria for social organization which one anticipates rational people would accept.	A scheme of cooperation that negates or neutralizes all arbitrary distribution of rights and responsibilities is the most equilibrated, for such system is maximizing the simultaneous benefit to each member so that any deviation from these rules would advantage some members at the expense of others.	The morality of nonarbitrary social cooperation: "How rational and impartial people would organize cooperation is moral."

Source: Rest (1983, p. 588). In P. Mussen (Ed.), *Handbook of Child Psychology*, Vol. IV. Copyright © 1983. Reprinted by permission of J. Wiley & Sons, Inc.

represents a coherent philosophy of *justice*. Justice is concerned with the balancing of moral claims based on equality, equity, desert, merit, and special circumstances. Moral situations involving problems of justice are quite varied and may involve competing concerns for human life and welfare, wealth, honor, loyalty, empathy, keeping contracts and one's word, retribution, restitution, and exchange arrangements. (4) The six stages depicted in Table 6.1 focus on the coordination of rules and expectations, schemes for balancing interests, and basic conceptions of rights and duties. Successive stages reformulate these three considerations in more abstract and comprehensive ways. (5) The stages are ordered according to a hierarchy. At the higher stages the range of social cooperation widens, moral considerations are increasingly differentiated from nonmoral considerations, and the divergent interests, needs, and concerns of the various moral actors are better integrated with each other and better balanced. It is assumed that persons tend to prefer the highest stage that they can understand because they intuitively realize that the higher stages represent more comprehensive forms of moral problem solving. (6) The stages of moral reasoning apply only to *deontic* reasoning, that is, to reasoning that asks: What should be done in such and such a situation? The stages do not describe metaethical reasoning (reflections on the general nature of morality); reasoning about the good life (What is of value in human lives?); or metaphysical-religious reasoning (What are the ultimate powers of the universe, and how are humans related to them?). The stages do not focus on moral character, personality organization, or mental health, nor should stage theories of moral reasoning be used to establish the comparative moral worth of persons or societies. Readers wishing to gain a more detailed understanding of Kohlberg's and Rest's stage theories are referred to Kuhmerker (1991), Kohlberg (1981, 1984), and Rest (1979). For an interesting stage theory of religious judgment, Oser and Gmünder (1991) should be consulted.

PRINCIPLED MORAL REASONING

At the postconventional or principled level of moral reasoning, a person has developed self-chosen, abstract moral principles that tend to focus on respect for individual dignity, benevolence, liberty, equality, human solidarity, and the maintenance of interpersonal trust. The person is able to take an outside-of-society perspective; that is, the person decides moral dilemmas from a point of view that could, ideally speaking, be adopted by any rational and impartial person in the given situation. Moral decision making is expected to be shareable or universalizable, representing an effort to reach consensus based on nonarbitrary social cooperation.

Moral principles are more broadly conceived than moral rules. While moral rules refer to specific injunctions such as You shall not steal, kill, cheat, lie, or rape, moral principles integrate specific moral rules and give them broader meaning. Moral principles enjoin us never to use another person merely as a means for our own purpose and pleasure, to consistently respect the human dignity of others and the self, and to take an attitude of *jen*—the Chinese virtue of human-heartedness—toward everybody (Roetz, 1992). Throughout the ages, principled concerns for justice have been recognized by moral leaders in Western and non-Western societies alike (Vasudev & Hummel, 1987). Sometimes, moral principles are summed up as the Golden Rule or the Silver Rule. The Silver Rule is recognized in India's *Mahabharata* ("This is the sum of duty: Do naught onto others which would cause pain if done to you"), in Chinese Confucianism ("Surely it is the maxim of loving kindness: Do not unto others that you would not have done unto you"), and in the Judaic *Talmud* ("What is hateful to you, do not to your fellow-man. That is the entire Law, all the rest is commentary"). Confucius combines the Golden Rule and the Silver Rule in the following saying attributed to him: "Do to everyman as thou would'st have him do to thee; and do not unto another what thou would'st not have him do unto thee." However, the Silver and Golden Rules must be universalized to all human beings, including women, children, and outgroup members, and to a broad variety of situations involving moral conflict, before they fully express the overriding moral principle of universal justice. In practice, persons as well as cultural traditions consistently fall short of the ideal of universal justice, but they may approximate it to varying degrees. Principled moral thinking is closer to the ideal than is conventional thinking, which in turn surpasses preconventional thinking.

MEASURING MORAL REASONING: THE DEFINING ISSUES TEST

In the cognitive-developmental tradition, the two most influential approaches to the measurement of moral reasoning have been Kohlberg's Moral Judgment Interview (MJI) and Rest's Defining Issues Test (DIT). This chapter compares data from studies employing the DIT. The DIT is an objective multiple-choice test that indexes moral development based on the recognition of, and preference for, 72 moral arguments. The DIT contains six moral and political dilemmas. Two examples are as follows: (1) Should a poor husband (Heinz) steal a drug in order to save the life of his very sick wife if he cannot get the drug in any other way? (2) A man escapes from prison and subsequently leads a model life. Should a neighbor who years later recognizes him report him to the police? In cross-cultural research, culturally inappropriate dilemmas may be deleted and details of the various stories adapted to cultural circumstances.

For each moral dilemma, the DIT provides twelve arguments that can be used to solve the conflict. The arguments reflect different moral stages. Respondents are asked to rate and rank order the moral arguments. Two examples of arguments pertaining to the first dilemma (the Heinz story) are as follows: Stage 3: Isn't it only natural for a loving husband to care so much for his wife that he'd steal? Stage 6: What values are going to be the basis for governing how people act toward each other?

The DIT is objectively scored and provides moral stage scores for Stages 2, 3, 4, 4½(A), 5A, 5B, and 6. Preferences for principled thinking (Stages 5A, 5B, and 6 combined) are expressed by the P%-Score. The P%-Score indicates the percentage of a person's rankings that falls in the principled range. The P%-Score is the most frequently used indicator of moral judgment maturity in the DIT literature; this chapter continues that tradition.

The DIT contains three validity and "consistency" checks to establish whether the person taking the test understands it and is reasonably careful in filling it out. Among the 72 items, there are a few "meaningless" items (M-items) based on lofty-sounding but senseless statements. Respondents endorsing a number of the pretentious-sounding but meaningless moral arguments are frequently removed from the research sample. A second checking procedure looks for consistency between items *rated* high and items *ranked* high. A third checking procedure determines whether a protocol reflects response sets on the rating task. Should there be too many "inconsistent" respondents in a cross-cultural study, the researcher may suspect a lack of cultural-cognitive fit between the task requirements and/or moral conceptions underlying the DIT and the minds of the respondents.

Rest (1979, 1986a, 1986b) has provided extensive evidence that documents the reliability and validity of the DIT in U.S.-American and selected cross-cultural settings. There now exist more than 1,000 studies employing the DIT, making it the most frequently used moral judgment test in the scientific literature. Because it is easier to judge moral arguments than to produce them, persons are usually 1 to 1½ stages "ahead" on the DIT when compared to Kohlberg's Moral Judgment Interview. Adolescents and adults frequently endorse principled moral arguments on the DIT, although they may be unable to construct such arguments in interviews. Just as recognition memory surpasses recall memory, and passive speech develops before active speech, so principled morality may be recognized and intuitively preferred before it can be actively produced in interviews. Therefore, the DIT can be used to establish the degree to which principled moral arguments are preferred over conventional and preconventional arguments in a given society or social group, even if most members cannot fully apply moral principles to concrete situations. In addition, cross-cultural studies using the DIT have asked whether preference for principled moral arguments increases as a function of age, gender, social class, educational level, intelligence, and other variables.

COMPARISON OF CROSS-CULTURAL STUDIES USING THE DIT

Development of Principled Moral Reasoning

The following comparisons are based on a survey of fifteen studies employing the DIT in fourteen countries. The studies include published and unpublished research projects by the first author, studies previously surveyed by Moon (1986), and additional studies that have since become available. Research data have been included in the present survey whenever scores for at least three age groups have been reported for a given country.

Moral maturity scores in all studies are expressed by the P%-Score. The P%-Scores have been taken from, or estimated on the basis of, the following studies: Australia (Watson, 1983); Ireland (Kahn, 1982); the United States (Rest, 1986); Greece (Gielen, Markoulis, & Avellani, 1994); Poland (Frackowiak & Jasinska-Kania, 1991); Belize (Gielen, Cruickshank, Johnston, Swanzey, & Avellani, 1986); Trinidad-Tobago (combination of scores reported by Beddoe, 1980, and by Gielen et al., 1986); Hong Kong (Hau, 1983); South Korea (Park & Johnson, 1984); Taiwan (Gielen, Miao, & Avellani, 1990); Sudan (Ahmed, Gielen, & Avellani, 1987); Kuwait (Gielen, Ahmed, & Avellani, 1994); Egypt (El-Shikh, 1985); and Nigeria (Markoulis & Valanides, 1997). The total number of male and female respondents included in the studies is N = 8,131, ranging from 50 respondents for Australia to 4,565 for the United States. All samples except those from Australia, Nigeria, and Belize include at least 240 students. The data for the United States are based on a composite sample that Rest computed on the basis of numerous individual studies.

Average ages for the various subgroups in the study range from 12 (South Korea) to 22½ years (Greece). The studies typically report data for junior high school, senior high school, and college students. The students' educational background in the various subgroups within the different societies is roughly comparable with respect to number of years of schooling. Age and years of schooling are completely confounded in these studies, but based on previous research evidence from the United States (Rest, 1979, 1986a, 1986b), Germany, and elsewhere, it may be surmised that educational experience rather than age per se is the crucial variable influencing P%-Scores. The fourteen countries listed in Table 6.2 represent a variety of Anglo-Saxon countries (Australia, Ireland, the United States), two European countries (Poland, Greece), two English-speaking countries located in the Caribbean (Belize, which is also a Central American country, and Trinidad-Tobago), three East Asian countries influenced by Confucian and Buddhist value systems (Hong Kong, South Korea, Taiwan), three Arab countries (Egypt, Kuwait, and Northern-Central Sudan), and one English-speaking country located in sub-Saharan Africa (Nigeria).

Table 6.2
Average P%–Scores of Students from Different Countries

Country	N	Age/Education	Average P%-Score
Anglo-Saxon Countries			
Australia (Watson, 1983)	50	14.7 years (8th-9th grade)	19.2%
		16.8 years (11th grade)	32.7%
		College/Univ. (Freshmen)	43.8%
		College/Univ. (Juniors)	47.5%
Ireland (Kahn, 1982)	508	12-13 years	20.0%
		15-16 years	20.7%
		18-19 years (College)	34.1%
USA (Rest, 1986a)	4565	Junior High	21.9%
		Senior High	31.8%
		College	42.3%
		(Graduate Students)	53.3%
European Countries			
Greece (Gielen, Markoulis, & Avellani, 1992)	353	13-15 years	21.5%
		16-18 years	29.1%
		19-21 years	40.3%
		22-23 years	43.8%
Poland (Frackowiak, & Jasinska-Kania, 1991)	286	14 years (8th grade)	23.9%
		15 years (High School Freshmen)	32.0%
		18 years (High School Juniors)	32.7%
		19.5 years (College-Freshmen)	39.9%
		22.5 years (College-Sophomores)	37.4%
Caribbean Countries (English Speaking)			
Belize (Gielen, et al., 1986)	118	12-14 years	19.9%
		15-16 years	18.7%
		17-19 years	24.3%
Trinidad-Tobago (Beddoe, 1980; Gielen, et al., 1986)	292	12-14 years	20.4%
		15-16 years	20.8%
		17-19 years	27.4%
		College	28.7%

Table 6.2 (continued)

Country	N	Age/Education	Average P%-Score
East Asian Countries			
Hong Kong (Hau, 1983)	242	7th-8th grade(Jr. High)	25.2%
		9th-10th grade (Jr. High)	29.3%
		11th-12th grade (Sr. High)	34.5%
		College	37.9%
South Korea (Park, & Johnson, 1984)	240	6th grade	25.0%
		8th grade(Jr. High)	30.2%
		11th grade(Sr. High)	37.4%
		College	41.5%
Taiwan (Gielen, Miao, & Avellani, 1987)	521	Junior High	30.4%
		Senior High	36.8%
		College	41.4%
Arab Countries			
Kuwait (Gielen, Ahmed, & Avellani, 1989)	313	High School (1st-3rd)	27.9%
		College (Fr. and Soph.)	24.6%
		Univ./College (Jr. & Sr.)	28.3%
		(MA level; N = 2)	(34.0%)
Sudan (Arab Students)(Ahmed, Gielen, & Avellani, 1987)	253	High School (1st-3rd)	25.1%
		College (Fr. & Soph.)	27.8%
		Univ./College (Jr. & Sr.)	24.5%
		(MA level; N = 4)	(39.6%)
Egypt (El-Shikh, 1985)	293	13-15 Intermediate School	21.5%
		15-18 Secondary School	22.0%
		18-21 Univ./College	22.6%
		21-22 One year Postgraduate (Special Diploma)	20.9%
Africa			
Nigeria (Markoulis & Valanides, 1997)	97	15-16 High School	11.5%
		17-18 High School	18.0%
		19-20 University	30.0%
		21-22 University	32.0%

Developmental Progression of P%-Scores

Bottom Effect. Except for the Nigerian study, no study reports average P%-Scores for any age group that go much below 18%–20%. This "bottom effect" probably indicates a situation where a good many students select moral arguments more or less randomly. It may well be that the DIT is too difficult a test for many junior high school students in countries such as Belize, Trinidad-Tobago, and Ireland. This conclusion is strengthened by the fact that the studies reporting P%-Scores for Belize and Trinidad-Tobago (Gielen et al., 1986) and for Nigeria (Markoulis & Valanides, 1997) also report the exclusion of a high percentage of respondents who failed to pass the various consistency tests.

Developmental Progression of P%-Scores. Apart from this bottom effect, all studies not conducted in Arab countries report that P%-Scores regularly increase with increasing age and educational level. The older, better-educated students endorse the principled arguments more frequently than the younger, less-well-educated students. Thus, the DIT appears to capture developmental trends in moral reasoning in a considerable variety of Western and non-Western countries.

High P%-Scores for East Asian High School Students. Among high school students, the highest scores are reported for Taiwan and South Korea, with Hong Kong not far behind. High school students from the United States (where the DIT originated) receive average scores.

High P%-Scores for Western and East Asian College-University Students. Among college and university students, respondents from North America, Europe, and the East Asian countries receive comparable scores, with the exception of the high-scoring Australian sample. However, the Australian sample is an unusually small sample, and it may not be fully representative of Australian students.

Industrialized versus Third World Countries. Students from Third World countries such as Belize, Trinidad-Tobago, and Nigeria tend to receive lower scores than students from the more industrialized countries located in North America, Europe, and East Asia. Thus, the main dividing line for the data is not between Western, Anglo-Saxon, English-speaking countries and non-Western, non-English-speaking countries but between industrialized Western or East Asian countries with demanding educational systems and Third World, less-industrialized countries with less-demanding educational systems.

No Developmental Trends in the Arab Societies. The three studies conducted in Egypt, Kuwait, and Sudan do not portray clear developmental trends. In addition, there are signs in these studies that the DIT may not be a satisfactory test of moral reasoning in these societies. In two of the studies, more than half of all students failed to pass the consistency check, sometimes ranking and rating the *same* moral arguments quite differently.

Even among the students who did pass the consistency tests (their scores are reported in Table 6.2), developmental trends are absent. It should be added that a different adaptation of the DIT was employed in the Egyptian study when compared to the studies conducted in Kuwait and Sudan. Thus, it is unlikely that the unconvincing results in the three Arab nations merely reflect linguistic problems related to the translation and adaptation of the DIT.

Gender Differences. Apart from the Nigerian study (test for gender differences not reported) and the Australian study (number of respondents too small to test reliably for gender differences), tests for gender differences are available for the remaining twelve countries. For six of the countries, namely, Belize, Trinidad-Tobago (study by Gielen et al., 1986), Kuwait, Sudan, Greece, and Poland, nonsignificant gender differences for P%-Scores are reported. In the Hong Kong, South Korea, and Taiwan studies, female students received significantly higher P%-Scores than the male students. Gender differences were small in size, however. In the United States, Thoma (1986) conducted a large-scale meta- and secondary analysis of DIT scores for 56 samples, including more than 6,000 male and female students. Female students at all age levels received slightly but significantly higher average P%-Scores than the male students. Gilligan's (1982) widely publicized claim that Kohlbergian theories and methods downgrade feminine concerns for care and empathy has fared poorly in North American research (Walker, 1991). It fares equally poorly in the cross-cultural research surveyed here.

Effects of Social Class Background. Several studies report correlations between measures of parental social class (SES) and the students' moral reasoning scores, with age and/or educational level statistically controlled. These studies were conducted in Belize, Greece, Kuwait, Sudan, Taiwan, and Trinidad-Tobago. It should be kept in mind that the studies try to evaluate the effects of social class on the moral reasoning scores of those high school or college/university students who attended the same educational institutions.

Taken together, the studies provide no support for the hypothesis that parental social class is linked in a clear way to the level of moral comprehension of adolescents. Correlations between indicators of social class and moral judgment maturity are very low and frequently statistically insignificant. In no study does social class account for an appreciable amount of the variance in the students' moral reasoning scores. This is an important finding: It means that, for instance, growing up in an upper-middle-class home rather than in a working-class home does not directly influence the adolescents' level of moral reasoning. Structures of moral reasoning are not learned from one's parents, nor are they the outcome of parental indoctrination. Instead, it is exposure to advanced levels of schooling that has a positive impact on the students' moral development.

Taken together, the DIT studies surveyed above suggest that an understanding of and a preference for principled moral arguments develops in systematic ways among high school and university students from both East Asian and Western backgrounds. In contrast, the DIT does not appear to be a good measure of the development of moral judgment in the Arab countries. While a variety of reasons may be adduced for these findings, we will argue in the following section that principled moral reasoning can already be found in the works of classical Chinese philosophers such as Confucius (551–479 B.C.E.), Mengzi (372–280 B.C.E.), and others. Consequently, societies shaped by Confucian and neo-Confucian value systems such as Taiwan, South Korea, mainland China, and Japan do not only place heavy emphasis on moral education (Gielen, 1990), but they also are heirs to an indigenous cultural heritage containing highly sophisticated and at times principled moral discussions going far back into history. A similar claim can be made about India, Western civilization, and various countries shaped by Buddhist theological and metaphysical traditions. These civilizations have their roots in reflective traditions of postconventional thought that first appeared in prototypical form during the "Axial Age."

THE AXIAL AGE AND POSTCONVENTIONAL MORAL THINKING

In his book *About the Origin and Goal of History* (1949/1953), the German existentialist philosopher and psychiatrist Karl Jaspers argues that humanity shares a common origin and a common goal in spite of the many cultural and religious differences that have both enriched and bedeviled its history. Between 800 B.C.E. and 200 B.C.E., certain fundamental transformations in religious-philosophical thought occurred in the three civilizations of China, India, and the West (Greece, ancient Israel), thereby laying the spiritual and cultural groundwork for many later developments in these civilizations. Jaspers names the period of 800 B.C.E. to 200 B.C.E. the Axial Age because during that age the philosophical-religious-cultural "axes" came into being around which many future developments in the three civilizations would turn.

India's basic metaphysical writings leading to Hinduism, Buddhism, Jainism, and other religious-metaphysical-philosophical systems, classical Greek philosophy, parts of the Old Testament, and the classics of Chinese philosophy are all representative of the Axial Age, and as such they constitute a breakthrough in the history of human thought. For the first time, highly reflective philosophies of human destiny begin to endorse and share an emphasis on universal human meaning, the replacement of myth by rational thought, a new conception of history, a pervasive questioning of traditional custom and traditional thought, the transcendence of traditional life and its customs, values, and norms, and new and much more reflective and interiorized conceptions of what humans are about, their inner nature, and their spiritual potentialities. Interwoven with these new philosophical and religious conceptions come higher, more abstract, and more differentiated levels of moral-ethical reflection.

For our purposes, the most important aspect of Jaspers's interpretation of universal history is this: Following the arguments of the German sinologist Heiner Roetz (1992, 1993, 1996), we may claim that *during the Axial Age, principled moral reasoning made its first appearance on the stage of world history.* It developed independently in Greece (Socrates and his successors), Israel (some of the prophets), and India (the Buddha, some of the Hindu and Jain theologians). In China, this stage of cultural evolution manifested itself in the works of Confucius (551–479 B.C.E.), Mengzi or Mencius (372–281 B.C.E.), Xunzi (ca. 310–230 B.C.E.), Mo Di (5th century B.C.E.), Han Fei (280–233 B.C.E.), the Daoist classics *Zhuangzi* and *Laozi* (3rd century B.C.E.), and others. The most detailed analysis of this revolutionary breakthrough in ethical thought has been presented by Roetz (1993) in his difficult but fascinating book, *Confucian Ethics of the Axial Age: A Reconstruction under the Aspect of the Breakthrough Towards Postconventional Thinking.*

According to Roetz, classical Chinese philosophy originated in a period of crisis during which the traditional norms and values underwent a process of disintegration: The *Dao* (the True Way) had been lost, and *luan* (chaos) threatened to engulf civilization. In response to this threat, the philosophers—themselves a footloose group of restless wanderers—began to search for overarching ethical and practical principles that could save the state and, with it, the common people who were seen as the victims of moral and societal chaos but could hardly be expected to fend for themselves. A hundred schools of philosophy began to blossom, each offering a different recipe to end the (supposed) moral chaos and the constant fighting between the various Chinese states and kingdoms. The romantic Daoists, for instance, argued that humans had lost their original place in nature and that only a retreat from corrupt society and a return to a natural way of life could bring about the return of the *Dao*. In stark contrast, the cynical Legalists favored a societywide and almost Skinnerian program of reinforcement in which, however, ruthless punishment for even the smallest transgressions of state law would predominate. In contrast, Master Kung (Confucius) proposed what in time would become the most influential program of moral philosophy and moral education in Chinese civilization, thereby making him perhaps the most important teacher-philosopher in history.

Confucius' original thought can be most clearly discerned in the book *Lunyu* (also known as *The Analects*) (Confucius, 1979). Here, we can see the postconventional nature of much of his thinking. Written in the form of terse aphorisms and teachings, the *Lunyu* describes various discussions between Confucius and his students in which Confucius upholds the ideal of principled moral uprightness and humaneness: The *chun-tze* (the noble one; the gentleman; the person upholding virtue) follows a path of moral autonomy guided by the principle of *jen* (*rén*), that is, benevolence or human-heartedness. Beholden to "heaven," he is morally autonomous in relationship to society but not at all individualistic or self-centered. Identifying with "heaven, earth, and the myriad things," he practices self-cultivation, self-awareness, and self-criticism while showing true justice to poor and rich alike.

The *chun-tze* seeks to discern and follow the *dao de* (the way of virtue) motivated by a sense of *inner shame* rather than being afraid of the conventional opinions of others. Reading all this one feels that it would be hard to find a more convincing philosophical-psychological portrayal of moral principledness than can be seen in some passages of the *Lunyu* or in the work of the later, idealistic Confucian scholar, *Mencius* (Mencius, 1970).

Let us now return to the main argument advanced in this chapter. We surveyed the cross-cultural empirical evidence and found that principled moral arguments are at least as frequently endorsed by Chinese and South Korean students as by American and other comparable Western students. Lei's (1994) recent longitudinal study employing Kohlberg's original Moral Judgment Interview with Chinese elementary, secondary, and university students from Taiwan provides additional support for this conclusion. Although Lei used a quite different methodology than the DIT, he found that his Chinese students received very high moral reasoning scores when compared to the scores typically seen in Western studies. To such empirical findings we may now add the historical evidence that principled conceptions of moral autonomy, justice, benevolence, and responsibility have long been a part of the indigenous Chinese philosophical tradition (even if they were frequently betrayed in history). In light of these findings, it would indeed be misleading to see in Kohlberg's theory nothing more than an expression of Western individualism as the Chinese-American psychologist Dien (1982) has urged us to do. While Dien argues that the collectivistic nature of Chinese society is at variance with Kohlberg's and Rest's notions of moral autonomy, the historical and experimental evidence suggests that moral autonomy (i.e., an inner guidance by universalizable moral principles) is compatible with, and even demanded by, the more advanced manifestations of Chinese moral thinking as these have influenced Chinese civilization for some 2,500 years.

SUMMARY AND CONCLUSIONS

Kohlberg and Rest have proposed that moral reasoning develops from an initial concern with the practical consequences of one's actions, to an identification with interpersonal and societal expectations, to a level where persons have worked out their own moral principles. The cross-cultural status of the level of moral principles is especially controversial. Critics have argued that Kohlberg's level of moral principles represents a Western, male-oriented, upper-class ideology of individualism that misrepresents the moral experience of non-Westerners, women, and members of the lower social classes. If the critics are right, we should find that samples of male Americans (and other Westerners) from upper-class backgrounds receive much higher scores on Kohlbergian tests of moral reasoning than samples from non-Western countries, especially if the latter include females and students from lower social class backgrounds. We also should find a lack of clear developmental trends in the non-Western studies.

Our review of fifteen studies in fourteen countries supports Rest's developmental hypotheses in European, North American, and East Asian societies, but the results of the studies conducted in the Arab and Caribbean societies are more ambiguous. Across all studies, gender differences tend to be small and, if significant, favor female students. Social class differences among students attending the same schools have little effect on their moral reasoning scores. Female students from collectivistic East Asian societies such as Taiwan or South Korea are especially likely to prefer principled moral arguments. Given these findings, it must be concluded that the DIT is not biased in favor of individualistic, male-oriented, upper-class, Western conceptions of morality. Notwithstanding this conclusion, the DIT in its present form does not adequately measure the development of moral reasoning in the Arab world, a finding that is discussed more fully in Gielen, Ahmed, and Avellani (1992).

One of the main findings of this survey is that the students from Third World countries such as Belize, Trinidad-Tobago, and Nigeria endorse principled moral arguments much less frequently than the students from industrialized East Asian and Western countries. This finding cannot be explained by theories of Westernization or by the influence of Anglo-Saxon individualism, since the English-speaking Caribbean nations have adopted British educational institutions and are pervasively influenced by North American culture. In contrast, the Republic of China, Taiwan, has kept its native languages and emphasizes "updated" versions of Confucian moral education. It is the overall complexity, modernity, and institutional integration of the East Asian societies, the rigor of their educational systems, and the "developmental pull" of complex ethical systems such as modern adaptations of Confucianism that can help explain the high P%-Scores of East Asian students when compared to the lower scores of the more Westernized, but morally more conventional, Caribbean students. The moral ethos of Caribbean societies appears to depend on conventional, role-oriented, interpersonal, yet individualistic, expectations which are frequently reflected in Stage 3 reasoning. This is especially true for traditional, face-to-face relationships in villages and small towns. In contrast, postconventional reasoning is furthered by involvement in tertiary education, active exposure to integrated but competing value systems, and sustained reflection on a widening sociomoral world. Postconventional reasoning also forms the moral basis of the worldwide human rights movement which appeals to principled and universalizable notions of justice, human dignity, and cross-cultural dialogue based on equality.

Critics of the cognitive-developmental approach have frequently confused the concept and ideology of rugged, masculine, rule-oriented individualism with the quite different philosophical idea of moral autonomy. Moral autonomy, as understood by Kohlberg and Rest, refers to an orientation toward internalized, *shareable* moral principles. These principles reflect schemes of cooperation rather than the arbitrary preoccupation with self-expression in the service of individualism. The very purpose of principled moral thinking is to create just solutions to moral problems based on ideal role-taking and shareable moral values. Ideal role-taking is usually supportive of "feminine" concerns for care and empathy. Moral autonomy and a concern for moral principles exist in collectivistic societies (e.g., Taiwan) just as much as in individualistic societies (e.g., the United States) (Gielen, 1990; Lei, 1994). Moral autonomy and shareable moral principles reflect moral ideals that to some extent transcend culture, gender, and religious ideology. They are not recent Western inventions but may already be found in some form in the sayings attributed to the Buddha, Confucius, and Socrates who became the teachers of humanity. They are ideals for all time, although they must be reinterpreted and divested of remaining biases as societies change.

Cultural ideals in their most developed forms give flesh to universal intuitions about the nature of moral excellence. While Western modern secular ideals emphasize the dignity and personhood of individuals, religious Tibetans emphasize the "Buddha-nature" inherent in everyone, Hindus uphold ideals of universal nonviolence (*Ahimsa*), and Confucianists focus on humanistic ideals of human-heartedness (*jen*). These cultural ideals are based on different metaphysical assumptions, but they all emphasize a concern for human dignity, solidarity, responsibility, and justice. Moral and cultural relativists have failed to perceive the underlying archetype that unites the moral imaginations of men and women living in different places and at different times. In contrast, Kohlbergian theories and methods are among the first sustained rigorous scientific attempts to capture the inherent nature and development of the age-old human search for justice and solidarity.

SOME SUGGESTIONS FOR FURTHER READING

Structural theories of moral reasoning are not easily comprehended since they focus on complex processes underlying the development of thinking rather than trying to identify more readily recognizable attitudes, opinions, and norms. The difficulty is compounded when we try to understand complex moral arguments advanced by members of other cultures. Given this situation, we would like to make some suggestions for further reading.

The reader interested in Kohlberg's theory should first consult the two volumes containing his essays: Lawrence Kohlberg (1981), *Essays on moral development, Vol. 1: The philosophy of moral development*; and Lawrence Kohlberg (1984), *Essays on moral development, Vol. 2: The psychology of moral development*, both published by Harper and Row. A more concise summary of Kohlbergian theory, methodology, and research may be found in Lisa Kuhmerker with Uwe P. Gielen and Richard L. Hayes (1991), *The Kohlberg legacy for the helping professions* (Religious Education Press; see especially chapters 2–4). Rest's Defining Issues Test and an early overview of the many studies based on it can be found in: James Rest (1979), *Development in judging moral issues* (University of Minnesota Press). A later summary of some additional DIT studies is included in: James Rest (1986a), *Moral development: Advances in research and theory* (Praeger).

Several summaries of Kohlbergian cross-cultural research are available. John Snarey's (1985) early article: Cross-cultural universality of social-moral development: A critical review of Kohlbergian research, *Psychological Bulletin, 97*, 202–232 remains a useful overview of studies employing Kohlberg's interview method. More recent surveys may be found in Uwe P. Gielen (1996), Moral reasoning in cross-cultural perspective: A review of Kohlbergian research, *World Psychology, 2* (3–4), 313–333; and in Lutz H. Eckensberger and Roderick F. Zimba (1997), The development of moral judgment, in W. Berry, P. R. Dasen, & T. S. Saraswathi (Eds.), *Handbook of cross-cultural psychology*, Vol. 2, *Basic processes and human development* (pp. 299–338) (Allyn & Bacon). A special issue of the new journal *World Psychology* (1996, Vol. 2 [3–4]; Focus on Lawrence Kohlberg) is highly useful in assessing the strengths and weaknesses of Kohlberg's approach to moral and religious development as seen through the eyes of some of his most creative followers.

Karl Jaspers' views on the Axial Age may be found in his book *About the origin and goal of history* (1953—Translation by Michael Bullock; published by Yale University Press). A special issue of *Daedalus* (1975, Vol. 104 [2]), titled *Wisdom, revelation, and doubt: Perspectives on the First Millennium B.C.* contains knowledgeable discussions of Jaspers' thesis by several cultural historians. Heiner Roetz's (1993) *Confucian ethics of the axial age: A reconstruction under the aspect of the breakthrough towards postconventional thinking* (SUNY Press) summarizes his attempt to reconstruct classical Chinese philosophy in the light of Kohlberg's theory. His article, Kohlberg and Chinese moral philosophy, in *World Psychology* (1996, Vol. 2 [3–4], pp. 335–363) updates this discussion and also contains his response to some criticisms that have been made of his interpretation. Some records of Confucius' teachings, *The analects*, have been translated and annotated many times. D. C. Lau's edition in the Penguin series is readily available, as is his translation of *Mencius* (also by Penguin).

NOTE

The first author is grateful to the H. F. Guggenheim Foundation, St. Francis College, the Pacific Cultural Foundation, and the Columbia University Faculty Seminar on Moral Education for grants supporting his DIT studies. Material drawn from this work was presented to the Columbia University Seminar on Moral Education. The chapter is dedicated to the memory of our colleague Joseph Avellani.

7

Women and Gender Roles

Leonore Loeb Adler

It has been stated that all over the world norms exist that describe and prescribe appropriate social behavior for both genders. These social expectations, or gender roles, for males and females vary with the stages during the life span. However, similarities as well as differences exist among and between cultures. Variations of the same behavior may occur within communities in the same country. And, as a matter of fact, individuals or different families may follow their own variations of generally accepted and expected behavior. Therefore it is well to repeat again the previous observation "with regard to the cultural and social effects of gender roles, it would probably be practically impossible to overestimate the exposure of different influences on people's behavior" (Adler, 1994, in press). Yet, that manners and customs of people all over the world may be adapted and adjusted to local habits, likes, and dislikes is a pertinent issue. For example, here is a paraphrased modified statement by Ian Robertson (1987), who reported that Americans eat oysters but not snails. The French eat snails but not locusts. The Zulus eat locusts but not fish. Russians eat fish but not snakes. Chinese eat snakes but not people. The Jales of New Guinea find people delicious (p. 67).

Just as there exists a variety of taste differences all over the globe, people around the world hold some norms in common. Those norms that are held in common seem to have a universal basis. One of the best known is the taboo against incest. "Parents are not to have sexual relations with their children, nor siblings with one another. Although the taboo apparently is violated more often than psychologists once believed, the norm is still universal" (Myers, 1996, p. 202).

A CLOSER LOOK AT GENDER ROLES

Gender roles are not only based on biologically determined structures and functions but may be based, in addition, on cultural norms that assign the gender roles for males and females throughout the life span. With regard to "gender-role ideology," Gibbons, Hamby, and Dennis (1997) recently suggested to examine the distinction between gender-related roles and gender-related traits. Their explanation of ideologies is identified as prescriptive or proscriptive instead of descriptive. An explanation of gender roles, advanced by Williams and Best (1990a, 1990b), states that these are culturally defined sets of behavior that are differentiated by gender. On the other hand, traits are thought to be relatively persistent qualities or characteristics that may differ between men and women. For example, in traditional as well as in modern societies, females are usually portrayed with nurturing traits, such as caring for their families and being busy with household chores inside their homes. On the other hand, men's usual activities are more characteristic of taking place outside their homes in order to bring home and supply the necessities for the families' subsistence. Of course, variations exist depending on the ecologies and whether the families reside in rural or urban environments. However, in modern settings, women have the choice of activities. Regardless of background culture, women living in modern countries have the option of working outside their homes. They can accept part-time or full-time jobs to help support the family and increase the income while still continuing with their traditional gender roles. Some of the crucial points of such modernization rest with the opportunities that are extended to women in the areas of education and modern technologies.

A FEW HISTORICAL NOTES

Some years ago, a conference and later its publication dealt with the question "Does *la différence* make a difference?" (Orasanu, Slater, & Adler, 1979). In this case, " *'la différence'* refers to a popular tagline in Western folklore. A debate among French cabinet ministers about the equality and fraternity [*sic*] of females and males ends with the following celebratory shout *'vive la différence!'* " Among the contributors to this volume are several authors who showed that many gender differences exist in language and speech.

The topic of gender equality does not seem to have universal appeal in other than modern, industrialized countries. Very little research has been conducted dealing with gender roles worldwide. However, even the same terminology does not represent equivalence between men and women. Alice Schlegel (1972), an anthropologist, wrote a book with the intriguing title *Male Dominance and Female Autonomy*. Describing the choice of the title, Adler and Clark (1999) explain Schlegel's reasoning, who does not see female autonomy as an equivalent to men's. Instead it represents a woman's control over her own thoughts and actions and, in addition, her meaningful contributions to her family and the society "beyond breeding and feeding" (p. 23).

However, under certain circumstances a type of equivalence may exist between men and women. During the 1940s in the United States, as a consequence of drafting young men into military service during World War II, women entered the workforce in great numbers to replace the men who had vacated their jobs. However, when the men came home, they returned to their prewar positions; therefore, the women were retired to resume their domestic roles of raising a family and taking care of the household. Yet many women did not find domestic work as satisfying as following a career and earning money to help upgrade the standards of living for the family. Equality seemed close at hand—though it still is a far way off!

During the 1970s, women gathered together in the feminist movement to achieve equal rights with men. Today, in most traditional as well as modern countries, men continue to occupy a higher status than women. Even though women have made strides toward equality during the twentieth century, particularly after World War II, they are not yet perceived as equal to men in any of their activities either in the family at home or away from home.

Of course industrialization has had a profound effect on women's roles in society. The importance of the woman's domestic role in the twentieth century has been diminishing (Denmark, Schwartz, & Smith, 1991, p. 2). For example, the introduction of polyester and similar fabrics and the availability of washing machines and dryers in industrialized societies have men as well as women taking care of laundry chores, which no longer need the laborious handscrubbing that had traditionally been performed by women. On the other hand, L. F. Lowenstein and K. Lowenstein (1991) propose that "the pendulum has certainly swung from women being in a very subordinate position in relation to men in society generally to one in which women are, if not equal, approaching equality and, in some cases have surpassed the role of the male totally" (p. 52).

While it may appear from a Western and modern outlook that, almost all over the world, women strive for equality with men, a great many women live in a male-dominated traditional world without any thought of change. The United Nations endorsed, however, the "Decade for Women 1978–1988," which was launched by the National Commission on the Observance of International Women's Year, in Washington, D.C. in March 1978. This was followed by the National Women's Conference in Houston, Texas, in November 1978. Of course, there were other outstanding women's meetings taking place periodically on different continents. Yet the analyses of their effects on the various populations still has to come in due time.

At this time it might be well to present a different type of example of a cross-cultural comparison. It is definitely an "exception to the rule" that has been reported by Singhal and Mrinal (1991) on the women of the Tharu tribe in northern India. There the Tharu women run the government. The men of the tribe are dependent and of lower status than women. In their communities, the status of a father is enhanced by the birth of a daughter, which of course is contrary to the custom in traditional Hindu families, where the birth of a girl is a less than fortunate event.

Another interesting situation exists in Western Samoa in the Southern Insular Pacific. By consensus of the adults of each household or family, women are appointed to be their chief and to represent them in the village council. The chief is responsible for all household members, overseeing family affairs, directing the use of family land, and assigning tasks according to age and sex of the members. Thus the chief holds great power over individual lives. Nearly 10 percent of the population of 160,500 inhabitants in Western Samoa hold the title of chief, and of these chiefs, 400 are women (Muse, 1991).

ASPECTS IMPORTANT TO EDUCATION

Education is one of the most crucial pivotal points for the progress of women's equality with men. Unfortunately, in many Third World countries, girls are not favored and their education is frequently nonexistent, inadequate, or too limited in terms of time spent in school. There are often different requirements for boys and for girls all over the world.

In most developed and some developing countries, school is compulsory for all children. In the United States and Canada, as well as in the countries of Europe and Australia and in New Zealand, elementary and secondary education is considered essential since almost all the countries offer children free education and provide free schools. Higher education in colleges and universities is viewed as prestigious, affording the opportunity to secure higher paying positions. In the United States and Canada, 51 percent of the student body are women, roughly the same proportion of the representation of women in the total population in these two countries (Denmark, Schwartz, & Smith, 1991). It seems that in most countries where the educational level of family members is high, husbands tend to be proud of their wives' achievements in areas other than just their financial contributions to the family income (Lowenstein & Lowenstein, 1991).

A different situation exists in Egypt, where, as in other Islamic countries, it was in the past believed—and practiced—that formal education was not for girls. When primary schools were finally opened to girls, most people perceived the schools as upper-class institutions. Later, intermediary and secondary schools were opened for girls. However, in rural districts, the dropout rate for girls has been much higher than for boys—at a two-to-one ratio. This accounts, to a great extent, for the illiteracy of the current population (Ahmed, 1991). In addition, Egyptian men often seek wives who are less educated than they are. Since Egyptian women are mostly homemakers, they do not take jobs outside their homes, and their educational level is not an important issue (Minai, 1981).

In the Sudan, however, enrollment in school has clearly affected the status of women favorably. Even though the enrollment of girls is increasing, it remains less than that of boys at all three educational levels, especially at the upper levels. There is also a smaller enrollment in rural areas, probably because of the dominant tribal values and strong Sudanese traditions against female education (Ahmed, 1991). Sudanese society should comply with the following slogan: "Educating girls may be one of the country's best investments toward future growth and progress" (Sudanow, March 1985, p. 7).

In Eastern Asia, for example, in the People's Republic of China, a similar situation may cause the illiteracy rate, especially in rural areas where school attendance is not compulsory. Children are generally encouraged to attend elementary schools but nonattendance and the school dropout rates are high, especially when the children have to help their families work in the fields (Yu & Carpenter, 1991).

In Taiwan, however, rules and regulations differ. There school attendance for children is mandatory until the ninth grade (Yu & Carpenter, 1991). Also, during recent years, the educational level of girls in Japan has increased. After high school, almost one-third of all female students go on to higher education, and one-fourth of the female students go on to a four-year college or university (Fukada, 1991). In addition, there are available opportunities for adult or continuing-education programs (Sukemune, Shiraishi, Shirakawa, & Matsumi, 1993).

With regard to adult education programs, there exists an ever-increasing trend—especially in modern countries in North America, Europe, Australia, and Eastern Asia, to name just a few of the geographical areas—to cater to the adult and elderly populations. However, the main purpose of education is still to concentrate on young school children and to provide them with a basic foundation of general knowledge.

C. J. Muse (1991) reports that in Western Samoa, the compulsory attendance laws require children to attend either the village, the district, or the denominational schools from ages 5 to 17. The curriculum is similar to that of New Zealand.

The traditions are quite different in India, where both middle-class boys and middle-class girls receive an education. It seems easier for parents to find husbands for their daughters when the daughters are educated because educated women can find higher-paying jobs, and the parents can therefore negotiate for smaller dowries (Kumar, 1991).

MATE SELECTION

An interesting study was conducted by Barry (1976) that related different aspects of marriage to childrearing practices. He based his findings on populations from 130 different societies. Barry notes that when large differences exist between the sexes, especially during the middle years of childhood, those societies usually insist on the virginity of the bride when she gets married. In addition, the possibilities of autonomous behavior and thoughts are suppressed during the girl's childhood years (Adler & Clark, 1999).

It was Murdock's (1964, 1967) major study based on 180 societies, which included many major cultural areas around the globe, that investigated premarital sex norms cross-culturally. His findings identified three distinct patterns: (1) *permissive societies* that are more or less permissive of unmarried girls' sexual behavior; (2) *intermediate attitudes* that represent the midpoint between permissive and restrictive societies; and (3) *restrictive societies* that do not permit premarital sex and therefore it occurs infrequently. This was followed by Goethals (1971) investigation of the same topic. Although he used different independent and dependent variables, the results were replicated. (See Broude, 1981.)

An important milestone in the life of young people is the selection of a spouse. In many modern or modernizing countries, young people of marriageable age select their own future marriage partners. However, in many traditional countries and communities, mate selection is handled by parents or matchmakers. In the United States and Canada, eligible young people tend to choose spouses who have similar social status, are of the same race or ethnic group, and belong to the same religion (Eckland, 1968). However, among Alaskan natives, marriages are frequently arranged between families in the same community (Fischer, 1991). When an agreement has been reached, the parents of the young girl present the young man with a gift, such as a knife, harpoon, or parka; in turn, the young man comes to the girl's family to work for them as his "bride service." This worktime may be shortened when the young man catches a seal and presents it to his future parents-in-law. The marriage could be consummated any time during this period, after which the young couple are considered married (p. 21).

In South America, mate selection is now a matter of choice and is no longer arranged by the parents or relatives. Ardila (1991) suggests that, given a choice between becoming a wife and mother or an executive, women would opt for the first choice. However, many women combine the two options. Yet even though the wife helps with the family financial support, the husband does not help with the household chores.

In Europe, Grzymala-Moszczynska (1991) reports from Poland that there exists an important age difference between rural and urban customs. Girls in most rural areas marry between the ages of 18 and 22, whereas those who live in a urban communities marry mostly between ages 21 and 26.

Many young farmers face difficulties in finding a prospective bride, because many rural girls "escape to the city" where they find more freedom and a less strenuous life. Therefore, many young farmers seek the help of a matrimonial agency—although not all are successful since many young women from the city are afraid to start a life in the country. These days the selection of prospective spouses in the city is done primarily by the young people without parental involvement. Yet the tradition in rural Poland is that the bride brings a dowry to the husband. Usually this dowry includes money and utensils for the future household. In addition, a featherbed (comforter), pillows, and kitchen utensils are almost obligatory. Of course, "more affluent families can give their daughters houses, some land, and a cow. Even a daughter who lives in the city might bring along a 'symbolic cow' in the form of money from the sale of a real cow" (Grzymala-Moszczynska, 1991, p. 61).

Islamic societies, including Egypt and the Sudan, among others, have remained strictly marriage-oriented. In addition, Islam prohibits premarital relationships between a man and a woman and instead encourages marriage. It also prohibits celibacy since Prophet Muhammed decreed that marriage is the only road to virtue (Ahmed, 1991, p. 121). Women in rural areas marry mainly between ages 16 and 18, whereas men marry between ages 20 and 25. However, in urban areas, young women are usually between the ages of 20 and 30 when they marry, and young men are usually between the ages of 25 and 35 at the time of their wedding. Within the last 20 years, matrimonial ads have appeared in Egyptian newspapers, where men and women look for spouses (Ahmed, 1991, p. 122). In an unpublished survey, Ahmed (1984) found that university men "tended to prefer that their future wives be less educated women, either from higher or lower secondary schools or primary schools, or possibly their illiterate village cousins" (Ahmed, 1991, p. 122).

The pattern of mate selection is quite different in India. Kumar (1991) reports that when a girl reaches puberty, her parents start arranging a match for her. Although at this time she attains a more important status in the family, she is also more restricted in her movements. "Unless she is with a group, interacting freely with boys of her age is prohibited. Male cousins and their friends may or may not be given access to her house." Resorting to "fasting or observing the ritual of tying a cord around the wrist of the young man proclaiming him as an 'adopted' brother are some traditional ways of coping with sexual feelings" (p. 150). The results of an informal study with female college students, related by Parul Dave to Usha Kumar, revealed some interesting views by the women students. They preferred their future spouses to be older, more intelligent, and of higher status and educational level than their own. The women unequivocally opted for marriage as the more desirable lifestyle rather than staying single or cohabiting (pp. 150–151). With parents looking for older and better educated husbands for their daughters, the trend has been for girls to marry earlier. Among Hindus the percentage of single women is almost nil, for marriage bestows on women their socially accepted role. Kumar (1991) also reports an increase of young newly married wives who continue their education, which she feels gives impetus to vocational orientation in female education. It appears that the working woman enjoys higher prestige in India and possibly greater self-esteem.

In Thailand in cities like Bangkok, a modernization of the old customs seems to prevail. Many young people reject arranged marriages, preferring to make their own choices. However, in rural areas, the traditional patterns of mate selection survive. "College women in Thailand were significantly more egalitarian in their marriage preferences (stressing shared decision making and female independence) than comparable groups of college women in India and the United States of America" (Gardiner, Singh, & D'Orazio, 1974, pp. 413–415).

In the two Chinas—Mainland China and Taiwan—vast progress in modernization has occurred. In 1950, the Marriage Law was passed in the People's Republic of China that freed women from the age-old system of bondage. Women were given free choice of a spouse, with monogamy and equal rights for both men and women. In the Republic of China, Taiwan, the Marriage Law abolished the feudal marriage system. From then on, women could choose their husbands. This law mandated monogamy and assured equal rights for both sexes. Women in today's Taiwan retain their family name after marriage. They are allowed to inherit property and keep it and the income in their name. Lucy C. Yu and Lee Carpenter (1991) describe the procedure of drawing up a contract for a woman to acquire any property; if this is not done, the husband gets all the belongings that became her property, either from before or during their marriage. On the other hand, women are held responsible for their spouse's debts.

Modernization has also left its mark in Japan by replacing traditional customs with new ones. Although young men and women are free to marry whomever they choose under the new law, parents generally hold on to old customs and habits. In general, marriages are arranged by mediators or go-betweens. This procedure is helpful, since the young people may not have adequate opportunities to meet eligible singles (Fukada, 1991).

In Western Samoa in the past, traditionally marriages were arranged; today, very few, if any, marriages are arranged. Instead, clandestine rendezvous are arranged by the young man's intermediary. After the formal announcement and engagement period, the wedding follows. However, the bride is only a probationary member of the groom's family until the first baby is born (Muse, 1991, p. 230).

FAMILIES

Some provocative and interesting topics were opened by Loeb (1962) when he discussed plural marriages. Several types of plural marriages are practiced. In all of them, it is the custom for one spouse to have more than one marital partner at the same time. In a polyandrous marriage, one wife has several husbands; these may be brothers (see Gielen, 1993). In a polygynous marriage, one husband has several wives. However, there exist two types of polygynies: one is a sororal polygyny, where the cowives are sisters or consanguinal (blood relatives), while the other is a nonsororal polygyny, where the women, who are the cowives, are neither related nor affinal kin (related by marriage). Loeb (1962) hypothesizes that sororal polygyny enhances female autonomy, since the sisters can present a unified front that enhances all of them. On the other hand, he suggests that in a nonsororal polygyny the cowives are jealous of each other, especially when they are competing for access to the center of power in the home, which is associated with the husband's authority and status. In reverse, Loeb feels that in a polyandrous plural marriage, the status and dominance of the husband is negatively associated with power, since the common wife can play one of her husbands against the others.

While the family is being established by the young couple, in modern communities the woman may have to work outside the home for economic reasons. The traditional role for women is that of a full-time homemaker who takes care of her husband, the children, and the home. However, such circumstances are becoming less and less common in modern times, even though such family constellations still have an aura of being women's first-role fulfillment. In the traditional role, the husband is the sole breadwinner, which makes the wife and children completely dependent on the man in the house—the husband and father. However in modern times, this double-role of the mother brings about a new situation. Markoulis and Dikaiou (1993) explain it as follows: "The daughter of the nuclear family is offered an inadequate female model for identification; she sees that her mother has shifted away from the traditional role of obedience and attendance to her husband's needs toward a vague and unclear perception of her role" (p. 90). Furthermore, it is the son as well who sees the father in an ambiguous role. In the current reality, the father is not the only one who contributes a salary to the family budget. Even though the mother's salary is probably less than the father's, she contributes the butter and jam for the daily bread. And at the same time the father probably does not provide any substantial help with taking care of the household chores. Situations such as these are probably quite common in modern and modernizing countries, where women have an opportunity to follow their own careers while still performing their traditional gender roles (Adler, 1998).

THE LATER YEARS

It was correctly pointed out by Denmark, Schwartz, and Smith (1991) that females are brought up to look attractive in order to find a husband and become mothers and that the aging process is often difficult for some women in the United States and Canada, as well as in other modern countries. The middle-age period in life may be particularly difficult for the woman when the grown children leave home, and she has no other major interests other than her husband, her children, and the home. Some of these women are identified as having the "empty nest syndrome." However, in a study of 160 women, only one showed the typical symptoms of depression (Rubin, cited in Greenberg, 1978, p. 75). The other women in this study expressed a "sense of relief," although a few had been ambivalent at the time of their children's departure.

Another trend of the time seems to be taking place. In this case it could happen that the young adult cannot secure a job after being away at college or earn a sufficient income to live independently. It could also be that the young newly married couple cannot make a go of their marriage; one way out may be to separate or get a divorce. As a consequence of such or similar situations, the young adult may return to the parents' home for support and understanding until such a time as the young adult can establish an independent existence. A situation of this type is usually identified as that of a "homing pigeon."

Health permitting, during older age, women as well as men may pursue hobbies, especially if their financial needs are provided for by family investments or by insurance, such as by retirement benefits. In the United States, early retirement at 62 years of age, with reduced Social Security benefits, is available; full retirement at age 65 is more or less standard procedure, although these ages are about to increase. In the United States, mandatory retirement at age 70 is scheduled to be instituted in the future.

Many women spend their last years in widowhood, since the life expectancy for women is generally longer than that of men. In Western societies, men who become widowers frequently remarry so that single-family households in the United States are overwhelmingly headed by women. During the past two or three decades, establishments of Golden Age Clubs, or leisure-time centers, have been on the increase in the U.S.A. and Britain in order to fill the free time of older people, left by shorter working hours and labor-saving appliances in the homes.

In other countries and cultures, the living arrangements may differ. Ardila (1991) writes that "aging is more positive in Latin America than in many other countries of the First and Second Worlds (p. 25). Grzymala-Moszczynska (1991) points out that after retirement, women live fuller and busier lives than men. "A grandmother, retired from professional duties, is still the most wanted solution (as a babysitter) for the majority of families in which young adult women, besides being wives and mothers, wish to continue their professional careers" (p. 65).

A special situation exists in Israel. Whereas elderly women in Israeli cities face conditions similar to those that exist in other Eastern environments, the kibbutzim in Israel present a different ecology. The economic structure of the kibbutz guarantees its members financial security; however, both men and women work as long as they are capable of doing so. Life expectancies of both men and women in the kibbutz are much greater (three years for women and six years for men) than that of the urban elderly in general. Part of this condition is attributed to the performance of work by all adult members. However, with increasing age, older workers may reduce their work hours and tackle less-exerting tasks (Safir & Izraeli, 1991).

In Egypt and the Sudan, health-care conditions and working environments have improved, which has contributed to the increasing number of elderly living there. In addition, the Egyptian Ministry of Social Affairs has established homes as well as clubs for the elderly in Cairo and in Alexandria, and since the 1970s, elderly people can receive monthly pensions, which are given to both men and women (Ahmed, 1991).

For a woman of the Yoruba tribe in Nigeria, the death of a husband does not end the marriage, unless she so wishes. Okafor (1991) reports that when a man dies, his marital rights go to his younger brother or to his son by another wife (pp. 140–141).

In the Tharu society in India, there is always a need for the elderly. Their families are productive units where everybody works together. The aged person is no burden to the family. The elderly women are experts in herbal medicine, which they use to treat a variety of ailments. They perform easier work in general, such as making ropes and cots, as well as drying fish and grain. An old man has the duty to guard the house against wild animals by sleeping at the main gate with a metal pipe in hand. The oldest members in the Tharu society also enjoy very special rights and privileges (Singhal & Mrinal, 1991).

The Japanese *rojin* (old people) are over age 65 and can receive a pension from the government. The amount, though, differs based on the individual's circumstances. Many elderly people in Japan prefer not to live with their children, yet about 70 percent of the women and approximately 59 percent of the men do so. In their leisure time they go to clubs and participate in sports; they do gardening, enjoy calligraphy, painting, arts and crafts; or they go to lectures on poetry, modern literature, or the classics.

The Japanese elderly who have a superior knowledge of a special ability in any field can register this information with the "Silver Bank," where records are kept. If anybody is in need of consultation, advice, or assistance, he or she can apply for such help and the Silver Bank will send a qualified *rojin* to the applicant. The *rojin* receives remuneration based on the regulations of the bank.

The *rojin* live in cities, towns, and villages, where shelter and rooms are provided for them. However, their most serious problems are financial and health. The suicide rate among the elderly in Japan is continuously increasing, and it is currently the third highest in the world (after Hungary and Austria) (Fukada, 1991).

As in Japan, the elderly in Western Samoa are respected for their knowl-edge and experience. At times, the chief will ask them for advice. Elderly parents are usually taken care of by their sons, who provide them with food and money; the daughters may take them to their own homes to care for them. The elderly have the privilege of being fed first and are given tasks that involve minimal physical labor, such as looking after infant grandchil-dren or weaving mats or thatch for their houses. Older women are also entrusted with traditional medicines and their appropriate dispensations and applications. Also, elderly "woman continue the traditional making of pig-ment for tatooing so essential to a young man's preparation for an eventual title. The candle nut burning for tatoo pigment is a ritual taught to younger women by older women. It is similar to the function of old men who meet to discuss the traditional Samoan myths and legends, educating younger men seated nearby" (Muse, 1991, p. 238).

SUMMARY AND CONCLUSION

To look at women cross-culturally and cross-nationally is to experience similarities and differences. The biological prerogative of giving birth to off-spring exists, of course, all over the world. However, women's status in their cultural groups differ, as do their functions and behaviors in the societies and communities in which they reside. In most of these ecologies, women follow stereotypical gender-prescribed customs, social conduct, and specific behaviors. Only during the last few decades has a movement toward gender equality been initiated, a movement whose goal has been to give women a more egalitarian existence with their male counterparts. So far that goal of equality between sexes remains nebulous. During the process of carving out a niche for their androgynous activities, women have made great progress in vocational and professional fields in most modern and modernizing coun-tries. However, the domestic spheres are almost solely delegated to women in practically all cultures, whether in developed or developing countries.

By regarding the activities of women in cross-cultural perspective, the enormous varieties and great differences in patterns and expressions of gen-der roles become more apparent (Adler, 1991). To attain a state of tran-scendence, to eliminate gender roles—where individuals of both genders can function regardless of their sexual determination, yet according to their own capabilities and potentialities—this is the hope and goal of most women cross-culturally.

8

Aging and Old Age in Cross-Cultural Perspective

Cynthia L. Frazier and Anthony P. Glascock

"All the world's a stage, and all the men and women merely players," Shakespeare wrote in his comedy *As You Like It* (Act II, Scene VII):

They have their exits and their entrances;
And one man in his time plays many parts,
His acts being seven ages . . .
Last scene of all,
That ends this strange eventful history,
Is second childishness and mere oblivion,
Sans teeth, sans eyes, sans everything.

Is old age merely a series of role enactments that result in nothingness? Was Shakespeare referring to mental and physical aging? Or does oblivion refer to the absence of meaning, fulfillment, accomplishment, status, or worth for one's life performance? Do all individuals experience old age as Shakespeare described? What are the universals and the variables of aging? Perhaps Shakespeare's description of old age was only a reflection of his own attitudes and perceptions about aging that were representative of sixteenth-century England. The best way to answer these questions is to examine the phenomenon of aging from a cross-cultural perspective, since it encompasses "all the world."

While aging occurs from birth until death, the lifecourse encompasses biological, psychological, and social processes that must be viewed within a specific environmental and historical context (Riley, 1979). As humans age over the lifecourse, variation and uniqueness increase due to the interplay of these multiple influences. "The longer they are here the more time they have to experience life and to become increasingly unique physically, psychologically, and culturally" (Fry, 1990). Since behavior and personality are continuously molded over the lifecourse, diversity within older adults defies generalization. In an early attempt at cross-cultural investigation of aging, Simmons (1945) concluded that all elderly the world over "seek to preserve life as long as possible, to be released from wearisome exertion, to be protected from physical hazards, to remain active in group affairs, to safeguard prerogatives—possessions, rights, prestige, authority, and to meet death honorably and comfortably." Havighurst (1952) postulated six late life developmental tasks requiring adjustment to declining physical strength and health, retirement and reduced income, changing roles, one's living arrangements, one's group affiliation, and death. Erikson (1963) proposed that the final phase of life was characterized by the psychosocial task of evaluating one's life and accomplishments for meaning. Meaning produces a successful resolution that is experienced as a sense of integrity. The negative resolution of this phase results in a sense of despair. Using these proposed universal characteristics and developmental tasks as a guideline, this chapter will review relevant research that illustrates the interactive process of biological, psychological, and social aging from a cross-cultural perspective.

When is a person considered old? In lifecourse research, cultural variation exists in the mere definition of old age. The Euro-American conceptualization of the lifecourse is a linear progression of time from birth to death. Fry (1980) found that adult Americans viewed the lifecourse as a horseshoe-shaped curve linked to personal independence. That is, youth was seen as a period of obligation to career and family. Middle-age was viewed as the peak of life. Old age was marked by a decline in independence and increase in frailty and dependence. For the Nandi of East Africa, age serves as the basis for social organization (Huntingford, 1960). Males have four age grades: small boys, initiates, warriors, and elders. Two age groups exist for females: girls and married women. Explicit behaviors accompany each age grade. Interestingly, the age grade of elders has four distinct age sets that define the expectations to marry, raise a family, and serve as a statesman and tribal advisor.

In most industrialized societies, one becomes old at an arbitrarily specified age (i.e., 65) regardless of one's biological condition or personality (including vitality, mental acuity, or aspiration). Old may be determined by the passage of a particular social milestone, such as retirement, inclusion in a community's council of elders or advisors, having a married child, or becoming a grandparent. Retirement in Ladakh begins when the eldest son marries. The parents, who are in middle-age chronologically, move from the main house into a smaller house nearby to "gradually withdraw from this world of illusion" and to "prepare themselves for a life of prayer and reduced worldly authority" (Gielen, 1993, 1997). Among the !Kung of Botswana, all elders by the chronological age of 45 are shown respect by the addition of *na* to their names. Guemple (1974) found that the Quiqiktamiut Eskimo is considered old when she or he has grandchildren who have begun to "learn basic work skills" (approximately age 8).

The determination of old age is often associated with changes in physical appearance (e.g., graying hair), biological changes (e.g., menopause), physical illness, and decline in functional capacity. In most nonindustrialized cultures, a person is considered old when she or he is unable to be fully productive. Biological and psychological factors are considered in the determination of old age. The elderly may choose to continue working at their own pace or select specialized duties that are more adaptive to their current capabilities. One may choose to stop working without risking loss of respect (Holmes & Holmes, 1995). The Gusii in western Kenya view the lifecourse in terms of three interrelated "subjective careers" the reproductive, the economic, and the ritual (Levine, 1978). Older men and women serve as diviners, healers, and witches in conducting traditional ritual when one's ability to have children and to earn a living has passed. In observing the Quiqiktamiut Eskimos, Guemple (1974) wrote: "When a man cannot hunt in midwinter, when the work is most rigorous, and when the need for food is most pressing, then he will be called "old" by his fellows."

Using health and social characteristics, Neugarten and Neugarten (1986) conceptualized aging in terms of *young-old* and *old-old*, with the old-old characterized as frail and in need of special care. In many nonindustrialized cultures, old age is differentiated between the *intact old* and the *decrepit old* (Glascock & Feinman, 1981). The intact old receive supportive behavior including food, shelter, and care. According to Glascock (1990), death-hastening behaviors are directed only toward the decrepit old who have become a burden to the family or community. Decrepit, then is linked to chronic disease that interferes with a person's ability to perform expected social roles. Broadly defined, death-hastening behaviors include withholding food and care, exposure to natural elements, abandonment, killing, and euthanasia. In an examination of 41 societies, Glascock found that 21 practiced death-hastening, or gerontocide, for the seriously ill. In such societies, decrepitude is conceived as a kind of death. Often, the same word is used both for death and for decrepitude.

A more recent form of treatment of the aged is *elder abuse* for which data has only recently been collected in some developed countries. While the definition varies, it appears that older adults who are impaired and dependent on others are at higher risk for abuse, neglect, and exploitation. Tartara (1990) found that neglect was the most common form of abuse, followed by physical abuse, and financial or material exploitation. The most frequent victims of abuse are elderly women. Adult children appear to be the most frequent perpetrators, accounting for 30 percent of the abuse. Other relatives account for 17.8 percent of the abuse, followed by spouses (14.8 percent). As a result, agencies for adult protective services and reporting systems have been instituted in the United States where elder abuse is considered deviant behavior.

In a cross-cultural comparison of two Native American communities, elder abuse was viewed as a community health concern rather than aberrant in-dividual behavior (Maxwell & Maxwell, 1992). On the reservation where alcohol abuse by young adults was more prevalent, elder abuse was higher. Furthermore, Pillemer (1985) found that violent physical abuse was linked to the abuser's dependence, emotionally and materially, on the elder. When elders are dependent on adult children for care, the type of abuse is more often neglect. Linking elder abuse to an individual or a family represents a significant cross-cultural issue. Western societies view "responsibility" as an individual choice, while non-Western cultures often perceive "responsibility" as a larger group concern (e.g., family, community).

The vulnerability of the elderly may be linked to physical and mental disability. The probability of physical and mental disability does increase with biological aging. Physical status (i.e., health and functionality) was found to be an important source of well-being (Keith et al., 1994). Project Age, Generation, and Experience (A.G.E.), sponsored by the National Institute on Aging, investigated the influence of social, cultural, and physical dimen-sions on the aging process and the elderly in seven locations: among the Zhun/wasi and the Herrero of Botswana; in Clifden, County Galway, and Bessington, County Wiclow, in Ireland; in Momence, Illinois, and Swarth-more, Pennsylvania, in the United States; and in four neighborhoods of Hong Kong. In every research site, the elderly viewed their health more negatively than younger adults, used health facilities more, described more chronic health concerns, and reported more frequent restrictions on behav-ior (e.g., ability to work). Actual illness, as well as anticipation of illness, was found to negatively affect well-being.

Since illness and impairment may interfere with one's capacity to function (i.e., perform activities of living), the impact of disability varies according to the type of activities one is expected to perform. According to Kaplan (1990), level of disability is a more powerful predictor of mortality than the number of disabling diseases. Disability has different meaning across cultures due to social norms and expectation. Keith et al. (1994) found that the relationship between health status and well-being is ameliorated by func-tional status (i.e., the ability of the individual to perform culturally relevant behavior). The results of Project A.G.E. demonstrate how differences in context account for variation in consequences. For example, in the Swarth-more, Pennsylvania, sample, the ability to remember, maintain a house, and manage finances determined functionality. Furthermore, functionality also determined whether an individual would remain at home in the community or would seek residence in health-related facilities, such as nursing homes. Successful aging in this Western culture was associated with the ability to remain independent and self-sufficient. Americans preferred to live alone in retirement housing or health-care facilities with access to peers or professionals, thereby exercising valued personal choice and independence.

In contrast, the culturally relevant behaviors that defined functionality among the Herrero of Botswana included watering cattle, gathering firewood, riding donkeys, and other physical tasks. When impaired by disability, older Herrero did not leave the village. Care giving was provided by younger relatives, and elders were not perceived as dependent. In Hong Kong, older subjects in the study were more likely to identify dependence, as opposed to independence, as a factor in well-being. Adult children and extended family played a major role in successful aging. Personal qualities that affect interactions with others, such as being "easygoing," were rated highest. Confucian tradition places great emphasis on the parent-child relationship, characterized by *filial piety* from the son and moral guidance from the father. According to Hsu (1971): "The son owes his father absolute obedience, support for his lifetime, mourning when he passes away, burial according to social station and financial ability, provision for the soul's needs in the other world, and glory for the father by doing well or even better than he."

According to Confucian tradition, support of one's aging parents is not a matter of choice but a moral duty. Hong Kong subjects reported doing well when interpersonal relations with children and relatives with whom they lived were stable (Keith et al., 1994). Tension was caused by the increasingly unwillingness of daughters-in-law to defer to the dominance afforded the mother-in-law by tradition. According to Yu (1989), daughters are now permitted to assume the duty of caring for elderly parents in the People's Republic of China. However, older Chinese preferred living with the son, rather than the daughter, as it fulfilled the tradition of filial piety. Both sons and daughters considered it their duty to provide financial support and shelter for elder parents. The extent to which children are now willing or able to meet their filial responsibilities is threatening the quality of old age in contemporary Asian societies (Ikels, 1980). For example, in modern-day Japan, security of old age is threatened by the shift away from the extended family and toward the nuclear family, the deterioration in traditional filial piety, and the lack of adequate housing and health-care facilities to accommodate the elderly (Tobin, 1987).

In most traditional societies, the care of the elderly is seen as a family responsibility, primarily that of the offspring. Thus, care received when one is young is reciprocated with respect and assistance when parents become old. As one Samian elder stated, "Old age is good if you have children to feed you" (Cattell, 1989). Moreover, in many cultures, the treatment of the elderly is a reflection of child-rearing practices. Harrell (1981) found that filial piety in Taiwan often produced a deep resentment and fear for sons toward their elder fathers while elder mothers received more affection and support from their sons. Prescott (1975) found a relationship between loving, nurturing care for children as well as the elderly. Similarly, de Beauvoir

(1972) found that in the Ainu and Yakut societies, where children were raised with little warmth or demonstration of affection, the aged were also mistreated and devalued. De Beauvoir wrote: "If a child is kept short of food, protection, and loving kindness, he will grow up full of resentment, fear and even hatred, as a grown man his relations with others will be aggressive—he will neglect his old parents when they are no longer able to look after themselves.

Since having children is generally viewed as a socially expected norm to ensure appropriate care in old age, how are individuals who are childless viewed? In some cultures, childlessness is considered to be no less than a betrayal of one's heritage, a condition that would put one's soul in serious jeopardy—the danger of becoming a "Hungry Ghost wandering alone in the Underworld" (Sankar, 1981). There are, however, ways in which childless couples or people who remain single can create special relationships that ensure support in elder years (Holmes & Holmes, 1995). In China, childless, single women can obtain domestic employment in another household. If she serves 20 years, she is legally entitled to full support in old age. Childless women and men can also join a religious order where care during old age is guaranteed. Couples who do not have children are sometimes cared for by the extended family if the financial means exist. Even couples who have only girls are considered the same as childless. This was sometimes remediated by having the daughter marry a husband (who was of lesser means) to reside with her and her parents. Donner (1987) found that lack of male offspring was viewed as "stopping up the family line" on Sikaiana atoll in the Solomon Islands. Those who were childless or had only daughters were distrusted by the community, who regarded childlessness as disinterest in the welfare of the kin group. As a solution, *fostering* is practiced whereby children may be reared by nonbiological parents called *tupana* (grandparents). Foster children (*tama too*) are encouraged to form emotional attachments and provide support for both their biological as well as foster parents. With increased mobility, many younger Sikaianans have moved, leaving older residents to rely on any foster children who have remained on the atoll. This practice of fostering demonstrates an important social adaptation in the care of the elderly.

In a review of childlessness in the United States, Rubinstein (1987) found that childlessness was viewed negatively. Childless people were perceived as "unhappy," "lonely," and "unfulfilled." However, childless, unmarried individuals (never married, widowed, and divorced) reported greater independence and ability to plan for old age. Childless couples appeared to be more "isolated" and "lonely." Those who are childless tended to develop stronger family ties with cousins, nieces, and nephews from whom support is often obtained. According to Rubinstein, childlessness has become a personal choice for women in the United States who desire greater personal freedom and a career. Successful aging in the United States is linked to the social value placed on individual choice versus social conformity. In westernized cultures, where individualism is valued, older adults experience greater satisfaction when given choice. In nonwesternized societies, older adults experience greater satisfaction as a result of conformity to group norms.

Marital relations, rather than relations with children, appeared to be the more salient factor in predicting successful aging in the American communities studied in Project A.G.E. (Keith et al., 1994). Being married consistently has been found to be positively related to well-being in the elderly Depner & Ingersoll-Dayton, 1985; Gove, Hughes, & Style, 1983; House, 1987). According to Lewittes (1982), the ability to develop and maintain relationships with others, family as well as friends, contributed to greater adaptability in old age. Residential stability—aging in a place surrounded by long-time friends and relatives—played a vital role in providing both security and emotional well-being (Keith, Fry, & Ikers, 1990). Butler (1982) suggested that long-term relationships with kin and friends serve as a connection to the past, which enhances a sense of continuity over time.

Social support, in the form of companionship, services, advice, and financial assistance from family members has been consistently found to act as a buffer against physical and psychological illness (Griffin, 1984). Relationships characterized by intimacy, reciprocity, and assistance have been found to be of greatest support to older women (Lewittes & Mukherji, 1989). Izraeli and Safir (1993) found that elderly living in a kibbutz community in Israel lived longer than those living near a relative. The social norms of the kibbutz encourage members to work as long as they are able, which is believed to promote the maintenance of a meaningful social role within the community. Physical care is then provided by other members of the community.

In a cross-cultural comparison of elderly in the United States and Haiti, Frazier and Douyon (1989) found that depression, self-esteem, and physical health were correlated with social support. That is, the more actual social support an individual received, the lower the level of depression, the higher the degree of self-esteem, and the higher the self-rating of healthfulness. Haitians relied most on social support from family members, while Americans depended more on friends. Interestingly, the better predictor of depression and self-esteem was not actual social support, but rather the perception of being supported. In a study comparing older adults in the United States and France, Antonucci, Fuhrer, and Jackson (1990) proposed that not all support is beneficial. The elderly may feel "overbenefitted" if one receives more support than one provides, or conversely, "underbenefitted" if one provides more support than one receives. The perception of reciprocal social exchanges was associated with greater life satisfaction. Overall, it appears that the maintenance of physical health (biological factor), self-esteem (psychological factor), and role (social factor) contribute to successful aging.

Elderly Americans and Japanese experienced more symptoms of depression when faced with the financial strain associated with living on a fixed income (Krause, Jay, & Liang, 1991). Interestingly, Americans showed an increase in both depressed affect and somatic symptoms of depression. The Japanese manifested depression only somatically. As financial strain increased, older adults in both cultures reported feeling less personal control over the events in their lives and a lowered sense of self-worth. While control of tangible resources such as wealth and property is considered an important factor in predicting status for older adults (Amoss & Harrell, 1981), esteem in old age may also be derived from possessing valuable information. For example, a major function of the older adult in Japan is to serve as a senior advisor for family problems. Silverman (1987) found that older adults derived greater esteem if they provided valued "information processing" (including administration, consultation, arbitration, reinforcement of behavior, entertainment, teaching, and instruction) more so than controlling property, having material wealth, or having social or supernatural resources.

Growing older also appears to be associated with several positive psychological changes. Lawton and Albert (1990) reported that older adults have less mood swings and more control of expression of emotion than younger adults. While speed of mental processing slows with age, greater command of vocabulary, increased confidence in decision making, greater reflection on issues, and greater tolerance for different views are associated with age (Baltes & Baltes, 1990; Labouvie-Vief, 1985). Creative ability, once believed to gradually decline after age 40 (Lehman, 1953; Wechsler, 1958) has been found to continue throughout life. Kogan (1973) suggested that physical and mental impairment, as well as loss of motivation and curiosity, may better account for decrements in creativity in later life. Dacey (1989) proposed that the period between ages 60 and 65 marks a peak of creative capacity that is contingent on the individual's successful adjustment of self-concept after retirement. Using improvisation as the definition of creativity, Holmes and Thomson (1986) studied 15 elderly jazz musicians to determine effects of age on performance, self-assessment of creativity capacity, and collegial evaluation of creativity. Their findings indicated that creativity did not decline or cease in advanced age. Maduro (1974) investigated whether artistic creativity declined with age in Brahmin folk painters from Rajasthan, India. Results of the study indicated that creativity peaked in middle-age and remained constant throughout old age. Furthermore, the artists reported becoming "more open to intuition" in the process of "unfolding of the self" with increasing age. Maduro linked creativity with the Hindu life cycle. Old age is termed the *forest hermit* stage when a man has "met his family obligations and performed his duties to caste and his society. He can turn inward and contemplate the inner light. At this time a man's powers of imagination increase fourfold because he has learned to reach into himself for light, bliss, and balance."

This shift from social to inner focus has been viewed as a universal aspect of aging by many researchers. In the longitudinal research of Field and Minkler (1988), level of social participation and need for friendship did decline with age. These results were thought to be consistent with psychological *disengagement theory* that postulates that elders withdraw from the world in preparation for death (Cummings & Henry, 1961). Maddox (1963) offered an *activity theory* that suggests that decreased social interaction was related to health limitations and loss of social partners due to death. Subsequent research, however, has shown that the elderly do maintain long-term friendships, which are related to higher levels of well-being (Albert & Cattell, 1994). When social endings are anticipated, the elderly are more selective in choosing friendships, prefer familiar friends over making new friends, and avoid taking affective risks (Carstensen, 1987; Fredrickson & Carstensen, 1990).

Social scientists have also considered retirement from *disengagement* and *activity* perspectives. In traditional societies where retirement does not exist, tasks are adapted to the current physical strength and abilities of the elderly that allowed continued productivity and sense of purpose and contribution. Roles, such as ceremonial director, storyteller, folk medicine specialist, and politician, illustrate the concept of "second career"—a social role adaptation to the individual abilities of older adults that provides continuity (Clark, 1972). Conversely, *activity theory* suggests that disengagement from certain roles and relationships does occur, but successful aging is characterized by role substitution and activity. In many societies where choice is permitted, older adults will choose to be active and productive (Holmes & Holmes 1995). While productivity has been linked to purpose and personal worth in many industrialized cultures, leisure time and idleness have been devalued. Holmes and Holmes (1995) have noted a shift toward productive or purposeful activity even during leisure time. In the United States, recreation is now acceptable if the activity is purposeful, such as promoting healthfulness. In an early study of residents of Fun City, a retirement community, Jacobs (1974) found that activity level varied by individual lifestyle preference and physical health. Of the 10 percent of residents who were actively engaged in the 92 planned recreational activities, all reported this activity level as a continuation of their lifestyle prior to retirement. Conversely, 15 percent were not active participants before or after retirement. A third group, constituting 25 percent of residents, were unable to participate due to physical health limitations despite interest and preretirement lifestyle. The remaining 50 percent of Fun City residents had chosen to withdraw socially (e.g., watch television, read, play cards, walk dog). Despite personal choice, this group was still viewed negatively as "vegetating" by active residents and outsiders. Lozier and Althouse (1975), who studied the phenomenon known as "retiring to the porch" practiced in the Appalachian region of the United States, found that idleness is condoned for men who have sufficiently contributed to the community. By earning the privilege, retirement is viewed positively and the individual experiences social acceptance because he has "paid his dues."

Based on his cross-cultural findings, Gutmann (1987) proposed a universal adaptation in personality style, which he observed in aging men and women. He described this shift in *ego mastery style* as a role reversal necessary for coping with one's changing social obligations (i.e., parental responsibilities). He wrote the following:

Where as adult males start from a grounding of *active mastery* and move toward *passive mastery*, women are at first grounded in *passive mastery*, characterized by dependence on and even deference to the husband, but surge in later life toward *active mastery*, including autonomy from and even domination over the husband. Across cultures, and with age, they seem to become more authoritative, more effective, and less willing to trade submission for security.

During one's parental years, men sacrificed their needs for comfort and emotional expression in the interest of enhancing competitive striving required in their role as breadwinner. Conversely, women sacrificed more aggressive characteristics to prevent alienation of the husbands, on whom they depended, and to protect the children. In some societies, older men may experience actual role reversal without stigma when performing domestic chores, such as babysitting, that are typically performed by women (Holmes & Holmes, 1995).

Overall, the older adult may not disengage but merely shift his or her interests and activities (e.g., from economic or parental requirements to spiritual or advisory strivings). Prestige and status are often reserved in old age for those who possess valuable information about tradition, religion, healing, history, folk lore, occupational skills, and arts (Amoss & Harrell, 1981; de Beauvoir, 1972; Lepowsky, 1985; Roscow, 1965; Shahrani, 1981). Among the Kirghiz of Afganistan, it is believed that as "one declines in strength one increases in wisdom and consequently respect and authority should increase" (Shahrani, 1981). Silverman and Maxwell (1978) developed a "Deference Index" to measure the "degree of esteem enjoyed by the aged in a given society." It included seven types of deference.

1. *Spatial deference*: An example is the practice of reserving "silver seats" for the elderly on public transportation in Japan.
2. *Victual deference*: An example is the Samaoan practice of feeding the elderly first or giving them the choicest foods.
3. *Linguistic deference*: An example is being honored by a specific title, such as the West African custom of addressing all older men as "Grandfather" regardless of kinship.
4. *Presentational deference*: An example is the Cambodian custom of avoiding sitting or standing higher than an elder.

5. *Service deference*: An example is any work performed for the elderly out of respect rather than disability (e.g., accompanying an older parent to a medical appointment, assisting with household maintenance).

6. *Presentative deference*: An example is the giving of gifts out of respect rather than reciprocal exchange, such as practiced in Japan.

7. *Celebrative deference*: An example is the American custom of inducting older sports figures into a Hall of Fame.

While a shift in role occurs with aging, the actual role opportunities and status afforded men and women appear to differ across cultures. For example, Simmons (1960) found significantly more respect for older men than older women. More men are permitted to seek political office or to serve on a community's council of elders. Maxwell and Silverman (1970) found that elderly women received similar levels of *service deference* as men in support of basic custodial care, which typically occurred within the immediate family. Men, however, received more *celebrative* and *presentational deference* outside the family. Across cultures, gender shapes attitudes and behaviors throughout the life course.

Cowgill and Holmes (1972) proposed that the status of the elderly is devalued as a society becomes modernized. In addition, modernization has greater negative impact on older men than older women. In modernized societies, elderly men often lose their position of authority and power, whereas women continue to function as matriarchs in the familiar role of homemaker and caregiver. For example, hunting is the single most impor tant skill and role expectation of men among the Chipewyan Indians of Canada. Women, on the other hand, perform three valuable roles: child-rearing, handicrafts, and food processing (Sharp, 1981). Since grandparents have the right to adopt a child from each of their children's marriages in the Chipewyan society, the maternal role is maintained well after menopause. Chipewyan women continue to perform a valuable role of teaching and supervising younger women in skills of sewing, beadwork, preparation of hides, cooking, and drying meats and fish. Likewise, women in contemporary Korean society experience less restrictions related to menstrual taboos and female sexuality, gain authority in making decisions and directing labor of younger family members, and obtain new opportunities for achievement and recognition outside of the home, such as participating in governmental affairs (Brown, 1982). Bart (1969) found that the position of women improved in societies with multigenerational living arrangements. For example, the *abuela* in Mexico plays a valuable role as grandmother in caring for the grandchildren while the mother is able to work outside the home (Díaz-Guerrero & Rodriguez de Díaz, 1993). The mother-in-law in India makes all decisions about the household and directs activities of the daughters-in-law residing in the same dwelling (Adler, 1993). The grandmother is the matriarch in Poland as well as Italy (Grzymala-Moszczynska, 1991; Merenda & Mattioni, 1993).

As illustrated throughout this chapter, the experience of aging defies generalization due to the interaction of multiple influences within each specific culture. One universal hallmark of old age that deserves inclusion is the experience of death and dying. "If old age is the final act of the human drama, then surely death is the final curtain" (Holmes & Holmes, 1995). While death can occur at any age, the probability of physical demise increases with chronological age. Gerontologists have begun to examine attitudes, perceptions, and anxieties pertaining to death across cultures. Becker (1973) suggested that humans are inherently fearful of death. Gorer (1967) coined the phase "pornography of death" that regards death as a taboo subject that fascinates and yet horrifies humans. In Papua New Guinea, where sorcery and magic are prevalent, death is not seen as a natural consequence of physical aging but rather caused by someone or some malevolent spirit (McKellin, 1985). In the United States, death anxiety was found to be inversely correlated with satisfaction with one's role (Schulz, 1980). That is, women whose role of homemaker remained constant and who were satisfied with their role tended to be more accepting of the inevitability of one's death than men. Schulz suggested that men in the study experienced greater disruption in role after retirement, which resulted in greater dissatisfaction and increased death anxiety. In westernized countries, advances in medicine have prolonged life but inadvertently perhaps, have raised the hope of delaying death indefinitely (Laungani, 1997). Death has become "medicalized" wherein people die outside the home (e.g., in a medical setting). Walter (1997) postulated that as humanism and secularization replace religion, death is distanced and viewed as the end of life.

The way in which the elderly cope with the prospect of one's own death and bereavement of loved ones depends on many cultural factors such as religious orientation, conception of an afterlife, and rituals and customs associated with death. In many traditional societies, death is not considered taboo, but is accepted as an inevitability—as a journey in a cycle of birth, death, and rebirth. In India, for example, the aged openly discuss death, including one's own (Laungani, 1997). Death is not viewed by all cultures as absolute or final. For the Kaliai of Papua New Guinea, the word *dead* has a range of meanings including: dying, unconscious, really dead, and completely dead (Counts & Counts, 1985). Death can occur when a sleeping person unexpectedly awakens during a dream before one's soul has returned to the body (Carucci, 1985). It is believed that the soul or spirit continues to live, to communicate with the living through dreams, and to influence future family members, particularly the lives of namesakes. Ancestors whose spirits are believed to be a part of the "continuum of existence" are an "ultimate source of blessings or misfortune." Rosenblatt (1997) described a common experience called "a sense of presence" of the departed reported among Westerners. For Buddhists and Hindus, death is not the end of human life, but the beginning of a new one through reincarnation. Since human suffering is caused by desire, humans are driven by false goals such as attaining material wealth and power. One may overcome this repetition or "burden of life" by being freed from the "fetters of individuality" (Laungani, 1997). The deceased's destiny is determined by one's self-created karma and by the positive prayers of loved ones and monks.

While grieving is a natural human process, the expression and meaning of loss is culturally determined. The funeral rituals for older adults in many cultures may be simple and restricted to the immediate family (Counts & Counts, 1985) or quite elaborate and extend over a period of time and include an extensive network of family and friends. In the Toraja region of Sulawesi, Indonesia, the soul of the departed cannot make the final journey to the land of the ancestors without a suitable feast befitting the status of the departed. The body of the departed is preserved in a shroud and placed in the traditional *tongkonan* (longhouse) and considered merely sick, while preparations are being made for a funeral celebration. Funerals may be delayed for two or more years. Once sufficient funding has been accumulated and the rice has been harvested, temporary housing is built for guests, and spotted water buffalo are purchased for ceremonial sacrifice during the week-long funeral rites. Celebratory dancing and feasting is integral to the successful passage of the deceased into the afterlife. A wooden effigy called a *tau-tau* is carved in the likeness of the departed and placed on a balcony carved into the side of a mountain with other effigies from one's family. The effigy is believed to be inhabited by the ancestor's spirit. The body is placed in a coffin shaped like a *tongkonan* and buried in a grave carved into the rock of the mountain. Mourners visit each year to replace the clothing of the effigy and to leave offerings for use in the afterlife including rice, money, and cigarettes.

Psychologists have been concerned about the increase in suicide among the elderly. In recent years, euthanasia (i.e., physician-assisted suicide) for the terminally ill has received increased publicity. In the United States, those over age 65 have the highest rate of suicide (i.e., more likely to succeed) than any other age group (National Center for Health Statistics, 1992). Men are more likely to commit suicide than women. Unmarried (single, widowed, and divorced) elderly have a higher rate of suicide than those who are married. Risk factors include diagnosis of depression, recent diagnosis of life-threatening illness, recent loss(es), past attempt(s), family history of suicide, and alcohol abuse. According to Judaism, suicide is viewed as a sacrilege by destroying the soul and ending the opportunity to "do good on this earth." The deceased may not be honored and, thus, may not be mourned by Jewish tradition if the suicide was deemed intentional. The deceased may not be buried within six feet of other graves in a Jewish cemetery. However, the rabbi is able to perform the customary funeral rites if the suicide was unintentional (i.e., not fully aware of his or her actions) (Levine, 1997).

The recent development of gerontology as a burgeoning area of study is due to the rapid growth of the elderly population. Advances in health technology, among other factors, has resulted in a worldwide trend known as *population aging*—a demographic shift in an increased percentage of individuals 60 and older. In 1991, the Population Reference Bureau estimated roughly 6 percent of the world population as elderly (Albert & Cattell, 1994). Kinsella (1988) assessed approximately 60 percent of the elderly live in developed countries while 40 percent reside in developing nations. Cowgill (1986) compared 180 countries according to the proportion of aging within the population. Countries were grouped as "young" (less than 4 percent elderly), "youthful" (between 4 and 6 percent), "maturing" (between 7 and 9 percent), and "aged" (greater than 10 percent). By comparing data collected in 1980 and 1986, a clear trend toward a more elderly population was demonstrated within just six years. In 1990, the country with the "oldest population" was Sweden (18 percent; the "youngest" was Kuwait and Quatar (1 percent respectively) (Albert & Cattell 1994). According to Torrey, Kinsella, and Taeuber (1987), the growth rate for the elderly population is 2.4 percent per year, which is greater than the rate for the global population. In less developed countries, the growth rate is assessed as 3.1 percent when the age criteria for old is lowered to 55. In the United States, the fastest growing segment of the population is 85 and older (Siegel & Davidson, 1984). This worldwide "graying" phenomenon has begun to alter our attitudes and perceptions regarding aging as healthy, active silver-haired individuals are more commonly viewed. Current images certainly challenge Shakespeare's description of old age.

Despite the search for commonalities to describe aging across cultures, older adults cannot be stereotyped as a distinct social category. While the process of aging is universal, the specific characteristics of old age are determined by the unique interaction between age as a biological factor of physical change with psychological and social (including economic, political, and historical) variables. Each person must be viewed within one's own cultural context to fully appreciate the meaning of aging. Myerhoff (1978) explains it best: "If any generalizations can be made, they point to the great variety of styles and forms of aging in different cultural settings. Here one is struck by diversity rather than uniformity; by variation rather than universality."

III

Emotions, Personality, and Belief
Systems in Cross-Cultural Psychology

9

Culture and Emotion

*Nathan Yrizarry, David Matsumoto, Chikako Imai,
Kristie Kooken, and Sachiko Takeuchi*

INTRODUCTION

The increasingly complex nature of economic, political, and social relationships between countries underscores this century's development of the "global community." It seems that industry and technology have introduced us to ourselves as a multicultural entity, and the human interaction born of demographic change has served to bring the global village home. For more and more of us, cultural diversity is part of the social landscape and cross-cultural interaction is an everyday experience.

Of course, the currency of human interaction is communication, in which we use complex code systems to exchange information, often unconsciously and effortlessly. Cross-cultural interaction, however, can bring to our attention communication processes that we might otherwise never notice. Attempts to establish a common "language" reveal similarities in communication style, some of which may be shared by all of us regardless of background, as well as differences. We may more readily notice cultural differences in verbal communication, or language, than in nonverbal communication, because language tends to be more explicit than vocal intonation, body movements, actions, or facial expressions. As such, language is more easily recognized as foreign than nonverbal communication processes, which may be afforded less attention and in which cultural differences may be less obvious, yet no less influential. Verbal and nonverbal communication modes tend to each be suited to, and predominate in the transfer of, distinct kinds of information.

Emotion is communicated primarily through nonverbal channels, and emotion research has largely focused on nonverbal communication, particularly through facial expressions. Other major research in the area of emotion has described social and cognitive processes, such as situational antecedents of emotions and dimensions of their appraisal. The role of culture has been central to much of this research activity, notably its influences on facial expressions of emotion and their perception, which have been shown to be basically universal. Indeed, the development of research on culture and emotion began with studies of universality and has spanned three decades of varied and active inquiry. Most researchers now agree that emotion communication processes are part universal and part culture-specific, and there are lively debates regarding the extent and nature of culture's influences on emotion expression and recognition, the language of emotion, and cognitive emotion processes.

This chapter will present the major contributions to the literature of the past 30 years through the present, addressing in detail universal and culture-specific components of antecedents, appraisal, expression, and perception and concluding with the detailed description of a current study that points to the future of research on culture and emotion. We will cover four areas that reflect the current knowledge regarding the role of culture in the non-verbal communication of emotion. First, we review major cross-cultural research, including early seminal studies on the universality and culture-specificity of facial expressions of emotion and their recognition. Second, we review research that examines emotion antecedents and appraisal processes. Third, we highlight a study that we consider to be at the forefront of important current research on culture and emotion. Fourth, we suggest an agenda for future research in this area.

MAJOR CROSS-CULTURAL RESEARCH ON EMOTION EXPRESSION AND PERCEPTION

Universal Recognition of Facial Expressions of Emotion

Research on culture and emotion has been conducted largely over the past few decades, but the concept that facial expressions are universally fundamental to the communication of emotion is not new. Darwin is typically cited as the first to have presented a comprehensive theory on the universality of facial communication of emotion in his book *The Expression of the Emotions in Man and Animals* (1872), where he proposed that facial expressions of emotion were innate and evolutionarily adaptive and also described certain nonemotion facial gestures of cultural origin. Although he presented examples of humans and animals that supported his theory, his data were largely observational. Since that time, a great deal of scientific research has been conducted with humans and nonhuman primates that supports Darwin's original theory (Ekman & Friesen, 1971, 1986; Ekman,

Sorenson, & Friesen, 1969; Ekman et al., 1987; Izard, 1971; Sackett, 1966).

The first major research in this area focused on the universal basis of facial expressions of emotion using studies where observers from many different cultures were shown facial expressions of emotion thought to be universal and asked to describe what emotion was portrayed. The framework under-lying these early studies was that if the facial expressions of emotion were universal, observers would agree on what emotion was being expressed, re-gardless of culture; disagreements within or across cultures would be evidence against the notion of universality. Influenced by Tomkins's (1962, 1963) theory of innate facial expressions of emotion that are subject to learned cultural variation, Ekman and Izard separately began research pro-grams to test the universality hypothesis via a set of studies now referred to as the "universality studies" and which produced the first scientific evidence supporting universality.

Original data supporting universality of emotion *recognition* were col-lected in literate and preliterate cultures (see Ekman, 1972; Ekman & Frie-sen, 1971; Ekman, Sorenson, & Friesen, 1969; Izard, 1971). Most of the studies involved the presentation of faces by photo, slide or videotape to observers who made categorical, scalar, or open-ended judgments. Ekman, Sorenson, and Friesen (1969) presented photographs to observers in the United States, Japan, Chile, Argentina, and Brazil who made *categorical* judgments, selecting from a prespecified list the term that they thought best described the emotion portrayed. Early studies by Izard (e.g., 1971) used this method as well. For literate cultures, there was high agreement about the association of emotion categories with specific facial expressions.

Support for these findings was also obtained with observers from pre-literate cultures (Ekman & Friesen, 1971; Ekman, Sorenson, & Friesen, 1969). Here, methods were modified due to language differences. For ex-ample, New Guineans were told short stories (in their native language) that suggested an emotion and were asked to point to the face (out of three possible choices) that portrayed the emotion being elicited. With the excep-tion of fear, often mistaken for surprise, participants were able to correctly identify intended emotions at levels well over chance.

Ekman (1972) reported data on five literate and two preliterate cultures and summarized a number of other studies that together convincingly evi-denced the universal recognition of six emotions (anger, disgust, fear, hap-piness, sadness, surprise) in specific facial expressions. These findings have been replicated across many other cultures using different methods and facial stimuli (Ekman et al., 1987). He also detailed a theoretical framework, de-veloped with Friesen (Ekman & Friesen, 1969), that addressed cultural spec-ificity and universality, blends of emotion expressions, elicitors and antecedents of emotion, and cognitive appraisal processes. The article served

to conclude the series of preceding judgment studies, spanning twelve literate and two preliterate cultures, as demonstrating the universal recognition
of facial expressions of emotion.

The early studies generally used judgment tasks that limited subjects' responses to the *forced choice* of one emotion label. Ekman (1972) had discussed the possibility of secondary emotions that, when present in blends
with the primary expressions of universal emotions, might represent the
larger set of emotions with which we are commonly familiar. Ekman et al.
(1987) allowed for the measurement of secondary emotions by introducing
a *multiscalar* judgment task. Observers in ten cultures viewed posed and
spontaneous expressions and first selected the emotion portrayed from seven
choices (the six emotion categories previously established as universal as well
as contempt). They then rated the expressions on each of the seven emotion
dimensions as absent or for level of *intensity*. The researchers compared
differences in judgments of relative intensity of different expressions of the
same emotion. In addition to that on categorical judgments, there was also
high agreement across cultures on the relative intensity of the expressions,
with the cultures agreeing 92 percent of the time on which expression within
each emotion was more intense. Agreement was also found regarding which
secondary emotion was portrayed. For disgust and fear expressions, there
was agreement across all cultures on the second highest-rated emotion, contempt and surprise, respectively. For anger, the second mode of response
varied depending on the anger photo, with disgust, surprise, and contempt
as second response choices.

Matsumoto and Ekman (1989) used the same multiscalar rating task as
above, but rather than performing the categorization task, subjects rated the
overall intensity of the expression without any reference to specific emotion
categories. The design was also extended to include comparisons of relative
intensity across different *poser types* by using a stimulus set that included
equal numbers of Caucasian and Asian posers and was also balanced for *poser
gender*. The design and development of this stimulus set are described later
in this chapter. Matsumoto and Ekman presented these stimuli to judges in
the United States and Japan. Looking at expression intensity comparisons
separately for each emotion (within culture and across gender and then
within gender across culture), they found that the Americans and Japanese
agreed on which photo was more intense in 24 out of 30 comparisons.

Thus, not only did early studies demonstrate consistent pan-cultural
agreement in judgments of which emotion was portrayed, taken to demonstrate universal recognition of certain facial expressions of emotion (anger, contempt, disgust, fear, happiness, sadness, surprise), but cross-cultural
agreement was also observed on other dimensions such as relative intensity
and secondary emotion portrayed.

Universal Expressions of Emotion

A limitation of early judgment studies was the assumption that cross-cultural agreements in recognition implicated pan-cultural *expression* of the same faces. The only way to address this limitation was to study the actual expressions themselves, examining cross-cultural similarities or differences in the components of the expressions for the different emotions.

Ekman and Friesen (1971) collected data in two preliterate cultures in New Guinea in order to control for the possibility of media exposure accounting for data favoring universality of emotion expression. Subjects were asked to show on their faces what they would look like if they felt the emotion suggested by simple stories designed to elicit the universally recognized emotions. Ekman and Friesen photographed the tribespeople's faces and showed the pictures to American subjects, who were able to recognize the intended emotions at accuracy rates well over chance. (Though, as in the judgment study findings, fear and surprise were often confused.) This indicated that the New Guineans generated specific facial expressions to express discrete emotions and associated them in the same way that subjects in Western cultures did in the judgment studies. Because the tribespeople were not exposed to the same visual input as were literate cultures, the findings provided evidence for the universality of facial expressions of emotion.

However, a criticism of this and earlier universality studies was the use of posed, rather than spontaneous, facial expressions of emotion. In order to address that criticism, Ekman (1972) and Friesen (1972) collected spontaneous facial expression data in a cross-cultural study conducted in the United States and Japan. Men in each country were videotaped with a hidden camera while they watched video clips designed to elicit extreme disgust. Although they thought that they were alone and unobserved, the Americans and the Japanese showed the same types and frequencies of negative facial responses, especially disgust. These results suggest that the men were exhibiting natural and spontaneous facial behaviors, independent of culture, that were expressed in reaction to the stimulus clips, rather than with any intent of communicating emotion to an observer. This study was the first of its kind to produce data that supported the universality hypothesis using spontaneous emotion expressions in a controlled setting.

Cultural Differences in the Expression of Emotion

The experimental data discussed so far largely supported the universality of facial expressions of emotion, but cultural variation was also present in most of the findings. Although this evidence was previously thought to refute universality, Ekman and Friesen (1969) addressed and reframed these questions and accounted for both universality and cultural differences with their *neurocultural theory of emotion*. According to this theory, universality of facial expressions of emotion occurs at the level of the facial muscles; certain patterns of facial muscle action associated with certain emotions are constant across cultures. When a specific universal emotion is elicited, a specific set of facial muscles is activated by a neural Facial Affect Program, a biologically innate center that stores the configurations of facial innervation corresponding to the universal emotions. Ekman and Friesen (1978) thus developed their Facial Action Coding System (FACS) as a means to explicitly define the particular muscle patterns by which universal facial expressions of emotion are characterized and pan-culturally recognized.

Differences in facial displays could occur because of learned cultural differences about the antecedents of emotions (e.g., the events that bring on sadness may differ across cultures) and culturally learned rules regarding the appropriateness of showing certain expressions in certain situations. Ekman and Friesen (1969) used the term *cultural display rules* to refer to socially learned rules of expression management that govern the modification of universal emotions and control of facial appearance; that is, rules that will act to intensify, deintensify, mask, or change a universal expression of emotion depending on social context (Ekman, 1972). Therefore, the facial expression shown in response to a stimulus will be jointly affected by factors operating at both the biological, or *neural*, and learned, or *cultural*, levels.

Ekman and Friesen (Ekman, 1972; Friesen, 1972) were the first to document how facial displays of emotion are modified by cultural display rules. The most convincing evidence for the existence of display rules was gathered in a separate part of Friesen's (1972) Japanese-American study described above. After the initial viewing of the negative films, subjects watched them a second time. This time the experimenter stayed in the room with them while they watched. Again, the subjects were videotaped with a hidden camera. Friesen found that the Japanese men showed considerably less negative facial expressions and even smiled when interviewed about the disgusting film. In the first condition, there were virtually no differences between the Japanese and American subjects; they showed the same types of negative facial expressions when they believed that they were alone. When there was an experimenter in the room with them, however, the culturally learned display rules (e.g., polite smiling for the Japanese) affected the natural reactions of the Japanese subjects.

This theoretical framework did not advance for several decades until Matsumoto (1991) suggested a new model based on Hofstede's (1980, 1983) dimensional approach to culture. In most cross-cultural studies, culture had been operationalized as either race (cross-ethnicity studies) or place of birth (cross-country studies). Culture is typically defined conceptually, however, as a set of shared beliefs, values, attitudes, and behaviors that are communicated from one generation to the next. In his large, extensive study of

IBM employees, Hofstede (1980) had identified dimensions of culture that could differentiate cultural groups on such conceptual bases. The dimensions he defined were Power Distance (PD) (Mulder, 1976, 1977), Uncertainty Avoidance (UA), Individualism (IN), and Masculinity (MA) (Hofstede, 1980, 1983).

Matsumoto (1991) presented a theoretical framework that combined Hofstede's cultural dimension of IN, or Individualism-Collectivism (I-C), a modified version of PD called Status Differentiation (SD), and the social distinction of *ingroup-outgroup*. He suggested that this model, by operationalizing culture on meaningful dimensions, could be used to not only explain but predict the influences of culture on emotion processes, representing an advance over the previous framework of cultural display rules, which lacked predictive power. According to the proposed model, "collective cultures will foster emotional displays of their members that maintain and facilitate group cohesion, harmony, or cooperation to a greater degree than individualistic cultures" (Matsumoto, 1991).

In a study of perceptions of display rules (Matsumoto, 1990), Japanese and American subjects rated the appropriateness of displaying emotions in different social situations that referred to ingroup and outgroup members. Americans, representing an individualistic culture, rated the negative emotions of disgust and sadness as more appropriate in ingroups than did the Japanese. In contrast, the Japanese subjects, representing a collectivistic culture, rated anger as more appropriate in outgroups than did the Americans. Americans also indicated that happiness in public (an outgroup) was more appropriate than did the Japanese, further supporting the theory. In a second study (Matsumoto & Hearn, 1991), subjects from the United States, Hungary, and Poland were presented with the same facial stimuli as in the previous study and likewise rated the appropriateness of displaying each of the emotions in various social circumstances. The judged appropriateness of emotion expressions was assumed to reflect display rules. Differences were found between the Hungarians and Poles (collectivists) and the Americans (individualists). For example, Poles and Hungarians reported that it was more appropriate to display negative emotions to casual acquaintances and in public (outgroups) and less appropriate to close friends and family (ingroups). The support for hypothesized differences between individualistic and collectivistic cultures illustrated the predictive strength of the theory.

Cultural Differences in Emotion Judgment

Cultural influences are obviously not confined to facial expressions of emotion and were also observed in emotion judgments. Ekman et al.'s (1987) study of ten cultures, for example, reported cultural differences in intensity ratings of facial expressions of emotion. Although cross-cultural agreement was found in overall recognition accuracy, relative intensity of emotion examples, and secondary emotion portrayed, certain cultural groups rated some universal emotion expressions more intensely than did other groups. Specifically, post hoc analyses revealed that Asian cultures gave significantly lower intensity ratings than did non-Asian cultures to happiness, surprise, and fear. This finding was unexpected, as Ekman (1972) had originally considered universality to extend to intensity ratings as well. One posited explanation was that the non-Caucasian subjects may have been rating the Caucasian posers less intensely in order to be polite. That is, the subjects were acting according to culturally learned rules about how expressions are to be perceived or attended to.

Thus, as different cultures have their own display rules of emotion, it was suggested that they may also have rules that govern emotion judgment. Observers of the emotional displays of others may make inferences about subjective experience based on how they believe the external display may have been managed vis-à-vis the internal experience, a sort of decoding of display rules. If a culture has rules about how a person is supposed to mask an expression based on, for example, the need to maintain group harmony, this may influence the assumptions that observers of faces make about internal emotional states. Culturally specific *decoding rules* (cf. Buck, 1984) would thus act to change, intensify, deintensify, or mask the perception of universal expressions of emotion. Biehl et al. (1997) suggested that such cultural decoding rules may interact with innate biological mechanisms of emotion communication in a manner similar to that theorized for display rules.

Although the effects of cultural decoding rules may have been implied by the intensity rating differences found by Ekman et al. (1987), the stimuli used in that study included only Caucasian posers. The post hoc finding may have been confounded by cultural or ethnic congruence between poser and observer; observers in the Asian cultures may have altered their judgments because posers were not of their own culture or non-Asian observers' judgments may have been affected by the similarity of poser race to their own.

To better examine possible interactions between race of posers and observers, Matsumoto and Ekman (1988) developed the Japanese and Caucasian Facial Expressions of Emotion (JACFEE) slide set of universal facial expressions of emotion, balanced for emotion, poser race (Caucasian and Asian), and poser gender. This was produced by requesting a large number of posers to individually perform the facial muscle movements associated with the prototypic expressions of anger, contempt, disgust, fear, happiness, sadness, and surprise while photographing their attempts. The photos were scored by independent FACS coders (using Ekman and Friesen's Facial Action Coding System); reliability was .91. Only those photos meeting the following criteria were included: (a) muscle movements and their intensity levels matched exactly those originally requested of posers, with no extraneous muscle movements; and (b) overall intensity of facial muscle inner-vation was of a moderate to high intensity and relatively constant with that of other posers of the same emotion (Matsumoto & Ekman, 1989). The current JACFEE set consists of 56 distinct faces presenting examples of the seven emotions, each posed by two males and two females of the two poser races.

Recall that Matsumoto and Ekman (1989) presented these stimuli to judges in the United States and Japan. Despite cross-cultural agreement on the relative intensity of different expressions of the same emotion, they found that, for all but one emotion (disgust), Americans gave significantly higher intensity ratings than the Japanese, regardless of poser race. These findings implied that the cultural differences reported by Ekman et al. (1987) were not explained by cultural congruence of posers and judges. Rather, Matsumoto and Ekman interpreted the intensity judgment differ-ences in both studies as a function of learned cultural decoding rules.

Furthermore, although the research demonstrating universality had shown that subjects were able to recognize emotions at well over chance rates, no study had ever reported perfect cross-cultural agreement and cultures dif-fered in the exact level of agreement in their judgments. Matsumoto (1989) reanalyzed those cultural differences reported in previous judgment studies by discriminating cultures according to Hofstede's dimensions of cultural variability. One hypothesis was that Individualism would be positively cor-related with the perception of negative emotions. Significant correlations between IN and intensity ratings of anger and fear bore out that prediction. These results were explained in terms of American-Japanese cultural differ-ences in decoding rules and perception of emotion intensity (Matsumoto & Ekman, 1989) theoretically consistent with the display rules described for these cultures.

Matsumoto (1992) subsequently compared Japanese and American sub-jects on their ability to recognize six universal facial expressions of emotion. Recognition rates ranged from 64% to 99%, consistent with those collected in earlier studies, but it was also observed that American subjects were better than the Japanese subjects at recognizing anger, disgust, fear, and sadness. Matsumoto interpreted these findings as a function of cultural decoding rules, suggesting that the differences were due to socially learned rules about how emotions could be displayed, recognized, or felt. Specifically, he looked at the major cultural differences between Japan and the United States that had to do with the allowance for individuality or conformity, or I-C. In Japan, because of the emphasis on group harmony and cohesion, the pres-ence of emotions that threaten group harmony would be discouraged and persons might tend to minimize the expression and recognition of negative emotions.

Other research has focused on how cultural rules can influence the mean-ings attributed to facial expressions of emotion. In some cultures, the smile is a common signal for greeting, acknowledgment, or showing acceptance, but, because the smile is one of the easiest facial movements to make, it can also be employed to *mask* an inappropriate facial expression. Cultures may differ in the use of smiles for this purpose, as appeared to be the case in Ekman's (1972) and Friesen's (1972) study in which Japanese men used smiling to cover up their negative expressions significantly more often than did the Americans. To further investigate the nature of those differences, Matsumoto and Kudoh (1993) tested the hypothesis that Japanese and American judges would make different assumptions about smiling vs. non-smiling (i.e., neutral) faces with regard to intelligence, attractiveness, and sociability. They found cultural differences in ratings of intelligence, with American judges rating smiling faces as more intelligent than neutral faces, whereas Japanese subjects showed no such rating differences. There was also a difference in degree of sociability; Americans and Japanese both found smiling faces more sociable than neutral faces, but for the Americans the difference was greater. Differences in the attributions of meaning to the smile of happiness or to other universal facial expressions of emotion represent major differences in communication styles across cultures. These results further suggest a direct relationship between cultural display and decoding rules and the attribution of meaning to facial expressions of emotion.

One recent study reported cross-cultural agreement in the perceived *expressivity* of people of different cultural (or racial) backgrounds (Pittam et al., 1995). Australian and Japanese subjects completed a questionnaire regarding overall level of expressivity of Australian and Japanese posers. The Japanese were rated as less expressive than the Australians by all subjects. These findings were consistent with cultural and ethnic differences in intensity ratings of emotion expressions. They also indicated that people of different cultures agree that there are cultural differences in emotion expressivity and that they tend to agree about who is more or less expressive.

In light of such similarities and differences observed across cultures, Matsumoto (1993) conducted a study that examined differences in affect intensity, emotion judgments, display rule attitudes, and self-reported emotional expression as a function of ethnicity within the United States. He reported ethnic-group differences in the perceived intensity of certain emotions, as well as differences in display rule attitudes. Specifically, African Americans perceived anger more intensely than did Asian Americans and disgust more intensely than did Caucasians and Asian Americans; Hispanic Americans perceived Caucasian faces more intensely than did Caucasian and Asian Americans; and African Americans perceived female expressions more intensely than did Asian Americans. Although these subjects all lived in the San Francisco Bay Area, they showed the kinds of judgment differences that one may expect to find across cultures. The delineation of such differences within an

American sample, a group often considered in cross-cultural studies to be culturally homogeneous, calls for a reevaluation of the way that culture is conceptualized in cross-cultural research and underscores the need to operationalize culture on meaningful sociocultural dimensions that are independent of country. Ethnicity may not best serve this purpose.

Recently, differences in the perception of emotion as a function of culture were found as a result of a meta-analysis conducted by Schimmack (1996). In a multiple regression analysis, he found that I-C was a better predictor of recognition of happiness than was ethnicity, operationalized as Caucasian/non-Caucasian. This finding suggests that sociocultural dimensions such as I-C, more than ethnic or racial distinctions, account for cultural differences in the perception of universal facial expressions of emotion.

Biehl et al. (1997) conducted a study designed to test the reliability of Matsumoto and Ekman's JACFEE slide set of universal facial expressions of emotion to produce pan-cultural agreement in emotion judgments as well as possible cross-national differences in judgments. Participants in the United States, Poland, Hungary, Japan, Viet Nam, and Sumatra made categorical judgments and intensity ratings of the photos. Despite high cross-cultural agreement by observers in identifying the emotions portrayed, cross-national differences were observed in level of agreement and in intensity ratings. Patterns of cross-national judgment differences were analyzed and could not be adequately explained according to a Western/non-Western dichotomy of culture, a division of the data consistent with both the regional/country and the racial/ethnic approaches to operationalizing culture. Rather, Biehl et al. discussed these differences in terms of possible underlying sociopsychological variables (i.e., those postulated by Hofstede, 1980, 1983) and the dimensional approach to culture advanced by Matsumoto (1989, 1990). Thus, based on the findings of this and the other studies presented above, the division of subjects into cultural groups cannot be operationalized solely as a function of country or ethnicity. Any theoretical explanations or further testing of the relationship of cultural specificity to universality in facial expressions of emotion and their recognition should define and approach culture according to meaningful sociopsychological dimensions above and beyond country, region, race, or ethnicity.

ANTECEDENTS AND APPRAISAL OF EMOTION

Another major area of research on culture and emotion addresses cognitive and social dimensions of emotional experiences. These include the ecology of emotions, regulation and control of emotions, types of antecedent situations, subjective evaluation of eliciting situations, cognitive appraisal, and verbal, nonverbal, and physiological reactions to emotional situations. These dimensions are also subject to the influences of culture and seem to interact with emotion expression and display rules, recognition and decoding rules, and cultural dimensions to form complex patterns of emotion processes.

Studies of these dimensions have largely relied on self-report questionnaires. This is partly a strategy to manage the practical problems involved in producing emotion phenomena in the laboratory or with observing them in natural settings; however, it may also be argued that this is as direct a path as any to measure such phenomena. Questionnaire methodology has yielded extensive, consistent, and interpretable results. For example, Wallbott and Scherer (1986) reported on several large cross-cultural studies of emotion antecedents and reactions that used open-ended surveys. Here, about 1,400 subjects throughout Europe were instructed to describe situations eliciting one of four emotions (joy, sadness, fear, anger) and then to detail aspects of these experiences. Results of these questionnaire data allowed the formulation of specific hypotheses for subsequent research on differences in the subjective experience of emotion.

Scherer et al. (1988) thus tested hypotheses based on that prior research in a study of cultural similarities and differences in the antecedents and determinants of different emotions, different emotional reactions to situations, and the amount of control or coping attempts to regulate different emotional reactions. As done previously, they collected open-ended survey data in which subjects described situations that led to the experience of joy, sadness, fear, and anger. The inclusion of subjects in the United States and Japan, two cultures commonly assumed to be more markedly different than those of Europe, allowed stronger tests of cultural specificity versus universality. The data clearly supported many of those predictions based on earlier results, such as pan-culturally consistent differences between the emotions in their frequency (e.g., inferred from anger and joy occurring more recently than sadness and fear) duration and intensity, as well as certain cultural differences in intensity and verbalization of respective emotions. Large differences between the Japanese and the European and American samples were observed in emotionality/expressiveness (Americans being very high and Japanese very low on this dimension) and the types of situations antecedent to emotion experiences (e.g., "stranger" situations antecedent to fear for American and European, but not Japanese, subjects). These were consistent with stereotypical notions of differences between these cultural groups.

Wallbott and Scherer (1986) had also generated hypotheses based on the results of those same European studies and tested them using a larger, more diverse sample and a closed-ended questionnaire. They also examined three additional emotions (disgust, shame, guilt). Their general questions were whether different emotions are elicited by different situation patterns, are accompanied by different physiological and expressive patterns, and involve different coping or control strategies. Surveys were completed by 2,235 subjects in 27 countries on 3 continents. Items assessed characteristics of emotional experiences, such as duration, verbal, nonverbal and physiological reactions, control of emotional reactions, and evaluation of the emotion-eliciting situation. The study's hypotheses were supported by significant differences between emotions, consistent across cultures, produced on these dimensions. Specifically, anger situations were more frequent than, in order, joy, sadness, and fear situations. Sadness situations were longer in duration, followed by joy, anger, and fear situations. Fear was more physiological in nature. Anger and joy were more active in terms of nonverbal behavior. Regarding tendencies to act, "moving toward" was typical of joy, "moving against" distinct to anger, and withdrawal descriptive of all negative emotions. Joy was less controlled than negative emotions. Sadness, guilt, and especially joy situations were more expected. Pleasantness was high for joy and undifferentiated for the negative emotions. Joy situations hindered plans the least and anger and sadness situations the most. Perceived unfairness of eliciting events was highest for anger-, followed by disgust-, sadness-, and fear-eliciting events. Finally, emotion differences in attribution of cause and coping, or reactive behaviors, were also reported.

Matsumoto et al. (1988) analyzed part of the data set of the above study of 27 cultures, focusing on American and Japanese responses to the closed-ended questionnaires designed to assess subjective experience of the seven emotions. Findings of cross-cultural agreement on emotion differences, such as in duration and intensity and many aspects of the antecedent/appraisal process, replicated those of the larger study and were discussed in terms of a model of emotion elicitation. American-Japanese differences were discussed in terms of stereotypical notions and Scherer et al.'s (1988) evidence of cultural differences in expressivity and cultural display rules.

Scherer and Wallbott (1994) reported an even wider sampling using such questionnaires in 37 countries and examined them in terms of universality of differential patterning of emotions versus cultural relativity of emotional experience. Looking at the same seven emotions as in the previous studies, they reported cross-culturally stable differences among the emotions with respect to subjective feeling, physiological symptoms, and expressive behavior. These results reflected those of similar prior studies and supported the universality of differential emotion patterning, concurrent with cultural differences, in emotion elicitation, regulation, symbolic representation, and social sharing.

The role of appraisal in emotion processing was the focus of a large cross-cultural study conducted by Mauro, Sato, and Tucker (1992). Differences between emotions were examined using a questionnaire on which 973 research participants from the United States, Japan, Hong Kong, and China were asked to recall and describe in detail emotional experiences and then rate them using a set of scales that assessed 10 dimensions of appraisal (e.g., Pleasantness, Control, Norm/self-compatibility). Dimensions of subjective experience of emotion were also analyzed. Cross-cultural differences were observed on a few, but not on most, of the dimensions of appraisal. Considerable pan-cultural consistency was reported on dimensions of subjective experience and their relationships to cognitive appraisals. Some culture effects were also reported. Extensive discussion was afforded to cognitive theories of emotion and the hypotheses and results were presented in terms of various theoretical models, including the sociocultural dimension of I-C.

IMPORTANT CURRENT RESEARCH: AMERICAN-JAPANESE CULTURAL DIFFERENCES IN JUDGMENTS OF EXPRESSION INTENSITY AND SUBJECTIVE EXPERIENCE

We have seen that prior research has consistently reported cultural differences in intensity ratings of facial expressions of emotion using single-choice and multiscalar rating instruments (e.g., Ekman et al., 1987; Matsumoto & Ekman, 1989). These differences have been explained according to learned rules of emotion display and interpretation (e.g., different cultural dimensions were correlated with emotion judgments in Matsumoto's [1989] study). However, all of these data are ambiguous in that methods did not specify the exact nature of the "intensity" ratings of "emotion" requested of observers. Previous discussions of the possible basis of cultural differences in intensity ratings have focused on two aspects of the stimuli: the external appearance of the expression and the subjective feelings of the poser inferred by observers. However, because judgments of these dimensions were not explicitly requested, it is unclear exactly what aspects of the stimuli the observers were actually rating and, consequently, whether previous findings of cultural differences refer to the dimension of external appearance, internal feeling, a combination of both, or neither.

In this study, Matsumoto, Kasri, Kudoh, and Kooken (1997) separated intensity ratings into these two components, a rating of the external expression and a rating of the subjective experience of the poser. American and Japanese observers were shown photos of the seven universal facial expressions of emotion and, for each stimulus, made a categorical judgment and the two intensity ratings. For the categorical task, observers selected a single category label from a list of alternatives (anger, contempt, disgust, fear, happiness, sadness, surprise) that they thought best described the emotion portrayed. For the next two ratings, observers used an eight point scale to separately indicate the intensity level of the facial expression and then the intensity level of what they thought the poser was actually feeling.

Prior studies (described above) showed that Americans rate "emotion" in facial expressions more intensely than do Japanese. It was speculated that this difference is specific to judgments of the external appearance of expressions. When, however, attributions of internal emotional experience are made, it was speculated that Japanese judges might actually give higher intensity ratings than Americans, since Japanese people might learn rules of emotion decoding that allow them to compensate for less intense emotional expressions. On the basis of this conceptual analysis, several hypotheses were constructed.

The first referred to country-level differences. It was predicted that (H1) Americans would give significantly higher ratings than the Japanese on external expression, but that (H2) the Japanese would give significantly higher ratings than the Americans on subjective experience. The next hypothesis was designed to uncover the basis for the cultural differences, if observed, in Hypotheses 1 and 2 and predicted that (H3) the Japanese would give higher ratings to inferred subjective experience than to external expression intensity, whereas there would be no difference between the two ratings by Americans.

Parenthetically, an issue common to cross-cultural research is exlpained by the results of a six-way ANOVA on the intensity ratings of judge country (2), judge gender (2), emotion (7), poser race (2), poser gender (2), and rating type (2). A significant and considerably large main effect was observed for culture (judge country), indicating that the ratings may have been confounded by *cultural response sets*, the presence of which would render findings inconclusive, since culture effects could then be explained as a function of cultural differences in use of the scales. To address this issue, each subject's ratings were standardized to their country mean and standard deviation across all items. The procedures were tested by a six-way ANOVA on the standardized ratings in which the country main effect was not significant. This procedure was chosen since any operative cultural response sets should affect all scales and all items on which ratings were done; standardizing across all items within country, however, still allowed for between-country differences in smaller portions of the data, for example on emotion differences (see Matsumoto, 1994, for a fuller discussion of this issue).

Hypotheses 1 and 2 were tested with a three-way ANOVA of judge country (2), judge gender (2), and rating type (2) conducted for each of the expressions. A significant two-way interaction between judge country and rating type would indicate that country differences varied as a function of rating. Across 56 analyses, 43 produced a significant interaction between these factors. For expression ratings, Americans had a higher mean than the Japanese 40 out of the 43 possible times, 30 of which were statistically significant. For subjective experience ratings, Japanese had a higher mean than the Americans 38 out of the 43 possible times, 23 of which were statistically significant. These results provided strong support for Hypotheses 1 and 2. Also, a significant interaction between judge country and rating type allowed the testing of country differences separately for each rating type collapsed across all photos. Americans gave significantly higher expression intensity ratings, whereas Japanese gave significantly higher subjective experience ratings.

Hypothesis 3 predicted country differences in patterns of intensity ratings. Fifty-six repeated measures ANOVAs were conducted between the expression and experience means, separately for each of the four poser types, seven emotions, and two countries. Contrary to prediction, significant effects were found on all 28 analyses for the Americans, and all indicated that the expression rating means were significantly greater than the subjective experience rating means. For the Japanese, only 9 of the 28 analyses were statistically significant, five of which indicated that the subjective experience rating means were greater and four of which indicated the reverse.

Although it was predicted that the Japanese would attribute greater intensity to subjective experience than to external expressions and Americans would attribute the same degree of intensity to both, instead it was the Japanese who attributed the same to both, while Americans gave higher ratings on expressions. This suggests that Americans learn to downplay inferences about subjective experience relative to judgments of display intensity. It could be that Americans learn such tendencies because they know that American display rules generally encourage more outward displays of emotion than may be actually felt. In this case, the cultural decoding rule may appear consistent with the cultural display rule. On the other hand, it may be that American display rules encourage the same level of expression congruent to the level of emotion felt, but that it is functionally more adaptive for Americans to infer less intense emotion felt by others. This tendency may arise because inferences of strongly felt emotions in others may interfere with the primacy of self-concerns characteristic of the individualistic American culture (Markus & Kitayama, 1991).

That the Japanese attributed the same degree of intensity to both external display and internal experience likewise suggests functional meaning in the Japanese culture. For example, it may be possible that emotional displays are deamplified in Japan, resulting in lower ratings of external display and that, because of this, inferences about the subjective experiences of others are raised in a compensatory fashion. Alternatively, the finding may simply be related to the fact that emotional displays are contextualized based on display rules, so that they correspond to the same degree of felt emotion as expressed. Thus, when they are observed, attributions about the faces could only be that the situation allowed the expressions to occur and that they correspond to that same degree of internal experience.

Also, this lack of differences may have been due to a lack of contextual information regarding the emotion expressions. Japanese culture tends to be highly contextualized (Hall, 1969), and judgments might have differed dramatically if contexts had been manipulated. For that matter, the American culture is not context-free, and such effects might have been obtained with the Americans as well. The manipulation of context, in addition to the inclusion of observers from other countries and cultures, is necessary to test the robustness of the ideas presented in this study.

FUTURE RESEARCH AGENDA

The findings of recent and current studies presented above clearly suggest several areas of inquiry for further research, specifically the manipulation of context and the measurement of sociopsychological dimensions of culture on the individual level. First, the highlighted study of American-Japanese differences in judgments seems best explained in terms of cultural decoding rules, their functionality in a culture, and factors that may affect their application, such as observers' knowledge of display rules. However, appropriateness of emotion display has been shown to vary cross-culturally based not only on the mere presence of others (Friesen, 1972), but on those others' ingroup versus outgroup membership (Matsumoto, 1990; Matsumoto & Hearn, 1991). Thus, context has been shown to interact with the perception of display rules. Testing of the effects of context on judgments of facial expressions of emotion is an important direction for future research.

Other recent research has yielded results that seem to be best explained according to sociocultural dimensions of culture such as I-C, rather than cultural group membership operationalized according to country, race, or ethnicity. However, a limitation of previous studies of cultural differences is the post hoc assumption of cultural constructs such as I-C to underlie the samples in the studies, without actually measuring I-C on the level of individual research participants. Incorporation of individual-level measurement of culture in studies of expression and judgment is critical to future research. On the individual level, Triandis refers to individualism and collectivism as idiocentric or allocentric tendencies, respectively (Triandis et al., 1986).

In this chapter, we presented major research on culture and emotion, culminating in the description of certain current research and how we believe it points to the future of study in the field. Extensive discussion was afforded to major cross-cultural research on emotion expression and recognition. This focused on universal facial expressions of emotion and the influences of culture on their display and perception. We traced work in this area from Darwin's first suggestion of universal facial expressions through the development of complex theoretical frameworks accounting for cultural differences in their expression and perception. We also described important research in the area of cognitive and social appraisal and antecedents of emotions. Finally, we detailed a current study that we consider to be at the forefront of research in the field.

10

The Influence of Culture on Stress: India and England

Pittu Laungani

Common sense often confirms the observation that stress varies from one individual to another, from one group to another, from one time to another, and from one culture to another. A situation (or a set of stimuli) perceived as being stressful on one occasion might be seen as exciting on another. Moreover, one individual's stress might be another individual's thrill. For those living in the Sahara Desert, the perception of stressors is likely to be significantly different from those living in the rain forests of the Amazon. Clearly, therefore, the ecology of each culture produces its own unique sets of stressors. However, cultures vary not merely in climatic conditions but also in terms of their political, social, economic, and environmental conditions, each exerting its own set of stressors. Moreover, cultures also vary in terms of their value systems. The existing value systems have a significant bearing on a variety of factors, including child-rearing techniques, patterns of socialization, development of identities, kinship networks, work habits, social and familial arrangements, and the religious beliefs and practices of people of that culture.

Thus, values play a dominant role in understanding the social behaviors of people in any culture. *Values may be defined as the currently held normative expectations underlying individual and social conduct* (Laungani, 1995). Our ideas of right and wrong, good and bad, virtuous and evil, normal and abnormal, appropriate and inappropriate, proper and improper, are to a large extent influenced by the values that are prevalent in our culture. Values are an integral part of our cultural atmosphere. Although we may not be consciously aware of their origins, we nonetheless imbibe them. They become part of our unique cultural psyche.

To understand the influence of culture on our perception of stress (and its management), it is desirable to examine sharply contrasting cultures, such as those of India and England. In this chapter therefore, we single out India (Eastern culture) and England (Western culture) for closer scrutiny. To do so, we concentrate on the values underlying the major parameters or factors that distinguish Indian culture from English culture. Insofar as the value systems within a given culture are relatively stable, one is able to deduce a variety of testable hypotheses concerning the salient behavior patterns of people within that culture. But when the dominant value systems undergo a rapid change or are in a state of flux, leading to a multiplicity of incongruent and incompatible belief systems—what Durkheim described as a state of *anomie* or normlessness—then the merit of deducing specific testable hypotheses becomes difficult, if not impossible.

CONCEPTUAL MODEL OF CULTURAL DIFFERENCES

Laungani (1990, 1991, 1991a, 1991b, 1992, 1993, 1994, 1995, 1996, 1997, 1998) has proposed a theoretical model arguing that four interrelated *core* values or *factors* distinguish some (but not all) Western cultures from some (but not all) Eastern cultures, and more specifically English culture from Indian culture in terms of their salient value systems. The proposed constructs are:

Individualism . . . . Communalism (Collectivism)
Cognitivism . . . . Emotionalism
Free will. . . . . Determinism
Materialism. . . . . Spiritualism

It should be noted that the two concepts underlying each factor are not dichotomous. They are to be understood as extending along a continuum, starting at, say, individualism at one end and extending into communalism at the other. A dimensional formulation has the advantage of allowing us to measure salient attitudes and behavior at any given point in time and over time. It also enables us to hypothesize expected theoretical and empirical shifts in positions along the continuum both within and between cultural groups, which may occur as a result of a variety of cultural or individual changes. Each of the hypothesized dimensions subsumes within it a variety of attitudes and behaviors that to a large extent are influenced by the norms and values prevalent within that culture. Let us now examine each concept briefly and trace its relationship to stress.

INDIVIDUALISM . . . . . COMMUNALISM (COLLECTIVISM)

Individualism

Several thinkers have written on the concepts of individualism and collectivism (Hofstede, 1980, 1991; Hui & Triandis, 1986; Kim, Triandis,

& Yoon, 1992; Matsumoto, 1996; Triandis, 1994; see also the chapter by Yrizarry et al. on culture and emotion in this volume). Insofar as the concept of collectivism is concerned, the author prefers the word communalism. The arguments for retaining the word "communalism" instead of "collectivism" have been discussed elsewhere (Laungani, in preparation). Suffice it to say that in employing the term "collectivism" there is the unvoiced danger of reintroducing the old notion of "group mind" which was abandoned several decades ago. Although the term "collectivism" appears neutral in its connotation, it does convey a vague impression of large, amorphous crowds of people gathered together to respond to collectivist values.

A distinguishing feature of Western society is its increasing emphasis on individualism. At an abstract level, the concept itself has come to acquire several different meanings: an ability to exercise a degree of control over one's life, an ability to cope with one's problems, an ability to change for the better, reliance upon oneself, responsibility for one's actions, self-fulfillment, and self-realization of one's internal resources. Triandis (1994) points out that individualism, in essence, is concerned with giving priority to one's personal goals over the goals of one's ingroup. Although Triandis (1995) distinguishes between vertical and horizontal individualism, Kim (1997) characterizes individualism in terms of three features, which he refers to as (1) emphasis on distinct and autonomous individuals, (2) separation from ascribed relationships such as family, community, and religion, and (3) emphasis on abstract principles, rules, and norms that guide the individual's thoughts, feelings, and actions. Individualism, according to Kim (1997), asserts the position of rationalism, universalism, detachability, and freedom of choice and rejects a traditional, ascribed, communal, and medieval social order.

Individualism has also been the subject of considerable debate among Western thinkers (Bellah, 1985; Kagitçibasi, 1997; Kim, 1997; Lukes, 1973; Riesman, 1954; Spence, 1985; Waterman, 1981). Some writers have argued that the notions of individualism are incompatible with and even antithetical to communal and collective interests. The "dog-eat-dog" philosophy is seen as being divisive and inimical in terms of promoting communal goals, and in the long run, it alienates fellow beings from one another. However, other writers—among whom Sampson (1977) is the most outspoken defender of individualism—extol its virtues, which are in keeping with the spirit of capitalism and free enterprise. Sampson (1977) sees no reason why the philosophy of individualism should not also nurture a spirit of cooperation and coexistence.

Whether or not the notion of individualism offers a satisfactory explanation of the dominant values that underlie Western cultures is an argument that lies beyond the scope of the present chapter. The questions that concern us here are as follows: How does the notion of individualism enable us to understand stress? Which factors within the philosophy of individualism are likely to lead to stress?

1. Individualism tends to create conditions that do not permit an easy sharing of one's personal problems and concerns with others. There is a close parallel between the notion of individualism and the philosophy of the absurd, which Camus propounded in his famous book, *The Myth of Sisyphus* (1955). Camus argued that individualism (although he did not refer to it as individualism) creates in people an existential loneliness that is compounded by a sense of the absurd, which is an integral part of the human condition. Camus warns us that there appears to be no easy escape from this human predicament. The emphasis on self-reliance, the expectation of being responsible for one's success or failure, which is integral to the notion of individualism, imposes severe stress on the individual.

2. The philosophy of individualism has a strong bearing on the notion of identity. In Western society, psychologists and psychiatrists of virtually all theoretical persuasions construe identity in developmental terms, which starts from infancy. In the process of development, one's identity—according to received wisdom—passes through several critical stages in adolescence into adulthood. The very process of acquiring an identity based in reality is fraught with stress. To acquire an appropriate identity that asserts one's strengths, that is located in reality, that reflects one's true inner being, and that leads to the fulfillment or the realization of one's potential results in conflict, which, if unresolved, leads to severe stress and in extreme cases to an identity crisis (Erikson, 1963; Maslow, 1970, 1971; Rogers, 1961, 1980). Individualism ensures that each individual is held responsible for his or her own development. Consequently, any failures with their attendant feelings of guilt are explained in individualistic terms.

3. A dominant feature of individualism is its recognition of and respect for an individual's physical and "psychological space." Vine (1982) has reviewed the major studies in the area related to crowding, the invasion of physical and psychological space, and has found that the effects of violating another person's physical and psychological space give rise to stress. In extreme cases, as Webb (1978) in a separate study has shown, it leads to neuroses and other psychosomatic disturbances.

4. Closely related to the notion of physical and psychological space is the concept of privacy. Privacy implies a recognition of and respect for another person's individuality (Laungani, 1995). It involves defining boundaries that separate the self from others—both physically and psychologically. Privacy is a valued concept in the West, respected and adhered to in all social relationships. The need to define one's psychological and physical boundaries starts virtually from infancy. The wish to respect another individual's privacy occasionally extends to those situations where it might be desirable (and possibly even therapeutic) to "intrude" on the privacy of another individual—as in the case of a recently bereaved individual, living on his or her

own. Several studies have demonstrated that the invasion of privacy often leads to severe stress (Greenberg & Firestone, 1977; Rohner, 1974).

5. At a social level, individualism has also had an effect on the size of the British family structure, which from the postwar period onward has undergone a dramatic change (Eversley & Bonnnerjea, 1982). Although the nuclear family is still seen as the norm, it is by no means clear how a "typical" British family should be defined. With the gradual increase in one-parent families—at present, around 17 percent—combined with the fact that just under 25 percent of the population live alone—the present nuclear family structure is likely to change even more dramatically. Changes in the size and structure of families, combined with high levels of social and occupational mobility, may have "destabilized" society, creating a sense of loss of community life, particularly in the urban metropolitan cities. Similar trends may be seen in other European societies as well as in the United States.

Communalism (Collectivism)

1. Indian society on the other hand has been and continues to be community-oriented (Kakar, 1981; Koller, 1982; Lannoy, 1976; Laungani, 1991; Mandelbaum, 1972; Saraswathi & Pai, 1997; Sinari, 1984; Sinha & Kao, 1997). Most Indians grow up and live in *extended family* networks. It should be made clear here that the term "extended family" subsumes within it not merely the structural and the functional features but also the psychological and relational features of the extended family. In the larger cities of India, such as Bombay, Delhi, and Calcutta, the structural features of the extended family are undergoing a visible metamorphosis. Because of a chronic housing shortage, the size of the extended family is dwindling rapidly. This, however, does not foretell the death of the extended family. Despite its structural weaknesses, the extended family is united by its psychological and functional features.

Indian society cannot be seen other than in familial and communal terms. It is, and has been for centuries, a family-oriented and community-based society. A community in India is not just a collection of individuals gathered together for a common purpose. A community in the sense in which it is understood in India has several common features. People within a group are united by a common caste-rank, religious grouping, and linguistic and geographical boundaries. The members within a community generally operate based on a ranking or a hierarchical system. Elders are accorded special status within the community, and their important role is clearly recognized. Elders, whether they come from rural areas or from large metropolitan cities, are generally deferred to. On important issues, the members of a community may meet and confer with one another, and any decisions taken are often binding on the rest of the members within the community. In Indian family life, one's individuality is subordinated to collective solidarity, and one's ego is suppressed into the collective ego of the family and one's community. Consequently, when a problem—financial, medical, psychiatric, or whatever—affects an individual, it becomes a joint family problem.

But the individual pays a price to remain part of the family and the community. The individual is expected to submit to familial and communal norms, and not to deviate to an extent where it becomes necessary for the deviant to be ostracized. The pressure to conform to family norms and expectations can cause acute stress in individual members in the family, leading, in some instances, to psychotic disorders and hysteria (Channabasavanna & Bhatti, 1982; Sethi & Manchanda, 1978). The authors point out that the very act of living together in crowded physical environments, with little room for physical privacy, creates its own sets of stressors. On the whole, however, it would appear that extended family networks provide built-in safety measures against stress and mental disturbances. The emotional and physical intimacy shared by all members within a family group acts as a buffer against the stressors, from which the European counterpart is not protected.

2. Several research studies undertaken in India, Hong Kong, Taiwan, and elsewhere have demonstrated that living together in overcrowded, unhealthy, noisy, and polluted urban environments tends to create severe environmental stress. These findings have been confirmed by several independent studies (Evans et al., 1989; Hwang, 1979; Jain, 1987; Lee, 1981; Nagar et al., 1988). The two major factors that lead to high levels of stress are associated with noise and overcrowding.

3. In an individualistic society, personal choice is considered to be extremely important and tends to take precedence over familial or communal choice (Triandis, 1994). Such is not the case in a communalistic or collectivist society. There, personal choice has less importance. This is evidenced by the fact that the majority of occupations in India are caste-dependent, and caste of course is determined by birth. One is born into a given caste and remains in it until death. One's friends, too, are an integral part of one's caste-related network. In addition to occupations, one has little choice even in terms of one's marriage partner. Although the "style" of arranged marriages has undergone a change within Indian society—largely among the affluent, urban sectors of the country—arranged marriages are still the norm.

With the exception of the caste system, which is a singularly unique feature of Indian society, other collectivist cultures, including China, Taiwan, Korea, Hong Kong, the Philippines, Thailand, Nepal, Pakistan, Iran, Turkey, Portugal, Mexico, Peru, Venezuela, and Colombia, also share most of the features described above (Cheng, 1996; Gulerce, 1996; Hofstede, 1980; Jing & Wan, 1997; Kim, 1997; Matsumoto, 1996; Sinha, Mishra, & Berry, 1996; Ward & Kennedy, 1996; Yang, 1997). For instance, Kuo-Shu Yang (1997), in his excellent analyses of the traditional Chinese personality, refers to the tight, close-knit bond between the individual and his or her family.

Table 10.1
Variations in Stress in Relation to Individualism and Communalism

INDIVIDUALISM	COMMUNALISM
Emphasis on high degree of self-control	Such emphasis unnecessary; dependence on elders and other family members
Emphasis on personal responsibility	Emphasis on collective responsibility
Emphasis on self-achievement	Emphasis on collective achievement
Pressure on individuals to achieve an identity	Identity is ascribed at birth
Stress is related to the acquisition of identity	Stress is related to the "imposition" of a familial and caste-related identity
Emphasis on nuclear families	Emphasis on extended families

He points out that "Chinese familism disposes the Chinese to subordinate their personal interests, goals, glory, and welfare to their family's interests, goals, glory, and welfare to the extent that the family is primary and its members secondary" (1997, p. 245). Again, Kuo-Shu Yang (1997) points out that in order to attain harmony within the family it is essential for the individual to "surrender or merge into his or her family, and as a result, lose his or her individuality and idiosyncrasies as an independent actor" (p. 245).

Pressures arising out of conformity to familial and communal norms, an inability or unwillingness to assert one's independence with regard to the choice of one's occupation and one's marriage partner, tend to create severe stress among individuals in collectivist societies. The major features of individualism and communalism are summarized in Table 10.1.

COGNITIVISM . . . . . EMOTIONALISM

This factor is concerned with the way in which the British (in particular, the English) construe their private and social worlds and the ways in which they form and sustain social relationships.

Cognitivism

Pande (1968) has suggested that British society is a *work-and-activity-centered society* and that Indian society, in contradistinction, is a *relationship-centered society*. These different constructions of their social worlds are not accidental cultural developments. They stem from their inheritance of their different philosophical legacies.

1. In a work-and-activity-centered society, people are more likely to operate in a cognitive mode, where the emphasis is on rationality, logic, and control. Public expression of feelings and emotions—particularly among the middle classes in England—is often frowned upon. The expression of negative feelings causes mutual embarrassment and is often construed as being vulgar.

Within a cognitivist framework, there is a cultural expectation that persons in most social situations will exercise a high degree of self-control. Stress in such a framework arises from two sources: (1) from the cultural expectation of reliance on self-control and (2) from the cultural embargo on the expression of feelings and emotions in public. Even in situations where it would seem legitimate to express feelings openly, without inhibition—at funerals, for instance—the English are guided by control, which suggests that one must not cry in public, one must at all times put on a "brave" face, one must, above all, never lose one's dignity. Dignity is preserved or even perpetuated through restraint. If one has to cry, one must do so in the privacy of one's home. The unwillingness or the inability to express emotions openly is a theme that has caused some worry to other writers in the field (Gorer, 1965; Hockey, 1993; Sarbin, 1986). Other Western societies such as Italy, however, allow more psychological space for the expression of emotions in the context of familial and friendship bonds.

Obviously, in a work-and-activity-centered society, a need often arises for the creation of professional and semiprofessional settings which permit the legitimate expression of specific feelings and emotions, and their handling by experts trained in the specific area. Thus, one sees in Western society the growth of specialist counselors, including bereavement counselors, cancer counselors, AIDS counselors, marriage guidance counselors, family therapists, rational-emotive therapists, and, last but not the least, psychotherapists and psychoanalysts of different theoretical persuasions.

2. Given the emphasis on work and activity, relationships in such a society are formed on the basis of *shared commonalities*. To a large extent, one's relationships also grow out of one's work. Thus, relationships become a byproduct of work. One is expected to "work at a relationship"—in a marriage, in a family situation, with friends, with colleagues at work, and even with one's children. In a work-and-activity oriented society, work defines one's sense of worth.

3. Work and its relation to self-esteem acquire meaning only when seen against the background of time. Our conception of time is both objective and subjective. At an objective level, time is seen as a dimension in which each hour is divided into fixed moments of minutes, seconds, and milliseconds. Each moment (at least on earth) expires at the same speed; an hour passes not a moment sooner, not a moment later. At a subjective level,

however, there are variations in our perceptions of time. In a work-and-activity-centered society, one's working life, including one's private life, to a large measure, is organized around time. To ensure the judicious use of time, one resorts to keeping appointment books, calendars, and computer-assisted diaries; one works to fixed time-schedules, and one sets deadlines; one tries to keep within one's time limits. One is constantly aware of the swift passage of time, and to fritter it away is often construed as an act of criminality. Time therefore comes to acquire a significant meaning in a work-and-activity-centered society. McClelland (1961) has shown that people in general and high achievers in particular use metaphors such as "a dashing waterfall" and "a speeding train" to describe time. *The fear of running out of time is seen as one of the greatest stressors in Western society.* Even casual encounters between friends and between colleagues at work are time-related and operate on covert agendas. One seldom meets people as an end in itself; meeting people is construed as a means to an end, with time playing a significant role.

Emotionalism

1. Many non-Western societies are *relationship centered* and operate in an *emotional mode*. The fact that people live in close physical proximity and share their lives with one another forces them into operating in an emotional mode. In such a society, feelings and emotions are not easily repressed, and their expression in general is not frowned upon. Crying, dependence on others, excessive emotionality, volatility, and verbal hostility, in both males and females, are not in any way considered signs of weakness or ill-breeding. Since feelings and emotions—both positive and negative—are expressed easily, there is little danger of treading incautiously on others' sensibilities and vulnerabilities, such as might be the case in work-and-activity-centered societies. Given the extended-family structure of relationships, emotional outbursts are, as it were, "taken on board" by the family members. Quite often, the emotional outbursts are of a symbolic nature—even highly stylized and ritualistic. To appreciate fully the ritualistic component of emotional outbursts among Indians, be they Hindus or Muslims, one must visualize it against the backdrop of living conditions in India. In urban areas—for those who are fortunate enough to live in brick houses—it is not at all uncommon for a family of eight to ten persons to be living together in one small room. Given the extreme closeness of life, the paucity of amenities, the absence of privacy, the inertia evoked by the overpowering heat and dust, and the awesome feeling of claustrophobia, it is not at all surprising that families often quarrel, fight, and swear at one another (and from time to time assault one another too). But their quarrels and outbursts are often of a symbolic nature; otherwise, such quarrels would lead to a permanent rift, the consequences of which would be far more traumatic than those of living together. There

is in such outbursts a surrealistic quality: at one level they are frighteningly real—the words and abuses hurled at one another, callous and hurtful—yet at another level they are bewilderingly unreal. They serve no function other than the relief which such "cathartic" outbursts bring.

In a hierarchical family structure, however, each member within the family soon becomes aware of his or her own position within the hierarchy, and in the process of familial adjustment, learns the normative expressions of emotionality permissible to the person concerned.

2. One major disadvantage of being in a relationship-centered society is that one is forced into relationships from which one cannot opt out without severe sanctions being imposed on the individual. Several studies have shown that one's inability to sever enforced relationships based on birth and caste often leads to severe stress and neurosis (Channabasavanna & Bhatti, 1982).

3. The factor of time which, as we saw, is so important in Western societies, does not have the same meaning in a relationship-centered society. At an objective level, time is construed in virtually the same way as it is in the West. But at a subjective level, time in India is seen in more flexible and even relaxed terms. Time, in Indian metaphysics, is not conceptualized in linear terms. A linear model of time signifies a beginning, a middle, and an end, or, in other words, a past, a present, and a future. Time, in Indian philosophy, is conceptualized in circular terms, which means that time has no beginning, no middle, and no end, or, if there is a beginning, it remains unknown. These differential conceptualizations have serious implications for our understanding of stress in both cultures.

For instance, at a day-to-day observational level, one does not notice among Indians the same sense of urgency that appears to have become the hallmark of Western society. Time in India is often viewed as "a quiet, motionless ocean," "a vast expanse of sky." It is interesting to note that in Hindi the same word—*kal*—stands for both yesterday and tomorrow. One gauges the meaning of the word from its context. Indians' flexible attitude toward time is often reflected in their social engagements: they tend to be quite casual about keeping appointments; being late for an appointment, keeping another person waiting, does not appear to cause them any undue stress.

There are, however, exceptions to this flexible construction of time. They occur in those situations that are considered auspicious: undertaking an important journey, and fixing the time of christening, betrothals, weddings, and funerals, in particular. In such auspicious situations, one is expected to consult the family Brahmin priest, who then consults an almanac from which he (most Brahmin priests are male) calculates the most auspicious time for beginning that particular activity. Because of their religious significance, such events are seldom left to chance; one seeks divine guidance in their planning and execution.

Table 10.2
Variations in Stress in Relation to Cognitivism and Emotionalism

COGNITIVISM	EMOTIONALISM
Emphasis on rationality and logic	Emphasis on feelings and intuition
Feelings and emotions kept in check	Feelings and emotions expressed freely
Emphasis on work-and-activity	Emphasis on relationships
Relations based on shared interests	Relations caste and family based

The major features of cognitivism and emotionalism and their relative differences are summarized in Table 10.2.

FREE WILL . . . . . DETERMINISM

The issues related to the nature of free will, predestination, determinism, and indeterminism are still being hotly debated in philosophical and scientific journals. No satisfactory solutions have been found to these age-old issues. Although the Aristotelian legacy has undergone several transformations, it has remained with us for over two thousand years (Flew, 1989). In the past, prior to Newton's spectacular achievements, determinism was entangled in its theistic and metaphysical connotations. After the publication of Newton's *Principia* in 1687, however, the concept of determinism was partially freed from its theistic connotations, and a nontheistic and mechanistic view of determinism in science, and indeed in the universe, gained prominence. A scientific notion of determinism, with its emphasis on causality, or conversely, its denial of noncausal events, found favor among the rationalist philosophers who embraced it with great fervor (Popper, 1972). It was not until the emergence of quantum mechanics in the early twentieth century that determinism in science, if not in human affairs, once again came to be seriously questioned. In keeping with his own views on the subject, Popper (1988) avoids the terms "determinism" and "free will" altogether. Instead, he proposes the term "indeterminism," which he argues is neither the opposite of determinism nor the same as free will.

Free Will

There is a peculiar dualism in Western thinking concerning free will and determinism. Scientific research in medicine, psychiatry, biology, and other related disciplines, including psychology, is based on the acceptance of a deterministic framework—hence the concern with seeking causal explanations and with predictability in accordance with rational scientific procedures of prediction. Yet, at a social, psychological, and common-sense level, there is often a strong belief in the notion of free will.

What do we mean by free will? Free will might be defined as a *noncausal, voluntary action*. However, at a common-sense level it is defined *as exercising voluntary control over one's actions*. Thus, free will allows an individual to do what he or she wills and, in so doing, take "credit" for his or her successes while accepting blame for his or her failures and mishaps. Thus, one is forever locked into the consequences of one's own actions. This feature of Western society entraps individuals in their own existential predicament from which there does not appear to be an easy way out.

Rotter (1966) offers a neat solution to the dilemma of determinism and free will. The concept of control is central to Rotter's ideas. He argues that some individuals explain their actions in terms of internal control (free will) and others in terms of external control (determinism). On the basis of a self-administered questionnaire, the Locus of Control Scale, he found that perceived control exists in individually varying degrees. He regards it as an enduring personality characteristic, and it seems that those who possess it to a high degree are able to moderate the impact of whatever stresses they encounter. Rotter sees perceived control as the principal coping mechanism for stress and other health-related problems. Studies suggest that those persons motivated by internal control—cognitive, informational, emotional, and behavioral control—are better able to cope with stress and other health hazards, including mental illness (Glass, Reim, & Singer, 1971; Mills & Krantz, 1979; Seligman, 1975; Thompson, 1981).

Determinism

Indians, by virtue of subscribing to a deterministic view of life—in a teleological sense at least—are prevented from taking final responsibility for their own actions. The notion of determinism plays an extremely crucial role in their thinking. The *law of karma*, which involves determinism and fatalism, has shaped the Indian view of life over centuries (O'Flaherty, 1976; Sinari, 1984; Weber, 1963). In its simplest form, the law of karma states that happiness or sorrow is the predetermined effect of actions committed by the person either in his present life or in one of his numerous past lives. Things do not happen because we make them happen. Things happen because they were *destined* to happen. If one's present life is determined by one's actions in one's previous life, it follows that any problem that affects an individual was destined to happen because of past actions.

A belief in the law of karma does not necessarily negate the notion of free will. As Christoph von Fürer-Haimendorf (1974) has pointed out, in an important sense karma is based on the assumption of free will. The theory of karma rests on the idea that an individual has final moral responsibility for each of his or her actions and hence the freedom of moral choice.

Pandey, Srinivas, and Muralidhar (1980) in a study of psychiatric patients in India found that psychotic disorders were most commonly attributed to sins and wrong deeds in their previous and present life. These findings have been corroborated by Srinivasa and Trivedi (1982) who, in their study of 266 respondents selected from three villages in South India, attributed, among other factors, "God's curse" as one of the most common causes of stress leading to mental disorders. Such a belief has its advantages: it takes away the blame that might otherwise be apportioned to the individual concerned.

A belief in determinism is likely to engender in the Indian psyche a spirit of passive, if not resigned, acceptance of the vicissitudes of life. This prevents a person from experiencing feelings of guilt—a state from which Westerners, because of their fundamental belief in the doctrine of free will, cannot be protected. The main disadvantage of determinism—and there are many— lies in the fact that it often leads to a state of existential, and in certain instances, moral resignation, compounded by a profound sense of *inertia*. One does not take immediate *proactive* measures; one merely accepts the vicissitudes of life without qualm. Although this may prevent a person from experiencing stress, it does not allow the same person to make individual attempts to alleviate his or her unbearable condition.

The major features of free will and determinism are summarized in Table 10.3.

MATERIALISM . . . . SPIRITUALISM

Materialism

Materialism refers to a belief in the existence of a material world or a world composed of matter. What constitutes matter is itself debatable; the question has never been satisfactorily answered (Trefil, 1980). If matter consists of atoms, it appears that atoms are made of nuclei and electrons. Nuclei, in turn, are made up of protons and neutrons. What are protons and neutrons made of? Gell-Mann (see Davies, 1990) coined the word "quarks." But quarks, it appears, have their own quirks. In other words, the assumed solidity of matter may indeed turn out to be a myth (Davies, 1990).

The notion of the solidity of matter was robustly debated by Heisenberg in his now famous research paper on indeterminacy in quantum theory in 1927 (Heisenberg, 1930). Such debates, however, are confined to journals of philosophy and science. At a practical day-to-day level, aided by empiricism, one accepts the assumed solidity of the world that one inhabits—but not without paying a heavy price. For such an acceptance gives rise to the

Table 10.3
Variations in Stress in Relation to Free Will and Determinism

FREE WILL	DETERMINISM
Emphasis on freedom of choice	Freedom of choice limited
Proactive	Reactive
Success or failure due largely to effort	Although effort is important, success or failure is related to one's karma
Self-blame or guilt is a residual consequence of failure	No guilt is attached to failure
Failure may lead to victim-blaming	No blame is attached to victim

popular myth that all explanations of phenomena, ranging from lunar cycles to lunacy, need to be sought within the (assumed) materialist framework. This is evidenced by the profound reluctance among psychiatrists, medical practitioners, and psychologists especially in the West, to entertain any explanations that are of a nonmaterial or supernatural nature.

A materialist philosophy also tends to engender in its subscribers the belief that our knowledge of the world is external to ourselves; reality is, as it were, "out there," and it is only through objective scientific enterprise that one will acquire an understanding of the external world and, with it, an understanding of "reality." Nonmaterial explanations are seen to fall within the purview of the *prescientific* communities, or in other words, *superstitious* and *backward* societies, to be found mainly in underdeveloped countries.

Spiritualism

In Indian thinking, the notion of materialism is a relatively unimportant concept. The external world to Indians is not composed of matter. It is seen as being illusory. It is *maya*. The concept of maya, as Zimmer (1989) points out, "holds a key position in Vedantic thought and teaching" (p. 19). Since the external world is illusory, reality, or its perception, lies within the individual and not, as Westerners believe, outside the individual. This, according to Zimmer (1989), tends to make Indians more *inward looking* and Westerners more *outward looking*. Also, given the illusory nature of the external world, the Indian mind remains unfettered by materialistic boundaries. It resorts to explanations in which material and spiritual, physical and metaphysical, natural and supernatural explanations of phenomena coexist. What to a modern Western mind, weaned on Aristotelian logic, nourished on a scientific diet, socialized on materialism, empiricism, and positivism might

Table 10.4
Variations in Stress in Relation to Materialism and Spiritualism

MATERIALISM	SPIRITUALISM
The world is "real", physical	The world is illusory
Rejection of contradictory explanations of phenomena	Co-existence of contradictory explanations of phenomena
Reality is external to the individual	Reality is internal to the individual
Reality perceived through scientific enterprise	Reality perceived through contemplation and inner reflection

seem an irreconcilable contradiction, leaves an Indian mind relatively unperturbed. To many Westerners if A is A, A cannot then be not-A. If dysentery is caused by certain forms of bacteria, it cannot then be due to the influence of the "evil-eye." The two are logically and empirically incompatible. But to Indians contradictions are a way of life. A is not only A, but under certain conditions, A may be not-A. One of the most interesting differences between traditional Indian thinking and many forms of Western thinking is this: Indians believe intuitively (and spiritually) the external world to be illusory without actually "knowing" it, whereas the Westerners "know" it to be illusory, without actually believing it. This differential construction of one's physical world has an important bearing on the perception of stress and the methods employed for coping with it.

Many Indian beliefs and values revolve around the notion of spiritualism. The ultimate purpose of human existence is to transcend one's illusory physical existence, renounce the world of material aspirations, and attain a heightened state of spiritual awareness. Any activity—particularly yoga—that is likely to promote such a state is to be encouraged. Table 10.4 summarizes the major features of materialism and spiritualism.

From Theory to Practice

Regardless of the elegance and plausibility of any theoretical formulations, it is essential that any hypotheses deduced from a theory be subjected to a series of rigorous and critical tests. Otherwise, the theory remains untested and consequently tells us little of any significant importance. Such a requirement is of greater importance in cross-cultural research. Given the cross-cultural nature of the theoretical formulations presented above, it is therefore essential that the empirical methods used in any empirical investigations be commensurable and valid.

Considerable research on stress has been undertaken in India. Given the sheer volume of work that has been undertaken, it would seem reasonable to expect that by now we should have found unequivocal answers to the fundamental questions related to the nature of stress, its etiology, and the tried and tested strategies related to stress management.

How has the notion of stress been conceptualized in India? Have Indian scientists developed their own culturally unique indigenous research methodologies and examined problems that are seen as representative of the Indian "scene"? Or have the researchers adopted the conceptual framework offered by Western researchers in the area?

Stress Research in India

Research on stress in India, to a large measure, has concentrated on two main types of studies: (1) a problem-centered approach; and (2) organizational stress.

Problem-centered Approach. Until the late 1970s many psychologists were concerned with investigating problems that were concerned with stress due to migration from rural to urban settings (Sharma, 1988). Most of the studies (Bhaskaran, Seth, & Yadav, 1970; Channabàsavanna, Rao, Embar, & Sharieff, 1970; Dube, 1970; Thacore, 1973) found a higher rate of morbidity among the migrant groups. Some of the studies also examined the coping strategies—in particular, yogic exercises and ayurvedic (traditional Indian medical) practices—which people living in rural areas adopt in times of famine, natural disasters, suicide in the family, economic deprivation, ill-health, and so on (Adityanjee, 1986; Kumar-Reddy & Ramamurty, 1990; Torry, 1986).

The importance of such types of studies is to be commended, for they concern themselves with issues that are not only indigenous to India but that have parallels in the recent large-scale migrations of displaced political and religious refugees in Russia, Bosnia, Croatia, Germany, the Middle East, and Africa. From a heuristic point of view, such studies are to be encouraged, for they attempt to promote a genuine understanding of the psychosocial variables associated with problems of migration, the process of acculturation, acclimatization, and adaptation, and the success or otherwise of the indigenous coping strategies employed by them. In India, however, such studies appear to be the exception rather than the norm.

Organizational Stress. The bulk of the studies on stress, however, have been concerned with organizational stress in general and role stress in particular (Pestonjee, 1992). These problems have been studied under a variety of work settings: senior and junior executives in large corporations, supervisors, academics in universities, officers in the Indian Administrative Services, managers in the public and private sectors, women in the public and private sectors, and so on. But, as Pestonjee remarks, "no attention has been paid to the stresses experienced by those below the level of supervisors" (1992, p. 82).

The research on organizational stress undertaken in India has been quite extensive. The findings from this type of research offer valuable insights into the personality characteristics of executives in large and medium-sized corporations and within the public sector. The research findings have also thrown light on the problems related to organizational structures, interpersonal relations within the organizations, and organizational role stress.

Several investigators in India have been concerned with administering a variety of psychometric instruments on a preselected sample of subjects, who may consist of college students, workers in a factory, middle managers in industry, psychiatric patients in a hospital, a team of social workers, and so on. This form of research which follows a correlational methodology is extremely popular in India. Its popularity would indicate that it is relatively easy to undertake and does not require a great deal of ingenuity in its design and execution. The data are then subjected to diverse forms of multivariate analyses, including regression analysis. Significant differences among test scores and other variables are then identified as indicators of stress. A high proportion of studies that have been undertaken are of a correlational nature, and notwithstanding the significant correlations between life stress and other variables which some studies have demonstrated, they do not permit any causal inferences being made (Pestonjee, 1992; Sharma, 1988).

The types of tests that are frequently used in such studies are Cattell's 16PF personality test, Rotter's Locus of Control Scale, Eysenck's Personality Questionnaire, measures of Type A and B Behavior, the TAT, the Rorschach Inkblot Test, the General Health Questionnaire, Spielberger's State and Trait Anger Scale, Witkin's Field Dependence/Independence measures, and the ubiquitous Stressful Life Events scale. The tests administered are often standardized translated versions, or in some instances, the original English versions are employed, depending on the type of samples making up a given research study.

It is debatable to what degree such tests have meaning in a culture that is sharply different from the one in which they have been designed. Several critics have argued that the use of psychometric tests in cross-cultural research poses serious theoretical and methodological problems. Not the least of these problems are those related to the conceptual and functional equivalence of the concepts being measured and the methodological issues surrounding the translation and standardization of psychometric instruments. (See also the chapter by Takooshian, Mrinal, and Mrinal in this volume.)

A close examination of the research literature reveals that, to a large extent, Indian researchers have accepted the conceptual framework provided by Western—in particular, American—investigators. Few attempts have been made to understand and conceptualize stress which would reflect Indian perspectives. The word "stress" itself is not easily understood in India.

With no equivalent word for it in the languages of India, its meaning has to be gleaned from a variety of social, philosophical, psychophysiological, and somatic-symptomatic indices.

Ramchandra Rao (1983) has highlighted two Indian concepts, *klesha* and *dukha*, which correspond closely to the Western concept of stress. He derived these two concepts from the Indian indigenous systems known as *Samkhya Yoga* and *Ayurveda*. The word "klesha" refers to the stressor aspect, and the word "dukha" refers to the range of sorrowful experiences that individuals go through in the course of their interactions with the world around them. However, when klesha is translated into common parlance it refers to life's unavoidable and inevitable vicissitudes, and dukha refers to sorrow or unhappiness. Since sorrow, within the Indian philosophical tradition, is the fundamental part of the human condition (Radhakrishnan, 1923/1989; Zimmer, 1951/1989), it does not arouse the same concerns among Indians as the word "stress" does among Westerners. Nonetheless, Ramchandra Rao (1983) proposes an interesting line of investigation, which, sadly, has not found a great deal of favor among Indian investigators. In general, Indian researchers tend to show a greater affinity for Western conceptual and methodological frameworks in their investigations into stress.

Clearly, therefore, the concept of stress needs to be reconceptualized and operationalized in a manner that will reflect the unique cultural arrangements of India and allow genuine and meaningful cross-cultural comparisons. Otherwise, one is left with borrowed Western concepts and Western research instruments (which include translated and standardized psychometric tests) that may be applicable only to the Westernized English-speaking, minuscule minority of the Indian population. The findings from such research studies offer valuable insights into the problems related to organizational structures and executive stress and the like. Unfortunately, however, such studies do not allow us other than in superficial terms, to draw any firm conclusions about differences (and similarities) either within cultures or among cultures. Even more importantly, they do not tell us a great deal about the nature and experience of stress in the rest of the Indian population, most of whom continue to live a more or less traditional village life.

The fact that the majority of studies on stress have made use of psychological tests—either borrowed, translated, or specially designed—raises serious methodological concerns, not the least of which are those related to language and levels of literacy.

Language. India, unlike England and America, is not a monolingual country. Its multilingual structure is extremely complex. It has 18 officially recognized languages, and in addition, it has 33 other languages, which though not officially recognized, are spoken by over 100,000 people. To these languages must be added 1,652 dialects, each of which is spoken by people inhabiting a given region. People from other regions are not always able to understand and converse in those dialects. Any research undertaking that involves the use of questionnaires or rating scales or standardized tests would make sense only to the people conversant in the particular language or dialect in which the test has been constructed.

The level of understanding that a subject brings to bear to a questionnaire is related to several other factors: past experience with questionnaires, level of education, a "culture" of test-taking, and so on. Americans are socialized into a culture of taking tests, which starts in their primary schools; as a result, they have internalized the norms and rituals related to test-taking. Indian subjects, on the other hand, are more likely to find the experience bewildering. To present a test to a person who has never taken one before, even though the test may have been designed in the language the subject is literate in, does not mean that the test will be of any great relevance to the subject. Test-taking is an isolated experience to which only a minority of the Indian population has been exposed. Second, given the multiplicity of languages spoken in India, not to mention the dialects, it may make translations of tests from one Indian language to another an extremely dubious enterprise. This in turn would raise serious doubts concerning any interregional or interlinguistic comparative analysis.

Levels of Literacy and Education. The overall literacy rate of India is about 52 percent. The average literacy rate of the male population in India is about 64 percent and of females about 39 percent. There are striking variations in literacy rates among different states. In Kerala (South India), for instance, the literacy rate is about 90.59 percent, whereas in Bihar (North India) it is only 38.54 percent. There are urban/rural differences in rates of literacy. The rates of literacy are lower in the rural areas. Regular, large-scale migrations of people from rural into urban areas would create formidable, if not insurmountable, problems in the design of appropriate sampling frames, questionnaires, and the like.

CONCLUSION

We have seen that stress is a common human and animal experience. It occurs when our coping resources are overstrained. It is an unhealthy or nonspecific response of the body to external and internal stimuli and, if unchecked, leads to severe psychological, physiological, and psychosomatic disturbances. People exhibit obvious personality differences in their reaction to stressors and their consequent susceptibility to cancer and coronary heart disease (Eysenck, 1994; Sapolsky, 1994). There are, as we have seen, vast cultural differences in terms of what constitutes stressors.

As a result, there are fundamental differences in the management of stress between the two cultures. The methods of stress management in Western societies are too well known to merit a detailed discussion here. They range from a variety of conventional individual and group psychotherapies, which include behavior modification, relaxation techniques, yoga, time-management, cognitive restructuring, rational-emotive therapy, and confrontational techniques, to nondirective client-centered therapies and Freudian and neo-Freudian psychotherapies. There are also less conventional techniques of stress management, such as dance therapy, Alexander technique, art therapy, physical exercises, aerobics, and sex therapy. The efficacy of many of these therapeutic processes remains an unanswered-question.

In India, stress is not seen as a major problem in itself, which would require the attention of experts. For a problem to be construed as a serious medical or psychiatric problem, there must be a set of other accompanying somatic and/or psychological symptoms. As Rao (1986) points out, India does not have the trained psychiatric and psychological personnel to offer Western-type therapies to the people in India, with its estimated population of 1 billion people. What, then, are the therapeutic alternatives available in India?

1. There is a greater reliance on indigenous therapeutic treatments. The World Health Organization report (1978) points out that there are over 108 colleges of indigenous medicine in India, with over 500,000 practitioners of one of the following indigenous forms of healing: Ayurvedsa, Unani, and Yoga.

2. Yoga in all its variants appears to be the most popular form of treatment for stress and other psychological disorders all over the country. The evidence on the efficacy of yoga therapy is quite convincing (Satyavathi, 1988). Encouraged by the results of yoga therapy, Vahia (1982) has even suggested that yoga represents a new conceptual model of health and disease. Although several studies point to the effectiveness of yoga therapy (Bhole, 1981; Dharmakeerti, 1982; Neki, 1979; Nespor, 1982), it is not seen as a panacea for all types of disorders.

3. In India, stress (with its accompanying somatic symptoms) is also explained in terms of sorcery, bewitchment, and spirits (Kakar, 1982). The belief in magical explanations is widespread, and persons specially qualified to remove spells and exorcise evil spirits such as *bhoots, balas,* and *shaitans* are summoned by the family members of the afflicted person (Kakar, 1982).

4. Throughout India one can find an army of faith-healers, mystics, shamans, *pirs, bhagats, gurus,* and practitioners of ayurvedic and homeopathic medicine, who are accorded the same respect and veneration as medically trained psychiatrists in India. It would not be uncommon to find the concerned relatives of a distressed person consulting some, if not all, of the above specialists for effective treatment.

5. One must take into account the influence of religion in the management of stress. A token offering to one of the many deities, a visit to the local priest, a pilgrimage to a well-known shrine, or *darga,* and a meeting with a guru in whose curative powers the family has unshakable faith, are

some of the familiar therapeutic routes taken by the family members of the afflicted person. Occasionally, the family may consult with an astrologer or undertake a visit to a shaman or a well-known *pir*. Psychotherapists in India do not have the specialized and important role to play in the treatment of stress and other mental disorders that they do in the West. A Western-trained psychiatrist or psychologist is one of many in the long queue of consultants—and by no means at the head of the queue.

We have seen that to design an appropriate research study in India would ideally involve the researcher considering a bewildering set of problems, some of which are the present unending strain on urban areas due to massive migrations, colossal differences in levels of affluence, climatic variations, environmental pollution, differential levels of education, multiplicity of languages and dialects, and conflicting religious beliefs and attitudes. All these factors—singly or conjointly—are likely to have a strong bearing on the choice of the research project and its appropriate methodology and execution.

To this must be added a catalogue of serious constraints under which researchers are often expected to work in India: lack of appropriate technological and information-gathering facilities, poor communication systems, draconian financial constraints, difficulties of travel, accommodation, food, and other such factors. Research on stress may itself become a stressful experience!

Given the sheer volume of difficulties involved, it is hardly surprising that most of the research workers in India have often played safe and have relied on Western models and methods in their research endeavors.

Many Western academics do not always understand the extremely severe financial, occupational, and other constraints under which academics in India and other developing countries work. It needs to be recognized (and internalized by Western academics) that no culture or society has all the answers concerning the problems related to stress and its variants. *It is only when cultures and researchers meet on equal terms and as equal partners and express a genuine willingness to learn from each other that one might find tentative answers to questions that concern us all.*

11

Personality across Cultures

Rogelio Díaz-Guerrero, Rolando Díaz-Loving, and
Maria Lucy Rodríguez de Díaz

INTRODUCTION

Personality, Allport (1937) said early in the game, is simply traits, and every trait provokes a multitude of stimuli to be functionally equivalent. In his recent review, Revelle (1995) describes three dimensions for personality theory: (1) level of generality, the distinction that Allport had made under the terms of idiographic: pertinent to the study of particular cases or individual instances (e.g., persons, works of art) and nomothetic: pertinent to the search of general laws or theories that can cover whole classes of cases. Trait theorists, Revelle points out, "focus on systematic individual differences and similarities among people" (1995, p. 299); (2) level of explanation: from the gene to the society; and (3) level of functioning: illustrating that personality theories are not only theories of normality but of dysfunctional and specific level behavior (e.g., prisoners, professionals).

This chapter deals essentially with personality across cultures from the vantage point of trait theorists. Additionally it subscribes to Díaz-Guerrero's (1979, 1990, 1995) culture-counterculture theory of personality that postulates that the individual personality emerges from a perennial dialectic in cognition, between the information provided by a given culture and the information outpouring from the biopsychical needs, in the context of the information prevalent in a given ecosystem. The idiographic portion is furnished mainly by individual needs, and the nomothetic, mainly by culture.

This conceptualization emphasizes culture over biology and the ethnopsychological (Díaz-Guerrero, 1989) over universal dimensions of personality. While it perceives culture as a reservoir of adaptive human behaviors, it is open to the demonstration of both universal (Díaz-Guerrero & Díaz-

Loving, 1990) and ethnopsychologically unique personality traits. In the *1996 Annual Review of Psychology*, Bond and Smith declare: "Studies of implicit personality theory in any language studied to date indicate that a five factor model can describe the organization of perceived personality" (1996, p. 216). They are discerning when they include the "any language," for the studies with the five factor model have relied, as we shall see later, on a lexical hypothesis.

The fundamental question for our chapter on personality across cultures is: Are there indeed universal personality dimensions? For this purpose we assess the American psychology of personality and the cross-cultural vicissitudes of the five-factor model, and then compare them with several ethnopsychologically derived personality dimensions. The nature of the comparison forces what may be a useful insight about the nature of personality study on its own and across cultures and about the strengths and limitations of personality measurement.

AMERICAN PSYCHOLOGY AND THE BIG FIVE

It is probably a good guess to state that between 80 percent and 90 percent of everything that has ever been written about the psychology of personality and the development of tests of personality is the work of American psychologists. As commonly used, the term *American* is inaccurate. Geographically, it would be far more correct to speak of Meso-North American psychology. North America includes Canada, the United States, and Mexico. Nevertheless, beginning about mid-century, after 50 years of productivity and enthusiasm, came a period of close to 30 years in which there proliferated negative criticism and skepticism about psychology's capacity to measure personality traits. It is during these years that Skinnerianism grew strongly. Among Skinnerianism's positive aspects could be found a negative one, namely, the denial of the existence of anything that could be called personality. In contrast, beginning in the 1980s, enthusiasm began growing about the measurement of persistent traits of personality and the scientific conviction that this would prove useful for understanding and prediction in every field of applied psychology.

In his chapter on personality for the *1989 Annual Review of Psychology*, Carson (1989) dedicated only a small section to the "so-called person-situation controversy," feeling that this was a closed issue and pointing out that even Mischel (1973) abandoned his radical situationist point of view in favor of what appeared to be a frankly interactionist perspective. In the third section of his chapter, Carson speaks of the problem of identifying "the elements or dimensional units comprising personality." Indeed, beginning in the 1980s (Goldberg, 1981, 1982), many U.S. personologists became preoccupied with determining, not to what extent the traits measured by personality inventories consistently predicted the behavior of individuals, but if there were a limited number of basic, universal dimensions that described personality. This was what researchers like McCrae and Costa (1985, 1986, 1987), Costa and McCrae (1985, 1988), and Digman and Inouye (1986), as well as numerous collaborators and colleagues, have been highlighting.

These researchers have published a number of studies using various methods and different sources of data and applying varied factorial analyses in their effort to demonstrate that within the enormous literature dealing with traits and within personality inventories, such as Cattell's or Eysenck's, there existed only five dimensions. These, they argue, were the only basic, universal dimensions of personality. Such a preoccupation with finding universals was remindful of Osgood's efforts (Osgood, May, & Miron, 1975; Osgood, Suci, & Tannenbaum, 1967) leading to the demonstration that there were only three essential and universal factors for the subjective meaning of concepts and the efforts of psychometricians to ascertain a fixed number of abilities in the structure of intelligence.

It is in this vein that Digman and Inouye (1986) confidently state that previous studies of personality trait organization have frequently suggested that a five-factor model not only would be sufficient to account for the observed correlations in many studies but also would stand the test of replicability. In order to further specify the five robust factors of personality, they provided teachers with 43 adjectival scales to rate 499 Hawaiian children. Each mentor had to rate between 20 and 30 children. So that the teachers would master the psychological meaning of the scales, every concept in the scales was defined for them. Thus, for instance, the scale concept *considerate* was defined as "thoughtful of others; sensitive to others' feelings; cannot do things which hurt others' feelings; sympathetic when others are in trouble and tries to help" (p. 20). The factor analyses of the results of this research end up supporting the five-factor model. The authors actually obtain seven minimum factors, but the sixth and seventh are explained away and there remain but five, albeit strong, factors. The authors labelled the factors, combining the definitions provided by Norman (1963) with their own.

Factor 1. Surgency, which the authors call extraversion and define according to the following adjectival scales: talkative-silent; sociable-reclusive; adventurous-cautious.

Factor 2. Agreeableness. Here the authors agree with Norman's label. This is defined by the following scales: good natured-irritable; mild, gentle-headstrong; cooperative-negativistic; not jealous-jealous.

Factor 3. Conscientiousness. The authors again agree with Norman's label. This is defined by responsible-undependable; persevering-quitting, fickle; fussy, tidy-careless; scrupulous-unscrupulous.

Factor 4. Emotional stability, which the authors call neuroticism. This is defined by the following scales: calm-anxious; composed-excitable; nonhypochondriacal-hypochondriacal; poised-nervous, tense.

Factor 5. Culture. This the authors call openness or intellectuality. Defining scales
            are imaginative-simple, direct; artistically sensitive-insensitive; intellectual-
            nonreflective, narrow; polished, refined-boorish.

All these investigators show the strong implicit assumption that *these* five
dimensions of personality are universal. The first column of Table 11.1 presents these five factors—which may well be the key only to an English lexical
structure of personality—in order to compare them with another scale regarding the dimensions of human behavior.

To get an idea of the heuristics that this type of research has stimulated,
consider the questions that Digman and Inouye ask and the way they answer
them. First they ask: What are these factors? How are they to be interpreted?
Some researchers, the authors do point out, are weary of seeing these factors
as anything other than five classes of connotative adjectives. However, they
assert, others have attempted to relate these big five to personality theory.

Digman and Inouye cite as an example Digman and Takemoto-Chock
(1981), who are of the opinion that these five factors are at the very least
personality constructs that have been in the personality literature for a long
time. The authors also refer to Hogan (1983), who made an ambitious
effort to utilize the five factors in encasing personality from a sociobiological
frame of reference.

What is fascinating is that Digman and Inouye consider no other way of
interpreting these five robust factors of personality. Not even their insistence
that these factors have been found again and again in personality constructs
from research in the United States lead them to say that the five-factor
model may be a U.S. culture-bound phenomenon,[1] bound, at least, to the
"culture" created by personality researchers. This "culture" defends the
proper ways to elucidate the fundamental characteristics of personality. In
the early days of research, professional needs as well as a knowledge about
human psychology led personality researchers to design personality inventories. In contrast, today researchers of the big five appear to follow the
psycholexical tradition initiated by Allport and Odbert (1936) and strongly
revived by Norman (1963) with his "adequate taxonomy" of personality
attributes. In this tradition, despite utilizing diverse sources of data from
diverse groups in the United States, these researchers have continued to find
these five basic factors. Yet they fail to consider the possible alternative, nor
do they cite any author who contemplates that alternative, namely, that
these five basic measures, and their relative importance according to the
amount of variance for which they account, may be diagnostic of the basic
dimensions of personality present specifically in the Meso-North America
culture. In this connection, let us advance the hypothesis that although some
of those dimensions may be universal, we will find that their importance,
that is, their variance, is different from one culture to another. Granting also
that the basic dimensions across cultures remain around five, it is quite pos-

Table 11.1
Are There Basic Universal Dimensions of Personality? A Cross-Cultural Comparison

Factors	The Five Robust North American Factors	La Rosa's & Díaz-Loving's Nine Factors of the Self-concept in the Mexican University Student
1	Surgency or Extraversion (talkative–silent; sociable–reclusive; adventurous–cautious)	Social Affiliative (courteous–noncourteous; well brought up–badly brought up; amiable–rude)
2	Agreeableness (good natured–irritable; cooperative–negativistic; not jealous–jealous)	First Emotional (happy–sad; depressed–joyous; bitter–jovial; frustrated–realized)
3	Conscientiousness (responsible–undependable; persevering–quitting; tidy–careless; scrupulous–unscrupulous)	Social Expressive (quiet–communicative; introverted–extroverted; reserved–expressive)
4	Emotional Stability or Neuroticism (calm–anxious; composed–excitable; poised–nervous, tense)	Emotional Interpersonal (romantic–indifferent; affectionate–cold; tender–rude)
5	Culture or Openness (imaginative–simple, direct; artistically sensitive–insensitive; intellectual–nonreflective, narrow; polished, refined–boorish)	Occupational (responsible–irresponsible; punctual–not punctual; keeps promises–does not keep promises)
6		Third Emotional (impulsive–reflexive; temperamental–calm; aggressive–peace loving)
7		Ethical Factor (honest–dishonest; loyal–disloyal; truthful–liar)
8		Initiative (active–passive; fearful–risk taking; slow–fast)
9		Accessibility (accessible–inaccessible; treatable–untreatable; understanding–nonunderstanding)

sible that only some will be universal, whereas others will be what cross-cultural psychologists call emic, or idiosyncratic, for a given culture, group, nation, or habitat.

The second question contemplated by Digman and Inouye asks: Are the five factors sufficient? Do they account for the observed relationships, or are additional factors necessary? Here the authors conclude: "The big five robust factors, then, are not necessarily the verities of personality description. They represent the degree of complexity, the *dimensionality* of the personality rating process. These five dimensions also provide us with a quite stable framework within which we propose all verbal descriptions of personality are likely to be found" (1986, p. 20).

The third and perhaps most interesting question is stated by the authors as follows: If the number of factors in this domain is five, what are the reasons for this? They consider the possibility that the five traits may indicate not actual behavior but only the rater's perceptions of behavior. That trait ratings have been correlated highly with behavior, .85 in one case (Small, Zeldin, & Savin-Williams, 1981), and are also correlated with other independent measures make it unlikely that the traits are only perceptions of behavior rather than the behavior itself. However, something remains impressed in the minds of human beings. The authors have this to say: "Consider the teacher-raters of the study reported here. Faced with the prospect of getting to know 20–30 children, a teacher-rater forms some mnemonic *impression* of a given child to differentiate him or her from the other children. We suggest that this impression has five (at most 6) aspects to it and that this number is related to limits in our capacity for information processing" (Mandler, 1967; Miller, 1956; Digman & Inouye, 1986, p. 120).

In a latter study, Botwin and Buss (1989) recaptured the five-factor model of personality utilizing a behavior methodology for the structure of act-report data. However, their discussion of the meaning of these five dimensions remains not only ethnocentric but extremely specialized. How much of ethnocentrism is exclusively a matter of excessive specialization and the complexity of the subject with which one is dealing? This would be very difficult to decide. What is unequivocal, though, is that this degree of specialization together with the assumption that what is discovered in U.S. subjects is universal is clearly shown in all of these studies.

Digman (1990) reviews the progress made by the Big Five model. Perhaps because it is obvious in the literature on the subject, he fails to dedicate a section to the fact that most, if not all, of these studies depart from the hypothesis that a lexicographic analysis provides the best avenue to select the qualifiers for a trait model of personality. At the end of his review he says: "The why of personality is something else . . . perhaps we shall have to study personality with far greater care and with much closer attention to the specifics of development and change than we have employed thus far" (Digman, 1990, p. 436). Perhaps these scientists could at least have proposed that a *sine qua non* for the existence of personality, as characterized, is the development of a language.

Digman refers to the first cross-cultural comparisons including the Bond, Nakasato, and Shiraishi (1975) study referred to previously and, acknowledging slight disparities, concludes that the Big Five have appeared in at least five languages.

Several studies about the Big Five model, conducted in Italy, are summarized by Caprara, Barbaranelli, & Livi (1994). The authors are enthusiastic regarding the importance and utility of a model requiring only five dimensions for the description of personality. The first and more pertinent study refers to the emergence of five factors in the Italian lexicon. They use for their search the *New Italian Dictionary*. Screening it for adjectives, they selected 8,532, then four expert judges selected 1,337 according to their mean scores in utility for describing personality. Next 22 lay judges evaluated the 1,337 adjectives, which led the authors to choose those 492 showing the highest utility mean score. When self-evaluations collected on these adjectives were subjected to a principal components factor analysis with varimax rotation, five factors were retained. These were named in order: Conscientiousness, Extraversion, Quietness vs. Irritability, Selfishness vs. Altruism, and Conventionality. They say: "This solution seemed to deviate slightly from the 'canonical' Big Five" (Caprara, Barbaranelli, & Livi, 1994, p. 9). As they indicate, the first factor was mainly loaded with adjectives referring to conscientiousness and the second with adjectives referring to extraversion. Third and fourth factors appeared to define two dimensions that related to different blends of Agreeableness/Hostility and Emotional Stability and the fifth factor seemed to be closer to Openness to Experience than to intellect.

Next, the authors applied a reduced version of 260 adjectives from the prior list to 862 subjects. Those adjectives that showed the highest commonalties with the U.S. five-factors structure were selected. They obtained the same factor solution, but in a different order. Extraversion, Conscientiousness, Quietness vs. Irritability, Selfishness vs. Altruism, and Conventionality. This interesting finding leads the authors to affirm: "Apparently the Big Five can be extended to the Italian Lexicon but not in the 'canonical' way" (Caprara, Barbaranelli & Livi, 1994, p. 10). The authors conclude that the Five-Factor Model can be considered a taxonomic framework to map the hundreds of personality constructs developed in personality and in social and clinical psychology.

THE RISE OF AN ETHNOPSYCHOLOGY
OF PERSONALITY

> "Information is knowledge. Knowledge is power." More than ever, this saying is acquiring compelling force. . . . But with the extension of rela-

tionships with societies, this maxim of Auguste Comte becomes even
more pertinent. Those who lack knowledge see their fate shaped by others in the light of their own interests. . . . Millions of human beings are
subjected to oppressive forms of domination, both covert and overt,
because they lack access to knowledge.

                                                                (Schwendler, 1984, p. 3)

It was primarily with the financial support from UNESCO's project on
the exchange of knowledge for endogenous development that the International Union of Psychological Science called for a special conference to be
held in conjunction with the Twentieth International Congress of Applied
Psychology in Edinburgh, Scotland, on July 24–26, 1982. The goal of the
small international working group brought together by the congress was, in
the words of the organizers, "to document and evaluate the transfer of
psychological knowledge and its impact on traditional thinking patterns and
value systems in the Third World" (Sinha & Holtzman, 1984, p. 1). It was
likely that in this conference, attended by distinguished scientists and scholars mostly drawn from the Third World, the terms *indigenous psychology* and
indigenous concepts were utilized for the first time, with greater or lesser
import, by several of the participants.

The International Association for Cross-Cultural Psychology (IACCP), at
first interested in testing cross-cultural differences of what were thought to
be universal theories and concepts and aware of the growing evidence for
idiosyncratic characteristics of the people of different cultures, organized in
1986 for its Seventh International Congress of the IACCP, a symposium
entitled "Indigenous Psychologies." The symposium's success prompted its
coordinators, John Berry and Uichol Kim, to edit a book with the same
title (Kim & Berry, 1993).

For a number of highly debated historical reasons, including the extensive
mixing of blood and culture between Spaniards and native Indians in Mexico, interest in the psychology of the Mexican has been aroused ever since
the beginning of this century. It is following this tradition that Díaz-
Guerrero (1971) declared, "The psychologist in a developing country must
therefore dedicate his attention to his own culture; paralleling the empirical
constructs developed in the Anglo-American culture, he must pore over the
peculiarities of his own people and develop concepts that will fit their specific
and idiosyncratic nature. . . . He must think about how he can construct
tests that are valid totally and specifically to the mental characteristics of his
own people" (p. 13). The blueprint was there. The first dimension typical
of the Mexican culture was reported a year later (Díaz-Guerrero, 1972).
The article was titled "A Factorial Scale of Historic-sociocultural Premises
of the Mexican Family" (translated from the Spanish). By 1977, a number
of indigenous studies permitted Díaz-Guerrero to say, "The universality—

not the scientific character of psychology—is challenged by data suggesting the need for a sociocultural psychology of personality" (1977, p. 934).

The story ever since has been long, but it has ended in the need to start developing a new discipline, an ethnopsychology. At the heart of this effort is the concept of the historic-sociocultural premise (HSCP). It is pointed out that the most significant part of the human subjective world is given in generalized statements that are defended by an operational majority or a psychologically significant minority of the people of a given culture, generalizations that govern the thinking, the feeling, and, if the situation permits, the behavior of individuals of a given culture.

Several papers (Díaz-Guerrero, 1982, 1986, 1987; Díaz-Guerrero & Iscoe, 1984) have described up to 13 preliminary factorial dimensions of HSCPs so far discovered in the Mexican culture. Among them is *machismo*, defined by items supporting the superiority of males over females and the attitude that submissive women are the best. Another is *virginity*, defined by beliefs such as: "To be a virgin is of much importance for single women," and "A woman should be a virgin until she marries." Besides prescriptive dimensions, others deal with preferred styles of coping with stress, among them *affiliative obedience versus self-assertion*. These coping dimensions derive from generalized HSCPs that command the appropriate way of dealing with problems. One of the conclusions of the vast longitudinal cross-cultural study of child development by Holtzman, Díaz-Guerrero, and Swartz (1975) was that

Americans tend to be more active than Mexicans in their style of coping with life's problems and challenges. . . . An active style of coping, with all its cognitive and behavioral implications, involves perceiving problems as existing in the physical and social environment. The best way to resolve such a problem is to modify the environment. A passive pattern of coping assumes that, while problems may be posed by the environment, the best way to cope with them is by changing oneself to adapt to circumstances. . . . Many of the cross-cultural differences in the present study can be understood in terms of this general dimension of active versus passive coping style (p. 339).

A proper ethnopsychology, it is proposed (Díaz-Guerrero, 1989, 1993), must show that the factorial cultural dimensions discovered for a given community must relate significantly and meaningfully to independent measures of cognitive, personality, and moral development; to vocational interests; and to consequential sociological and economic variables measured in the same subjects. In the cited papers there are several tables with data obtained in earlier studies confirming various aspects of this assertion. An ethnopsychological approach demands that the studies be carried out to discover the crucial dimensions for every culture. The methods to be followed are not as important as the fact that the discovered dimensions are cogent, valid, and will bear meaningful relationships to psychological and other social science constructs in the given culture.

It is in this ethnopsychological context that La Rosa (1986) and La Rosa and Díaz-Loving (1988) decided to approach the problem of the dimensions in the self-concept of the Mexican. This was done with a methodology different from the historic-sociocultural premises approach. Their procedure is also different from what was utilized in the work dealing with the five fundamental dimensions, the big five. It is valuable to present it step by step.

La Rosa and Díaz-Loving defined the self-concept in abstract terms and then carried out several brainstorming sessions in which samples of Mexican senior high and university students of both sexes (N = 118) participated. In this way they identified five dimensions of the self-concept: *physical* (appearance and functioning); *occupational* (role and functioning in any type of work); *emotional* (intraindividual feelings and interpersonal interactions); *social* (satisfaction and dissatisfaction in social interactions); and *ethical* (congruence or incongruence with personal and cultural values). Next, using these extracted dimensions of the self-concept, they applied a questionnaire soliciting all the adjectives, positive and negative, that came to the minds of a more heterogeneous sample of 358 students of both sexes from the senior high and university levels. From the several thousand adjectives that resulted, those with highest frequencies and least synonymic overlap were selected (35 to 40) for each dimension. Next were two pilot studies with 200 subjects each, heterogeneous samples of students from high school to university level, in order to determine the most adequate antonyms for the adjectives. In one case, the antonyms selected were those most frequently chosen by students; and in the other, those with the highest negative correlation with their opposites (provided that they were psychologically significant). Then, with a semantic differential (SD) format and the concept *I am*, 418 students, again from heterogeneous samples, responded to 54 scales of selected pairs of adjectives resulting from the previous steps. A factor analysis was carried out to verify the construct validity. From 13 factors, 8 explained 59 percent of the total variance; being conceptually congruent, these 8 were selected. The pairs of adjectives for the physical dimension, which were rather heterogeneous, did not produce any physical factor. There were three emotional, two social, two ethical, and one occupational factor.

After careful psychological analysis of this pilot study, and the addition of congruent adjectival scales of the self-concept, a questionnaire containing 72 adjectival scales on a SD format were administered to the most heterogeneous sample, containing 1,083 students of both sexes. These had a mean age of 21 and a standard deviation of 4.32. From the factor analyses that followed, there resulted 9 congruent factors explaining 49 percent of the variance.

Factor 1 turned out to be a social affiliative factor with high loadings on courteous-discourteous; well brought up-badly brought up; amiable-rude.

Factor 2 was one of three emotional factors with highest loadings in happy-sad; depressed-contented; bitter-jovial; frustrated-realized. This was labeled intraindividual emotions or mood states.

Factor 3 was a social expressive factor with highest loadings in quiet-communicative; introverted-extroverted; reserved-expressive.

Factor 4 turned out to be an emotional interindividual factor. Its determinants were romantic-indifferent; affectionate-cold.

Factor 5 an occupational factor, has as its determinants responsible-irresponsible; punctual-not punctual.

Factor 6 the third emotional factor, had as its determinants impulsive-reflexive; temperamental-calm.

Factor 7 was an ethical factor, its determinants were honest-dishonest; loyal-disloyal.

Factor 8 was considered to be an initiative factor. Its determinants were apathetic-dynamic; slow-fast.

Factor 9 was the third social factor, defined by accessible-inaccessible; understanding-nonunderstanding (comprensive-incomprensive).

Importantly, La Rosa and Díaz-Loving (1988) connected these nine factors not only with the results of most previous ethnopsychological work but, cogently, with ordinary, quotidian personal and particularly social behavior of Mexicans. It is difficult not to conclude that hidden in these nine factors are the Mexican "big five."

It is interesting to add that La Rosa (1986), among other studies, included a correlation with Díaz-Guerrero's (1972) original scale of HSCPs of the Mexican family. All but one of the factors in his self-concept correlated significantly with affiliative obedience, but the first two correlated more.

ARE THERE UNIVERSAL PERSONALITY DIMENSIONS?

We have purposely selected two different research approximations to the understanding of human behavior. Personality can be defined in at least 50 different ways (Allport, 1937). James (1968) spoke of a social self and advanced that each individual has many a social self, each appearing in relation to different social groups. We feel that the Big Five in any culture may represent the modal quotidian behavior. We are convinced, however, that although this everyday behavior may approach universality, the five fundamental dimensions will be ordered differently in different cultures. Thus, for example, as is clear in Table 11.1, factor 1, socially affiliative, for the Mexicans may correspond with factor 2 for the Americans, though with a different tonality, and there is little doubt that factor 3 in the Mexican study is factor 1 of the Big Five.

In one case, exploring intracultural variation of the pathological correlates of sadness, and in the other comparing clinical patterns of depression with Holtzman Inkblot scores across Mexican and U.S. students, Díaz-Guerrero (1984, 1985) concludes that depression should be more prevalent in Mexico and anxiety in the United States. The only psychopathological factor among the Big Five is Factor 4, calm-anxious. The only factors resembling it among the nine Mexican factors are factors 2 and 6, but factor 2 has far more variance and is defined by sad-happy, depressed-joyous. Here there is not only a different tonality but the implication of a different etiology for possible pathological manifestations.

The United States factor 3 and the Mexican factor 5 have as their first determinant the adjectival scale responsible-irresponsible, with the interesting possibility that the Mexican factor 9 represents the U.S. factor 5. Readers will undoubtedly realize that in spite of these similarities, the Mexican patterning with two social and three emotional dimensions is interestingly idiosyncratic.

It is the strong impression of the authors of this chapter that apart from the five factors that describe the quotidianness of personality so well, the dimensions that critically intervene in specific human habitats like home, school, church, business, industry, and government do vary. One of the insights that can be gained from the present comparison across cultures is that clinical, educational, industrial, criminal, and social as well as other specialized psychologists must develop appropriate inventories that permit quantification of the behavioral dimensions functional in their respective realms. Thus, the big five factors of personality and the nine Mexican factors of the self-concept may aptly summarize expected ordinary, everyday personal and social behavior. The Big Five factors appear more useful to clinicians; the nine Mexican ones, to educational and industrial psychologists.

To detect and properly quantify universal traits across cultures requires a rigorous methodology, even if the order of factors, and thus their cross-cultural variance, obviously differs. In addition to maintaining a consistent focus and procedure, and conforming to the usual requirements of the cross-cultural endeavor, one should clearly define and enumerate the critical functions and behaviors typical of the ecosystems and/or habitats selected.

A recent study (Rodríguez de Díaz & Díaz-Guerrero, in press) can help illustrate many of the theoretical considerations in this chapter. Avendaño-Sandoval and Díaz-Guerrero (1990, 1992) had demonstrated construct validity for a trait of abnegation in senior Mexican high school students and in a laboratory experiment; behavioral abnegation. Abnegation had been defined as the behavioral disposition that others be before one or to sacrifice in their behalf. In addition, Flores-Galaz, Díaz-Loving, and Rivera Aragón (1987) had unexpectedly found, when trying to validate for Mexico, Rathus's (1973) 30-item schedule for assessing assertive behavior, that even when adding Mexican items to increase its reliability, the first factor, explaining 35.5 percent of the variance was one of no assertiveness! All of these characterizations were strongly remindful of the self-modifying coping style when facing problems expounded before.

Thus, Rodríguez de Díaz and Díaz-Guerrero (in press) felt that a radical test of the canonical Big Five would be to determine if they could explain the traits of abnegation and nonassertiveness found in several studies in Mexico.

First they consulted Dr. Lewis Goldberg regarding marker adjectival scales for the Big Five. He sent his very pertinent article "On the Development of Markers for the Big Factor Structure" (Goldberg, 1992). The criteria utilized in selecting the marker scales were that they loaded high on the factor and that they were easily translated into Spanish, thereby preserving their psychological meaning. A Big Five Inventory resulted with five to seven marker scales for each factor. These inventories, the Abnegation Inventory, developed by Avendaño-Sandoval and Díaz-Guerrero (1990) and the Nonassertiveness Inventory by Florez-Galas, Díaz-Loving, and Rivera Aragón (1987) were administered to 300 senior high school students (half females, half males, half in a government high school and half in a private high school).

A factor analysis of principal components with varimax rotation was carried out independently for each of the inventories. For the inventory of the Big Five there appeared nine factors with Eigen values above one. Only the first and the fifth factors could be fully interpreted by the canonical five. The first was defined by talkative-nontalkative (.71), reserved-demonstrative (.59), and introverted-extroverted (.59). The fifth, which apparently made good sense to these students, was clearly reproduced by three of its scales. The canonical factor 2 disappeared in this sample, factor 4 of the Big Five showed as second, defined by calm-angry (.75), relaxed-tense (.70), and steady-moody (.63). Factor 3 became a combination of scales of the U.S. factor 3 and factor 5.

The surprise was the fourth factor in this sample. It put together, independently of the other factors, hard-working (translated as *estudioso*)-lazy (.72), intellectual-nonintellectual (.60), and cooperative-uncooperative, a schooling factor very pertinent to their habitat.

Correlations between the factors of the Big Five in this study and the dimensions from the abnegation and nonassertiveness inventories showed factor 1 extraversion, correlating .19 with no abnegation and −.28 with nonassertiveness. Even scales were not included in a factor if they correlated less than .40. The Big Five failed to explain the largest part of the variance of the presumed typical Mexican traits.

We cannot forget the wise premise of a computer science teacher who said: "If a computer is fed garbage, the output will be garbage." If you feed a lexicographic model of personality to the computer, you will get a lexi-cographic understanding of personality. But if you feed it the adjective scales resulting from the brainstorm of literate Mexicans, you will get an idiosyn-cratic understanding of their personality. The latter appears far more func-tionally valid and more vernacular than the learned. Only research can ascertain the extent to which the lexicographic and the brainstorm models agree.

Given the importance, but also the complexity, of both universal and idiosyncratic dimensions for a comprehensive human psychology of "human nature," cross-cultural research on personality should be aware of and, when justifiable, utilize the two models in every effort. But this endeavor must remain parallel, in every culture, with the ethnopsychological that, as illus-trated in this chapter, may demand the development of interrelated idiosyn-cratic cultural, social, and personality dimensions.

NOTE

1. This in spite of the fact that Bond, Nakasato, and Shiraishi (1975), in an early study dealing with the results of the administration of a translation of Norman's (1963) 20 original scales to Japanese and Philippine students and comparing their results with Norman's, conclude that Factors 4 and 5 are construed in culturally specific ways.

12

Beliefs and Cultural Social Psychology

Albert Pepitone

The study of human history leaves little doubt about the importance of beliefs in the affairs of our species. We need only recall the accounts of the Holy Crusades, the witch trials, the strange concoctions that are said to cure cancer, the reading of horoscopes to foretell the future, the searches for elixirs of love, to realize that much of our cultural evolution over the past fifty thousand years may aptly be described as social behavior organized around beliefs. Despite their importance in the social life of human beings, however, the literature of social psychology contains little theory and research on the subject.

The neglect derives, to some degree, from the natural science "ideology" widely adopted by psychology in general and experimental social psychology in particular. The basic prescription of the ideology is that theoretical statements must be general across content domains and universal across cultural samples (Pepitone & Triandis, 1987). Accordingly, the processes and structures that constitute major theories of mainstream social psychology are assumed to hold whatever the content of the independent and dependent variables may be. Such theories are also viewed as universal; they hold in whatever culture the sample of subjects is embedded.

There is another related characteristic of contemporary social psychology that inhibits the study of beliefs—its "individuocentrism." Most theoretical processes and structures are conceived to operate in the autonomous individual mind (Pepitone, 1976, 1981). The structures and dynamics that exist in groups such as status hierarchies and shared culture play only a minor role in theories of social psychology or are ignored altogether.

Although content generality is a desideratum of theory, it is not easy to suppose that a meaningful theory of beliefs could be absolutely content-free.

Indeed, the content of beliefs is what appears to be of major theoretical interest. Thus, we would like to answer precisely such questions as why some people believe that illnesses are caused by the evil eye, whereas other people believe that the same illnesses are the wages of sin. To consider all beliefs as theoretically equivalent precludes the hypothesis that different beliefs serve different functions.

Finally, there is an ontological premise in contemporary social psychology—again derived from the natural science paradigm—that generates a disincentive to study beliefs. Many beliefs—for example, the belief in witches, in the soul, in angels—refer to entities that are not real in terms of any measurable material existence. Therefore, it is argued, beliefs are beyond the bounds of legitimate scientific inquiry! The crucial point missed in this "argument" is simply that people hold such beliefs. Whether or not the referents of the beliefs exist in an objective material order does not alter the reality that people believe in their existence. It is not merely the phenomenological reality for the believer that makes beliefs a legitimate subject of scientific study but the objective reality of their effects. It is relevant to note here that the large number of experiments in psychology on extrasensory perception (ESP) and other paranormal phenomena have been designed to refute the claim that extraordinary, unnatural psychic powers exist and rarely to show how and why people believe in such powers (Alcock, 1981).

Although the concept of belief is not entirely absent from the literature of social psychology, it has few if any distinctive conceptual properties and is connected only vaguely if at all to the phenomena of everyday life such as prayer, superstition, and fate. For example, in the field of decision making, belief refers to the individual's view of the "state of the world," specifically, the probability and the "payoff" (valence) of the possible outcomes. In social psychology proper, beliefs represent the cognitive dimensions of an object, the probability of its existence (Fishbein & Raven, 1962). In this meaning, beliefs have to be taken into account as a necessary variable in predicting behavior from attitudes.

THE DEFINITION AND CLASSIFICATION OF BELIEFS

The idea of the existence of things captures the essential meaning of beliefs and brings us to a working definition: Beliefs are relatively stable cognitive structures that represent what exists for the individual in domains beyond direct perception or inference from observed facts. More particularly, beliefs are concepts about the nature, the causes, and the consequences of things, persons, events, and processes. Such concepts are more accurately described as social constructions that are part of a culture and have guided the socialization of those who share that culture. In this definition, beliefs are conceived as cognitive structures that are more or less adopted from

Table 12.1
A Classified Sample of Important Beliefs

SUPERNATURAL	
Religious	god(s), human soul, resurrection, reincarnation, angels, devils, holy shrines, faith healing
Secular	fate/destiny, good or bad luck, superstition, witchcraft, evil eye
Paranormal	telepathy, precognition, psychokinesis, animal magnetism, orgone
Personality	ability to control life events, genius, sexuality, characterology
Society	origins of class structure, economic systems
Culture	ethnicity, race
Moral Justice	distribution of resources, punishment of bad deeds and reward of good deeds

what is already there in the culture rather than entities formed from the raw material of social perception, inferred through empirical observations, or deduced via a system of logic from premises and assumptions. We would have to add an obvious feature of valuation to this essentially cognitive definition. To "believe in" means to endorse, to favor, to be committed to, and so on. The conflation is not always the case, however, and there is a necessary conceptual distinction to be made between the belief about "what is" and the value "what should be." Finally, consistent with the cultural origin of beliefs, we may observe that beliefs are exclusively human; no orangutan believes in witchcraft or in the Second Coming of the Messiah.

The task for the cultural psychologist is to construct empirically based theories that support general propositions about the structure of beliefs, their origins, and their psychological functions in individuals and groups. As in the study of other psychological phenomena, the first order of business is to organize and classify the phenomena. In a field that is as yet so uncultivated, there are several options in undertaking this first step. One provisional classification—which can be elaborated and corrected as knowledge accumulates—can be seen in abbreviated form in Table 12.1. Arguably, included in the principal categories and subcategories are the most important beliefs in the human repertoire, beliefs that have had the greatest influence in the history of the species. Although the categories in Table 12.1 are neither exhaustive nor independent of one another, they have a common denominator: The objects, agents, processes, powers, and so on, to which the beliefs in these categories refer are nonmaterial and not verifiable by the logic and methods of physical or social science. They contrast with the vast body of material beliefs about the natural world of physics and biology. The distinction is not always clear-cut, but we may set aside the boundary issue in order to pursue the analysis of nonmaterial beliefs.

The plan of this chapter is to survey a number of important beliefs and their essential properties, to specify research and theoretical issues, and to present some recent research findings that bear on such theory, specifically on the functions of beliefs.

RELIGIOUS BELIEFS

Besides the variety of deities, holy spirits, angels, the soul, and other divine agents and powers, the large category of religious beliefs includes sacred objects, places, and supernatural processes such as resurrection and reincarnation. Religious beliefs have a special quality that beliefs in the other categories lack, an awesome and mystical quality connoted by the terms *holy*, *sacred*, and *divine*. In the cognitive structures of the members of most religious groups, the beliefs—in divine laws, in the efficacy of prayer, in life after death, and in holy objects, places, and events—tend to exist together in organized structures. At the center of such structures is the belief in a God or Gods who are thought to be more or less omniscient and omnipotent spiritual agents, and the belief in the soul, the spiritual center of the person. Also in this more or less organized structure are beliefs about the functional relations among beliefs—belief theories. For example, through prayer, sacrifice, propitiation, and obedience to God's laws, the soul may be purified and qualify for salvation and admittance to an eternal afterlife or higher spiritual order of reincarnated existence.

A psychological question of deep interest is how such religious beliefs, built as they are on intangible beings, powers, and insubstantive spirits utterly outside the material realm, can be so widely diffused in the world and so resistent to extinction. How can people continue to believe when what they believe in cannot be perceived or empirically demonstrated in terms of objective criteria? One observation relates to the definition of beliefs given previously: The maintenance of a belief or of faith in general (faith may be regarded as a metabelief in the truth of beliefs) does not depend in any simple way on empirical evidence. What is called religious experience—for example, feeling the presence of God or seeing tears in the eyes of statues—may reinforce beliefs and may convert predisposed individuals into full-strength believers, but no such sensory events are necessary to maintain the belief that God and saints exist. Indeed, according to dissonance theory, beliefs about God and salvation can be strengthened following an objective disconfirmation of the latter's existence (Festinger, Schachter, & Riecken, 1958). Nevertheless, from a theoretical perspective, one can assume that beliefs are maintained because they serve functions for individual and group.

A key objective for theory and research is the specification of such belief functions.

SECULAR SUPERNATURAL BELIEFS

Compared with religious beliefs, the supernatural beliefs classed as secular are less a part of organized, differentiated structures; typically, they are relatively simple structures independent of one another. Secular supernatural beliefs also lack the special qualities of holiness, sacredness, and so on. However, the secular-religious distinction is not always consistent. In one culture, a belief may be secular whereas in another the same belief is religious. We will briefly examine some important secular beliefs and their properties.

FATE

Fate is probably one of the oldest and most influential beliefs in the human repertoire. Its relationship with systems of religious beliefs is not uniform. In the Islamic religion, fate is that which is ordained by Allah. More generally, fate is an impersonal power that is part of a cosmic belief system; hence the close link to astral movements. In many cultures certain life events and outcomes are normatively and ritually believed to be determined more or less by fate: when and how one will die, who one will marry, whether there will be children, and so on. Whether actual life events of such kind are attributed to fate appears to depend on their characteristics. Everyday observations suggest that the life events interpreted as products of fate are unexpected and perceived as coincidences with uniquely meaningful outcomes for those affected, outcomes that are particularly relevant to their past experience ("uncanny") or contrary to what might reasonably be expected ("perverse" and "ironic") and, therefore, apparently purposive and predestined. Generally, such "meant to be" outcomes could not have been avoided or controlled. In regard to future events (destiny), however, horoscopes and various forms of divination may help to find out what fate has in store and so provide some possibility for avoiding or, in the case of positive outcomes, facilitating the occurrence of the event. At the concrete cultural level, one finds varieties of fate-beliefs. In the Hindu belief system important conditions of life such as one's caste position, chronic illness, or state of poverty are functions of one's Karma, a metaphysical index of the individual's spiritual purity based on past deeds. Karma is an inexorable law of fate; one reaps what one has sown. With respect to one's future existence, the form of one's reincarnated life outcome is determined by the Karma that one is creating by the deeds of the present. The belief in Karma is thus both a belief in fate and a belief in individual control.

We may note that many important and unexpected events of life are attributed to a purposive God rather than to fate, including illnesses, accidents, failures, and successes, even when those who experience such outcomes are in no way deserving, when it is not a matter of divine justice; that is, when it is not God's punishment or reward. It is commonly believed that "God moves in mysterious ways." In most such instances it is a powerful and absolute belief in God that constrains this preferential interpretation. We would not be surprised to find, however, that characteristics of the outcome have an influence. Thus, for example, God is chosen over fate when the unexpected outcome makes no connection to past experience, or when it is not an ironic coincidence, thus precluding the idea that it was predestined.

WITCHCRAFT

The belief in witches including varieties of "satanism" still flourishes in many parts of the world, and there is evidence that it was an element in the culture of our Cro-Magnon ancestors. In its essential form, witchcraft refers to supernatural powers employed by extraordinary persons through incantations, curses, trances, and other "black magic" for the purpose of harming persons or damaging their property. Unlike fate and God, conceived as supernatural agencies, witchcraft is practiced by real human beings, albeit "special" ones. Like the belief in fate, the belief in witches is sometimes connected to religious beliefs. Thus, in the period of the European witch trials, from the fifteenth to the seventeenth centuries, the witch was believed to be the creation of the Devil (Trevor-Roper, 1967), and as such, a threat to the Church. It was symptomatic of the evil of Manicheanism, which placed the Devil on a par with God in a titanic struggle for the human soul. Although such diabolism has declined and the Church no longer holds inquisitions, there are today priests who specialize in exorcising witches and other evil corrupters. African types of witchcraft, on the other hand, do not involve diabolism and are not connected with institutional religion.

The belief in the evil eye—in the power of the eye to harm—may be included in the category of secular supernaturalism. The evil eye is a concept similar to that of witches in that it is a supernatural power exercised by human beings against human beings with harmful consequences. Whereas witches operate in many modalities and have a special talent for evil that makes them extraordinary persons, the evil eye operates only through the visual medium, and the carrier or launcher of the eye is no one special. Those who have the eye are not easy to identify; indeed, those who have it may not know it. There are as many varieties of the beliefs about how to avoid the eye or minimize its effects as there are about who possesses the eye, what causes it, and who are its favorite targets (Maloney, 1976).

LUCK

The most common secular supernatural belief, which in one form or another is widely diffused throughout the world, is the belief in luck, a mysterious power that affects outcomes favorably or unfavorably, over and beyond the influence of ability, motivation, and chance. The power of luck is implicit in the great store of superstitions that make up a culture's folklore. If X happens (a mirror breaks, a black cat crosses your path, and so on), then an unspecified misfortune will befall you. The agent of fortune or misfortune is rarely identified or is conceived to be semihuman, an organism with some humanoid features, yet of a distinct species such as elves or fairies. The belief in luck plays a prominent role in gambling contexts, where outcomes are determined by objective laws of chance. In such contexts, the deliverer or withholder of luck is often personalized, as are the ways designed to invite positive interventions. Thus, bigtime gamblers make "side bets" of only respectful size and magically importune the favors of the mysterious Lady Luck by, for example, blowing on dice or wearing a lucky article of clothing. It is also commonly believed that luck is bestowed upon certain individuals like an endowment. When we say, "She is a lucky person," we imply that she is characteristically favored by the agent of good fortune. Omens, auguries, and auspicious signs are beliefs about mysterious powers that are of the same type as luck. Luck tends to be attributed to life events and outcomes that are inexplicable in terms of chance ("against the odds"), to ability (a case of "dumb luck"), or to drive ("I wasn't even trying hard"). Moreover, luck is not usually attributed to the most tragic misfortunes of life. The unexplained death of a child, for example, would rarely be blamed on an unlucky day or on the mischief of an evil elf. Further, the attribution to luck is not necessarily symmetrical between negative and positive outcomes. Although a major tragedy is not likely to be a matter of bad luck, winning $10 million in the state lottery could be assigned to luck. Such a gratuitous outcome would hardly seem to be the work of God.

CHANCE

In everyday discourse *luck* and *chance* are often used interchangeably; even the dictionary defines one in terms of the other. As beliefs, however, the two concepts are different. When we consider the belief in chance, we leave the realm of the supernatural, although psychologically we do not necessarily enter the material realm of science. The ordinary believer does not internalize statistical inference theory or the probabilistic laws of quantum theory. To the believer in chance, there are no personal or impersonal agencies responsible for the outcome; the characteristics of the person affected by a chance outcome cannot have had anything to do with the outcome. Only at a given point in time did random and independent elements concatenate to produce the outcome. Before or after the outcome, the random assembly would have been different. Finally, the belief in chance does *not* usually refer to life events that are extremely improbable and extremely important. Even in the domain of natural events like earthquakes and volcanic eruptions, the belief that chance is the exclusive cause is rare among the numerous attributions that people spontaneously make.

PSYCHOSOCIAL BELIEFS

The psychosocial category encompasses a large variety of beliefs that refer to individual abilities and the structure and dynamics of groups, crowds, and institutions, as well as to culture (beliefs that people hold about their own cultural traits and those of other groups). Psychological beliefs most commonly refer to mental or personality processes or underlying structures that enhance existing abilities or create special and unique ones. In addition to beliefs in so-called paranormal abilities, the category includes the ability to induce trances in oneself or others and to circumvent, or break down, another's will. Historically, the belief in animal magnetism, Mesmer, Svengali, and Rasputin illustrate the psychological genre. Beliefs in phrenology and similar concepts about the structure of the mind are also assignable to this category. More generally, the belief that self and others in certain ways and in certain areas have the ability to control to some degree life events and outcomes, including one's ultimate destiny, properly belongs to the psychosocial category of beliefs. It is understood, of course, that such events and outcomes—a successful career, a long and healthy life, a durable marriage and devoted children, and so on—are judged to be the result of multiple agents of control such as political and social support, fate, biological assets, or God's help. It is quite common to observe that when measured against objective criteria, the attribution of the source of control as well as the amount of control is distorted, sometimes either extremely exaggerated or underestimated. In such cases we may talk of "illusory" control (Langer, 1975). A distinction should be made, however, between such distortions and beliefs that are wholly supernatural. The latter are based on insubstantive and unmeasurable psychic energies, abilities, and powers, either indigenous or accessible from external sources, such as beliefs about "will power," "mind over matter," or therapeutic crystal. The distinction is relevant to the recent explosion of beliefs about diet, exercise, and health, particularly in the United States, which may be described as a revolution of consciousness in which people believe that they have almost unlimited control over their bodies, health, and longevity. Although such beliefs may have some validity, they are often illusory, some even falling frankly into the category of magic, alongside beliefs about fountains of youth, the rejuvenating effects of ground rhinocerous horns, and the cancer-curing properties of apricot pits.

Beliefs about society abound, including beliefs about the origins of class and caste system, economics, organized religion, conflict between groups, and political power dynamics. Beliefs about culture include beliefs about the "kind of people" we or they are—how good, how intelligent, how much control they have over specific life events, and so on.

MORAL BELIEFS

In general, moral beliefs are concerned with states of goodness and rightness, and the ways to achieve those states. One prominent set of beliefs or values in the moral domain relates to justice. Justice is not a unitary concept; there are several quite distinct states to which this belief refers, including, for instance, the alleviation of political oppression, equal treatment in juridical judgments about criminal penalties, and the distribution of resources in proportion to merit. In the context of religion and ethical philosophy, justice may refer to a moral order in which the good are rewarded and the bad punished. Such concepts are often connected directly or indirectly with beliefs in God. Justice in all human affairs is believed to be a major preoccupation of the Judeo-Christian and Muslim God. God not only is just but also believed to have more or less control over the world to bring about justice.

METHODOLOGY, THEORY AND RESEARCH

The beliefs described in the foregoing survey have to be seen as part of normative prescriptive systems that evolve and function in cultural and subcultural groups. This view that beliefs are shared norms that operate in groups raises an important question about whether universal theories are possible. If the beliefs of any culture are unique, are we not locking ourselves into a cultural relativism in all things? It is true that the social psychologist who adopts the position that beliefs are cultural products of groups cannot assume a priori that belief theories are universal, but it would be equally fallacious to rule out the possibility of universality (Pepitone, 1986). For one thing, inasmuch as culture is created to address basic biological needs, there is the presumption that at some deep level cultures are the same. Second, it must be kept in mind that theory is an abstract representation of phenomena. Even though beliefs may vary in many aspects across cultures, theories may be stated in terms of more abstract universals such as belief categories used in the present analysis or belief functions. Finally, there is ethnographic evidence that religious, magical, and other supernatural beliefs exist everywhere in the cultural atlas (Murdock, 1945). In any case, it is a premise of cultural social psychology that cross-cultural research is necessary to formulate hypotheses and to determine empirically the degree of their generality. The final section of this chapter discusses research that focuses on the functions of beliefs.

THE PSYCHOLOGICAL FUNCTIONS OF BELIEFS

As with beliefs themselves, there are many ways to classify their functions. Four functions may be specified in simple propositional form.

1. Emotional: Beliefs serve directly to reduce emotional pain or stress associated with fear, hope, anger, awe, uncertainty, and so on. For example, the belief in the efficacy of prayer provides a feeling of security.
2. Cognitive: Beliefs provide cognitive structure that gives a sense of control over life events. Thus, as Evans-Pritchard (1937) has hypothesized, the belief in witches provides an explanation of misfortunes.
3. Moral: Beliefs function to create a sense of moral order and certainty, the impression that goodness begets good effects and badness has bad effects; they also function to reduce moral "pain" through regulating the allocation of moral responsibility between self and others. For example, the belief that a misfortune was caused by fate allows the believer to disclaim responsibility for it.
4. Group: Beliefs serve to enhance group solidarity by providing people with a common identity. Emil Durkheim's (1912/1915) analysis of ancient totemic religions concluded that totem worship was the symbolic expression of societal identity and power. In modern society, social affiliations are often based explicitly on religious creed and practice.

Research on Belief Functions

The direct emotional stress-reducing function of beliefs is perhaps the most intuitively obvious—especially in the case of religious beliefs. Beliefs in God, saints, faith-healing, and life after death are indeed explicitly recommended by spiritual leaders for the lifting of hopes and the relief of despair and suffering. Surprisingly, there has not been much empirical documentation of this commonly supposed function in the research literature. A recent experiment, however, allows for the inference that religious beliefs have an anxiety-reducing function. Shrimali and Broota (1987) studied two groups of patients in a Delhi clinic—those awaiting what doctors classified as major surgery, and those awaiting minor surgery. A third sample of subjects was randomly selected from among healthy nonhospitalized persons. Questionnaire items selected from a standardized religiosity scale were administered before and after the surgery (successful in all cases) to measure the strength of belief in God, prayer, and so on. In addition, part of an anxiety scale was administered before and after the surgery. Shrimali and Broota found that preoperatively, those patients expecting major interventions scored significantly higher on religiosity than those about to have minor surgery and the healthy subjects. After surgery, however, their religiosity was no different from that of the other samples. The pattern of mean scores on the anxiety scale was parallel; that is, the patients awaiting major surgery were significantly more anxious than the other samples, whereas after surgery their level of anxiety was no different.

The compelling and straightforward interpretation of these results is that the patients in the sample subjected to the strongest life threat most strongly affirmed their religiosity. When the threat passed, the belief weakened and returned to baseline.

Although this functional interpretation is intuitive, there is what appears to be an inconsistent effect commonly observed. After avoiding an almost certain injury or death in an accident—after a "close call" or "near miss"—it is sometimes observed that religious beliefs often become *stronger*—at least for the period immediately after the threat has passed. There is no inconsistency here, however. In contrast to successful surgery that in most cases did away with the medical problem once and for all, avoidance of injury and death in what are classed as accidents does not necessarily preclude future dangers, particularly when they are created by others. The Shrimali and Broota research, of course, has to be repeated in a way that rules out demand characteristics; but if their findings hold up, they would be consistent with other common observations that when people reach old age and begin to contemplate the nearness of death, especially if they suffer from infirmity or progressively debilitating disease, they become more religious. That the religious impulse is felt when people face serious danger can be observed in a wide range of situations—prayer for the desperately ill, by those on a sinking ship, and on the battlefield.

Of deeper theoretical significance than the conclusion that beliefs are functional is the proposition that beliefs are *selectively* functional. The idea comes from an evolutionary perspective. In the beginning of human history, shared beliefs about animistic and naturistic powers, as well as magic, served to reduce the emotional stress of our primitive ancestors and provided cognitive structure about the large domain beyond perception about which there was complete ignorance. Further, such prescriptive belief norms that evolved from primitive religion and magic were retained and modified on the basis of their effectiveness in increasing the welfare of groups or important members of groups. Finally, we assume that like tools, beliefs became increasingly specialized to deal with the important events of life around which ignorance flourished. In a recent experiment, Saffiotti (1990) tested the hypothesis that for people who share a culture, beliefs function selectively to provide cognitive structure about life events, that a selective correspondence exists between certain kinds of events and beliefs. Members of a culture do not themselves have to believe in a given agent or power to know the normative functions of the belief and define the kinds of events for which the beliefs are functional.

Saffiotti presented to her sample of more than a hundred middle- and lower-middle-class college students a set of audiotaped descriptions of life events that the subject was to imagine happened to him or to her. (We ignore here other conditions of the experiment). There were two variations of each of eight types of life events, for which, on the basis of pilot research and common observation, certain beliefs were hypothesized to be most effective in providing cognitive structure. After hearing each event, subjects were asked to comment, to "interpret" what had happened. These open-ended comments were then reliably analyzed and coded into categories representing explanations and theories as to why the event occurred, attributions of responsibility for the event, evaluations of the event in moral or material terms, and other cognitive structure. More specifically coded in such categories were agents, powers, and processes such as God, fate, luck, chance, and laws of moral justice. Before presenting some of Saffiotti's results, it will be useful to highlight some of the hypothesized properties of beliefs and the corresponding kinds of events for which such beliefs selectively provide cognitive structure. It should be understood that the properties specified are not exhaustive, nor are they stated in their final, most precise form. It is also important to note that Saffiotti's results are based on a culturally diffuse North American sample. Preliminary results from West European studies, however, are on the whole consistent with Saffiotti's basic hypothesis. (Studies conducted in the Netherlands and Italy confirm the hypothesis that beliefs function selectively to provide explanations, but show variation in the beliefs used in Saffiotti's life event cases.)

God. For most believers, even if they are not strong believers, God would be the agency selected to explain sudden recovery from a fatal illness that cannot be explained in medical, material terms—miracles. For instance, cases of spontaneous remission of tumors that are medically inexplicable are typically attributed to God's intervention.

Fate. Fate-determined events are those that are perceived to be predestined and purposive. The attribution to fate is likely when important events are unexpected but meaningful so that they can be interpreted as meant to be. For instance, when long-lost brothers meet in a place where neither has been before, attribution to fate is likely.

Luck. Events for which luck is the normative interpretation are against the odds or beyond chance, and yet not the result of ability, motivation, or social agency. Winning nine out of ten consecutive card games is what the power of luck would explain to a player with only average skill.

Chance. The belief in chance selects for events that are not "against the odds," not of world-shaking significance—for example, winter colds, accidents on roads during rush hour, or where alternatives to an event are few (e.g., the roulette wheel stopping on black) and appear to have no determinative agent behind them.

Table 12.2
Percentage of Subjects (n = 103) Who Select Given Beliefs in Interpreting
Given Life Events

Life Event	God	Fate	Luck	Chance	Justice (neg)	Justice (pos)
miracle recovery	<u>49.5</u>	2.9	4.9	0.0	0.0	3.9
contrary to expectation	11.7	<u>31.1</u>	12.6	18.4	0.0	1.9
against odds	4.9	10.7	<u>53.4</u>	6.8	0.0	0.0
casual meeting	1.9	1.0	2.9	<u>45.6</u>	0.0	0.0
embezzler has losses	1.0	1.9	8.7	4.9	<u>66.0</u>	0.0
good person is rewarded	3.9	5.8	13.6	5.8	0.0	<u>52.4</u>

Justice. Events that are interpreted by beliefs in justice are those associated with definitely positive (morally attractive) or negative (morally unattractive) character or behavior on the part of the person who is affected by the event. Thus, a "positive" law of justice is attributed to an unexpected, ad hoc event that results in a large benefit to a person with a positive character or history of positive deeds. A "negative" law of justice is cited when an event is punishing or causes losses to a person with negative moral standing. Justice is sometimes mediated by transcendental impersonal agencies similar to fate or by God.

Table 12.2 presents the percentage of subjects whose comments on each of six life events were coded as the primary or only explanation or causal attribution that explicitly mentioned God, fate, luck, or the laws of justice. Because of space limitations, omitted are descriptions of the events that select for the belief in material causation and the belief that moral transgression can lead to self-destruction. The results are consistent with what is presented in the table.

If one inspects the diagonal of Table 12.2, a clear correspondence is seen between the life events listed in the left column and the beliefs selected by subjects to explain or otherwise provide cognitive structure about them. The beliefs predicted to provide what was hypothesized to be the normatively appropriate explanations and other cognitive structure for given life events, which we have described above, were in fact selected for this purpose more often than other beliefs. Indeed, Saffiotti found such selective correspondence—when the modal frequency of subjects mention the normatively appropriate belief—in all but two of the sixteen life events presented to the subjects for interpretation.

CONCLUDING COMMENT

This chapter has specified some of the properties of a small number of the most important beliefs in the human repertoire, from the diverse categories of the supernatural, secular, psychological, and moral. It has emphasized the view that beliefs are norms, shared concepts about agents, powers, events, psychological processes, and states of goodness and rightness. It has also described some research findings that lend support to the theory that beliefs are selectively functional. This chapter, of course, is only the beginning of an analysis of belief systems. Much needs to be explained; but first much more needs to be observed.

IV

International Interactions

13

Multinational Enterprises

Justin P. Carey

The bird of time has but a little way
To flutter—and the bird is on the wing.
> Omar Khayyám, *Rubáiyát* (c. 1100), trans.
> by Edward Fitzgerald, 1857

These are the times that try men's souls.
> Thomas Paine, *The American Crisis* 1776

Plus ça change, plus c'est la même chose.
> French proverb

Mandarin Chinese does not have a single ideograph to express the concept written in English as *crisis*; instead, it uses two: *wei gee*, translated as "dangerous opportunity." As psychologists confront the dual crises of growing bureaucratization and politicalization of our profession, the *wei* aspect of our situation is obvious. It is the *gee* to which this chapter is dedicated.

A GLOBAL PHENOMENON

The current opportunity for psychologists is the Multinational Enterprise, or MNE, with positions opening now and benefits predicted to continue well into the present century. The MNE is a cyclical occurrence, rising, growing, maturing, and dying throughout recorded history. Consider the ancient Phoenician traders and the more recent British East India Trading Company (1600). The modern phenomenon is the exponential growth rate in the number of organizations entering the MNE category, from relatively few companies at the end of World War II to an extrapolation of close to 100 percent by the year 2001.

MNEs may be any type of organization: for profit, nonprofit, private, governmental, manufacturing, distributing, servicing, and so on. All share the characteristic of conducting business across national borders. Wherever the home office is located, one or more host countries will be involved in production or marketing of goods and/or services. An increasing number of MNEs are moving into the upper range of "multinational" and are becoming truly *global* in their scope.

MANAGEMENT PROBLEMS AND PSYCHOLOGICAL SOLUTIONS

As an MNE adds more nations to its enterprise, management problems develop, not by arithmetic but by geometric progression. This is so because management is essentially the task of managers getting things done through other people, and the behavioral performance of those other people is going to be influenced by their culture. As the MNE interacts with multiple cultures, it becomes aware that the reliable and validated operational procedures standardized for successful business in the home country are not working as projected. If management is not culturally sensitive, it may not become aware of the cultural basis of the problem in time to create an effective solution.

This problem area of cross-cultural conflict is built into the nature and concept of the MNE. The relevance of effective resolutions and solutions to success or failure of the enterprise in a given host nation is receiving increasing emphasis in business school curricula. The objective is to train managers who are aware of cultural diversity, who respect those whose culture is different from their own, and who seek solutions that are compatible with both the demands of the host culture and the legitimate needs of the MNE.

The business schools are not training cross-cultural psychologists; that mission belongs to psychology. But the business schools are educating MNE managers to the need for expert advice and guidance on cross-cultural matters to safeguard their operations across cultural borders. This opens the door to countless opportunities for a professional position with an MNE as staff officer or consultant for cultural relations, for psychologists who are competent in cross-cultural psychology by virtue of training, knowledge, and experience. Responsive departments of psychology will offer courses in cross-cultural psychology to their undergraduate and graduate students.

Students of cross-cultural psychology who are interested in affiliation with an MNE will be well advised to also take, at a minimum, the undergraduate Introduction to Management course and either the undergraduate or graduate course in International Management. Practical work experience in business or industry, domestic or foreign, will be helpful. A minor in Management to accompany the major in Psychology is valuable. It is realistic to say that some business background will significantly improve the perception of you by the MNE interviewer as not only a cross-cultural expert but as a colleague who can speak the language of management and who has an appreciation of the needs and objectives of the organization.

ORGANIZATIONAL BEHAVIOR

Every human being belongs to multiple organizations—from family to firm—each with its own collection of cultural characteristics. The categories of these variables are shared in common by the organizations, for example, values and attitudes, ethics and morality, perceptions and misperceptions. But each organizational culture is unique in having its own combination of specific differences within those general categories. As not a few frustrated multinational managers have exclaimed, "The devil is in the details!"

Frustration is the bitter fruit of ignorance. The antidote is knowledge of Organizational Behavior (OB). OB is the study of the behavior of individuals and groups in organizational environments. People (and their cultures) are different; no matter how much physical, emotional, or intellectual similarity is perceived, people are still different. Psychologists know this; many managers need to learn it.

OB is the ultimate interdisciplinary study, drawing with varying degrees of emphasis from the theories and practices of other subjects: anthropology to zoology. A welcome trend in recent OB courses and textbooks is attention to the importance of multinational variables in the operations of organizations today. As the trend continues, the multinational dimension will be integrated into every aspect of OB, replacing the back-of-the-book and end-of-the-course treatment that marked its birth.

Traditionally, the study of OB has emphasized theories, research findings, and practical applications that were "made in the U.S.A." The subjects were drawn from U.S. population groups, for example, employees and employers, the output of U.S. educational and vocational systems. The longstanding assumptions of similarity of people, that is, a worker is a worker (even though bosses are different!), led to problems with the workforce rather than to solutions derived from new perceptions. Productivity, meaning profit, was at stake. Necessity mothered the invention of OB research and development centered on the awareness and acceptance of multicultural influences and differences affecting the behavior of people in their organizational environments.

What started as a caveat to the student of OB—to beware of generalizing from the national and organizational cultures of the United States to those in the rest of the world—may soon be a recommendation instead. How do we resolve this seeming paradox? The answer is found in the rapid cultural evolution of the United States of America from a relatively homogeneous national culture to one marked by a degree of diversity and multiplicity not found within any other national environment, mainly occurring during the latter half of the twentieth century. Although the United States is truly described as "a nation of immigrants," the earlier influx of new and different cultural groups was episodic, usually with adequate time for a given wave to be assimilated within the dominant national culture before the next wave reached the shore. OB was managed, taught, and practiced on a foundation of assumed generalizations about the behavior of people as members of organizations.

This simplistic reliance on what seemed to work in the past as being a valid guide for the present, and even the future, is still held by too many U.S. managers today; very simply, they are relying on false premises. Organizations today are populated by professional, scientific, technical, and operative members comprising a mix of cultural attitudes, values, and behavior patterns, resulting in cross-cultural conflict with those holding the outdated traditional false premises. The growing number of culturally sensitive organizational managers has learned to appreciate cross-cultural enhancement and enrichment contributed by newcomers to the nation. These managers have learned how to work within the parameters of the unassimilated portion of the cultures represented in their workforce. This is the good news to balance the earlier-described caveat for U.S. managers. The extreme cultural heterogeneity now present in many U.S. organizations provides the best possible internship for those planning on a career with multinational, or even global, enterprises, either as employees or consultants.

The professionally competent cross-cultural psychologist working for an MNE will work to enhance the cross-cultural awareness, sensitivity, and appreciation of organization members within the context of OB. Among the many relevant facets of OB that deserve inclusion on the cross-cultural goals agenda a sample of three—communication, motivation, values—will demonstrate the need and significance for the MNE to have a cross-cultural program. (As should be obvious, this is equally true of domestic organizations in the United States.)

Communication

A communication checklist includes the following points:

- Communication is the transfer of information and understanding from a sender to a receiver.
- Communication is what the receiver understands, not what the sender sends.
- Effective communication is a two-way process.

- Feedback (the receiver sends a response to be received by the original sender) is essential to validate congruency between the sender's understanding of what was sent and the receiver's understanding of what was received.
- Cross-cultural barriers to effective communication breed misperceptions, for example, semantic barriers, beginning with language diversity.
- International business depends on effective communication for growth and profitability; the global air traffic control system, for example, has an even more vital impact for the survival of human lives, achieved by replacing language diversity with a mandated single language (English) for system use worldwide.
- Psychological mindsets and perceptual filters, often originating in cross-cultural ignorance, distort decision making and may lead to lowered organizational efficiency and competitive disadvantages. Examples include selective listening (perceiving only what supports existing beliefs and blocking out what is new or contrary) and stereotyping (holding an overgeneralized set of assumptions about a group, attributing them without question to any individual perceived or misperceived to be a member of the group).
- Pictures can be a helpful medium for effective cross-cultural communication.
- Nonverbal communication ("body language") carries more weight than verbal communication, especially if it is perceived as inconsistent or there is language diversity.

Motivation

A motivation checklist includes the following points:

- One culture's motivator is another culture's inhibitor.
- Even within a culture, one motivator does not stimulate all.
- Managers maximize their motivational effectiveness in improving individuals' job performance along the path to achieve organizational goals by matching their knowledge of theories of motivation with their knowledge of both cultural differences and individual differences.
- Individuals, including managers, differ in their needs and goals, with consequences reflected in their organizational behavior.
- Effective managers consider the consequences before implementing their motivational decisions.
- The consequences of the behavior of all organization members will influence their subsequent behavior in similar organizational environments.
- Effective self-management utilizes the same principles and practices to motivate individual behavior to satisfy personal needs and goals.

Values

A values checklist includes the following points:

- Right and wrong are universal concepts, found both within and across cultures; the specifics of what, when, for whom, how, where, and why create the contingencies and situations resulting in cross-cultural values conflict. For example, consider the lack of universality between organizational cultures regarding the creation, preservation, or termination of human life.
- Values are the sets of positive and negative perceptions and misperceptions, prejudices, biases, and rational or irrational beliefs that determine our understanding of reality.
- Values help to clarify and determine the attitudes of organization members.
- Attitudes are positive or negative feelings (affect) and/or thoughts (cognition) that influence the individual's response (behavior) to specific aspects of reality, for example, other people in various relationships, things, and situations, whether generalized or particularized, for example, labor and management, my coworker, and my boss.
- Values and attitudes over time become internalized as components of personality, along with other cultural, hereditary, social, and environmental factors.
- When values are internalized, they can be held either consciously or unconsciously.
- When values are shared by a group regarding what is desirable, they will influence group decision making and group behavior, determining, for example, which of the available behavioral paths will be selected as the chosen modality to achieve the desired goal, and which means will be used among alternatives.
- Values, attitudes, and behaviors are also components of culture.
- The desirability of ethical and socially responsible behavior may be a value component of an organization's culture, providing guidelines for the OB of its members internally and externally.
- Ethical values equate with right behavior, not wrong. Even within a culture, country, or organization, there may be diversity in what is right, not wrong, depending on. . . .
- Between cultures, countries, and organizations, there will be ethical value diversity; just consider the United States Foreign Corrupt Practices Act as a classic example.

CROSS-CULTURAL BUSINESS

Even before crossing national borders, when we consider the composition of the contemporary workforce in the United States, we should appreciate the importance of cultural sensitivity on the part of those responsible in purely domestic enterprises for moving workers along the path of achieving organizational objectives. No country today has as heterogeneous a workforce as does the United States. At the other extreme, with maximum homogeneity, is Japan. It is interesting to note that Japan, with little need for cross-cultural sensitivity at home, is among the world-class leaders in multinational enterprises.

The cross-cultural psychologist has opportunities for an MNE position both abroad and at home. Just as United States organizations are becoming

MNEs, or are expanding their MNE operations to additional countries, so foreign corporations are becoming MNEs, or expanding, by crossing the national boundary of the United States of America to carry our their business operations. There is equal need for the skills of the cross-cultural psychologist on the part of both the United States and the foreign MNE.

THE ROAD TO MNE

Why does an organization adopt as a corporate strategic objective the goal of acquiring (or expanding) MNE status? Cross-cultural psychologists seeking affiliation with an MNE should first do some homework research on the specific company; convenient sources are the business reference section of your local library, stockbroker offices, or the firm's annual report by request to the public relations department. These sources may answer the above question on strategy for a given corporation but should be preceded by acquisition of fundamental background knowledge on the nature, birth, and growth of MNEs in general. Seeking to build a multinational career track should be preceded by a survey of the road MNEs follow in their various operations, its pitfalls, barriers, and detours, all of significance to the affiliated cross-cultural psychologist. The basic characteristics of this sequence will be highlighted as we examine the major phases of operation that a business implements as it travels along the road to becoming a multinational enterprise.

The decision to engage in business across one or more national borders is part of the organization's strategic plan, rooted in necessity: to defend, to maintain, or to expand when confronted by threats and/or opportunities. The threats to present profits may be either foreign or domestic and may be found in the decisions of our own or other governments, of competitors or labor unions, of consumers or suppliers. Opportunities may also arise as a consequence of changes in any of these same areas. The organization with "smart" management is prepared to take advantage of the opportunities and to neutralize or compensate for the threats. This includes utilization of cross-cultural psychologists as a component for effective multinational moves.

The type of business action decided on will determine the need and extent of cross-cultural orientation required. Modern MNE actions go beyond the traditional roles of importer or exporter. They include, for example:

• building or buying a foreign manufacturing plant

• creating or acquiring a foreign distribution system for exported products

• developing a joint venture with one or more host country partners and/or with other MNEs

- licensing arrangements whereby the licensor grants the licensee the right to use something possessed by the licensor (e.g., management skills or cultural expertise)
- management contracts to provide specific managerial skills to one party for an agreed upon fee (e.g., in the special functions of personnel or purchasing)
- manufacturing contracts with a host country manufacturer to produce or assemble parts in compliance with MNE specifications
- franchising to market and sell goods or services already well-developed by the MNE (e.g., McDonald's Big Mac in Tokyo, Japan).

Most psychologists are not aware of the full potential for employment of cross-cultural consultants by MNEs implementing any of the above strategic actions. The cost of such a consultant may be seen as an insurance premium to cover a real business risk at the interface of different cultures. Psychologists should also know that the estimated volume of international trade for 1991 is more than 3 *trillion* and still growing. Consider the continuing growth of MNE activity in the Pacific Rim, the fully operational impact of the European Economic Community in 1992, and the move to a market economy, free enterprise, and entrepreneurship of the newly liberated countries of Eastern Europe. All these events comprise strategic career opportunities for cross-cultural psychologists with an interest in the applied aspects of their specialty. It is, perhaps, easier for the applied practitioner of cross-cultural psychology to also perform research as an incident of their practice than for the researcher to move into practice, and this chapter is mainly addressed to those with a primary interest in practice.

GEOCENTRIC ORIENTATION

Our recommendation to the MNE cross-cultural psychologist is to understand, accept, and endorse the *geocentric* orientation for human resource management by the MNE. The best MNEs have adopted this policy position as a comprehensive management perspective. Geocentric means world-centered; when applied to personnel, as in calls for a vacancy to be filled by the best qualified available person, it means wherever in the world that person may be and wherever in the world the vacancy may be.

The majority of MNEs do not yet have this global approach, but the cross-cultural psychologist may serve as a facilitator in encouraging its adoption. Even though the logic of the geocentric view may be appreciated by management for its rationality, for it to be successfully applied, management is required to have an international information system that may be costly to acquire and is difficult for managers to master.

What are the more popular, but not better, perspectives? The *polycentric* orientation is held by MNE managements whose perspective has not moved to the geocentric or who reject it as too difficult or impossible for their managers. In fact, they regard the culture of any foreign (host) country as too difficult for home country managers to understand and apply in business decision making. The practice under polycentrism is for MNE operations in each host country to be managed and staffed to the maximum extent by nationals of that host country. The rationale is that local people know the local culture, work force, and customers best. The polycentric approach has some advantages under its premises, but there are also disadvantages: All host nationals are not equally and interchangeably expert in local culture, and career development and advancement within the MNE for local managers is automatically limited to opportunities arising inside their own national borders. MNE management with a polycentric orientation is a prime candidate for the services of a cross-cultural psychologist, to evaluate and select the best host nationals under polycentrism and to educate management toward at least a limited geocentric perspective.

The *ethnocentric* orientation is deservedly in last place. Executives with the ethnocentric philosophy of management assume as a basic premise that the way management is practiced in the home office in the home country is beyond criticism because it is obviously the best and only right way to conduct a business. A corollary of this position is that only home country managers will be competent to conduct MNE affairs in any other country. The fallacies in ethnocentrism are clear to a cross-cultural psychologist, but the MNE management that holds them as truths may not be interested in your bid to educate them to reality until the MNE has suffered a major financial loss directly traced to an ignored cross-cultural variable. The more successful the MNE has been as a domestic enterprise, the greater the temptation to transfer the self-image of national champion to world-class know-it-all. Take Procter & Gamble (P&G), for example. In the domestic American retail marketing industry, P&G expertise was the standard by which others were found deficient. This was a valid reputation, believed and appreciated by P&G executives, since they knew it all, including consumer psychology and the application of consumer research to product marketing. When an advertising campaign worked well, there was no need to fix it, even when transferred to another culture.

Philosophical premises die hard, particularly those of an ethnocentric nature. It took 13 years and losses estimated at a quarter of a billion dollars for P&G to learn that cultural variables in Japan are not necessarily the same as those in Europe. Where was the cross-cultural psychologist as insurance against that loss? Actually, a Japanese employee warned of the cultural conflict, but P&G knew better, as reported by J. A. Trachtenberg in *Forbes*, 15 December 1986, pp. 168–169 ("They Didn't Listen to Anybody").

SELECTION AND TRAINING FUNCTIONS

The skilled cross-cultural psychologist should have a role from the beginning in the selection of MNE managers who will be functioning at the international level and stationed in other than their own home country. This includes the preselection determination of recruitment policies—deciding what sources will be used in recruiting suitable candidates for actual selection. Such policy decisions will be seen to reflect top management's orientation: ethnocentric, polycentric, or geocentric.

Working closely with the MNE human resource department, the cross-cultural psychologist will have been told what kind of positions need to be filled and where in the world they are located. He or she will review the *job description*, a comprehensive statement of the details comprising the work to be performed in the position; also provided will be the *job specification*, listing the qualifications (education, experience, skills, etc.) required for the person holding the position to perform at an acceptable level.

Decisions to be made include the use of sources that are internal or external to the organization: there are advantages and disadvantages to each. A specific choice must be made on which source country to use for a particular position. When a foreign source is used, recruitment itself becomes an international operation subject to all the cross-cultural complications and potential conflicts common to routine business in an MNE. Newspaper ads and employment agencies are common sources, but the cross-cultural psychologist might recommend recruiting international management trainees from the graduating students of business schools in the MNE home country who are nationals of foreign countries where the MNE is planning operations. A supplement to this source would be graduates of foreign business schools, especially in countries where the MNE already has a presence.

Women are significantly underrepresented and underutilized in the ranks of international management. The cross-cultural psychologist can recommend taking advantage of this source of high-quality managerial talent and skills, and also use his or her own psychological skills to overcome resistance and neutralize prejudice frequently found in MNEs regarding recruitment and selection of female managers for foreign assignment.

The failure, turnover, and replacement rate for expatriate employees is higher than for any other employee category, ranging from 30 percent to 70 percent, depending on the cultural distance between the employee's home country and the host country to which he or she is assigned. Since MNEs by their complex and costly nature usually originate in developed countries, the higher failure rates are found with MNE home office employees who are dispatched to lesser developed countries, thereby experiencing relatively greater culture shock—a stress reaction stimulated by an individual's perception of unfamiliar, strange, and different cultural components: people, places, customs, values, and so on.

High turnover rates equal high costs for relocation and replacement expenses, which reduce profits, plus additional significant losses in business and possibly customer satisfaction engendered by the usually deteriorating quality of performance and service by the unhappy and dissatisfied expatriate employee. Again, the solution for the MNE is found in the services of a competent cross-cultural psychologist who will practice psychologically sound selection procedures to prevent, or at least minimize, the usually high degree of job dissatisfaction.

Greater culture shock and expatriate dissatisfaction correlate with lower ratings for adaptability, tolerance, and understanding. The pattern of these variables provides an initial basis for screening applicants or nominees for foreign assignment. Cross-cultural sensitivity is a prime requisite for the satisfied expatriate. When eligibility for further consideration has been determined by application of the above general criteria, specific information should be provided to the candidate, using the comprehensive job analysis plus up-to-date research on the particular country and culture relevant to the vacant position. As more and more specific data are disclosed to the candidate, his or her responses are continually monitored by the psychologist for evidence to support a valid negative judgment, which would preclude further screening and orientation. Although skill in the local language is a big positive factor, its absence should not exclude the candidate. What would be sought is skill in any other language or interest in learning the local language as indicators of cultural sensitivity.

Assuming the applicant's candidacy has survived the above screening hurdles, most MNEs would consider the person ready for transportation to the foreign culture. Some MNEs have an additional phase in the eligible candidate's orientation, which would call for explicit participation by the cross-cultural psychologist. Managers with prior experience in the country relevant for the candidate make presentations and answer questions to give a picture of what may be expected from a cultural viewpoint; this may be supplemented by invited nationals from the host country, obtained from within the MNE, from diplomatic and industrial missions, universities, and others.

The goal of the cross-cultural psychologist is to do what is necessary to have the MNE provide a *realistic* job preview for the applicant as the final step before the official assignment. It would probably prove to be long-term cost-effective to send the successful candidate on a temporary trial assignment in the country as the final screen *by the candidate* before accepting the company's offer.

FAMILY ADJUSTMENTS

Most MNE assignments to foreign countries are for a term of years. For the married manager under consideration for such a position, all that has been stated regarding the screening variables applied to the employee is equally valid and relevant for the candidate's family. The family usually accompanies or shortly follows the new expatriate employee to the host country. When the employee fails and has to be repatriated, the probable causes of low adaptability, low tolerance, and cultural sensitivity very frequently originate in one or more of the other family members.

For the cross-cultural psychologist, the solution to this problem is clear: Bring the family of the applicant in for screening regarding the culture shock potential of the new environment, along with evaluation of personality characteristics compatible with good adjustment to strange people, language, and customs. The solution, however, has a problem: Family members are not MNE employees and, if required to undergo screening and psychological evaluation, some will protest it as an invasion of privacy.

The psychologist as problem solver neutralizes this by altering the requirement to a persuasive invitation, acceptance being truly optional, but with the valid benefits to all parties—employee, family, MNE—being spelled out in detail. It is assumed that the employee is technically competent to do the job. Therefore, the thrust of the screening, the information provided, the in-depth interviews, the testing, the presentations, and the previews are to minimize the probability of an outcome assignment that will result in a failing employee and an unhappy, dissatisfied, and even frightened family. Conversely, the procedure may result in an eager, interested, enthusiastic family group, fascinated by the opportunity to make new adjustments, learn new words, meet new people, and understand new cultural behaviors.

The cross-cultural psychologist who has not had personal experience with the candidate's proposed host country should make every effort to borrow a repatriate from that country to participate in the interviews. The orientation for the family members should include videotapes giving an approximation of a *realistic culture preview*, not a traditional travel tape to entice tourists. This should also be given or loaned for home use as a basis for private family discussion and decision. The psychologist knows and should emphasize that a supportive, satisfied family is essential for the expatriate employee to succeed. And the MNE should know that the cross-cultural psychologist is a key person to help the MNE to succeed.

14

Intercultural Contact and Communication

Richard W. Brislin

INTRODUCTION

There are certain predictions about people's lives that psychologists can offer with certainty, and one is that people will increase their contact with individuals from other cultural backgrounds. This contact can include people from other countries as part of life-changing events, such as an overseas assignment, or it can include interactions with people from other cultural backgrounds within large and complex nations, such as the United States or Canada (Cushner & Brislin, 1996; Landis & Bhagat, 1996; Pettigrew, 1997). Some of the reasons for increased contact are now familiar, and others will assume increasing importance with the continued development of new technologies such as e-mail and teleconferencing. Many college students have their first interactions with people from other countries given their contact with international students. They may continue this type of interaction as part of overseas business assignments, employment in their countries' foreign services, or as technical assistance advisers assigned to less industrialized nations. Within a country, people will surely have contact in schools and workplaces given legal requirements that all of a country's citizens must have access to education and employment regardless of race, ethnicity, religion, gender, and other markers that historically have been reasons for discrimination. Furthermore, people from different cultural backgrounds are demanding not only legal access to society's benefits but also respect for cultural traditions and practices. These demands for respect take the form of language and dialect use, celebration of holidays, and integration of traditional garb into dress codes. Especially difficult demands include respect for intercultural communication issues that are more often the topic of college-level courses than everyday expectations of the lay public. These include respect for cultural differences regarding eye contact, voice tone, body language, and typical boss-subordinate communications. When there are members of multiple cultural groups represented in the same workplace, it is easy to sympathize with executives who say they are expected to have different sets of cultural sensitivities for each group whose members want respect for their traditions. Further complexities are added when other groups not traditionally considered in studies of intercultural contact also demand recognition and use the word "culture" in their communications: the deaf, people with various disabilities, gays and lesbians, and females and males in gender-stereotyped occupations (e.g., female construction workers, male nurses).

A Hotbed of Potential Misunderstandings

When people from different cultures come into extensive contact, there are many reasons for miscommunications and negative attributions about observed behaviors. Many of these reasons stem from the nature of culture itself. Standard definitions of culture include elements such as shared attitudes and values that are transmitted generation to generation and that give guidance to behavior. Culture can be both objective and subjective (Triandis, 1994), with the latter leading to especially difficult interactions. Subjective culture includes norms, mores, manners, and various behaviors known to be shared by people with the label "socially skilled." Difficulties arise when behaviors considered polite and effective in one culture are seen as rude and inept in another. Problems are compounded when most people do not have a vocabulary to discuss misunderstandings. While they can say, "I'm sorry, but I forgot the date of your party" in their own culture, they don't have the words to say, "I'm sorry that what is polite in my culture is rude in yours" as a step in patching up misunderstandings.

The issue of "concept absence" is best explained through the use of examples, and the best examples consist of "well-meaning clashes." Such clashes, incidentally, are the basis of one of the most effective intercultural relations training tools, the culture assimilator (Cushner & Brislin, 1996; Triandis, 1995). In these types of intercultural interactions, people are trying to communicate effectively and to be pleasant by the standards of their own culture, but there is a clash given cultural differences in these standards. Given that the individual differences of purposeful ineffectiveness and unpleasantness are ruled out, the reasons for resulting clashes inevitably have a cultural basis. Variants of the following anecdote have been reported to me a number of times, and I have experienced its major cultural theme on various occasions.

Dr. Jack Douglas, a faculty member at the University of Massachusetts, had developed a very good working relationship with Dr. Zhou Chao, a faculty member at Beijing University. During his visits to China, Dr. Chao had been an excellent host, introducing Dr. Douglas to high-level people and seeing that his days were filled with interesting professional and free-time opportunities. Dr. Chao was serving as the mentor of a younger colleague, Haiyan Wang. As part of one of their communications, Dr. Douglas mentioned that he was expecting to hire a research assistant for a cross-cultural research project and asked Dr. Chao if he had any recommendations. In this communication, Dr. Douglas mentioned that he would be asking other senior people for their recommendations. Dr. Chao recommended Ms. Wang and was severely disappointed to the point of entertaining feelings of betrayal when he heard that Dr. Douglas had hired a Japanese-American for the assistant's job. Dr. Douglas was surprised and hurt at Dr. Chao's reaction. Are there cultural reasons for this misunderstanding?

The answer to this question is yes, and the exact reasons are admittedly difficult to communicate in any attempt to patch up the relation between Drs. Douglas and Chao. Dr. Douglas is reacting from his individualistic socialization (Triandis, 1995) during which he learned to pursue his own goals (hiring the best person). In addition, he has learned to participate in a society whose laws protect as many pursuits of individual goals as possible. Requirements call for Dr. Douglas to advertise the position openly and to consider seriously all applicants who meet the qualifications stated in the advertisement. Dr. Chao, on the other hand, is reacting from his collective socialization during which he learned to integrate *his* goals with *others who are members of his collective.* Ms. Wang is a member of Dr. Chao's collective and consequently Dr. Chao is expected to look after her interests.

In terms used by Bhawuk (1995) in analyzing 51 such potential difficulties, a further difference stems from a contrast between a rational and a relational approach to decision making. Dr. Douglas was socialized to accept a rational approach: careful description of qualifications, advertisements, selection committees, and so forth. Dr. Chao was socialized to accept a relational approach where there is more emphasis on taking care of people to whom one is close. Given this socialization, unless he had a reason to pay especially close attention to Dr. Douglas's remark, that he "would be asking other senior people for their recommendations," Dr. Chao would not have processed this input given that he does not have well-developed categories to capture the information.

In addition to this general analysis that follows from an understanding of individualism and collectivism (Triandis, 1995), there is also culture-specific information. In China, *guanxi* is a complex concept that includes relationship development over a long time period and the exchange of favors (Luo & Chen, 1996). The favor exchange can draw from different domains and does not have to follow from the original favor (money does not have to follow money). Participation in the favor giving and receiving can be passed on to others, summarized in the phrase, "*guanxi* is transferable." In this clash, Dr. Chao felt that his contributions to Dr. Douglas's success in China could be repaid through the hiring of Ms. Wang. In addition, Dr. Chao felt that since Ms. Wang was clearly his protégé, the concept that his *guanxi* could transfer to her should be clear. The difficulty is that Dr. Douglas does not have access to this concept given that it was not part of his socialization.

Addressing Problems: The Complex Contact Recommendations

Incidents such as this one involving misunderstandings and ill feelings are common when people from different cultures interact frequently. Problems are compounded when people start thinking about these interactions with a set of negative stereotypes or prejudicial attitudes. What positive recommendations can be made? The most common answer to this question centers on a set of recommendations for complex types of intercultural interaction. I want to emphasize "complex" because researchers and practitioners have long moved beyond the simple "contact hypothesis" that suggests bringing people together to reduce negative stereotypes and prejudices (moves toward increasing complexity were made as early as Allport, 1954, and Amir, 1969). The use of the word *complex* is a reminder that contact alone may not yield positive results and may simply reinforce old hostilities, as can be seen in Northern Ireland, Israel, and parts of North America where prejudice toward outgroups is still part of the socialization of many children.

Before discussing complex contact, however, there has to be a discussion of people's desires regarding intercultural interactions. People must have desires *other than* maintaining ancient hostilities passed down by their ancestors, keeping outgroups "in their place" so that the favored ingroup has more access to society's benefits, and demonstrating to others that the ingroup already has discovered correct answers to life's questions and so its members don't have to interact with anyone else. People's desires have to possess a more positive connotation, such as increasing civility in society through pleasant everyday interactions, putting into practice a culture's values such as "all people are created equal," or expanding one's own outlook by making a point to seek out the differences that intercultural contact inevitably brings. Other desires may seem less noble, but working toward them can have positive outcomes. Businesspeople may want to expand into areas where people from other cultures live. These same businesspeople may want to avoid lawsuits by setting up various types of affirmative action programs that encourage culturally diverse people to be hired and promoted. Educational institutions may seek contracts and grants from funding organizations whose goal is to promote the interests of culturally diverse groups. Given any of these desires, the complex contact recommendations can be consulted (features of contact drawn from Amir, 1969; Brislin, 1981; Pettigrew, 1997; Stephan, 1985). Problems stemming from the absence of these desires will be discussed later in this chapter.

Superordinate Goals. People desiring improved intergroup relations should seek commonly desired, or superordinate, goals. Such goals are desired by all people involved *and* demand the efforts of all people. One of the processes that leads to better relations is that when jointly pursuing shared goals, people often set aside their preexisting negative feelings since goal attainment is more important than maintenance of ill-will. Businesspeople from Germany and Israel may want to enter into joint ventures, and this shared goal and necessary mutual effort may cause hostile feelings stemming from World War II to be downplayed. Professors in large universities and their international students share the goal of preparing for a successful career, and all have to work together to see that steps, such as exam completion and thesis preparation, proceed apace. Members of diverse groups living in the same neighborhood often work together in the pursuit of good after-school programs for children and adolescents. In many cases, the development of close friendships or romances across cultural boundaries becomes the superordinate goal. Such close relationships are often difficult, and their development and maintenance demand joint time and effort.

Opportunities for Contact. As discussed previously, contact alone will not guarantee improved intercultural relations, but it is a necessary first step. The more opportunities people have for intercultural encounters, the more chances there are to experience *other* aspects of the complex contact under discussion here. A recommendation, then, is to bring people together but to give immediate attention to what people do during contact, such as the identification of and joint effort surrounding, superordinate goals. Contact opportunities will depend on time, populations, and place. In cities, they will include neighborhoods that have been integrated in recent years. In organizations, they will include the development of work teams as well as company softball games. In schools, they will include integrated teams in various sports. In government-run low cost housing projects, they will include common laundry rooms and playgrounds where children bump into each other. When people have overseas assignments, they will include sites where common interests are pursued, such as gyms, spas, musical gatherings, and bridge or chess clubs.

Perhaps a summary of a discussion I once had with a university foreign student adviser will communicate my arguments about contact. The adviser complained that there was little interaction among international and American students, and consequently people were not learning from each other. We then discussed activities that would involve both, such as a talent show. She said, "I'll entertain the possibility of a talent show, but not an international fashion show where students walk around a stage in their traditional dress" (saris, kilts, kimonos, etc.). Her arguments included the points that such activities were clichés, reinforced traditional stereotypes, were unchallenging for her to organize, and were frowned on by her advisory board who have been to eight or nine in past years and now find them boring. My arguments were that such activities bring people together, and this includes both the fashion models as well as backstage crew people, members of the publicity and refreshment committees, and so forth. Many of the support staff can be Americans, and a guaranteed crowd pleaser is the American who comes out on stage in jeans and a T-shirt. It does not take a great deal of effort, a point to keep in mind since students have their coursework to keep up. It *does allow* the introduction of superordinate goals, since everyone has to work together to meet deadlines and (to use a line from Hollywood movies) to "put on a show." It may not be challenging to oversee the fashion show, but it can be challenging to introduce other aspects of complex contact (more to be reviewed, below). When the advantages that can stem from the fashion show are carefully communicated to the advisory committee, they may approve, and if not interested in seeing men in kilts, they might look for evidence of complex contact.

   Stereotype-breaking Contact. One of the foreign student adviser's complaints about fashion shows is correct. There is the danger that seeing people in their native dress will not be much of a mental challenge and will simply reinforce preexisting stereotypes. The most effective intergroup contact encourages culturally diverse people to be seen in social situations that challenge stereotypes and that force individuals to think about outgroup members with a fresh perspective. Do not introduce African Americans as basketball players: arrange for contact with African American professors, physicians, and lawyers. To follow up the fashion show example, the international graduate students who work with me once added an element to the fashion show that tried to address this issue. While in their native dress, they asked for questions from audience members of the type, "What cultural difference or previous puzzling intercultural encounter would you like us to explain?" I will admit that the first few questions were planted by friends, but after these models, actual audience members asked about topics such as arranged marriages, eye contact, and speaking up in public, all of which are topics covered in treatment of intercultural communication. The question-answer session allowed the international students to be seen in a fresh light, and this is necessary to challenge stereotypes.

   Intimate Contact. Opportunities for intercultural interactions can lead to the possibility of more intimate contact. *Intimate* does not refer to romantic or sexual interactions. Rather, it refers to the exchange of personal information and thoughts that move people beyond their status as "members of a culturally diverse group" to complex and distinct individuals with hopes, desires, and concerns about the future. As people exchange intimate observations about their lives and life in general, previous barriers that separated "us" from "them" become less rigid. As people discover that individuals from other groups have well-thought out opinions about the quality of elementary school education, the growing disparity between "haves and have-nots," and increases in the cost of living, previous stereotypes based on the simplistic notion that outgroup members think alike become untenable.

In a seven-country study involving adult respondents drawn from national probability samples, Pettigrew (1997) found that having a friend from another cultural group was the best predictor of a generalized lack of prejudice toward outgroups. He suggested that at least two processes may work together. One is that in developing this type of friendship, people may develop an appreciation for the norms, mores, and values of people in other cultures. This appreciation of other cultures has long been an argument in favor of extensive intercultural contact opportunities, such as study years abroad for both high school and college students (Brislin, 1993). A second process is that these friendships may lead to an examination of one's own culture with the resulting realizations that there are different ways of achieving similar goals and that one's own culture does not have a monopoly on truth. In fact, the friendships may cause an active questioning of certain features of one's own culture. Americans, for example, might question the widespread and easy availability of guns, pornography, and supermarket tabloids with questionable journalistic standards if they develop friendships with people from cultures where the sun rises and falls quite efficiently without these societal features. This questioning of one's own culture does not lead to a lack of patriotism (Kosmitzki, 1996). Rather it contributes to the development of complex thinking summarized by the term "cultural relativity" and its connotations of understanding imperfections, tradeoffs among desirable goals, and the inevitability of ethical dilemmas.

Equal Status Contact. As much as possible, administrators should take pains to ensure, within the contact setting, that the people involved have equal access to any rewards or benefits. Equal status, then, means that there are no differences among people in their ability to reap the benefits of the social setting in which contact is taking place. Any benefits, of course, are specific to different settings in different parts of society. In the workplace, members of diverse groups should have equal access to employment interviews, hirings, merit raises, and promotions. In school, people should have equal access to attention from teachers, good grades, and other benefits such as scholarships and recommendation letters for posteducation employment. In neighborhoods, people should have equal access to homes with the best views, membership in desirable clubs, and favorable mortgage terms from lending agencies.

If intercultural contact is taking place in a country where there are general and widespread status differences, it is especially important to ensure equal status within the contact situation under scrutiny (e.g., the specific workplace, school, or neighborhood). Administrators should look on their contact situation as a jewel to be constantly polished, even if the jewel exists among the rubble of widespread prejudice, discrimination, and status differences. This assumes that a goal within the contact situation includes being a model of what is possible, not an imitator of the generalized status quo. Discussions of this goal also introduces the next feature of complex contact: the role of administrators.

The Choice of Administrators and Facilitators. People within the contact situation must be convinced that administrators are genuinely concerned with positive intercultural relations and aspects of complex contact such as equal status and the development of superordinate goals. In the three examples introduced above, administrators would refer to company executives, school principals and superintendents, and elected politicians who want the votes of people in the culturally diverse neighborhoods. People are extraordinarily skillful in their ability to distinguish lip-service treatments about the need for positive intergroup contact and true commitment to fairness, equal status, and a zero-tolerance for discrimination. What are needed, then, are high-level administrators with leadership ability and charisma who communicate in no uncertain terms that effective intergroup relations will be a high priority.

A related need is for effective intercultural facilitators. I am making a distinction between administrators who will vigorously support positive intergroup relations and the staff members who will do most of the day-to-day work ensuring that this policy becomes implemented. This type of distinction between decision makers and implementers is common. A company president may decide to build a bridge or decide that workers should be covered by a comprehensive health care plan, but he or she may not have the necessary expertise and so makes sure that these tasks are completed by a specialist. The analogy with engineering and health care is no accident. Intercultural relations has become an increasingly specialized and complex field, and there are many dangers that face amateurs and neophytes. For example, discussions of intercultural relations are often very intense since they often threaten people's perceptions of themselves, the culture of their socialization, and their reputations among peers. When changes in policies involving intercultural contact are introduced, there are often challenges to preexisting values and perceived threats to familiar ways of life. For example, certain people may feel that the hard work they have invested in an organization is less important than the ethnic group membership of newcomers looking for a handout. Or certain people may feel that they will be the losers if affirmative action plans are adopted and wonder if they should search for heretofore unexamined cultural diversity in their ethnic backgrounds so that they can qualify for perceived benefits.

These frustrations are often projected onto people involved in the day-to-day efforts surrounding improved intercultural communication, people sometimes called "facilitators." I was a member of a team that collected advice from more than 100 experienced facilitators (Ptak, Cooper, & Brislin,

1995), and the resulting "mentoring wisdom from the trenches" included the necessity to remain emotionally calm when one becomes the target of projected frustrations. No matter what a person's gender or ethnicity, it can be used against them. Questions phrased in unpleasant tones, such as "What does a Caucasian male know about . . ." or "How can a pretty %*#@* like you argue that . . ." must be expected. Choosing facilitators who know intercultural communication and who have the social skills to remain emotionally stable and to model tolerance is a necessary part of complex contact.

A disturbing feature of the 1990s is that facilitators have been chosen for reasons other than their expertise in intercultural communication, complex contact, ethnic relations, or other relevant knowledge areas. For example, organizations that feel that they have intercultural communication difficulties hire consultants. Ideally, the consultants would have relevant education and extensive experience and would make such credentials clear. But instead, people sometimes advertise themselves and are chosen based on demographic features such as their ethnicity, gender, or country of origin. These often have taken precedence over expertise and lead to terribly amateurish and harmful interventions. Some of these consultants seem to feel that a speech with the theme, "What it was like for me to grow up as a minority person in this country" will be effective. Or they feel that an intense seminar with the theme, "You are all racists and I must confront you with this fact" will change patterns of intercultural communication in favorable directions. A glance at the features of complex contact necessary for change, however, demonstrates that these approaches will not be effective.

Anticipating Difficulties. Another reason for choosing facilitators based on expertise rather than demographics is that improvements in intercultural communication and arranging for complex contact are not easy and there will inevitably be roadblocks to overcome. Many of these problems are known givens that have been documented in research studies and consequently well-read facilitators can help people overcome the likely difficulties.

Assume that administrators decide that complex contact will be introduced in their organizations and they hire knowledgeable facilitators. Certain difficulties can be predicted. One is that complex contact may have benefits within the organization, but people's time in the organization does not take up 24 hours of each day. People spend time in other places, such as within their families and in informal activities with friends, and positive intercultural communication may not be valued in these other places. The danger is that the positive approaches to communication learned in the organization may be balanced out by a norm of skepticism toward interacting with "those others" encountered outside the organization. Good facilitators, then, introduce organizational members to this possibility and introduce ways of coping with such skepticism and prejudice.

Other difficulties stem from problems in changing any well-entrenched attitudes (Petty, Wegener, & Fabrigar, 1997). People do not change easily, and good facilitators know this. In the example of the seminar with the message, "you are racists," several basic mistakes are being made. People need time to engage in elaboration of attitude-change messages and to consider implications for themselves. If they do not engage in such personalized elaborations, the communication is forgotten along with the hundreds of other messages received but forgotten each day. Examples of forgotten messages include those in television advertisements, communications from coworkers considered low priority when heard, and the content of one's junk mail and phone calls. The message that "you are racist" often puts people on the defensive, stops elaborative thinking, and causes people to put their cognitive efforts into discounting the facilitators as unreasonable and unhelpful agitators.

Another set of difficulties stems from points that may be so obvious that they are underdiscussed. Many people want to have effective intercultural interactions but they do not have the skills to do so. Rather, they attempt interactions but find that they make mistakes, feel clumsy, and become generally anxious about future intercultural interactions (Stephan, 1985). For complex contact to succeed, then, people need to know about and to practice behaviors that are considered appropriate among hosts. Putting people into complex contact, even with such desirable features as superordinate goals, equal status, and the possibility of intimate contact, is much like throwing a two-year-old into a swimming pool. Some children may paddle their way to limited success, but others will not do well and will become anxious about ever learning to swim.

Often, necessary skills follow from an understanding of cultural differences. In discussing the critical incident involving Drs. Douglas and Chao earlier in this chapter, the concepts "individualism" and "collectivism" were introduced. In individualistic societies, people learn skills that allow them to pursue their own goals *without* the automatic support provided by membership in a long-lasting collective. In collectivist societies, people are more attuned to developing long-term relations with others, with the possibility that some of these others will become part of people's collectives. Imagine a social gathering to welcome the new president of a company. The skill individualists find valuable is to "circulate," spending time with many different people. From such interactions, a person develops a network whose members offer and return favors, but without the obligations of permanent membership in a collective. The skill collectivists find valuable is to find an interesting person or small group of people and to spend all their time with this person or group. Given the greater amount of time invested, it is more likely that long-lasting relationships will develop. Such understandings lead to skills that can be practiced so that people feel comfortable when the type of social gathering under discussion involves intercultural contact. Collectivists would be encouraged to develop skills that allow them to circulate.

Individualists would be encouraged to downplay any tendencies to circulate since these lead to attributions of "flighty" and "superficial" by hosts. Rather, they can be encouraged to find interesting people with whom they might spend several hours, and they can practice discussing topics appropriate for these long interactions. These suggestions follow from studies (e.g., Cushner & Brislin, 1996) that collected and organized sojourners' reports of difficulties and adjustments. Collectivists complain about the need to circulate, to introduce themselves, or to arrange introductions, and to develop a supportive network. Individualists complain about the amount of personal information they have to share during these interactions and the inability to talk to all the important people at the gathering.

Specific Intervention Methods: Using Critical Incidents and Culture Assimilators

When administrators feel that intercultural relations in their organizations are poor, they sometimes call for formal interventions. The facilitators chosen to design and implement the interventions then make choices among many methods, techniques, and educational pedagogies that have been shown to encourage positive changes (Landis & Bhagat, 1996). Before making their choices, facilitators often complete needs analyses of organizations so that specific problems can be diagnosed and intervention plans introduced. Often, the needs analyses yield findings consistent with themes discussed in this chapter: An organization's members want effective intercultural interactions but do not know much about cultural differences and are clumsy when attempting such interactions. In such cases, the use of critical incidents and culture assimilators (Cushner & Brislin, 1996) can be helpful.

Critical incidents for intercultural interventions are short cases involving people from different cultures in various types of interactions. Despite good intentions, there are misunderstandings, and people in the incidents are puzzled as to the exact reasons. Readers choose among various alternatives, most of which sound reasonable, and are then told which alternatives make contributions to an understanding of underlying reasons for the misunderstandings. These reasons are then placed into frameworks based on well-established findings concerning cultural differences and people's reactions to extensive intercultural interactions. Often, the incidents identify the types of behaviors that people might practice so that they feel comfortable during their intercultural interactions. Ideally, then, the sophisticated use of critical incidents leads to reactions of "I understand the cultural differences going on" and "I know and have the opportunity to practice appropriate behaviors." When multiple critical incidents are combined into an integrative package that covers a wide range of cultural differences, together with integrative frameworks that help people organize myriad pieces of specific information, the term "culture assimilator" (Cushner & Brislin, 1996) is used as a label for the package.

The use of critical incidents and culture assimilators becomes clearer if examples are examined. The following is from a collection by Bhawuk (1995, p. 169) designed to prepare people for intercultural interactions in cases where differences due to individualism versus collectivism are likely to be impactful.

UNINTERESTING RESEARCH

Professor Folk, a psychology professor from an American university, was visiting China for a week-long seminar. He was very excited about the research findings he was going to present at a Chinese university. He started his presentation by introducing the research as follows: "This is a unique study in two ways. First, it uses a methodology that has not received much attention, and second, it addresses a problem that has baffled social scientists . . . for a long time. I think the findings of this research are going to set the pace of research in this field in the future." He presented his paper and was sure that a lively discussion would follow the way it always had during his presentations in the United States of America. To his surprise, people did not ask him any questions. Dr. Folk was quite disappointed. What is happening here?

a. Dr. Folk bragged about his research, which has upset the audience.

b. Dr. Folk's cutting-edge research is too complicated for the Chinese audience.

c. Dr. Folk's study is impeccable and people did not have much to say.

d. Chinese researchers do not ask serious questions in a seminar.

In the complete culture assimilator, there are explanations for each alternative, and readers can learn a great deal of information by analyzing more and less appropriate alternatives. Here, the best answer is a: Dr. Folk's behavior is seen as that of a braggart. The cultural differences stem from individualism and collectivism. In his culture, Dr. Folk does not have an automatic collective whose members push him forward and say positive things about him. He had to learn to take these steps, necessary for professional development, himself. In a collective society such as China, people have a supportive group to say positive things about a person, and so any one person can communicate in a modest manner.

By using multiple incidents, cultural differences can be introduced and immediately applied to real cases with a human interest appeal, and these features undoubtedly improve the chances of retention in people's memories. Behaviors that might better lead to positive reactions from hosts can also be identified, and these can be practiced if necessary. In this incident involving the lecture in China, for example, a more modest initial statement would be more appropriate. Dr. Folk might say, "Thank you for taking the trouble to come to this lecture. I hope I will be able to make one or two points to make your time worthwhile." The incident can also be used for "the other direction," Chinese scholars traveling to the United States, and here the advice would be to decrease modesty. "I am trying to make a methodological and theoretical contribution to the important issue of . . ." is more appropriate in an individualistic culture. General points of wide-spread usefulness can also be introduced. In collective societies, modesty extends to people and organizations with whom one is surrounded. "My son is not very bright," or "My work is very ordinary," are the types of comments frequently heard. These can have devastating impacts if people are unprepared for them. An individualist newlywed woman who has slaved in the kitchen all day may become upset on hearing her collectivist husband say to dinner guests, "Please excuse this poorly prepared meal. My wife is not a very good cook." If the couple is living in a collectivist culture, it would be wise for the wife to practice dealing graciously with comments such as these. If they are living in an individualistic culture, it would be wise for the husband to avoid such comments because they can cause the dinner guests to make extremely negative attributions.

Future Directions: Attention to Differing Viewpoints

A great deal is known about intercultural communication, complex contact, and methods for improving intercultural relations, three of the topics discussed here and in book-length treatments (Allport, 1954; Cushner & Brislin, 1996; Landis & Bhagat, 1996). At times, it is frustrating that this knowledge has not had more impact. A glance at newspapers, magazines, and television news indicates tremendous problems involving intercultural relations all over the world. In addition, basic mistakes continue to be made in business dealings, diplomacy, and the effective integration of international students on college campuses. Why haven't intercultural relations specialists had more impact? Several reasons will be considered here as part of recommendations for more attention in future research and applications.

Differing Goals. Intercultural relations specialists often assume that people fall short of the ideal if they do not have multiple close friends from different cultural backgrounds. In actuality, people have a variety of goals and these must be understood if reality rather than idealization is to be addressed. Some people are willing to be effective, tolerant coworkers with culturally different others, but they do not envision themselves spending voluntary free time with these others outside the workplace. Further, the culturally diverse people may want only minimal interactions outside their own group. They may be quite satisfied if others simply stay out of their way and do not actively interfere with goals such as workplace promotions, education of children, and purchase of homes in certain neighborhoods. Consideration of different people's goals brings to mind the American saying, "It takes two to tango." Both sojourners and hosts have to desire the types of complex contact previously described. In a study of sojourner experiences in Japan, Tsai (1995) pointed to difficulties that make complex contact difficult, such as the Japanese fascination with industrialization, leading to little respect for sojourners from less industrialized countries. Interestingly, Tsai suggests that the Japanese may offer a red-carpet treatment to Americans and others from industrialized nations, but such treatment is also discriminatory and does not allow for equal status and intimate contact. Shortly before he died, Yehuda Amir told me that there were limits to the contact programs he could introduce into Israel's high schools. With complex contact, Jewish young men might want to go to social occasions with Arab young women, and this is an outcome desired by neither traditional Arabs nor Orthodox Jews.

Challenging the Tolerance of Intercultural Specialists Themselves. Whenever multiple sets of goals are considered seriously in analyses of intercultural relations, specialists themselves will have their own tolerance for others challenged. Many times, they will find themselves entering into conversations much like political negotiations in which compromises must be sought. In politics, a common saying is that "a half a loaf is better than none." It is better to have an impact on an organization, symbolized by a half rather than a full loaf of bread, than to leave the organization without having made a contribution. Consider the business world. A company may have an excellent affirmative action policy, but what happens when important customers want to deal only with male Caucasian salespeople? The temptation may be to recommend that such customers be dropped, but how many customers can be dropped by a company that wants to continue in a highly competitive business world? It may be better to seek alternative responses, such as using the stimulus of customer preferences to open markets in areas where culturally diverse salespeople have advantages. Or consider international education. Professors may encourage students from certain countries to expand their horizons by engaging in intercultural contact. They may be rebuffed, however, with the response: "Except for high technology, which is what we are studying, we already have the correct way of life and don't need any expanding." Various types of intercultural contact can be forced by professors with their rewards/punishments of As and Fs, but it may be wisest to work with the existing interest in high technology and to introduce intercultural skills through the formation of multicultural groups whose members work together on various high-technology projects. The desire for successful project completion may provide the type of superordinate goals that allow effective interactions today that may be expanded tomorrow with the addition of other types of complex contact. While intercultural friendships may be a rarity, the half-a-loaf outcome of "effective working partners" may be a realistic possibility. The concept of identifying realistic goals bears similarities to the advice given to teachers at all educational levels: Know where your students are now. Statistics professors, for example, may eventually expect an understanding of analysis of variance, but they need to start with college students who are still vague about means and standard deviations. Similarly, intercultural specialists may want smooth, effective, and respectful communication, but will often have to start with people's more self-centered goals such as preparation for the job market.

CONCLUSIONS

Intercultural specialists know a great deal and can make major contributions in diverse settings such as workplaces, schools, hospitals, and social service agencies. When interacting with nonspecialists, it is important for them to remember one of their own central tenets: There must be respect for differing viewpoints. As intercultural specialists help others achieve their goals such as better customer service, health care delivery, and educational programs, these *others* are likely to accept another central tenet. Effective intercultural communication is not just a pleasant luxury. Given the reality of a shrinking world and the frequency of intercultural contact, it can be central to the profitable and successful company, the respected hospital, and the prestigious educational institution.

15

Psychological Aspects of Immigration

Paul G. Schmitz

Worldwide, the flux of immigration increases, and not only traditional immigration countries of the "second world" such as Australia, Canada, and the United States but also countries in the "first" and the "third world" are confronted with this issue. Whereas traditional immigration countries have developed their immigration policy, European countries mostly do not possess such sophisticated policies, and the consciousness to be a de facto immigration country is only weakly developed. The scientific literature and research on immigration reflect this state: We find proportionally more publications on immigration in anglophone countries, in particular Canada and the United States, than in other countries of the world. Theoretical concepts and empirical findings seem to be more mutually related to each other, and there are attempts to elaborate general frameworks (cf. Berry, Poortinga, Segall, & Dasen, 1992; Segall, Dasen, Berry, & Poortinga, 1990; Triandis, 1994). During the last 10 years, the number of publications is also increasing in Europe, but more investigations are published by educational scientists and sociologists than psychologists and cross-cultural psychologists. Anglophone literature concerning theoretical aspects and empirical findings is mostly not taken into consideration, and the generalizability of empirical findings across cultures is not investigated (cf. Nuscheler, 1995). During the last decades, European psychologists have been becoming more and more interested in research on psychological aspects of immigration: for example, Abou (1978), George (1986), Oriol (1981) in France; Bagley (1968, 1969, 1971, 1993), Burke (1977), Cochrane (1977, 1980), Furnham (1986—cf. Furnham & Bochner, 1996), Gupta (1977), Hemsi (1967), Watson (1977) in Great Britain; Boker (1981), Cropley, Ruddat, Dehn, and Lucassen (1994), Suzuki (1981), Schmitz (1994a, 1994b) in Germany;

Georgas and Papastylianou (1994, 1996) in Greece; Boski (1994) in Poland; and Neto (1986a, 1986b, 1988, 1989, 1993) in Portugal.

Investigations in cross-cultural psychology during the last decades illustrate that human behavior, in particular social behavior, is strongly influenced by sociocultural factors (Berry et al., 1992; Segall et al., 1990). With regard to immigration, an interesting question arises: What do we find when a group of persons or individuals socialized or enculturated in one society immigrate into another culture and attempt to stay there over a longer period of time? Do immigrants continue to behave in the same way as they did before, do they acquire new behavior forms, or do they modulate or modify their behavior to find a compromise between their own traditional behavior patterns and behavior forms practiced in the country of immigration? Cross-cultural research demonstrates that each of the three solutions is chosen, but most frequently encountered is the last type, which includes both continuity as well as changes of behavior patterns. Further, we discover marked differences in behavior modifications across immigrant groups and individuals. Moreover, it can be observed that the degree of behavior change varies across social fields, such as family life, school, job, and leisure activities. Some behavior patterns are easier to change than others; central value systems are more resistant to changes than overt behavior (Rokeach, 1973). We do not only find changes in the behavior repertoire for reason of cultural contact between ethnic groups from different cultures within immigrant groups, but also with members of mainstream societies. In recent history, we find these mutual influences in typical immigration countries, such as Australia, Canada, and the United States, but they can also be discovered during the last decade in Europe. Europe's history over centuries is an excellent example of mutual sociocultural acculturation processes, such as assimilation and integration, as it is illustrated for example in the *Histoire de France* edited by Jean Favier (1984).

The term acculturation refers to cultural changes that result from cultural contact between different cultural groups. Acculturation is a phenomenon groups or individuals experience when they are confronted with changes in their cultural surrounding (Berry et al., 1992). It refers to both adaptive processes and adaptation as outcomes and includes psychological, social, and cultural aspects (Berry, 1992). Acculturation cannot be understood as a simple process of reaction to changes in the cultural context but rather as an active and sometimes a creative dealing with challenges experienced by immigrants when confronted with cultural changes. Process and outcome of acculturation can be circumscribed by different strategies of adaptation, which are preferred by a society and by its members (Berry, 1988, 1994a). In the cross-cultural literature we find a distinction between group level of acculturation and psychological adaptation (i.e., acculturation at the individual level), a distinction first made by Graves (1967) (cf. also Berry et al., 1992). This distinction is important insofar as it allows one to investigate, first, the relationship between acculturation forms at both levels, and second, the nature of conflicts if beliefs about acculturation differ between acculturative individuals and their own ethnic group. Psychological adaptation is defined by Berry, Kim, and Boski (1986) as "the process by which the individual changes his psychological characteristics, changes the surrounding context, or changes the amount of contact in order to achieve a better fit (outcome) with other features of the system in which he carries out his life." These strategies can lead to different adaptive outcomes. The adequacy and effectiveness of a strategy depends on a variety of variables, which will be discussed in the following section.

THE INFLUENCE OF STRESSORS

One group of variables relates to the influence of perceived stress during the process of acculturation and to those situational characteristics that cause stress, the so-called stressors. Research findings (e.g., Bagley, 1968, 1969; Berry, 1988; Berry, Kim, Minde, & Mok, 1987; Cochrane, 1977, 1980; Neto, 1993; Oriol, 1981; Schmitz, 1992a, 1992b, 1994a, 1994b; Zheng & Berry, 1991) show that individual efforts to acculturate can be experienced as stressful life events. Immigrants are confronted with a variety of problems concerning maintainance or change of their own identity. They are dealing with different systems of values, beliefs, and behaviors than those of the mainstream society and use their own ethnic or cultural group and their own personal system in resolving everyday routine problems such as housing, finding a job, and so on. Interview data show that individuals apply different coping strategies or reaction forms to deal with these challenges (Schmitz, 1994a). Reaction forms are hierarchically organized in a person, are often situation specific, and are subject to change over time (Thomae, 1988). Acculturation strategies can be considered as specific forms of such individual reaction forms.

The amount of stress, immediate reactions to stress, and long-term outcomes, such as adaptation or maladaptation, vary markedly across acculturating persons. Recent research demonstrates that acculturation processes do not lead inevitably to stress in its negative sense and to social and psychological problems (Berry & Kim, 1988; Jayasurija, Sang & Fielding, 1992; Westermeyer, 1986). Instead of distress we find sometimes eustress. Berry and coauthors, in their 1992 book *Cross-Cultural Psychology*, write: "Acculturation sometimes enhances one's life chances and mental health and sometimes virtually destroys one's ability to carry on; the eventual outcome for any particular individual is affected by other variables that govern the relationship between acculturation and stress" (p. 285). The degree of experienced psychosocial problems depends on the amount of behavior changes requested during the process of acculturation: It varies from psychosocial learning of mostly overt behavior forms, described as "behavioral shifts" (Berry, 1980), "cultural learning" (Brislin, Landis, & Brandt, 1983) or "social-skill" acquisition (Furnham & Bochner, 1986/1989), over changes requested in more central areas of personality, such as changes in a person's value system, called by Oberg (1960) and later by Furnham and Bochner (1986/1989) "culture shock" or named by Berry and coauthors (1987) "acculturative stress," to more severe psychopathological disturbances and somatic diseases (Bagley, 1968, 1971; Cochrane, 1977, 1980; Malzberg & Lee, 1956; Murphy, 1965). Pathological reactions are found when the amount of stress exceeds the individual resources to cope with highly stressful situations and a pathogenic personality structure exists.

No doubt, the immigrant's experience of stress and reactions to stress depend on given objective factors, for instance characteristics of the society of settlement, the society of origin, and social groups an immigrant belongs to. Relevant characteristics distinguishing societies of settlement are orientation toward immigration, pluralism, multicultural ideology (Berry & Kalin, 1995), history of immigration (Sabatier & Berry, 1994), geography and population density, number of immigrants and immigrant groups in a country, immigration policy, prosperity of the host society, social support systems, value systems, and others (Furnham & Bochner, 1986/1989). With regard to the society of origin, we find characteristics such as social, political, economic, demographic structures, culture, and value system. All these factors have an influence on the degree of stress experienced by an immigrant, but Thomae (1988) argued, referring to his extensive research, that the individual's "cognitive representation of the world" may be psychologically more relevant than the objective facts a person is confronted with. So the perceived stress, the reaction forms applied, the way of acculturation a person chooses differ among individuals. The role of intervening cognitive processes is also dealt with by Lazarus and colleagues (1984, 1993) in their transaction model of stress. The extent of the perceived stress, the coping strategies, and the consequences in the area of individual well-being and health depend on two main classes of cognitive processes. One cognitive process refers to how the situational stressors are perceived and interpreted. Lazarus calls this process "primary appraisal." For instance, the more a situation is perceived as threatening, the more stress is experienced by a person. The second cognitive component is called "secondary appraisal" and is defined as a cognitive process referring to the individual's belief about his or her own strategical resources and the effectiveness of these coping strategies in a stressful situation. A third component is also relevant, the so-called "reappraisal." A person judges how effectively he or she has coped with a situation. The perceived consequences have an impact on the individual's cognitive structure and on his or her inner organization of available coping strategies. The amount of the experienced acculturation stress and the effectiveness of the applied acculturation strategies determine the individual well-being and health behavior.

Empirical findings presented by Schmitz (1992b, 1992c) point to the relevance of these cognitive appraisal processes or cognitive representations of the immigrant's situation as central intervening variables. The data were collected among migrants from the former German Democratic Republic. Migrants who scored high on rating scales that related to the degree of experienced discrepancies between their own belief and value system and that of the mainstream society as well as to the degree of perceived difficulties showed higher correlations between acculturation strategy and psychosomatic complaints than those scoring low on these scales. Interview data demonstrated migrants scoring high on these scales experienced these situations as uncomfortable and threatening. These types of behavior can be considered as primary appraisal processes according to Lazarus's model. An example for secondary appraisal and reappraisal processes, respectively, turns up if we look at rating scales referring to the perceived own chance to resolve their own adaptation problems effectively and relating to the perceived effectiveness of applied strategies in the past, respectively. Low scorers on both scales showed a higher degree of psychosomatic complaints than high scorers did.

In Berry's framework of acculturation, presented in 1992 in his article "Acculturation and Adaptation in a New Society" and at the conference of the International Association for Cross-Cultural Psychology (IACCP) in Pamplona (1994b), the central components of the model refer to a sequence of acculturation processes: acculturation experience, appraisal of experience, strategies applied, immediate outcome or effect, and long-term outcomes. He relates the model developed in earlier years (Berry et al., 1987) to Lazarus and colleagues' stress model (1984, 1993). Acculturation experience relates to Lazarus's variable "life events," apraisal of experience to "primary appraisal of stressors," strategies used to "secondary appraisal" (coping resources), immediate outcome to "stress-reactions," and long-term outcomes to "adaptation." Appraisal processes determine immediate outcome as well as the quality of long-term outcomes such as behavioral shifts, the degree of acculturative stress, or the severity of psychopathological disturbances. Acculturation experiences (an immigrant's life events), influenced by factors belonging to the "group-level" of the model, such as society of origin, acculturating group, and society of settlement. The process of acculturation resulting in immediate and long-term outcomes is highly shaped by a variety of variables including moderator and intervening variables. Berry attempts to classify these variables by distinguishing between "moderating factors prior to acculturation" and "moderating factors during acculturation" belonging to variables at the "individual level" of the model. The first group of factors includes age, gender, education, preacculturation, status; migration motivation, expectations; cultural distance (language, religion), value systems; and personality (locus of control, self-identity, flexibility). The second group contains variables such as phase of acculturation (contact, conflict, crisis, adaptation); acculturation strategies: attitudes and behaviors; coping styles; social support (offered by the society of settlement and by the immigrant's acculturating group(s); social attitudes (prejudices, discrimination); and personality characteristics.

A huge amount of empirical findings demonstrates that, first, all these variables influence the process of acculturation and adaptation, and, second, each variable itself is also shaped by the influence of other variables presented in the model (Berry & Sam, 1996; Brislin, 1990; Furnham & Bochner, 1986/1989; Furnham & Shiekh, 1993; Segall et al., 1990, Ward & Kennedy, 1995). Berry's framework is heuristically of great value because it offers a taxonomy and guidelines for how to organize future research. But it also illustrates the complex interrelationship of variables involved. The model has to be more elaborated in the future with regard to how the variable groups are dynamically related to each other.

MODERATING FACTORS PRIOR TO IMMIGRATION

The literature on acculturation shows a series of studies referring to variables "prior to immigration and acculturation" that have an impact on the motivation to immigrate (e.g., Mullet & Neto, 1991; Neto, 1993), on acculturation processes, and on acculturation outcomes (Furnham & Bochner, 1986/1989). Most of these investigations show the character of correlational studies and are retrospective. They do not tell us in a more concrete way how they influence ongoing acculturation processes. It may be assumed that they interfere as components belonging to the individual's "system of constructs" (Kelly, 1955), "system of beliefs" (Rokeach, 1960), or "system of cognitive representations" (Thomae, 1988) or basic personality system (as the result of the interaction of genotype and phenotype [Eysenck & Eysenck, 1985]).

The age of an immigrant seems to be an important variable: Early immigration facilitates adaptation (Beiser, 1994; Beiser, Barwick, Berry, da Costa, Fantino, Ganesan, Lee, Milne, Naidoo, Prince, Tousignant, & Vela, 1988), whereas late immigration may impede effective adjustment (Beiser et al., 1988; Ebrahim, 1992).

Gender also shows an influence on acculturation (Berry et al., 1992), but data show that the influence of social status, education, and culture of origin has to be controlled. In general, females experience more acculturative stress and cultural conflicts than males (Moghaddam, Ditto, & Taylor, 1990; Naidoo, 1992).

Migration motivation, contact to immigrants and precontacts to the immigration country, and knowledge of the language of the host society are also considered as relevant moderator variables (Neto, 1988, 1991, 1993; Schmitz, 1996). In particular, the distinction between push/reactive and pull/proactive motivation seems to be of interest with regard to difficulties of psychological adaptation (Furnham & Bochner, 1986/1989; Kim, 1988; Richmond, 1993).

The cultural distance concerning the value system, general belief system, and language has also an important impact on the immigrant's adaptation. The greater the cultural distance between the society of origin and the society of settlement, the more difficulties we find during the process of acculturation (Schmitz, 1996; Ward & Kennedy, 1992; Ward & Searle, 1991).

Personality traits are also considered as moderating factors prior to acculturation. There is little research showing which role they play during the time prior to immigration (Furnham & Bochner, 1986/1989). It may be assumed that basic dimensions such as sensation seeking, activity, neuroticism, and anxiety (Zuckerman, 1994) affect the motivation to emigrate and after immigration influence positively or negatively psychological adaptation. We will discuss this in the following sections in connection with other moderating factors becoming relevant during the process of acculturation, such as phase of acculturation, acculturation strategy, coping styles, and personality.

INFLUENCE OF PHASE OF ACCULTURATION

Cross-cultural psychologists have attempted to link levels of acculturative stress and psychological adaptation to phases of acculturation (cf. overviews given by Berry & Kim, 1988; Furnham & Bochner, 1986/1989). Several models distinguish the following phases: precontact, contact, conflict, crisis, and adaptation (Berry & Kim, 1988). Phases of acculturation and acculturative stress are seen to be related to each other in the form of an inverted U-curve. However, research findings show that there is little evidence of the correctness of this assumption (Church, 1982; Furnham & Bochner, 1986/1989). The relationships found are weak and sometimes even contradictory. Even if investigations show some changes of stress experience over time, these fluctuations cannot be related to fixed time intervals. It seems to be that we have to deal with a continuous process of stress and adaptation. Stress fluctuations over time were observed in several studies (Hurgh & Kim, 1990; Schmitz, 1996; Ward & Kennedy, 1995; Zheng & Berry, 1991).

It can be assumed that the first months of an immigrant's life in a new society, while he or she is trying to find the best way to acculturate, are experienced as stressful. The amount of the experienced stress and the outcome for the individual's well-being will depend, within Thomae's and Lazarus's stress models, on the cognitive representation or appraisal of the acculturation situation. The first months are stressful in particular because the immigrant is confronted with a variety of objective and psychological problems (e.g., finding and defining his or her identity) and, probably, adequate adjustment strategies are not yet developed.

Empirical findings illustrate this: Independent of the particular acculturation mode a person prefers, excessive and exaggerated efforts to acculturate are accompanied by feelings of stress and feelings of psychological unwellbeing (Schmitz, 1992c). A high degree of stress experienced by a person over a longer period of time may result in impairment of the individual's psychological and physical health, particularly if no adequate coping strategies are available and if personality characteristics, such as neuroticism, psychotic behavior and closed-mindedness, tend to impede an effective adjustment. But otherwise, acculturative stress experienced by a person does not necessarily lead to lowered psychological and physical health if task-oriented rather than emotion- or avoidance-oriented coping styles (Endler & Parker, 1990) are applied and if coping modes are flexibly used with regard to specific challenges of situations.

ACCULTURATION STRATEGIES

In Berry's model of acculturation processes, acculturation strategies as well as coping strategies are considered factors moderating a chain of processes related to a person's adaptation to a new culture, such as acculturation experience, perception of a situation as stressful, and reaction to stress (Berry et al., 1992; Zheng & Berry, 1991). The individual acculturation style a person may choose is a product of a variety of factors that are related to each other in a very complex way.

Berry, Kalin, and Taylor (1977) and Berry (1988) present a conceptual framework of acculturation styles that serve as the basis for describing different types of acculturation attitudes and behavior strategies of persons belonging to ethnic groups as well as to the mainstream society (Schmitz, 1992b). The model contains two continuous dimensions: Dimension I can be described as "cultural maintenance" and Dimension II relates to "contact and interaction." The former refers to the question: "Are their own cultural identity and customs of value to be retained?" and the latter refers to the question: "Are positive relations with other groups considered to be of value, and are they to be maintained?" If for purposes of presentation the answers to both questions are restricted to the responses yes or no, four combinations that define different acculturation strategies are obtained. Answering both questions affirmatively describes the option of "integration," which is defined by Berry et al. (1986) as maintenance of the cultural integrity of a group, as well as the movement by the group to become an integral part of a larger societal framework. "Assimilation" implies the abandonment of the cultural identity and the maintenance of positive relations with the other group, while "separation" (when chosen by members of the nondominant group) or "segregation" (when required from members of the dominant group) signifies the maintenance of his or her own cultural identity with no interest in building up positive relations with other groups.

The fourth option is called "marginalization." This option is defined by Berry as "giving up his own cultural identity and not being interested in positive relations to another cultural group."

Berry's model of acculturation is of great interest in cross-cultural psychology, as it offers several advantages: First, it allows us to analyze acculturation processes at different levels, namely at the society, group, and individual level, and it offers the opportunity to relate data collected at one level to data gathered at another (Berry et al., 1992). Second, the model serves as an excellent basis for categorizing and describing different types of acculturation attitudes and behavior strategies of persons belonging to a minority group as well as of those who are members of the mainstream society (Schmitz, 1992b). Third, concerning acculturation at the individual level, acculturation styles are clearly and consistently related to basic personality dimensions. Schmitz (1992c, 1994b, 1994c) found that different modes of acculturation are clearly related to a variety of individual differences such as basic personality dimensions, cognitive styles, and cognitive structure. Berry's model is frequently used in acculturation research (Georgas & Papastylinanou 1994, 1996; Neto, 1993; Sabatier & Berry, 1994; Sam & Berry, 1995; Schmitz, 1994a; Ward, 1996).

Acculturation strategies can be assessed by different measures (Berry, Kim, Power, Young, & Bujaki, 1989). Attitude scales are used by Berry et al. (1997) in their research project "Multiculturalism and Ethnic Attitudes in Canada." Most of the scales developed later are based on items from these scales. Schmitz (1987, 1992b) developed the MCI Scale (Multi-Cultural-Ideology Scale), which is based on indicators formulated by Berry and coworkers (1977). Other instruments are self-ratings (Schmitz, 1996), observational methods, and interviews (Neto, 1993; Schmitz, 1992b, 1992c).

ACCULTURATION OUTCOMES

As we have seen, many immigrants have to cope with situations they experience as stressful. Any acculturation strategy immigrants prefer can be experienced as stressful if they have to strive hard to realize their aims regarding successful adaptation to a new culture, particularly when the mainstream society or their own ethnic group does not support them in achieving their goal (Berry, 1992; Berry & Sam, 1996; Schmitz, 1994a).

The amount of acculturative stress experienced by an immigrant and the effectiveness of acculturation strategies applied determine the individual's well-being and health behavior. If we consider the long-term outcome of the four acculturation modes we may assume that integration as well as assimilation can be considered effective strategies in most cases. Both techniques lead to an arrangement with the mainstream society and clarify the relationship with the own ethnic group. If case integration is preferred, a compromise between mainstream society and the ethnic group has to be found. If assimilation is chosen, an immigrant has to assimilate him or herself to the mainstream society on the one hand and has to give up the ties with the own ethnic group on the other. In case segregation is chosen, the relationship to the mainstream society is mostly perceived as negative and remains unclear (Berry & Kim, 1988; Berry et al., 1992; Schmitz, 1992b). A possible conflict between needs and expectations by the mainstream society and those by one's own ethnic group often remains unresolved for a longer period of time, and this situation may be experienced as continuous stress. Consequently, health problems can arise (Berry, 1988). Marginalization, if it is not a temporary phenomenon, is considered by most researchers as the worst situation because it tends to be accompanied by major psychosocial disturbances (Berry, 1990; Schmitz, 1994a, 1994b).

COPING STRATEGIES AND ADAPTATION

Another group of moderator variables has to be considered, namely coping. Coping strategies are considered relevant factors in moderating the relationship between acculturative stressors and stress outcomes (Berry et al., 1992; Zheng & Berry, 1991). Taft (1977) also considers coping as a central variable in acculturation and adaptation processes. In Taft's model, coping includes components such as ethnic and national identity, social-emotional adjustment, social absorption, cultural competence, and role acculturation. Berry et al. (1992) see a close relationship between Taft's coping styles and acculturation styles. There is some empirical evidence that Berry's acculturation strategies are related to a person's general coping system (Schmitz, 1992b). The acculturation strategies integration, assimilation, segregation, and marginalization can probably be considered as situation-specific forms of the individual's general coping system. Schmitz (1992b) presented data showing that integration, assimilation, and segregation are significantly correlated with scales from Endler's Coping Inventory for Stressful Situations (CISS). The inventory measures task orientation, emotion orientation, and avoidance orientation (Endler & Parker, 1990). Integration was positively correlated with task orientation, assimilation was positively correlated with both task orientation and emotion orientation, but correlated negatively with avoidance orientation, whereas segregation is positively correlated with emotion and avoidance. Emotion orientation as well as avoidance orientation can be considered helpful in specific situations for a short term, but they are less effective because they do not help to resolve problems for the long run at all. So Schmitz stated: "These data confirm our expectation that in most cases segregation could not be considered as an effective strategy in adjusting to a new culture. The problems a person is confronted with remain unresolved, the stress situation continues, and its possible consequences may be psychosomatic complaints and diseases" (p. 368).

Further evidence of the close relationship between acculturation strategies and coping behavior results from findings reported by Schmitz (1994a). Schmitz correlated acculturation strategy scales of the MCI with scales of the Psychosocial Stress Inventory (PSI) (Grossarth-Maticek & Eysenck, 1990). The PSI scales measure six different types of coping reactions with psychosocial stress. In this context, the four types of particular interest are labeled "neurotic approach behavior" (Type I), "neurotic avoidance behavior" (Type II), "flexible response behavior" (Type IV), and "evasive behavior" (Type VI). Immigrants confronted with stressful situations attempt to cope effectively with these situations by applying specific acculturation strategies. Each strategy applied can be experienced as not effective and frustrating if an immigrant has to strive hard and in vain over a longer period of time to adjust successfully. This is the case if the mainstream society, or his or her own ethnic group, does not support him or her in achieving his or her goal. The behavior can be considered as nonadaptive or pathogenic if a person is not able to change his behavior. "Neurotic approach" and "Neurotic avoidance" belong to this class of behavior. The findings confirmed the hypotheses that Berry's acculturation strategies were related to the PSI scales in the following way: "Neurotic approach behavior" showed a positive correlation with assimilation, "neurotic avoidance behavior," with segregation. In contrast, "flexible response behavior," a healthier form of coping, correlated with integration. "Evasive reactions" showed a correlation with segregation. The strength of correlations varied across ethnic groups.

The PSI scales are of interest in so far as these scales are related to different types of diseases (Grossarth-Maticek & Eysenck, 1990) that allow one to make a prediction about the relationship between acculturation strategies on the one hand and patterns of psychsomatic complaints on the other. Empirical findings confirm these assumptions. These findings will be discussed later.

With regard to the question of relevance of the individual's coping system during acculturation processes, it can be concluded that coping strategies covarying with integration can be considered to be the most effective ones concerning a successful adjustment to a new sociocultural surrounding. Research findings demonstrate the marked superiority of the integration strategy in most societies (Berry et al., 1977, 1987; Neto, 1993, Schmitz, 1992b, 1992c, 1994a; Ward, 1996), but Berry argues that in some societies other modes of acculturation may be more effective if they are able to match conceptions of the host society and those of the acculturating population (Berry et al., 1987).

ACCULTURATION AND PERSONALITY

Basic personality dimensions have to be considered as factors that, in addition to situational factors, strongly influence social behavior (Costa & McCrae, 1992; Eysenck & Eysenck, 1985; Zuckerman, 1979, 1994). Personality dimensions belonging to Eysenck's "Giant Three Model," to Costa and McCrae's "Big-Five Factor Model," or to Zuckerman's "Alternative Big-Five Model" are called "basic" because they possess a genetic and a biological basis with regard to the genotype level of the models, whereas at the phenotype level, they may be shaped by environmental factors (Eysenck, 1967; Eysenck & Eysenck, 1985; Zuckerman, 1994). These basic traits are also closely related to coping styles and health behavior as Schmitz (1993) was able to show. It may be assumed that basic personality dimensions are also related to migration motivation, experience of acculturative stress, acculturative strategies, and psychological adaptation. This network of relationships between both personality and acculturation variables allows some predictions concerning adaptation and health behavior as we will see later.

The potential influence of personality factors is frequently discussed in the literature (Berry et al., 1992; Furnham & Bochner, 1986/1989), but there is relatively little empirical research concerning the relationship between personality and acculturation. Some studies refer to the relationship between self-concept, self-identity, and self-efficiency, but it is often quite difficult to see what these constructs mean exactly because it is unclear how they are related to the structural models of established personality theories.

Ward and Kennedy (1992) consider extraversion-introversion and locus of control as both risk and protective factors. Schmitz (1987) found, when comparing different immigrant groups, marked differences with regard to the acculturation strategies most preferred by acculturating groups. But within each group he found also marked individual differences in acculturative behavior and adaptation. Acculturation strategies were consistently related to a variety of personality characteristics. The data were collected with immigrants belonging to different ethnic groups. Several instruments to measure personality were applied: EPQ-R (Eysenck & Eysenck, 1985) measuring neuroticism (emotional instability), extraversion, and psychoticism (psychopathic behavior, assertiveness, aggressiveness); KZPQ (Zuckerman, 1994) assessing five basic factors: impulsivity-sensation seeking, sociability, neuroticism-anxiety (neurotic), aggression-hostility, and activity; Open-Closed Mindedness (D-) Scale (Rokeach, 1960), and field-dependence tests (EFT and RFT, cf. Witkin, 1965; Witkin & Berry, 1975). Integration correlated negatively with neuroticism, neuroticism-anxiety, psychoticism and field-dependence, and correlated positively with extraversion, activity, and open-mindedness. Assimilation showed positive correlations with neuroticism, anxiety, closed-mindedness, and field-dependence. Segregation was positively correlated with psychoticism, neuroticism, impulsivity-sensation seeking (in particular the components impulsivity and unsocialized behavior), and (neurotic) aggression-hostility, and negatively with extraversion (Schmitz, 1994a, 1994b). These findings make sense: Persons preferring integration are open-minded and flexible; they are able to break up existing behavior patterns and integrate elements belonging to different cultural belief and behavior systems into a new behavior system (Witkin, 1965). Emotional stability and a low degree of anxiety facilitate this process. Immigrants favoring more assimilation or segregation do not show this degree of flexibility and openness, and probably they are not able or willing to construe more complex behavior systems that combine elements of behavior patterns belonging to different cultural backgrounds. They attempt to avoid conflicts between their own traditional belief and value systems and that of the society of settlement by identifying either with the culture of the mainstream society (assimilating) or by joining their own ethnic group and by minimalizing the contact with the majority culture (segregating).

Persons preferring segregation are less extraverted, which makes it difficult for them to open new social contacts; their higher degree of aggression-hostility may be interpreted as defensive.

ACCULTURATION AND HEALTH

Acculturative behavior and its outcome are related to health, psychological well-being, psychosomatic complaints, and diseases as research findings illustrate (Bagley, 1971, Berry, 1994, Brucks, 1994; Burke, 1977; Schmitz, 1994a, 1994b, 1994c). Schmitz (1994a) presented findings that can be discussed with regard to three aspects: (1) acculturative stress and general feelings of psychosocial unwell-being; (2) acculturative stress and general index of psychosomatic complaints, and (3) acculturative stress and strategy specific patterns of psychosomatic complaints.

1. General feelings of being stressed and incapacity to detach are positively correlated with each acculturation mode, in particular during the active process of acculturation. Probably, it may be concluded from these data, that in case situational conditions are negative or less promising and if there is a high personal commitment (i.e., in particular during the first months an immigrant lives in a new society), each acculturation mode can be experienced as stressful.

2. The data showed that each acculturation style is more or less positively correlated with a general index of psychosomatic complaints. This can be explained by the fact that the experience of acculturative stress over a longer period of time may cause health problems, which becomes plausible if we consider the positive correlations found between acculturation styles and psychosomatic complaints in general; this is likely to happen during the first time an immigrant stays in a new country.

3. Specific predictions concerning the relationship between the different acculturation styles and specific patterns of psychosocial complaints and diseases, both as potential long-term outcomes of unsuccessful adaptation, can only be made if we take into consideration findings regarding the relationships between types of reactions to social stress and acculturation strategies as well as relationships between types of reaction to social stress and psychosomatic complaints. "Neurotic approach behavior" is related to proneness to infections and allergic reactions; "neurotic avoidance behavior," to cardiovascular complaints, anger, and irritability;

"evasive behavior," to alcohol and drug addiction; and "flexible behavior," to well-being and health. As predicted, research findings demonstrated the following relationships between acculturation strategies on the one hand and specific psychosomatic patterns on the other: assimilation (related to "approach behavior" as we have seen) correlated positively with proneness to infection and allergies; segregation (usually related to "avoidance behavior") with cardiovascular complaints, anger, and irritability; and integration (related to "flexible behavior"), with well-being and health. But data from these investigations illustrate also, first, that there are obviously differences concerning the strength of correlations across ethnic groups, and second, that the correlation coefficients are relatively high during phases of active coping with situations experienced as stressful and enduring over a longer period of time. These findings were also confirmed by data from interviews regarding frequency of visits to the physician, medical prescriptions, and medical treatment.

Research findings can be summarized in the following way: In most cases, integration as acculturation strategy is more effective than assimilation and segregation with regard to psychological and social adaptation. But there exists also some evidence that under certain sociocultural conditions—for example, psychosocial support is offered by the mainstream society or by the ethnic group—each style (except marginalization) can be adaptive and may be related to feelings of well-being (Berry, 1992; Furnham & Bochner, 1986/1989). On the basis of these findings we may conclude that individual differences in coping styles have to be considered as relevant determinants of individual well-being and health in addition to factors at the sociocultural and political level. These findings are in agreement with those reported by Berry and Kim (1988).

CONCLUSION

Research in the field of immigration, acculturation, and adjustment has provided a huge amount of findings that are relatively consistent. As we have seen, immigration is frequently related to the experience of stress. Whether acculturative stress can be interpreted as eustress or distress, whether the stress outcome is positive—for example, enhancing the immigrant's life chances and giving feelings of well-being—or the outcome is negative, impeding effective adjustment and probably being responsible for diseases and mental health problems, depends on a huge number of interdependent sociological and psychological factors. More research is needed to better understand the dynamic relationship of variables involved in the process of acculturative adjustment. To investigate the generalizability of findings we need to have more comprehensive studies in which behavior patterns of various acculturating groups having their origin in the same or in different cultures across different societies of settlement are compared, the same constructs are used, and the same instruments are applied. When scientific research has helped to better understand the complex relationships between sociocultural factors, acculturation strategies, adjustment, and health, then social scientists will be able to offer proposals as to how current problems concerning immigration can effectively be resolved.

V

Applications of Cross-Cultural Psychology

16

Psychopathological and Clinical Aspects of Personal Experience: From Selves and Values to Deficits and Symptoms

Juris G. Draguns

How much do abnormal patterns of behavior and experience vary across cultures? Are the differences in these manifestations of psychological disturbance basic or trivial? Moreover, what, if anything, about mental disorder can be realistically compared across culture lines? What, if any, aspects of psychological disorders are universal and invariant around the world? And how are any cultural differences relevant for the practical tasks of intervention and treatment across culture lines?

This chapter attempts to provide answers to the above questions on the basis of the current state of knowledge on the cultural variations and constancies in abnormal behavior. In the process, the weight of cultural factors in some of the major mental disorders, such as schizophrenia and depression, will be addressed. The chapter will also concern itself with cultural influences on such social phenomena relevant to adjustment and disturbance as alcohol and substance abuse, suicide, borderline personality disorder, and anorexia. Of necessity, coverage will be selective rather than comprehensive; the topics chosen correspond to the foci of both curiosity and investigation in this young yet rapidly growing field.

The term *culture* as used in this chapter and throughout the volume has two distinct yet related referents. It pertains to the ways of life or the humanmade environment, in Herskovits's (1948) famous phrase, of people linguistically, historically, and sometimes racially distinct whose habitats are geographically removed. In this sense, we speak of the Japanese, Brazilian, or Swedish culture. In the United States and, increasingly, in many other countries around the world, including Australia, Israel, India, Singapore, and Canada, we encounter the situation of several culturally distinct groups of people living side by side. Cultural diversity, then, evokes remote and exotic locations, yet in many parts of the world it is part and parcel of daily life and is observable around the block. This chapter addresses cultural diversity near and far. The practical implication of its existence not only in remote locations but in our neighborhoods is that the interplay of culture and abnormal psychology is relevant to the activities and techniques of the members of the mental health professions.

CULTURE AND SCHIZOPHRENIA: CONSTANCY AND VARIATIONS

Perhaps the most serious and challenging mental disorder is schizophrenia. Its causes are multiple and complex; it does not predictably yield to any single mode of treatment, although it is helped by a wide range of modes of intervention, and theories about its origin, manifestations, course, and outcome abound. In reference to culture, one might speculate whether this disorder is unique to or at least characteristic of the cultures of Western Europe and North America, where it was originally described and named. Conversely, if it is a biological disorder with disruptive psychological manifestations, as an influential current of contemporary professional opinion maintains, does that leave room for culture to shape or influence its manifestations, and if so, to what degree?

A series of studies sponsored by the World Health Organization (WHO) provide empirically grounded answers to these questions (World Health Organization, 1973, 1979; Sartorius, Jablensky, Korten, & Ernberg, 1986). The WHO research team applied a standardized diagnostic schedule in nine countries designed to maximize the cultural and historic contrast and to encompass the major existing political and economic systems. Specifically, the following cultures were included in this investigation: China (Taiwan), Colombia, Czech Republic, Denmark, India, Nigeria, Russia, Great Britain, and the United States. The principal result of this ambitious research project was the identification of a core syndrome of schizophrenia that was observed at all research sites. This common pattern was characterized by a restricted range of affective expression, inadequate insight, thinking aloud, poor rapport, incoherent speech, nonrealistic information, and delusions with bizarre and/or nihilistic features. This finding left open the question of any variation of schizophrenic symptoms across the nine research centers. It solidly substantiated, however, the notion that the same symptoms were observed in a large proportion of schizophrenics at all the participating research locations. The initial research report did not inquire into any cultural differences, although such differences were identified in the subsequent publications of the WHO project (World Health Organization, 1979; Sartorius et al., 1986). First, somewhat counterintuitively, the WHO researchers reported that the outcome of schizophrenia was more favorable in the three centers in developing countries, Colombia, India, and Nigeria, as opposed to the other six, located in more industrialized and prosperous regions. A variety of interpretations can be advanced for this unexpected finding. Moreover, this positive result does not stand alone (e.g., Murphy & Raman, 1971), even though there have also been a few refutations (cf. Westermeyer, 1989). The second result by the WHO team reverses one of the most solidly established conclusions based on research in the Western world: The schizophrenics' prognoses are inversely proportionate to their educational and occupational level (Dohrenwend & Dohrenwend, 1969). In the WHO study, it was the poorer and less-educated patients in the developing countries, exemplified by India and Nigeria, who recovered more rapidly and readily. Thus, the series of WHO studies reinforce the notion that schizophrenia occurs in a substantially similar form across a wide range of countries. Yet the same project also contributed information on the cultural shaping of the disorder. In this respect, the WHO report does not stand alone; there is a wealth of comparisons, observations, and reports that testify to an impressive variety of schizophrenic manifestations across cultures (cf. Al-Issa, 1995a; Draguns, 1995; Draguns, 1997; Tanaka-Matsumi & Draguns, 1997). Later in the chapter, the meaning and nature of these differences will be addressed.

   The feature that is allegedly identical around the world is the incidence rate of schizophrenia, provided that this disorder is objectively, cautiously, and conservatively diagnosed. Upon the application of such precautions, the allegedly constant rate of schizophrenia amounts to 0.3 percent (Odejide, 1979). This conclusion would accord well with the currently prevailing majority opinion in the field according to which the sources of schizophrenia are fundamentally biochemical rather than psychological or social. Murphy (1982), however, questioned the validity of these conclusions and pointed to a number of cultural groups, large and small, that were shown to have high or low rates of schizophrenia. In the former category, he included western Ireland and the Istria peninsula in northwestern Croatia. To the latter category he assigned the Hutterites, a pacifist sect found in western Canada, and the Tongas of the South Pacific. He even identified two additional tribal groups in which the incidence of schizophrenia changed from low to high in the course of a generation. On the basis of a searching analysis of all of these groups, Murphy concluded that the claim of worldwide constancy of rates of schizophrenia is premature. Moreover, he tentatively identified a social pattern of influence that is likely to be responsible for cultural variations in the incidence of schizophrenia. According to Murphy, the few regions characterized by a high rate of schizophrenia exhibited social ambivalence toward its inhabitants, on the one hand pushing them to succeed and emigrate while, on the other hand, reproaching them for any lapse in loyalty toward their home region by leaving it. A parallel to the well-known dynamic of double-bind within the schizophrenic's parental family is readily recognizable. Murphy's contribution has been to transpose the double-bind from the family to the culture. Since the original double-bind formulation has not fared well in light of systematic empirical research, skepticism is warranted concerning Murphy's promising and intriguing formulation. So far, however, it has been the only comprehensive explanation advanced to account for any cultural variations in schizophrenia.

In a reference to the more specific symptoms that occur in schizophrenia, Al-Issa (1995b) has proposed that the sudden appearance of visual, auditory, or other imagery in cultures in which imagination is neither valued nor cultivated may provoke intense anxiety and lead to the external attribution of such experiences. As a result, an unexplained random image is crystallized into a hallucination. Al-Issa's formulation is at this point hypothetical. It should stimulate research on the cultural contexts in which reality is ascribed to imaginary experience and in which fantasy tends to be confused with reality.

Another relevant variable that has emerged in cross-cultural research is the construct of expressed emotions (EE). EE refers specifically to the negative emotional states, such as criticism, hostility, and intrusiveness that are often directed at a schizophrenic person by his or her family (Vaughn & Leff, 1976). Levels of EE have been found to vary across cultures. In India, for example, EE has been reported to occur in only 23 percent of schizophrenic families, compared with 48 percent in families with a schizophrenic member in Britain (Wig, Menon, Bedi et al., 1987). Could the greater acceptance of schizophrenics by their families in India be responsible for their better prognosis in that country, as documented by WHO (Sartorius, Jablensky, & Shapiro, 1977)? On the basis of the available findings, this possibility is worth pursuing systematically and testing rigorously.

To conclude, there is an impressive amount of evidence pointing to the existence of schizophrenia, the constancy of some of its basic features, and its tendency toward occurrence at about the same rate at a great many sites around the world. None of these conclusions can negate the cultural influences upon this disorder, especially in its manifestations, course, and outcome. These influences have been established by means of increasingly systematic and objective investigations; it is unlikely that their results will prove to be artifactual. The degree and meaning of the cultural shaping of schizophrenia, however, continue to be subjects of debate and controversy.

DEPRESSION AND CULTURE: A COMPLEX PATTERN OF INTERACTION

On an intuitive basis, most professional observers would probably argue for a greater weight of cultural factors in major or disabling depression than in schizophrenia. The available research evidence generally supports this judgment. However, worldwide, or at least widely encountered, features of depression have also been identified. Studies by means of a variety of methods converge in suggesting that depression is not the exclusive property of Judeo-Christian cultures, even though such cultures are especially susceptible to the experience of guilt. The more basic and universal components of depression are the vegetative and related symptoms that occur at the interface of psychological and organismic experience, such as lethargy, inability to concentrate, loss of enjoyment, fatigue, loss of sexual interest, and reduced appetite with or without the resulting weight loss (Murphy, Wittkower, & Chance, 1967; World Health Organization, 1983). Sad affect and feelings of worthlessness should be added to this list of depressive symptoms found in cultural milieus as different as those of Canada, Switzerland, Iran, and Japan (Jablensky, Sartorius, Gulbinat, & Ernberg, 1981; World Health Organization, 1983). In a recent epidemiological comparison of rates of depression across ten nations (Weissman et al., 1996), insomnia and loss of energy were found to be the most common symptoms at all sites of investigation. Guilt, however, has shown a great deal of cross-cultural variation in the comparison of the four cultures investigated by the World Health Organization (1983) and in many other cross-cultural studies. The pivotal role assigned to guilt feelings in a number of influential Western conceptualizations of depression may be called into question on the basis of cross-cultural data (Binitie, 1975; Diop, 1967; German, 1972; Peltzer, 1995; Zeldine et al., 1975). So far, the cross-cultural study of depression has not yet progressed to the point of being able to pinpoint the worldwide invariant manifestations of depression. Moreover, depression has both an elusive core and fuzzy boundaries. Both of these features raise the question of depressive equivalents in a cross-cultural perspective. Kleinman's (1982) extensive observations of depression in China have led him to conclude that a pattern of fatigue, discouragement, and weakness constitutes the contemporary Chinese mode of depressive manifestations in mainland China.

China is not the only country in which somatization has been identified as a prominent avenue of experiencing and communicating personal unhappiness and psychological distress. It is widespread in other East Asian cultures such as Japan and Korea as well as in Africa and Latin America. It is also frequently encountered among patients in the United States, even though, because of the psychodynamic orientation of a great many North American mental health professionals, it is not highly valued. All of these observations have caused Kirmayer (1984) to conclude that "at present there are insufficient data to support the claim that some cultures are more prone to somatization than others" (p. 170). At the same time, he concedes that "the nature and meaning of somatic symptoms vary widely across cultures" (p. 170). Among other features, bodily symptoms of depression may vary across cultures in prominence and visibility. While the bias of numerous North American clinicians would be in favor of psychological manifestations of distress, as opposed to physiological ones, Kirmayer (1984, p. 170) cautioned that "the other face of somatization is psychologization, the tendency

to perceive distress in psychological terms and to seek psychological treatment. Just as both interpersonal and intrapsychic problems can be expressed
through bodily complaints, so somatic disease and social conflict can be
cloaked in psychological guise." Leff (1977, p. 74) went so far as to say that
"only in the contemporary West is depression articulated principally as an
intrapsychic experience (e.g., 'I feel blue')." These considerations may fore-
stall an ethnocentric, deficiency-oriented explanation of the somatic experience of depression and other modes of distress. The Chinese and other
depressive patients who voice physical complaints may be genuinely more
perceptive of negative bodily sensations that accompany depression than are
their Euro-American counterparts.

Like many other psychopathological phenomena, depression can be construed as a transaction (Kleinman, 1986). In such a view, the social perception and communication of depression assumes prominence. Moreover,
these social components of depression are subject to cultural shaping. Thus,
it has been demonstrated that affective symptoms are often missed by di-
agnosticians in patients who are members of a different cultural group (e.g.,
De Hoyos & De Hoyos, 1965; Kiesling, 1981). These findings are sometimes cited in connection with the demonstrated tendency to label members
of other cultural groups schizophrenic or to assign them to the various
personality disorders. Some observers (e.g., Fernando, 1988; King, 1978)
have ascribed this phenomenon to prejudice, rejection, or racism. A more
general explanation (Draguns, 1990) posits that the subtle clues that are
indispensable for the perception of depressive experience in another person
are easy to miss across a cultural gulf. Moreover, empathy does not travel
well across culture lines (Draguns, 1996a & 1996b). In the face of behaviors
that are both strange and disturbed, clinicians fall easily into the trap of
opting for the most disturbed and deviant category, which in psychiatry is
schizophrenia. Recognizing genuine distress, despite the obtrusive trappings
in which it is cloaked, and experiencing its affective reverberations are a
challenge to clinicians who work in culturally pluralistic settings. Specula-
tively, the lag that transcultural investigators experienced in acknowledging
depression in Africa, South and East Asia, and other locations may be traceable to discerning depressive affect in culturally alien contexts. By this time,
it is generally recognized that some aspects of depressive experience are
encountered over a wide range of cultures and that no major region of the
world is free of its manifestations. It would be premature to assert, however,
that depression is a human universal that is present in all cultural groups.
Such a statement not only would gloss over the complexity of pinning down
the essential features of depression but would also be vulnerable to refutation by a single well-documented negative instance. At this point, I am not
aware of such a refutation so that one can say that depression has so far
been found wherever it was studied.

Subject to these complexities, it can be stated on the basis of the available evidence that the incidence rates of depression are subject to cultural variation. The most ambitious comparison of rates of major depression was undertaken in a recent epidemiological study of ten nations (Weissman et al., 1996) in which the diagnosis of depression was based on uniform criteria derived from DSM-III. The differences across nations in this project proved to be substantial, but they were not easy to explain. In the authors' words (Weissman et al., 1996, p. 297), "the rate of major depression for Korea is twice as high as compared to Taiwan, two Asian industrialized nations. Paris, with a temperate climate, stable economy, and political structure has a rate of major depression almost as high as Beirut, a city that had been besieged by war for the past 15 years. Much has been said about the blending of Canadian and United States identities and cultures, but the rate for major depression is generally twice as high in urban Edmonton compared with four urban catchment areas of the United States." Certainly, these findings should be taken seriously and be further pursued. As yet, it is premature to accept them as definitive.

Depression, though present, occurs less frequently and, according to some observers, is expressed less elaborately in various regions such as the Far East and South of the Sahara in Africa (Kleinman, 1982; Yap, 1965; German, 1972; Peltzer, 1995). Its mode of presentation and the nature of its experience have less to do with self-castigation or guilt than with total and overwhelming distress, expressed through both psychic and somatic channels.

Along somewhat related lines, Rädar, Krampen, and Sultan (1990) explored cultural differences in internal versus external locus of control (Rotter, 1966), that is, in attributions of events and happenings to self or to others. Their subjects were hospitalized depressed patients in Egypt and in Germany who were compared with their nondepressed and nonpsychiatric counterparts hospitalized for medical reasons in the two countries. Rädar et al. found that external orientation was more prevalent in Egypt than in Germany in both depressed and control patients. This study illustrates the potential in going beyond the symptoms in investigating the more subtle variations in mood disorder across cultures.

Less can be said of the opposite extreme of the affective spectrum: abnormal excitement, mania, and euphoria that often occur within the context of bipolar affective disorder. In the recent ten-nation epidemiological comparison (Weissman et al., 1996), bipolar affective disorder was found to vary considerably less than the unipolar variety of major depression. Still, the range of cross-national variation was substantial. At this point, these findings are preliminary and need to be replicated. In the case of the Pennsylvania Amish, Egeland, Hofstetter, and Eshleman (1983) have documented the tendency of the local psychiatrists to misdiagnose the manics in their midst chizophrenics, another instance of using schizophrenia to cover instances of extreme deviance in people who are generally "different" and little understood.

SUICIDE: A CENTURY OF COMPARING RATES

Emil Durkheim (1951), the great sociological theorist, is usually credited with having inaugurated the international comparison of official suicide statistics. Moreover, he proposed an explanation of differences in suicide rates across countries that remains viable, though not uncontested, to this day. What Durkheim proposed was that social cohesion counteracted suicidal tendencies and that social isolation, loneliness, and alienation promoted suicidal tendencies. A prominent variant of suicide was traced to anomie, a condition in which human behavior is ineffectively regulated and insufficiently integrated into a social setting. As a general explanatory principle, lack of integration into culture has, however, held up exceedingly well in light of the comparison of suicide statistics around the world (Desjarlais, Eisenberg, Good, & Kleinman, 1995). In a comparison of ten countries of Western Europe and North America, a positive relationship between rates of suicide and those of unemployment has been established (Bloor, 1980), as predicted in Durkheim's formulation. Anomie as a social condition has proved to be exceedingly difficult to assess, so that it is more often invoked post hoc than predicted as a determinant of high suicide rates. Durkheim's idea that Protestant countries would have higher suicide rates than Catholic ones, presumably because of the difference in the levels of anomie, did not lead to clear-cut positive results, although several Catholic countries, such as Ireland and Spain, showed extremely low suicide rates, and a number of Protestant countries, such as Denmark and Sweden, had high suicide rates. At this time, close to a century after Durkheim's formulations, the generalization is even less valid. Consider three countries with some of the highest suicide rates in the world: Austria, Czechoslovakia, and Hungary, all of which have a substantial majority of Catholics, even though the influence of the Church over the lives of the people in these three states has experienced a considerable decline over the last few decades. Obviously, the nominal religious affiliation of the majority of the inhabitants is, at best, a very uncertain guide to the social cohesion of their country, and lack of social integration is only one of the factors that determine the frequency of suicide, although, at this point, it is the variable that has been most intensively and successfully investigated. Inversion of aggression or suicide as anger turned inward has proved to be less universally valid as an explanation of mainsprings of suicide (Desjarlais et al., 1995). Undoubtedly, a great many cases of suicide are traceable to this dynamic and may in part account for the elevation of suicide rates in countries racked by civil strife and violence, such as Sri Lanka in the last decade (Desjarlais et al., 1995). Other characteristics come into play, such as the proportion of aged and/or unattached persons in the population, which in turn is related to a country's birthrate. Old people are at risk for suicide, especially if they live alone. Another vulnerable segment of the population is composed of young people, and observations in the recent decades have generated a lot of concern with the increase in the suicide rate of adolescents and young adults. According to Jilek-Aal (1988), this is an international trend, observable in the same time span in cultures as different as those of Norway and Japan, and of the Indians and Inuit of northwestern Canada. Paris (1991) has gone further and linked these recent age-specific increases to social disintegration within the family. As social cohesion has broken down, there has been, according to Paris, a virtual epidemic of behavioral and affective turbulence among young people, which in North America is typically diagnosed as borderline personality disorder. These personality patterns are associated with an increased proportion of suicide attempts. As the family environment restabilizes, Paris (1991) predicts, the rash of impulsive suicide attempts mainly occurring among the young will also subside, and some tentative indication of a decline of suicide rates in this age group has been observed in Canada and the United States in the last few years. Tseng and McDermott (1981) have concluded that the rates of completed suicide for the entire population of a country reflect enduring cultural factors and are typically subject to relatively little change over time. By contrast, rates of attempted suicide are much more sensitive to disruptive and discontinuous social change.

Suicide rates, then, are an index of several coalescing cultural characteristics. It is generally recognized that they are an imperfect indicator contaminated by the distortions of suicidal statistics that are brought about by embarrassment, concern for the survivors, or sheer administrative and clerical sloppiness. It should be added, however, that much progress has been made since Durkheim and others blazed the trail in using suicide statistics as a social indicator. At this time, the available statistics are used with a sophisticated awareness of their imperfection.

ANXIETY DISORDERS IN OTHER CULTURES: THE CASE OF JAPAN

On the whole, a disproportionate share of cross-cultural information on abnormal behavior is focused on the most disabling disorders: major depression and schizophrenia. Ironically, these disorders may be among the ones least susceptible to cultural shaping. This is especially true of schizophrenia. The urgency of studying and understanding these debilitating states is probably a major reason for their prominence in the transcultural research literature. The other reason, more down to earth, is the availability of hospitalized patients for international comparison. By the same token, anxiety states, which are with few exceptions ambulatory, have been relatively neglected, at least in major comparative international studies. There is as yet no research parallel in scope and penetration to the WHO international comparisons of depression and schizophrenia. What multinational studies have been conducted (Lynn, 1971, 1975; Lynn & Hampson, 1975, 1977) are based on indirect, ingenious, but arguable indicators of anxiety in the general population. For these reasons, the relevance of this research for the understanding of the interplay of cultural factors and *clinical disturbance is not clear*. On the basis of the worldwide composite of clinical and anthropological investigations, Pfeiffer (1994) concluded that separation anxiety, fear of the unknown, and fear of solitude are readily observable in traditional small-scale cultures, such as those of Australian aboriginal tribes (e.g., Cawte, 1964). Cultures based on hunting and gathering provide a lot of conditions that trigger intense avoidance reactions and panic states (Pfeiffer, 1994).

The descriptive literature on the culturally distinctive manifestations of some of the anxiety disorders is well worth noting. In Japan, for example, psychiatrists have described the syndrome of *taijin-kyofushu* (Russell, 1989; Tanaka-Matsumi, 1979), a variant of social anxiety that often occurs in young men who are insecure about social status. Transitions from adolescence to adulthood, or changes in job or residence, are among the conditions that precipitate this disorder. Its principal manifestations include extreme self-consciousness often accompanied by negative concerns or beliefs about one's physical appearance and bodily odor. Sometimes these convictions reach a delusional elaboration and intensity. In reference to the official diagnostic manual used in the United States, the DSM-IV (American Psychiatric Association, 1994), this disorder is rather difficult to classify. Several components of it have been empirically established (Kirmayer, 1984 & 1991). They range from a relatively simple stress-related anxiety state, through a social phobia of varying severity, to a clearly psychotic delusional state that would be diagnosed as paranoid schizophrenia by Western clinicians. What these observations suggest is that the current official U.S. catalogue of mental disorders can accommodate a prominent disorder from another culture only with difficulty. Perhaps this conclusion is both obvious and trivial, but it does point to the range of cultural plasticity in expressions of distress. Social anxiety is experienced in both North America and Japan; its respective expressions show more than a culture tinge.

CULTURE-BOUND SYNDROMES

In this connection, the general problem of culture-bound reactive syndromes may be addressed briefly. Over a century or more, reports of indigenous manifestations of psychological disturbances from remote and exotic lands have been accumulating (Murphy, 1982; Prince, 1985). Such behavior patterns as *amok* and *latah* have been identified. Without describing any one of these syndromes in detail, what can be said is that many of their manifestations are dramatic and conspicuous. Their onset is sudden, and the symptoms of the disorder are often dangerous to self and others. The immediate need is for restraint. If the person is protected from his or her frenzy, the disturbance quickly subsides. Chronicity is rare. Such is the case with amok, which can be described as a combination of excitement and fury, often set off by a relatively mild interpersonal slight or disappointment. The apparent disturbance is extreme, but this impression is belied by the quick disappearance of its symptoms. Moreover, it is not clear whether all the culture-bound syndromes really belong within the rubric of abnormal behavior as the term is commonly understood. In same cases, they constitute ritualized and consciously controlled responses, usually to a stressful situation (e.g., Salisbury, 1966). In other instances, there are serious doubts whether the behavior in question, such as *Windigo*, an alleged attack of cannibalistic frenzy among Ojibwa Indians, ever actually occurred (Marano, 1982). The alternative construction, supported by copious evidence and persuasive argument, is that a mythical belief and an observable behavior pattern were confounded.

The challenge to Western observers is to find for these syndromes appropriate and flexible slots in their diagnostic system, which originated at a point in space and time that yet aspires to comprehensiveness and universality. This effort has recently been gathering strength (Kirmayer, 1991; Prince, 1985). As a result, in the current version of the official American psychiatric diagnostic manual, DSM-IV (American Psychiatric Association, 1994), both the impact and the range of cultural factors are explicitly recognized as important influences on the experience and manifestations of mental disorder. The consensus of experts in this field is that culturally distinct syndromes are not necessarily entities *sui generis* but, rather, slightly to moderately different variants that can be fitted into the existing slots of the diagnostic system. Often they are psychotic in appearance but on more thorough observation and analysis have closer affinity to anxiety and/or stress disorders. The flip side of the coin is the emerging recognition that some of the disorders in the DSM-IV may be the culture-bound conditions of their place and time. Among the candidates for such status are some of the prominently diagnosed syndromes of contemporary North America, such as the borderline personality disorder and anorexia nervosa.

THE CULTURAL FACTORS IN EATING DISORDERS

In the 1970s and 1980s, speculations were voiced about the cultural sources of the dramatic burgeoning of the incidence of self-induced starvation, or anorexia nervosa. Why did this disorder mushroom and spread across the United States and Canada, a phenomenon apparently paralleled in other economically developed countries? Prince (1985) was among the first to recognize the potential role of the culture in the development of this syndrome, although data on ethnic differences within the United States and other pluralistic cultures remain inconclusive, as do also the results of international comparisons. Selvini Palazzoli (1985) identified anorexia nervosa as the syndrome of the affluent society, and DiNicola (1990) was able to confirm this relationship in a searching review of the pertinent evidence. In his words, "Anorexia nervosa shows a developmental gradient across cultures, with predominance in industrialized, developed countries. . . . Both the social class and cultural bias of anorexia nervosa share an association with affluence" (DiNicola, 1990, p. 286).

Consistent with this conclusion, case studies and descriptive research have begun to appear from countries and regions to which affluence has spread in recent decades, for example, Hong Kong (Lee & Hsu, 1995). Chinese anorexic adolescent girls experience less fear of becoming fat, and the gamut of depressive symptoms is less frequently encountered among them by comparison with their counterparts in Great Britain and North America. Instead, their complaints are more somatically oriented, as exemplified by intolerable fullness in the stomach, fear of acne, and distaste for food. Descriptions of anorexics in India (Khandelwal & Saxena, 1990) are compatible with these findings. These observations highlight the relationship of anorexia nervosa to the variations in culturally mediated standards for a socially acceptable or ideal body image. Moreover, the findings recapitulated call into question the Western notion that fear of obesity constitutes the fundamental dynamic of anorexia nervosa.

VARIATIONS IN ALCOHOL ABUSE AND THEIR CULTURAL MEANING

Ethnic and cultural differences in alcohol consumption and in the rates of alcohol-related disorders are well-established topics of cross-cultural study. Over the years, much information has been collected on the cultures that produce a disproportionate amount of alcohol abuse. Cultures that are characterized by a low percentage of problem drinkers have also been investigated. In the latter category are Jews, Chinese, and Italians, both in their countries of origin as well as in the United States and other New World locations. The former category includes the Irish (Stivers, 1976) and several Native American (Mail & McDonald, 1980) groups. The differences between these two types of culture pertain to the manner in which alcohol consumption is socialized and controlled (MacAndrew & Edgerton, 1969). Contrary to what one might expect on a common-sense basis, the child in the Jewish, Italian, or Chinese family is often introduced to alcoholic beverages early in life. This, however, usually occurs in a ritualized, festive context at which the amount of alcohol consumed is at most moderate (Snyder, 1958). By contrast, alcohol in many other ethnic groups, including those with a reputation for excessive consumption, is first tasted in secret, outside of the family setting, and often in the context of rebellious adult and/or masculine self-assertion. Alcohol in low-consumption cultures is regarded as food, in those characterized by heavy use it is viewed as akin to a drug, designed to produce changes in mood and consciousness. In more extreme cases, alcohol becomes a general antidote against frustration, as a universal means to drown out sorrow, insecurity, or helplessness. If such an attitude is widespread within an ethnic group and if, moreover, it is transmitted by explicit instructions or implicit modeling, its members are likely to be at risk for alcohol abuse. Other factors no doubt play a role, such as the perceived uselessness and the resulting low self-esteem of many Native American and some African American young men, deprived and cut off from their traditional male roles. Alienation fosters heavy drinking: Aboriginal alcoholics, removed from their customary habitats, yet not integrated into modern Australian urban life, come to mind in this connection.

And yet it would be a mistake to conclude that all the pieces in the above picture fall neatly into place. Above all, it is easy to succumb to the stereotype of the alcohol-prone Irish and of the Jews or Chinese who are immune to this problem. Historical research has shown that the Irish reputation for heavy drinking originated in the eighteenth century (Stivers, 1976). The contemporary Irish-American figures for alcohol consumption tend to approach the national average and the statistics on the consumption of alcohol in the Republic of Ireland are not extreme. Conversely, as Jewish family life in the United States loses its distinctive traditional characteristics and approximates the general norm, some of the built-in safeguards against heavy alcohol consumption are likely to weaken. Indeed, there are some tentative indications that the alcoholism rate among the Jews in North America and of the Chinese on the mainland, in Taiwan, Hong Kong and the diaspora is gradually rising (Desjarlais, et al., 1995).

Similarly, volumes have been written about the major problem of alcohol abuse in France (e.g., Sadoun, Lolli, & Silverman, 1965) and about the low number of alcohol abusers in Italy (Lolli, 1958)—both nations that are Latin, Catholic, and wine producing, but the hidden, yet crucial difference between these two countries remains to be discovered. However, in the largest international epidemiological study as yet undertaken, Helzer and Cannino (1992) documented the low rates of alcohol abuse in China, by comparison with high prevalence rates for the United States. Interestingly, alcohol abuse was found to be widespread in Korea which shares with China values of self-control and self-restraint and other aspects of a family-centered orientation. This contrast between the two countries remains to be further explored. More generally, reviewers (Desjarlais et al., 1995; Heath, 1986) are in agreement that alcohol abuse around the world defies being traced to a unitary cause. Disentangling the multiple determinants of excessive and problematic alcohol consumption is a challenge for future investigators.

FROM FINDINGS TO EXPLANATIONS:
THE MEANING OF CROSS-CULTURAL DIFFERENCES
IN PSYCHOPATHOLOGY

This chapter's cursory survey of cross-cultural differences has now been completed. It has hit some of the highlights but omitted a lot of the details. The time has come to explain these findings. What general principles would account for the data just summarized? If possible, the nature of the relationship between culture and psychological disturbance should be identified and the differences in abnormal behavior traced to their corresponding cultural features.

In reference to the first objective, one possible link between modal and abnormal behavior within a culture is that the latter represents an inappropriate exaggeration of the former. Typical and adaptive patterns of behavior are applied at the wrong place and time or in the wrong way. They become a reduction to absurdity or a caricature of culturally prevalent modes of coping. Two examples will suffice. Díaz-Guerrero (1967, 1994) identified passive versus active responses as the characteristic modes of coping with stress in Latin American and Anglo-American milieus, respectively. Several comparisons of Latin American and North American psychiatric patients have demonstrated that passive symptoms are prevalent among the former and active symptoms among the latter (Draguns, 1990).

External locus of control (Rotter, 1996) emerged as a significant differentiator of both depressed and psychiatrically unimpaired medical Egyptian patients from their respective German counterparts (Räder, Krampen, & Sultan, 1990). This finding was corroborated and extended in a tricultural comparison of Afghan, Egyptian, and German patients (Shakoor, 1992). Of particular interest is the similarity of Egyptian and Afghan results, and their contrast to the German data. In a parallel fashion, Tseng, Asai, Jieqiu, Wibulswasd, Suryani, Wen, Brennan, & Heiby (1990) noted a resemblance between the responses of anxiety disorder patients in the two politically distinct, but culturally similar Chinese locations of Shanghai and Taiwan, which set them apart from the Indonesian, Japanese, and Thai patients who were also included in the same comparison. Thus, both cultural differences and similarities appear to be reflected in the verbal reports and behaviors of identified psychiatric patients. Three relatively recent studies (Räder et al., 1990; Radford, 1989; Tseng, Asai, Jieqiu, Wibulswasd, Suryani, Wen, Brennan, & Heiby, 1990), which included both normal and clinically diagnosed samples in two or more cultures, are compatible with a more general conclusion, that is, that the characteristic psychiatric symptoms of a culture reflect its prevailing or typical personality traits.

As far as the second objective is concerned, progress in this field has for a long time been stymied by the absence of empirically based dimensions on which various cultures could be placed. This lack has now been remedied by the well-known major study by Hofstede (1980; 1991) in which four such dimensions were identified. This was done by means of multivariate statistical procedures applied to the analysis of responses of several thousand subjects from more than 40 countries of all regions of the world. The four dimensions derived in this manner were individualism-collectivism, uncertainty avoidance, power distance, and masculinity. A recent attempt was undertaken to extend these four variables to the domain of abnormal psychology (Draguns, 1996b). Individualistic cultures, as exemplified by the United States and the countries of Western and Northern Europe, were found to be characterized by internalization of distress, experience of guilt, chronicity in schizophrenia, and predominance of cognitive symptoms. In collectivistic cultures, such as Japan, China, and several Latin American cultures, psychiatric symptoms revolved around specific human relationships. If guilt was felt, it occurred in the context of such relationships, rather than in reference to violations of absolute and abstract principles (Kimura, 1995). Uncertainty avoidance was discovered to be associated with manifestations of anxiety, whereas masculine cultures tended to promote catastrophic responses to failure, for example, in the form of suicide. These leads are at this point few and isolated, but they should be extended if research is initiated to test explicitly the relationships between Hofstede's four dimensions and the features of psychological disturbance.

At the same time, a start has been made toward connecting these four basic variables with the culturally distinctive components of psychotherapeutic intervention (Draguns, 1990). That psychotherapy differs across cultures has been solidly established (cf. Prince, 1980), even as the cross-culturally constant ingredients of psychotherapy have been identified. The interplay of the cultural and the universal transactions in the psychotherapeutic encounter is sometimes conspicuous and at other times subtle and barely perceptible. It has been proposed but as yet not demonstrated that psychotherapeutic intervention in individualistic cultures would emphasize self-understanding and insight, together with themes of guilt, alienation, and loneliness (Draguns, 1996a). In collectivistic cultures, in contrast, a more expressive and close relationship between the therapist and client would be promoted, with the goal of enhancing well-being rather than festering self-understanding. Cultures with a high need for uncertainty reduction would stress scientific and objective explanations, whereas in low uncertainty-avoidance cultures, variety and spontaneity in psychotherapy would prevail and immediate experience would be prized. Power distance in a culture would be characterized by emphasis on the therapist's expertise; low power distance would go hand in hand with egalitarianism, confrontation, and improvisation in the conduct of psychotherapy. In masculine cultures, the therapist would facilitate the client's adjustment to the culture. By contrast, therapists in feminine cultures would foster the client's self-realization and self-expression in preference to the culture's rules and concerns. These expectations have as yet not been systematically tested, even though they are compatible with descriptive accounts of psychotherapy in various cultural settings characterized by low or high placement on the above four dimensions.

Finally, cultural variations in self-experience and self-concept may be relevant, or indeed crucial, to consider. In recent years, the self has evolved as a central concept in linking psychology and culture (Chang, 1988; Landrine, 1992; Markus & Kitayama, 1991; Kimura, 1995; Nathan, 1994; Roland, 1988; Triandis, 1989). Many theorists emphasize the contrast that exists between the sociocentric and autonomous selves, which are purportedly prevalent in collectivistic and individualistic cultures, respectively. A sociocentric self is typically an aggregate of experiences, skills, and practices that come into play in specific social interactions with significant figures in a person's life. The person's uniqueness is expressed in the distinctiveness of these encounters. As Chang (1988) put it, a sociocentric self binds or ties the person to his or her family, reference group, or community. By contrast, the individualistic self marks a sharp boundary between the person and the rest of the world. This distinction reverberates in the psychiatric symptoms of collectivistic and individualistic cultures, respectively. The full implications of these variations—and of subtler distinctions in self-experience, such as those identified by Roland (1988) between Japan and India or by McClelland, Sturr, Knapp, and Wendt (1958) between the United States and Germany—remain to be described and pinpointed.

CONCLUSIONS

The investigation of the interplay between culture and mental disorder is a young but rapidly developing area of inquiry. Much progress has been achieved in the past 30 years, and these advances are reflected in the preceding pages. The extent and limits of cultural influences on the manifestations of abnormal behavior have been identified, and a much clearer panoramic picture has emerged of the manner in which these influences operate. Furthermore, links have been suggested between the way in which cultures construe self-experience and the mode of expression of psychiatric distress, distortion, and dysfunction. Within the last two decades, cultural dimensions have been described that are very likely to be reflected in psychiatric symptomatology, even though the details and the specifics of this relationship are only gradually coming to light. Certainly gaps and ambiguities remain, but an agenda for the systematic exploration of the field is being implemented. It will keep investigators active for decades to come.

17

Mental Health Treatment and Service Delivery in Cross-Cultural Perspective

Harriet P. Lefley

In most societies, the form and content of mental health service delivery has been based on a constellation of cultural variables and socioeconomic realities. Belief systems, values and value-orientations, religious and medical practices, family structure, economic organization and resources, and societal needs for protection and order have all affected both identification and treatment of persons defined as needing mental health treatment. In some countries, the political philosophies of persons in power have also had a significant impact on the structure of mental health service delivery (Al-Issa, 1995).

Across cultures, practitioners differ in their explanatory models of disorder or illness, their diagnostic practices and treatment technologies, and often in the types of patients their particular specialty is designed to serve. Although in many traditional cultures the priest and healer are one, most distinguish between religious practitioners and herb doctors. The latter, however, functioning on the principle of mind-body unity, can usually cure afflictions of the spirit as well as physical illness or disability. Almost all cultures in the world, from tribal units to nation states, acknowledge an officially sanctioned Western medical system as well as a traditional healing system. They also recognize the types of cases their respective practitioners are trained to serve. In cases of persistent behavioral deviance, or psychotic behavior, indigenous healers typically recognize when Western medicine is indicated and make appropriate referrals (Lefley, Sandoval, & Charles, 1997).

Paradoxically, the training of mental health professionals in Western industrialized nations has often been less specialized and more diffuse. There is greater reliance on a core body of etiological theories and standardized diagnostic procedures rather than, as in native healing, on specific precipitants and correlative cures for individual cases. In Western education, although psychotropic medications are in the purview of those who are medically specialized—psychiatrists and psychiatric nurses—all core professions have been trained in psychotherapies oriented toward treating persons with ordinary problems in living or impediments to self-actualization. In many programs there is a far greater training emphasis on this clientele than on treatment and rehabilitation of persons with serious mental disorders (National Institute of Mental Health, 1990). In developing countries with scarcer resources, the tendency is to orient both training and services toward the most needful populations and to integrate these services with primary health care at the village level (see Asuni, 1990; Nagaswami, 1990; Yucun, Changhui, Weixi et al., 1990).

The treatment techniques of indigenous and Western healers inevitably differ, although both will use medications and somatic therapies as needed. In healing disorders of the mind/spirit, native healers look to supernatural causality or external malevolence, focus on immediate precipitants, and help afflicted individuals direct their behavior toward propitiating gods, performing requisite rituals, or balancing unequal forces. Western healers look to internal causality and individual history or behavioral patterns. They focus on eliciting verbalization, abreaction, insight, and/or behavioral or cognitive change. Western psychodynamic therapies have often been lengthy, costly, and elitist, and except for the affluent and educated few, are not frequently practiced in non-Western societies. In these cultures, Western psychopharmacologic and rehabilitative technologies are usually directed toward those people whose psychotic symptoms and incapacity for self-care have overtly identified their need for professional intervention.

In another chapter in this book, Juris Draguns has spoken of cultural concepts of psychopathology and correlative issues of diagnosis. It is evident from a proliferating body of biological research that certain core diagnostic entities such as schizophrenia appear to be found in all human groups (Jablensky et al., 1991; Sartorius et al., 1993; Warner, 1994). However, problems of differential diagnosis continue to abound. There is a very large literature on cultural aspects of diagnosis such as those relating to the use of assessment instruments and interviewing techniques, language and psycholinguistics, understanding culturally normative and deviant behavior, and other issues involving social distance between clinicians and patients (Lefley, 1990a, 1991). Diagnostic clarity may be confounded by cultural differences in behavioral manifestations of psychosis (Mezzich, Kleinman, Fabrega, & Parron, 1996). This is why such studies as the International Pilot Study of Schizophrenia are so important, since they develop mechanisms for diagnostic uniformity across cultures (Jablensky et al., 1991; Leff, Sartorius, Jablensky et al., 1992).

This chapter deals primarily with the structures that cultures have developed to deal with the mental health needs of their populations. It discusses the development and interface of community and institutional mental health systems, and the interface between Western medicine and indigenous healing systems. Commonalities of traditional and modern cultures are described.

Differences in approach derive from differing world view and belief systems, kinship structure and caregiving roles, and cultural attitudes toward dependency and disability. Enculturation within the matrix of sociocentric or collectivist versus individualistic societies affects both self-perception and the way society treats persons perceived as behaviorally deviant or as mentally ill (Triandis, 1995). Social structure and world view also affect caregiving roles and family-professional relationships—particularly the manner in which professionals perceive and interact with their patients' kinship network (Lefley, 1985). Longitudinal changes in the Western world and cross-sectional changes as nations begin to modernize are linked in projecting the cultural context of future mental health systems throughout the world.

COMMUNITY MENTAL HEALTH IN DEVELOPING COUNTRIES

In 1975, the World Health Organization (WHO) began a collaborative study on strategies for extending community-based mental health care in developing countries. Services were to be offered by primary health care workers in pilot study areas in selected countries as part of general medical care. The study found that these primary health care workers indeed could deliver mental health care at the community level. According to the major investigators, the research itself was a catalyst that "has served to change attitudes toward disease and health in general as well as toward mental illness; it has served to sensitize workers to important wider psychosocial issues" (Sartorius & Harding, 1983, p. 1462). Further collaborative research has continued with respect to optimal dosage and duration of psychotropic medications; effectiveness of psychosocial interventions at the primary care level; management of common psychiatric problems of patients visiting primary health care facilities; home management of the mentally retarded; and factors that influence help-seeking and attitudes of health personnel toward mental health problems (Sartorius & Harding, 1983).

In most countries of the world, mental health and health care are merged, long predating the "linkage model" that became popular in the United States in the 1970s and continues today in health maintenance organizations and other types of managed care. Private mental health care in the United States, however, is oriented toward acute hospitalization and time-limited interventions. It does not address the needs of chronic patients, who are largely handled in the public sector. In most settings, medical and psychiatric services continue to be segregated both conceptually and physically. On the other hand, integrated medical, mental health, and case management services have long been incorporated in the more fluid and less compartmentalized systems of the developing countries. Presently, there is an initiative to include psychosocial rehabilitation in the national health care programs of developing countries (Nagaswami, 1990).

Despite the relative advantages of Western nations in funding, facilities, and professional personnel, several areas of relative strength are apparent in the service delivery systems of developing nations. First is the more efficient utilization of scarce resources, with providers often offering home services that are typically unavailable in the clinic-based systems of industrialized countries. Second, culturally syntonic diagnostic and treatment procedures merge indigenous healing systems with scientific modalities. Third, and extremely important, is the inclination of most practitioners in the developing world to welcome and integrate their patients' families, their natural support systems, into the treatment process. In fact, in a series of mental health program descriptions in various developing countries, there is not one that fails to mention that families are viewed as the central supportive resource in caregiving and treatment (Lefley, 1990b).

The planning process and training of skilled paraprofessionals facilitate some efforts from which Western systems could learn a great deal. For example, a few trained primary health workers doing a field survey for a "community mental health care net" in a district in China with 190,000 population—about the size of a community mental health center catchment area in the United States—were able to identify all individuals needing help for severe psychiatric problems (Yucun et al., 1990). This is certainly more direct and efficient than our customary needs assessments. With far greater resources, American systems target estimated percentages of at-risk populations, rather than identified individuals in need of mental health care, and would consider direct case-finding an extraordinary luxury.

Anthropologists generally agree that in most non-Western societies, traditional healers are the first resort in mental health problems, and they continue to be used even after psychiatric systems are enlisted (Jilek, 1993). In many countries, there is a respectful acceptance of dual and sometimes mutually referring modern and traditional medical/mental health systems. In Chinese hospitals, a pharmacopaeia of herbal remedies coexists with the latest in psychotropic medications. A center for Ayurvedic medicine is found among the buildings at the National Institute of Mental Health and Neurosciences in Bangalore, India, an important modern training center for psychiatrists and other mental health disciplines. In many African countries, indigenous healing is integrated with modern psychiatry.

The ARO village system in Nigeria and other African countries was started by World Health Organization psychiatrist Lambo (1978). Here, after treatment in a Western mental hospital or clinic, psychiatric patients live with a relative in a traditional village close to the mental health facility. Treatment is organically related to village life, combining native healing rituals with psychotropic medication and group therapy. Asuni (1990) has described a similar system run solely by traditional healers. This "involves the active participation of relatives of the mentally ill. In fact, the relatives have to live with their ill member in the compound of the traditional healers to provide creature needs of the patient and also to participate in the healing rituals" (pp. 35–36). The treatment consists of administration of herbs (which typically include *Rauwolfia Serpentina*, which has known antipsychotic properties, as an active component), performance of rituals, and recitation of incantations. Initially kept under restraints, patients are given greater freedom of movement and are involved in household chores and other village community activities as their mental state improves. Asuni notes that "even though it is not identified as such, rehabilitation is built into the system of care and treatment by traditional healers" (p. 36).

Among certain ethnic groups in the United States, indigenous healing not only provides an explanatory model for the patient and family, but may functionally permit mastery through manipulation of the powerful gods (Lefley, Sandoval, & Charles, 1997). Equally important are the human resources found in "cult houses" such as those of Haitian *Vodou*, Afrocuban *Santeria*, or Hispanic *Espiritismo*. For many transplanted immigrants, the communal practice of ritual provides an extended kinship network augmenting or replacing missing family ties. There is ample evidence that, as in traditional cultures, persons with psychiatric problems will use biomedical and supernatural healing systems simultaneously in order to meet different needs (Gaw, 1993; Jilek, 1993; Lefley, Sandoval, & Charles, 1997).

When community mental health centers started expanding in the United States in the early 1970s, there was widespread recognition of the need for culturally appropriate services. A number of centers around the country developed innovative programs to serve specific cultural groups (Dana, 1982; Lefley & Bestman, 1991; Ruiz & Langrod, 1976). In many of these centers, there was a principled attempt to link patients with indigenous healers when necessary, and there are many examples of successful healing that integrated biomedical and spiritual interventions (Lefley, 1991; Lefley & Bestman, 1991). In Puerto Rico, anthropologist Koss-Chioino (1992) had a longstanding Therapist-Spiritist Training Project, which brought together mental health professionals, medical doctors, and spirit mediums to educate each other about disease concepts and models of diagnosis and treatment.

Western therapists treating newly entrant groups such as Southeast Asians will try to use psychoeducational approaches and explanatory models that incorporate salient elements of the clients' belief systems (Jordan, Lewellen, & Vandiver, 1995). We have long known that in most traditional cultures, Cartesian mind-body dualism is unknown, so many patients do not conceptualize mind and emotions as distinct from bodily experience. In dealing with Southeast Asian refugees who have gone through multiple traumatic transitions in their escape and subsequent entry into the United States, Kinzie (1986) and his associates have developed an extremely creative therapeutic technique. Utilizing the principle of mind-body unity, they have patients link a history of their experiences with a drawing of the human brain and body. The patients recall stressful transitional periods such as a fearful sojourn in a displaced persons camp, or a difficult boat journey. The therapists then point out visually on the drawing what was happening in the patients' brain and body as they responded to these stressors and what is happening as they relive the experience.

Other innovative approaches are used in clinics that treat immigrants from diverse cultures. The Department of Psychiatry of the University of California, San Francisco, maintains ethnic minority focus units in their teaching hospital, San Francisco General, training residents in transcultural psychiatry in an inpatient setting (Zatrick & Lu, 1991). In the same hospital, "a Cambodian woman complaining of insomnia was offered sleeping pills and also encouraged to seek a blessing from a krou khmer, a native healer. . . . Illiterate hill tribesmen from Laos are taught how to take their pills, which are taped to an index card under pictures of the sun and moon at different places in the sky" (Gross, 1992). In many clinics, staff have learned the importance of humoral medicine concepts, such as taking pills with warm water rather than cold to balance *yin* and *yang* for Chinese patients, and hot-cold elements of disease in the belief systems of many Hispanic and Caribbean patients.

CULTURAL FACTORS IN REHABILITATION AND PROGNOSIS

In the United States, community development has sometimes been conceptualized as a means of primary prevention to raise the mental health levels of entire catchment area populations (Lefley & Bestman, 1991). In other countries, creative deployment of community resources is a means of providing tertiary rehabilitative care for persons already identified as mentally ill. Dunlap (1990) has described activities and programs that operate at the interface of community development, rehabilitation services, and community reintegration of mentally ill persons in countries as diverse as India, Micronesia, and Australia. Here community resource development is "conducted for the purpose of making normative roles of living, working, socializing available to persons with mental illness that is of a disabling nature" (p. 67). One of the most intriguing examples of this is the experiment attempting deinstitutionalization in Italy.

The Italian Experiment

In 1978, under the leadership of Italian psychiatrist Franco Basaglia, Italy passed Law 180, which banned all new admissions to public mental hospitals, converted all inmates to voluntary status, and decreed that in place of state hospitals, psychiatric units of 15 beds per 150,000 population would be established in all general hospitals (figures considerably below the need established in the United States, where there are 130 psychiatric beds per 100,000 population). Mental health policy in both the United States and Italy has exemplified the politicization of illness. In the United States, deinstitutionalization was endorsed by an unlikely alliance of civil libertarians and fiscal conservatives. In Italy, Law 180 was pushed through by left-wingers who merged antipsychiatry with Marxism, in consort with right-wing Christian Democrats who viewed deinstitutionalization as a money-saving measure.

In some parts of Italy, the former government-run hospitals have been taken over by the Catholic Church, and approximately 35,000 patients are still institutionalized. Community mental health services have since developed very unevenly, with great disparity in the resources available in northern and southern Italy. In many parts of Italy, families are greatly burdened with a major caregiving role and inadequate clinical supports to deal with grossly psychotic behavior (Jones & Poletti, 1985). An overview of studies of the Italian reform movement found that in the south, community support services were virtually nonexistent compared with other parts of Italy (Bollini & Mollica, 1989).

In northern Italy, however, in Trieste, Brescia, and Verona, some resources are on the cutting edge of psychiatric rehabilitation. According to M. Farkas, an international trainer of rehabilitation workers affiliated with Boston University's Center for Psychiatric Rehabilitation, there are almost 100 work cooperatives for people with mental disabilities (Farkas, 1992, personal communication). In contrast to employment conditions in the United States, patients work in first-class industries producing high-quality products of which they can be proud. All businesses are small with no more than 15 to 20 people. Since psychiatric patients have difficulty tolerating overstimulating or high-demand environments (Lefley, 1992), here they can work without excessive interpersonal stimulation and at their own pace.

A 15-year study looked at the long-term psychosocial outcome of patients with schizophrenia in southern Italy (Sardinia) who were discharged after the 1978 reform. The investigators found that 70 percent of the patients showed poor or very poor adjustment or severe maladjustment. Most were single, and 85 percent were unemployed. Their treatment histories were marked by a large number of hospitalizations and rare or irregular outpatient contacts (Fariante et al., 1996). The researchers noted that their 1996 study confirmed earlier findings that patients treated in areas with inadequate services had the worst outcomes, while good outcomes in social performance are found in regions with good rehabilitative services such as those in northern Italy (Mignolli, Laccincani, & Platt, 1991).

The Italian findings tell us something about the potential of well-designed rehabilitative models to change the lives of people who would otherwise be hospitalized. They also highlight the relationship of good and poor mental health services to relapse and rehospitalization. Other studies from the World Health Organization point to the larger social context as a predictor of prognosis and outcome.

The World Health Organization Studies

The International Pilot Study of Schizophrenia (IPSS) of the WHO was a nine-culture study that demonstrated transcultural agreement on the symptom clusters diagnosed as schizophrenia. Continuing WHO studies of ten cultures found a similar incidence rate in developing and developed countries (Sartorius et al., 1993). These findings have tended to reinforce growing evidence from neuropathology, neuroradiology, neurochemistry, hematology, and genetics that schizophrenia is a biologically based pan-human disorder. At follow-up, however, the WHO studies have found significantly better prognosis in the developing countries than in the industrialized West (Leff, Sartorius, Jablensky, et al., 1992).

It should be noted at this point that even in the developing countries, there is a core group of individuals who do not have a good prognosis. Studies from various sources suggest that approximately one-third do not stabilize and do poorly over the long-term (Lin & Kleinman, 1988; Mendis, 1990; Westermeyer, 1989). Nevertheless, the developing countries seem to provide a more favorable climate for many patients to avoid progressive social disability.

Explanations for the more benign course of illness have usually postulated lower stress and higher social support in the developing countries, together with a worldview that both expects recovery and frees the patient and family of blame. Opportunities for productive labor, supportive families and extended kinships networks, and externalization of causality have all been considered factors in lowering stress levels and facilitating recovery (Lin & Kleinman, 1988; Lefley, 1990a; Warner, 1994). A brief summary of these views regarding the relationship of culture and prognosis follows.

Externalized causality. In traditional cultures, psychiatric symptoms are typically viewed in terms of a somatic or supernatural model of etiology. This generates less social rejection and less self-devaluation of patients and creates expectations that this is a temporary aberration. Because there are many culture-bound syndromes that are brief and self-limiting (see Draguns' chapter, this book), this expectation leads to lack of stigmatization in first-episode or short-term cases of major disorders and facilitates remission of symptoms. (In cases of recurrent episodes, however, and particularly when there is a long history of bizarre antisocial behavior, the person becomes defined as chronically mentally ill and then is highly stigmatized in many traditional cultures.)

Different concepts of selfhood. Major psychotic disorders such as schizophrenia tend to fragment the self, but cultural concepts of personhood are a key to how self-disorganization is experienced and evaluated. In less individualistic cultures, people's concept of self is merged with that of the group. This tends to mitigate a sense of responsibility and guilt for personal deficiencies, unless they are connected with the group's common good. Fabrega (1989) has suggested that in Western culture, with its highly individualistic ethos, the loss of the sense of self in conditions such as schizophrenia involves a loss of control, autonomy, and meaning that makes it difficult for afflicted persons to distance themselves from their disorder. There is a fusion of identity with the illness. The person self-identifies as a mental patient, a "loser," which leads to alienation and despair and induces chronicity.

Estroff (1989) similarly has argued that culture affects prognosis by mediating the relationship between the self and the sickness. In Western cultures, persons are seen as unique beings with an enduring core of meaning and knowledge; thus, the loss of the former personality and of positive social roles are seen as chronic conditions that fundamentally alter the person. Because self-disorganzation is viewed as a temporary condition in traditonal cultures (particularly those in which trance possession and other ritual dissociative states are common), self-evaluation and interpersonal relationships are not so readily affected.

Work. One of the big problems in rehabiliation in the United States is that mental patients, many with education and skills, often have to work in demeaning entry-level jobs and sometimes find even that work too demanding in terms of hours or pace of activity. In developing countries, patients can work in agrarian economies in normalized roles and usually at their own pace. Thus there is no message from the culture that diminishes their value as productive human beings.

Different concepts of dependency and interdependence. According to noted anthropologist Francis Hsu (1972), the overarching American core value is fear of dependency. The emphases on self-reliance and personal autonomy that so characterize the U.S.-American value system have been generalized to the most basic treatment philosophies. Throughout the deinstitutionalization and rehabilitation literature, the phrase "return the patient to independent living" appears constantly, regardless of whether the goal is realistic or even advisable for all classes of patients. Emphasis on self-reliance carries over into psychotherapy. An African psychologist from an interdependent tribal background expressed his concern at reconciling his own cultural norms with the major psychotherapeutic goal of loosening dependency ties on significant others (Uzoka, 1979). The Japanese psychiatrist Takeo Doi (1973), describing the central Japanese concept of *amae*—a reciprocal honoring of adult dependency roles—reported his surprise at finding the concept entirely missing from the English lexicon.

In community-based treatment for persons with severe mental illnesses, aftercare planning in the United States has rarely made provisions for supportive networks. Day treatment and rehabilitation programs have had high-expectancy goals based on the implicit value of a client's attaining ultimate separation from the program. The linguistic terminology of mental health programs embodies expectations of linear progress: "transitional," "step-level," or "half-way" and "three-quarter way."

Experiences with severely mentally ill people suggests that this orientation may be far too demanding and may exacerbate precisely those feelings of anxiety and apartness that are central to their illness. A "transitional" policy in mental health planning imposes a built-in impermanence in the lives of people who may need long-term stability in order to remain intact. In traditional societies, families provide this stability through a permanent caregiving role. The concept of interdependence, which characterizes most sociocentric societies, provides roles for mentally ill people. It also enables them to accept and benefit from familial caregiving without the personal and interpersonal conflicts that plague dependent adults in many Western cultures.

Family structure and differential family burden. The extended family network in traditional cultures has also been postulated as a factor in prognosis (Greenley, 1995; Leff & Vaughn, 1985; Lin & Kleinman, 1988). In many cases, this provides a large and benign support system for the mentally ill person. In most nuclear families, there are typically only two adults and often only one person with the major responsibilities of caregiving. In contrast to the charged atmosphere of most overburdened nuclear households, the extended family provides both financial and emotional buffering mechanisms to dilute the problems of living with a dysfunctional adult whose difficult behavior must be tolerated and forgiven. The network may also have a greater capacity for providing occasional work or other productive roles.

In the West, a growing literature indicates extensive family burden in caring for persons with severe and persistent mental illness (Greenley, 1995; Lefley, 1996). This may involve dealing with bizarre or abusive behavior, curtailment of social activities, disruptions of household functioning, and constant crises that often involve the police and psychiatric emergency rooms. Families are caught in an ongoing tension of balancing their own rights and those of other family members with those of the person with mental illness, and in balancing expectations that may be too high or too low. They also suffer empathic pain for a loved one, perhaps once bright with promise, who typically leads an impoverished life and must relinquish former aspirations.

In the United States, a critical aspect of family burden, reported by many families in surveys of their experiences, has come from frustrating and often humiliating interactions with mental health service providers (Greenley, 1995; Lefley, 1996). Although family education is standard procedure when patients are hospitalized for medical conditions, for many years relatives of persons with mental disorders, seeking this type of education, experienced responses from professionals ranging from evasiveness to outright rejection. Professional-family relations are now changing in the West, but these types of interactions have been quite unknown in traditional cultures (Shankar & Menon, 1991).

CULTURAL DIFFERENCES IN
FAMILY-PROFESSIONAL RELATIONSHIPS

In all societies, long-term hospitalization in remote institutions has tended to isolate mentally ill persons from their families and to foster abandonment. In the West, however, for many years patients were deliberately distanced from their relatives because of theories of family pathogenesis and requirements of psychodynamic treatment models. To avoid contamination of transference and preservation of the therapeutic alliance, pychotherapists rejected contact with families and excluded them from any involvement in treatment. Under an all-inclusive definition of confidentiality, families were often denied essential information needed for the caregiving role. Some professionals agreed to meet and then expressed open hostiliy toward families because of their presumed roles in causing their patients' illnesses (Greenley, 1995; Lefley, 1996).

Later, family systems models catapulted family members into family therapy, on the premise that psychotic symptoms would cease when they were no longer needed to maintain homeostasis of a dysfunctional family system. With little empirical support and unsatisfactory outcomes, most systemic family therapies moved away from the treatment of schizophrenia and other severe mental illnesses toward nonpsychotic disorders. Family members who had experienced this earlier therapeutic approach recalled bewilderment and anger that their expressed needs for information, support, and illness management techniques were consistently ignored (Greenley, 1995; Lefley, 1996). Subsequently, psychoeducational family interventions were developed that did meet these needs and that were not based on any presumptions of family psychopathology. They also provided empirical research evidence of their effectiveness (Dixon & Lehman, 1996).

The present era has seen some remarkable changes in the West as a result of developments in several domains. The proliferation of biological and genetic research findings has led to widescale abandonment of theories of family causation of major disorders such as schizophrenia or major affective illnesses. Corollary research on family burden has alerted professionals to the devastating experience of living with mental illness in the household. The pragmatic needs of deinstitutionalization have made it necessary for professionals to work more closely with family caregivers.

Perhaps the most notable advances have come from the emergence of powerful advocacy movements for the mentally ill composed largely of family members. At this writing, at least 35 nations have organizations focusing on support, education, and promotion of adequate services (Johnson, 1995). In the United States, the National Alliance for the Mentally Ill (NAMI) has more than 1,000 affiliates. Similar organizations have emerged throughout Europe, Asia, and Australia.

Focusing on advocacy for basic research, increased funding for services, public education, destigmatization of mental illness, patients' rights, insurance parity, and similar issues, NAMI has become a powerful political force in less than two decades. State and government funding sources have mandated family and consumer participation on mental health planning and governance bodies, and mental health professionals have found it beneficial to ally with large constituencies of NAMI groups for legislative advocacy. When they meet the families of their patients in different roles, moreover, professionals have reported that their former prejudices have changed to admiration for families' coping strengths under conditions of extreme stress (Johnson, 1995; Lefley, 1996).

Relations In Traditional Cultures

In non-Western cultures, relationships between families and practitioners have been quite different. In both traditional healing and in psychiatric practice, family members have been welcomed as partners in the therapeutic process (Asuni, 1990; Lefley, 1985, 1990a; Report of a World Health Organization [WHO] Meeting, 1990). Family members typically accompany their ill relative to the hospital and often live in nearby compounds provided by the hospital, fulfilling an auxiliary nursing and feeding role until the patient is discharged (Lefley, 1985). In traditional cultures, it would be inappropriate for a healer to withhold information from a patient's relatives, so the family is almost always informed of diagnosis, indicated therapeutic modalities, and prognosis. Above all, in cultures that have different explanatory models of mental illness, theories of family pathogenesis present cognitive dissonance and family-blaming is largely unknown. Two prominent Indian psychiatrists describe relationships of families and professionals in India:

The family has always been regarded by professionals as a working partner. . . . [There is] an absence of conceptual dogma dictating professional-family interaction. In contrast to those in the West, mental health professionals in India generally have not dealt with families on the basis of any etiological presupposition regarding their role in the causation of illness. Because of this, professional-family interactions have been on a relatively even keel and the ideological see-saw from viewing families as schizophrenogenic in the 1950's to viewing families as equal treatment partners in the 1980's has not taken place. (Shankar & Menon, 1991, p. 86)

Culture and Expressed Emotion Research

Some important clues to both treatment and etiology have come from the international research on expressed emotion (EE). Early work of Brown, Birley, and Wing (1972) in Great Britain suggested that family members' responses to the Camberwell Family Interview (CFI) were associated with certain types of patient outcome in schizophrenia. Remarks indicating criticism, hostility, or emotional overinvolvement above a certain cutoff point on the CFI were scored as high EE, while those below the cutoff were scored as low EE. A consistent association was found between high EE of at least one family member and relapse in patients, a finding since replicated in numerous studies throughout the world.

An extensive literature has emerged regarding EE as a construct and as a predictor (Lefley, 1992). Despite attempts to control for patients' level of psychopathology, researchers are still conflicted about whether familial EE levels actually predict relapse or whether patients' characteristics mediate both familial EE and their potential for relapse. Moreover, although the correlation between high EE and relapse remains constant in the short-term (typically one-year follow-up), a large number of recent studies indicate that the association seems to disappear or diminish over time (Lefley, 1992).

All EE researchers have explicitly denied any implication of family pathogenesis, but rather have ascribed relapse to "ordinary family interactions" that may be too stressful for persons with the core deficits of schizophrenia. Some major investigators have described high EE families as intrusive, excitable, critical, and overprotective and low EE families as empathic, calm, patient, and respectful (Leff & Vaughn, 1985), while others dispute any type of trait definitions. Clinicians and researchers have suggested that high EE is not specific to families and that EE analogues should be sought in clinical and rehabilitative environments.

Despite the misconceptions of many clinicians, studies from Scotland, India, England, Denmark, and from Mexican-descent families in the United States have demonstrated that the majority of persons with schizophrenia live in low EE families (Jenkins & Karno, 1992; Lefley, 1992). It was primarily among urban Anglo-Americans and urban Australians that the number of high EE relatives exceeded those of low EE relatives. In terms of the trait definitions previously cited, the majority of families of persons with schizophrenia are empathic, calm, patient, and respectful, disputing a vast clinical literature on family characteristics.

Leff has linked the better prognosis in developing countries to lower EE in families (Leff & Vaughn, 1985). He suggests that criticism, hostile remarks, or emotional overinvolvement are more likely to be found in the overwhelmed nuclear family, whereas the extended families are better able to diffuse the burden. This may be one piece in the tapestry of variables that affect the course of serious mental illness. It is important to note, however, that family structure is embedded within cultural systems that determine how people view illness roles and the obligations of human beings to each other.

INDIVIDUALISTIC AND SOCIOCENTRIC CULTURES

The concepts of selfhood, views of dependency and disability, and attitudes toward patients' families are closely interrelated with the degree of importance assigned to the individual versus the group and the responsibility of the group toward its members (Triandis, 1995). These types of cultural norms are very much related to how a society conceptualizes and cares for its disabled, dysfunctional, and dependent citizens—in this case, persons with long-term mental illnesses. They determine the rights and prerogatives of these individuals, society's obligations to care for them, and the type of mental health system developed to serve them.

In traditional cultures, adults typically live in the parental home until they marry, and there is no specific age ceiling for leaving. Disabled adults continue living with their families of origin, and families are expected to care for them. The question of individual autonomy is unrelated to these living arrangements. The notion that it is pathological for adult children to remain under parental supervision, a basic premise of some family therapies, is culturally dystonic in many traditional societies. Paternalistic concern with the affairs of an adult child would be considered appropriate behavior, rather than emotional overinvolvement. In such cultures, there is little evidence of the independence-dependency conflicts that are so characteristic of family-patient relationships in Western society and that frequently consume the therapeutic hours of Western practitioners.

In certain political systems, however, individualist philosophy has been suppressed. A visiting Russian psychiatrist captured the perils of a sociocentric model that minimizes the rights of individuals in comparing psychiatric treatment in the United States and in the former Soviet Union (Yegorov, 1992). He marveled that "contrary to Soviet practice, it would never occur to anyone in a U.S. psychiatric hospital to monitor patients' outgoing mail or impede its delivery, no matter how deranged its content may be" (p. 8) but also noted that Russian psychiatrists feel that "the strict guarantee of the rights of the mentally ill that is required by American laws may result in certain negative medical and social consequences to some patients" (p. 12). Our cultural emphasis on the rights of individuals has spurred a large number of lawsuits and generated new legislation in many areas of the United States. Many of these have been initiated by advocacy groups for persons with mental illnesses.

PATIENTS' RIGHTS AND THE RISE
OF CONSUMERISM

Societies that are sociocentric or collectivist by tradition, religion, or political ideology generally expect the subordination of individual rights to those of the group or the body politic (Triandis, 1995). Thus, there may be a commonality of views among the traditional cultures of developing countries and those of industrial countries such as the former Soviet Union and Japan. These tend to be sociocentric vis-à-vis the more individualistic views of Western Europe, the United States, and Canada. Sociocentric cultures are far less likely to be concerned with the balance between rights and needs of mentally ill persons, a problem of increasing concern in the Western world.

The rights of mental patients have been a prominent issue in the United States and various Western European countries since deinstitutionalization began. Vigorous advocacy for the civil liberties of people with mental illness was long overdue. In the United States, for example, for many years citizens were stripped of their civil liberties when they entered a state hospital. Regardless of their willingness to seek treatment voluntarily, persons who had committed no crime were deprived of their right to vote, marry or divorce, keep bank accounts, or sign contracts. In institutional settings, they often had no redress against abuse.

With the forward surge of deinstitutionalization in the United States, our cultural emphasis on the rights of individuals spurred a large number of lawsuits and generated new legislation. The result has been rigorous limitations on involuntary commitment and treatment. In 1986, federal legislation set up protection and advocacy centers in each state to ensure that patients were not being mistreated and were receiving appropriate services in public institutions. Concomitantly, organizations of present and former psychiatric patients, termed consumers, were developing and are now growing rapidly throughout the world. In the United States, many of their efforts were devoted to patients' rights and in the most radical wing, opposition to any involuntary treatment.

It is precisely in the area of forced treatment that the differences between individualistic and sociocentric worldview becomes highly salient. Protection of civil liberties and individual self-determination are among the most cherished cultural traditions of democratic societies, but may be at odds with society's obligation to protect others and to care for the disabled. This is a very special issue when the population in question consists of persons who are cognitively impaired and lack the capacity for informed judgment. The debate about the rights of severely mentally disordered people to reject treatment, to remain homeless, or to live under conditions of life-threatening self-neglect continues to pose a major value conflict in Western cultures (Lefley, 1997).

The development of the consumer movement, however, has also provided a forum for the destigmatization and growth of many people who formerly would have languished in institutions or been isolated in homes. With great encouragement and funded support from the Community Support Program of the National Institute of Mental Health, formerly hospitalized mental patients are now functioning as paid research assistants, knowledge disseminators, case managers, operators of residences and drop-in centers for persons with mental illnesses, and support persons in crisis management teams. Consumer-operated enterprises include housing and residential placement services, case management, peer counseling programs, social centers, job placement, crisis respite houses, and special programs for the homeless (Lefley, 1997).

A European network of consumer movements, based in Rotterdam, has held several large meetings. Consumer groups are also found in Australia, Japan, New Zealand and are beginning in Latin America. In Eastern Europe, some consumer groups are developing the types of consumer-run facilities already implemented elsewhere, such as half-way houses, drop-in centers, and sheltered employment. These consumer efforts are concordant with longitudinal research that has demonstrated unexpectedly good prognosis many years after psychiatric hospitalization in both the United States and Europe (Harding, 1988). The current era has also seen a remarkable social change in the way mentally ill persons are portrayed in the media. Empirical and media validation of the potential for recovery from mental illness may begin to fertilize the ground for the gradual process of destigmatization.

Meanwhile, the WHO is showing support and encouragement for consumer involvement in mental health services throughout the world. At a WHO meeting in Germany on consumer involvement in mental health services, there was strong affirmation of patients' empowerment, rights to representation, and access to medical records, as well as the rights of consumers to participate actively in the planning and implementation of mental health services. However, the conference specifically took note of cultural differences. Mindful of the debate in the United States between families' emphasis on patients' right to treatment and the emphasis of some consumer groups on patients' right to reject treatment, the WHO report warned against developing patient advocacy groups that might pit their agenda against those of their families (Report on a World Health Organization Meeting, 1990).

FUTURE DIRECTIONS

In the United States, we are seeing the growth of managed care to control rising medical and mental health costs. Some countries with national health insurance show similar curtailment or slow growth of needed services because of rising costs. The acute care model of managed care may have highly damaging effects on the long-term rehabilitative services needed by persons with severe and persistent mental illness. Alternatively, however, the cost restrictions and medicalizing emphasis of managed care may focus more on the treatment of disorders viewed as biologically based.

Funding cuts and managed care restrictions may have a corollary impact on clinical training—on the number of future mental health professionals and the focus of their education. Predictions for psychiatric education in the

United States are for greater emphasis on treating major mental illness and neurobehavioral disorders rather than psychological problems in living; more attention to psychosocial rehabilitation for the disabled rather than psychotherapy for the general population; and more emphasis on psychopathological aspects of medical conditions (Lieberman & Rush, 1996). With third-party payers refusing to pay for more than a few psychotherapy visits (increasingly assigned to lower paid social workers) there will be less training in psychoanalytically oriented psychodynamics.

The adaptation of psychiatric training to focus on biologically based disorders, develop a non-Cartesian view of psychological and physical illness, and retreat from long-term psychotherapy functionally moves American practice more toward the mental health systems of the developing world. Conceptually also, there seems to be a merger of Western scientific thought and its correlative healing systems with implicit folk models of a seamless psyche and soma. Western theoreticians for many years ascribed mental illness to psychogenic or sociogenic factors. The proliferation of research findings pointing to biogenesis of the major psychiatric disorders has led to a biopsychosocial model. This is a more holistic view in which somatic vulnerabilities interact with psychosocial stressors that can affect the course of illness, without attributions as to causality. Increasing utilization of treatment modalities such as massage and acupuncture also lessen the distance between Eastern and Western therapeutic approaches.

The WHO research findings suggest that the course of a mental disorder may be profoundly affected by the culture in which it is experienced. Cultures differentially provide social acceptance, support systems, appropriate work opportunities, and balanced expectations of persons with core cognitive and perceptual deficits in attention and information processing. Western nations are beginning to understand the benefits of extended support systems and normalizing productive roles for persons with variable levels of functional impairment.

Worldwide, the growth of consumer movements indicates that many persons once impaired enough to have required hospitalization are able to offer services, counseling, role-modeling, and hope to less functional peers. Data from multiple sources, from the international longitudinal research (Harding, 1988), from the cross-sectional WHO Collaborative Study on Determinants of Outcome (Jablensky et al., 1991; Sartorius et al., 1993), and the successful cooperative ventures of northern Italy (Fariante et al., 1996), tell us much about what persons with mental illness are able to accomplish given the right cultural context. With decreased stigmatization, adequate support systems, and appropriate expectations—all culturally determined—together with increasingly perfected psychopharmacy and rehabilitative technologies, the future for persons with mental illness may be brighter in the years ahead.

Epilogue

That this second edition of *Cross-Cultural Topics in Psychology* so closely
follows the publication of the first edition in 1994 is testimony to the increasingly rapid advances in cross-cultural psychology and international psychology on a worldwide scale posited by Denmark (1994). Further evidence
of the growing interest among psychologists, universally, is the steady rise
of international psychological and cross-cultural associations, the significant
increases in the structure and membership in these associations, and the
founding of new professional journals devoted to these interests. Foremost
among such advances currently and in the very recent past are, respectively,
to mention only a few:

1. Until quite recently, going as far back as 1920, there were only three major
   international psychological associations, IAAP, ICP, and IUPsyS, and only one
   major cross-cultural psychology association, IACCP (Merenda, 1995). Now, there
   are innumerable such formal associations, many of them organized within specific
   areas of psychology.

2. The first international psychological association to be formally organized in 1920
   was the International Association of Applied Psychology (IAAP). The first IAAP
   division was not established until 1978, and the second, in 1982. Today, there
   are 13 divisions. For most of its history, the International Union of Psychological
   Science (IUPsyS) had a membership of fewer than 50 national societies. In 1995,
   the membership rose to 51 nations. Today, there are more than 60 national members and the number is increasing (Ritchie, 1996).

3. *World Psychology*, the official journal of the International Council of Psychologists
   (ICP), was first published in 1995.

In light of the foregoing, it becomes evident that this important updated
book fulfills a need, which is to keep the reader abreast of rapid develop-

ments and global interests in psychology. The editors, Leonore Loeb Adler and Uwe Peter Gielen, have long been recognized as international and cross-cultural psychologists. Most of the authors likewise have been so recognized internationally. Many of them are not only charter members of the new American Psychological Association (APA) Division of International Psychology, they have also spearheaded the drive within APA to establish Division 52.

The second edition of the book retains the same format as the first edition. There are five parts, each presenting a collection of topics ranging from the history of cross-cultural studies to the applications of cross-cultural psychology. The authors of the chapters are essentially the same as those who authored the chapters in the first edition and who expanded on and updated the themes they expounded initially. Three new chapters have been added, and one chapter has been eliminated. In this second edition, the Foreword and the Epilogue were contributed by well-known international psychologists, Dr. Florence L. Denmark and Dr. Peter F. Merenda.

Mainly significant among the additions is the chapter by Brislin, "Intercultural Contact and Communication." For the last quarter of this century, Richard Brislin has been recognized as one of the most outstanding and prominent cross-cultural psychologists. In fact, he is a renowned *patriarch* in the field. His seminal book as senior author (Brislin, Lonner, & Thorndike, 1973) is considered a precursor to the many books on comparative studies in the behavioral sciences that have followed and are yet to follow.

An additional chapter, "Psychological Aspects of Immigration," by Paul Schmitz of Bonn, Germany, is of great current interest in the field and should be well received by scholars and students of cross-cultural psychology.

A third new chapter by the bicultural psychologist Pittu Laungani discusses the influence of culture on the nature and experience of stress by comparing the value systems and social life of India and England.

Cross-cultural psychology and cross-cultural research have always been important to students of psychology, especially at the graduate level. It is hoped and expected that the vital contents of this book will serve to stimulate further interest in the topics that are so well presented by eminent cross-cultural psychologists. It is further hoped that a book such as this will stimulate graduate departments of psychology to develop courses on the topics and related ones as well, and to begin to consider seriously developing programs leading to graduate degrees in cross-cultural psychology.

References

Abou, S. (1978). Integration et acculturation des immigrés: Un modèle d'analyse (Integration and acculturation of immigrants: A model of analysis). *Migrants-Formation, 29/30*, 35–39.

Adityanjee, D. (1986). Suicide attempts and suicides in India. *International Journal of Social Psychiatry, 32* (2), 64–73.

Adler, L. L. (1975). *Issues in cross-cultural research.* Conference sponsored by the New York Academy of Sciences, New York, October 1–3.

Adler, L. L. (Ed.). (1977). *Issues in cross-cultural research.* New York: Annals of the New York Academy of Sciences, *285.*

Adler, L. L. (Ed.). (1982). *Cross-cultural research at issue.* New York: Academic Press.

Adler, L. L. (1989, April). *A personal appreciation of Wilhelm Maximilian Wundt.* Paper presented at the Annual Meeting of the New York State Psychological Association, New York.

Adler, L. L. (1989). *Cross-cultural research in human development: Life-span perspectives.* New York: Praeger.

Adler, L. L. (1991). In appreciation of Wilhelm Maximilian Wundt. *The Psychologist, 42*, 18–19.

Adler, L. L. (Ed.). (1991). *Women in cross-cultural perspective.* Westport, CT: Praeger.

Adler, L. L. (1993). (Chair). *Research on human behavior: The shift from universality towards cultural diversity.* Symposium at the American Psychological Association, Toronto, August.

Adler, L. L. (1993, February 19–21). *Gender roles of the elderly in cross-cultural perspective.* Paper presented at the Annual Convention of the Society for Cross-Cultural Research, Washington, DC.

Adler, L. L. (1994, August). Collaborating with researchers across countries and cultures. *International Psychologist*, 18–19.

Adler, L. L. (1994). Women and gender roles. In L. L. Adler & U. P. Gielen (Eds.), *Cross-cultural topics in psychology* (1st ed.) (pp. 89–101). Westport, CT: Praeger.

Adler, L. L. (in press). Gender identity, gender roles, and gender differences. In U. P. Gielen & A. L. Comunian (Eds.), *Cross-cultural and international dimensions of psychology*. Padua, Italy: UNIPRESS.

Adler, L. L., & Clark, S. P. (1999). Female autonomy in life-span and cross-cultural perspective. In M. Nadien & F. L. Denmark (Eds.), *Female autonomy: Life-span perspective*. New York: Allyn & Bacon.

Adler, L. L., Denmark, F. L., & Ahmed, R. A. (1991). A critical evaluation of attributes toward mother-in-law and stepmother: A cross-cultural study. In W. Oxman-Michelli & M. Weinstein (Eds.), *Conference 1989 Proceedings: Critical thinking: Focus on social and cultural inquiry*. Upper Montclair, NJ: Montclair State College.

Adler, L. L., Denmark, F. L., Miao, E.S.Y., Ahmed, R. A., Takooshian, H., Adler, H. E., & Wesner, R. W. (1992). Cross-cultural comparisons of projected social distances toward family members: A programmatic study. In U. P. Gielen, L. L. Adler, & N. A. Milgram (Eds.), *Psychology in international perspective* (pp. 260–270). Lisse, The Netherlands: Swets & Zeitlinger.

Adler, L. L., & Gielen, U. P. (Eds.). (1994). *Cross-cultural topics in psychology*. Westport, CT: Praeger.

Adler, L. L., & Graubert, J. G. (1976). Projected social distances as cross-cultural measure of attitudes toward mental patient-related simuli. *Society for Cross-Cultural Research Newsletter, 4* (1), 9.

Adler, L. L., & Mukherji, R. B. (Eds.). (1995). *Spirit versus scalpel: Traditional healing and modern psychotherapy*. Westport, CT: Greenwood.

Ahmed, R. A. (1989). The development of number, space, quantity, and reasoning concepts in Sudanese schoolchildren. In L. L. Adler (Ed.), *Cross-cultural research in human development: Life-span perspectives* (pp. 17–26). New York: Praeger.

Ahmed, R. A. (1991). Women in Egypt and the Sudan. In L. L. Adler (Ed.), *Women in cross-cultural perspective* (pp. 107–133). Westport, CT: Praeger.

Ahmed, R. A., Gielen, U. P., & Avellani, J. (1987). Perceptions of parental behavior and the development of moral reasoning in Sudanese students. In Ç. Kagitçibasi (Ed.), *Growth and progress in cross-cultural psychology* (pp. 196–206). Lisse, The Netherlands: Swets & Zeitlinger.

Akimoto, H., Sunazaki, T., Okada, K., & Hanashiro, S. (1942). Demographische und psychiatrische Untersuchung über abgegrenzte Kleinstadtbevölkerung. [Demographic and psychiatric investigation of a delimited small-town population]. *Psychiatria et Neurologia Japonica, 47*, 351–374.

Albert, S., & Cattell, M. (1994). *Old age in global perspective: Cross-cultural and cross-nation views*. New York: G. K. Hall.

Alcock, J. (1981). *Parapsychology: Science or magic?* Oxford: Pergamon Press.

Al-Issa, I. (1995a). Culture and mental illness in an international perspective. In I. Al-Issa (Ed.), *Handbook of culture and mental illness: An international perspective* (pp. 30–52). Madison, CT: International Universities Press.

Al-Issa, I. (1995b). The illusion of reality or the reality of illusion: Hallucinations and culture. *British Journal of Psychiatry, 166*, 368–373.

Al-Issa, I. (Ed.). (1995). *Handbook of culture and mental illness: An international perspective.* Madison, CT: International Universities Press.

Allport, G. W. (1937). *Personality: A psychological interpretation.* New York: Holt.

Allport, G. W. (1954). *The nature of prejudice.* Reading, MA: Addison-Wesley.

Allport, G. W., & Odbert, H. S. (1936). Trait names: A psycholexical study. *Psychological Monographs, 47,* (1, Whole No. 211), 1–177.

American Psychiatric Association (1994). *Diagnostic and statistical manual of mental disorders* (4th ed.). Washington, DC.

Amir, Y. (1969). Contact hypothesis in ethnic relations. *Psychological Bulletin, 71,* 319–342.

Amoss, P., & Harrell, S. (1981). *Other ways of growing old.* Stanford, CA: Stanford University Press.

Anastasi, A., & Urbina, S. P. (1997). *Psychological testing* (7th ed.). Upper Saddle River, NJ: Prentice Hall.

Antonucci, T., Fuhrer, R., & Jackson, R. (1990). Social support and reciprocity: A cross-ethnic and cross-national perspective. *Journal of Social and Personal Relationships, 7,* 519–530.

Aptekar, L. (1989). Colombian street children: *Gamines* and *chupagruesos. Adolescence, 24,* 783–794.

Aptekar, L. (1994). Street children in the developing world: A review of their condition. *Cross-Cultural Research, 28* (3), 195–224.

Ardila, R. (1991). Women in Latin America. In L. L. Adler (Ed.), *Women in cross-cultural perspective* (pp. 27–37). Westport, CT: Praeger.

Armstrong, S. (1991). Female circumcision: Fighting a cruel tradition. *New Scientist,* February, 42–47; *Psychological Bulletin, 71,* 319–343.

Aronoff, J. (1967). *Psychological needs and cultural systems: A case study.* Princeton, NJ: Van Nostrand-Reinhold.

Aronson, E., Ellsworth, P. C., Carlsmith, J. M., & Gonzales, M. H. (1990). *Methods of research in social psychology* (2nd ed.). New York: McGraw-Hill.

Aronson, L., Tobach, E., Rosenblatt, J. S., & Lehrman, D. S. (1972). *Selected writings of T. C. Schneirla.* San Francisco, CA: W. H. Freeman.

Asuni, T. (1990). Nigeria: Report on the care, treatment, and rehabilitation of people with mental illness. *Psychosocial Rehabilitation Journal, 14,* 35–44.

Avendaño-Sandoval, R., & Díaz-Guerrero, R. (1990). El desarrollo de una escala de abnegación para los Mexicanos. In AMPESO (Eds.), *La psicología social en México* (Vol. 3, pp. 9–14). México, D. F.: Asociación Mexicana de Psicología Social.

Avendaño-Sandoval, R., & Díaz-Guerrero, R. (1992). Estudio experimental de la abnegación. *Revista Mexicana de Psicología, 2* (1), 15–19.

Bagby, J. W. (1957). A cross-cultural study of perceptual predominance in binocular rivalry. *Journal of Abnormal and Social Psychology, 54,* 331–356.

Bagley, C. (1968). Migration, race and mental health: A review of some recent research, *Race, 9,* 343–356.

Bagley, C. (1969). A survey of problems reported by Indian and Pakistani immigrants in Britain. *Race, 11,* 65–78.

Bagley, C. (1971). Mental illness in immigrant minorities in London. *Journal of Biosocial Science, 3,* 449–459.

Bagley, C. (1993). Mental health and social adjustment of elderly Chinese immigrants in Canada. *Canada's Mental Health, 41,* 6–10.

Baldry, H. C. (1965). *The unity of mankind in Greek thought.* Cambridge, MA: Cambridge University Press.

Baltes, P. B., & Baltes, M. M. (1990). *Successful aging: Perspectives from behavioral science.* Cambridge, MA: Cambridge University Press.

Banks, E. (1989). Temperament and individuality: A study of Malay children. *American Journal of Orthopsychiatry, 59,* 390–397.

Barber, T. X. (1976). *Pitfalls in human research: Ten pivotal points.* New York: Pergamon Press.

Barker, R. G. (1963). *The stream of behavior: Explorations of its structure and content.* New York: Meredith.

Barker, R. G. (1968). *Ecological psychology: Concept and methods for studying the environment of human behavior.* Stanford, CA: Stanford University Press.

Barnouw, V. (1963). *Culture and personality.* Homewood, IL: Dorsey Press.

Barry III, H., (1976). *Cultural variations in sex differentiation during childhood.* Typescript.

Barry III, H., & Paxson, L. M. (1971). Infancy and early childhood: Cross-cultural codes 2. *Ethnology, 10,* 466–508.

Bart, P. (1969). Why women's status changes in middle age: The times of the social ferris wheel. *Sociological Symposium, 3,* 1–18.

Beatty, J. (1980). An analysis of some verbs of motion in English. *Studia Anglica Posnaniensia.* Vol. 11. Poznan, Poland.

Beatty, J., & Takahashi, J. (1994). *Bunka to Komyunikeeshon.* Machida, Tokyo: Tamagawa Daigaku Press.

Becker, E. (1973). *The denial of death.* New York: Free Press.

Beidelman, T. O. (1971). *The Kaguru: A matrilineal people of East Africa.* New York: Holt, Rinehart & Winston.

Beiser, M. (1994). *Longitudinal study of Vietnamese refugee adaption.* Toronto: Clarke Institute of Psychiatry.

Beiser, M., Barwick, C., Berry, J. W., da Costa, G., Fantino, A., Ganesan, S., Lee, C., Milne, W., Naidoo, J., Prince, R., Tousignant, M., & Vela, E. (1988). *Mental health issues affecting immigrants and refugees.* Ottawa: Health and Welfare Canada.

Bellah, R. N. (1985). *Habits of the heart: Individualism and commitment in American life.* Berkeley: University of California Press.

Bem, L. (1974). The measurement of psychological androgyny. *Journal of Consulting and Clinical Psychology, 42,* 155–162.

Bendix, E. H. (1979). Linguistic models as political symbols: Gender and the generic "He" in English. In J. Orasanu, M. K. Slater, & L. L. Adler (Eds.), *Language, sex and gender: Does "La Différence" make a difference?* Annals of the New York Academy of Sciences, Vol. 327.

Benedict, R. F. (1934). *Patterns of culture.* Boston, MA: Houghton Mifflin.

Benedict, R. F. (1946). *The chrysanthemum and the sword.* Boston, MA: Houghton Mifflin.

Berlin, B., & Kay, P. (1969). *Basic color terms: Their universality and evolution.* Berkeley: University of California Press.

Bernard, H. R. (1994). *Research methods in anthropology* (2nd ed.). Thousand Oaks, CA: Altamira.

Berry, J. W. (1969). On cross-cultural comparability. *International Journal of Psychology, 4*, 119–128.

Berry, J. W. (1976). *Human ecology and cognitive style*. Beverly Hills, CA: Sage.

Berry, J. W. (1980). Introduction to methodology. In H. C. Triandis & J. W. Berry (Eds.), *Handbook of cross-cultural psychology: Vol. 2. Methodology* (pp. 1–28). Boston, MA: Allyn & Bacon.

Berry, J. W. (1980). Social and cultural change. In H. C. Triandis & R. Brislin (Eds.), *Handbook of cross-cultural psychology. Vol. 5. Social* (pp. 211–279). Boston, MA: Allyn & Bacon.

Berry, J. W. (1988). Acculturation and psychological adaptation: A conceptual overview. In J. W. Berry & R. C. Annis (Eds.), *Ethnic psychology: Research and practice with immigrants, refugees, native peoples, ethnic groups and sojourners* (pp. 41–52). Amsterdam: Swets & Zeitlinger.

Berry, J. W. (1990). Psychology of acculturation. In J. Berman (Ed.), *Cross-cultural perspectives: Nebraska symposium on motivation* (pp. 201–234). Lincoln: University of Nebraska Press.

Berry, J. W. (1992). Acculturation and adaptation in a new society. *International Migration, 30*, 69–85.

Berry, J. W. (1994a). Acculturation and psychological adaptation: An overview. In A. M. Bouvy, F.J.R. van de Vijver, P. Boski, & P. Schmitz (Eds.), *Journeys into cross-cultural psychology* (pp. 129–141). Amsterdam: Swets & Zeitlinger.

Berry, J. W. (1994b). Immigrant psychological adaptation: An introduction. In P. G. Schmitz & J. Georgas (Chairs), *Adaptation Processes of immigrants: New empirical findings*. 12th International Congress of Cross-Cultural Psychology, Pamplona, Spain.

Berry, J. W., Dasen, P. R., & Saraswathi, T. S. (Eds.). (1997). *Handbook of cross-cultural psychology. Vol. 2. Basic processes and human development* (2nd ed.). Needham Heights, MA: Allyn & Bacon.

Berry, J. W., & Kalin, R. (1995). Multicultural and ethnic attitudes in Canada. *Canadian Journal of Behavioral Science, 27*, 301–320.

Berry, J. W., Kalin, R., & Taylor, D. M. (1977). *Multiculturalism and ethnic attitudes in Canada*. Ottawa: Government of Canada.

Berry, J. W., & Kim, U. (1988). Acculturation and mental health. In P. Dasen, J. W., Berry, & N. Sartorius (Eds.), *Cross-cultural psychology and health: Toward applications* (pp. 207–236). London: Sage.

Berry, J. W., Kim, U., & Boski, P. (1986). Acculturation and psychological adaptation. In Y. Y. Kim & W. B. Gudykunst (Eds.), *Current studies in cross-cultural adaption* (Vol. 2 of Intercultural Communications Annual). London: Sage.

Berry, J. W., Kim, U., Minde, T., & Mok, D. (1987). Comparative studies of acculturative stress. *International Migration Review, 21*, 491–511.

Berry, J. W., Kim, U., Power, S., Young, M., & Bujaki, M. (1989). Acculturation attitudes in plural societies. *Applied Psychology: An International Review, 38*, 185–206.

Berry, J. W., Poortinga, Y. H., & Pandey, J. (Eds.). (1997). *Handbook of Cross-cultural psychology. Vol. 1. Theory and method* (2nd ed.). Needham Heights, MA: Allyn & Bacon.

Berry, J. W., Poortinga, Y. H., Pandey, J., Dasen, P. R., Saraswathi, T. S., Segall, M. H., & Kagitçibasi, Ç. (1997). (Eds.). *Handbook of cross-cultural psychology* (2nd ed.). Needham Heights, MA: Allyn & Bacon.

Berry, J. W., Poortinga, Y. H., Segall, M. H., & Dasen, P. R. (1992). *Cross-cultural psychology: Research and applications.* New York: Cambridge University Press.

Berry, J. W., & Sam, D. (1996). Acculturation and adaptation. In J. W. Berry, M. H. Segall, & Ç. Kagitçibasi (Eds.), *Handbook of cross-cultural psychology.* Vol. 3. *Social behavior and applications* (pp. 291–326). Boston, MA: Allyn & Bacon.

Berry, J. W., Segall, M. H., & Kagitçibasi, Ç. (Eds.). (1997). *Handbook of cross-cultural psychology.* Vol. 3. Social behavior and applications (2nd ed.). Needham Heights, MA: Allyn & Bacon.

Best, D. L., & Ruther, N. M. (1994). Cross-cultural themes in developmental psychology: An examination of texts, handbooks, and reviews. *Journal of Cross-Cultural Psychology, 25* (1), 54–77.

Beveridge, W. M. (1935). Racial differences in phenomenal regression. *British Journal of Psychology, 26,* 59–62.

Beveridge, W. M. (1940). Some differences in racial perception. *British Journal of Psychology, 30,* 57–64.

Bhaskaran, K., Seth, R. C., & Yadav, S. N. (1970). Migration and mental health in industry. *Indian Journal of Psychiatry, 12,* 102–116.

Bhawuk, D. (1995). *The role of culture theory in cross-cultural training: A comparative evaluation of culture-specific, culture-general, and theory-based assimilators.* Unpublished doctoral dissertation, University of Illinois. Ann Arbor, MI: UMI Dissertation Services (UMI No. 9624287).

Bhole, M. V. (1981). Concept of relaxation in *shavasana. Yoga Mimamsa, 20,* 50–56.

Bickman, L., & Henchy, T. (1973). *Beyond the laboratory: Field research in social psychology.* New York: McGraw-Hill.

Biehl, M., Matsumoto, D., Ekman, P., Hearn, V., Heider, K., Kudoh, T., & Ton, V. (1997). Matsumoto and Ekman's Japanese and Caucasian facial expressions of emotion (JACFEE): Reliability data and cross-national differences. *Journal of Nonverbal Behavior, 21,* 3–21.

Binitie, E. (1975). A factor analytic study of depression across cultures. *British Journal of Psychiatry, 127,* 559–563.

Bird, L. (1991). Life in the South Pacific: New Zealand/Aotearoa. In L. L. Adler (Ed.), *International handbook of gender roles* (pp. 218–227). Westport, CT: Greenwood Press.

Birdwhistle, R. (1970). *Kinesics and context.* Philadelphia: University of Pennsylvania Press.

Blass, T. (in press). The Milgram paradigm after 35 years. *Journal of Applied Social Psychology.*

Bloom, A. H. (1977). Two dimensions of moral reasoning: Social principledness and social humanism in cross-cultural perspective. *Journal of Social Psychology, 101,* 29–44.

Bloor, M. (1980). Relationships between unemployment rates and suicide rates in eight countries, 1962–1976. *Psychological Reports, 47,* 1095–1101.

Bochner, S. (1986). Observational methods. In W. J. Lonner & J. W. Berry (Eds.), *Field methods in cross-cultural research* (pp. 165–202). Beverly Hills, CA: Sage.

Bock, P. K. (1980). *Continuities in psychological anthropology*. San Francisco, CA: W. H. Freeman.

Bock, P. K. (1988). *Rethinking psychological anthropology: Continuity and change in the study of human action*. San Francisco, CA: W. H. Freeman.

Bogardus, E. S. (1925). Measuring social distances. *Journal of Applied Sociology, 9*, 299–308.

Boker, W. (1981). Psycho (patho) logical reactions among foreign labourers in Europe. In L. Eitinger & D. Schwartz (Eds.), *Strangers in the world*. Bern: Huber.

Bollini, P., & Mollica, R. (1989). Surviving without the asylum: An overview of the studies of the Italian reform movement. *Journal of Nervous and Mental Disease, 177*, 607–615.

Bond, M. H. (Ed.). (1989). *The cross-cultural challenge to social psychology*. Newbury Park, CA: Sage.

Bond, M. H., Nakasato, H., & Shiraishi, D. (1975). Universality and distinctiveness in dimensions of Japanese person perception. *Journal of Cross-Cultural Psychology, 6*, 346–357.

Bond, M. H., & Smith, P. B. (1996). Cross-cultural social and organizational psychology. *Annual Review of Psychology, 47*, 205–235.

Bornstein, M. H. (1995a). Parenting infants. In M. H. Bornstein (Ed.), *Handbook of parenting* (Vol. 1, pp. 3–39). Mahwah, NJ: Erlbaum.

Bornstein, M. H. (Ed.). (1995b). *Handbook of parenting* (Vols. 1–4). Mahwah, NJ: Erlbaum.

Bornstein, M., & Bornstein, H. (1976). The pace of life. *Nature, 259*, 557–559.

Bornstein, M. H., Tal, J., & Tamis-LeMonda, C. S. (1991). Parenting in cross-cultural perspective: The United States, France, and Japan. In M. H. Bornstein (Ed.), *Cultural approaches to parenting* (pp. 69–90). Hillsdale, NJ: Erlbaum.

Bornstein, M. H., & Tamis-LeMonda, C. S. (1989). Maternal responsiveness and cognitive development in children. In M. H. Bornstein (Ed.), *Maternal responsiveness: Characteristics and consequences* (pp. 49–61). San Francisco, CA: Jossey-Bass.

Bornstein, M. H., Toda, S., Azuma, H., Tamis-LeMonda, C. S., & Ogino, M. (1990). Mother and infant activity and interaction in Japan and the United States: II. A comparative microanalysis of naturalistic exchanges focused on the organization of infant attention. *International Journal of Behavioral Development, 13*, 289–308.

Boski, P. (1994). Psychological acculturation via identity dynamics: Consequences for subjective well-being. In A. M. Bouvy, F.J.R. van de Vijver, P. Boski, & P. Schmitz (Eds.), *Journeys into cross-cultural psychology* (pp. 197–215). Amsterdam: Swets & Zeitlinger.

Botwin, M. D., & Buss, D. M. (1989). Structure of act-report data: Is the five-factor model of personality recaptured? *Journal of Personality and Social Psychology, 56* (6), 988–1001.

Bourguignon, E. (1979). *Psychological anthropology: An introduction to human nature and cultural differences*. New York: Holt, Rinehart & Winston.

Bowman, M. L. (1989). Testing individual differences in ancient China. *American Psychologist, 44*, 576–578.

Boyer, P. (1994). Cognitive constraints on cultural representations: Natural ontologies and religious ideas. In L. A. Hirschfeld & S. A. Gelman (Eds.), *Mapping the mind: Domain specificity in cognition and culture* (pp. 391–411). Cambridge, UK: Cambridge University Press.

Boyes, M. C., & Walker, L. J. (1988). Implications of cultural diversity for the universality claims of Kohlberg's theory of moral reasoning. *Human Development, 31,* 44–59.

Brill, A. (1913). Pibloktoq or hysteria among Perry's Eskimos. *Journal of Nervous and Mental Diseases, 40,* 514–520.

Brislin, R. (1981). *Cross-cultural encounters: Face-to-face interaction.* Elmsford, NY: Pergamon Press.

Brislin, R. W. (1983). *Handbook of intercultural training.* New York: Pergamon Press.

Brislin, R. W. (1986). The wording and translation of research instruments. In W. J. Lonner & J. W. Berry (Eds.), *Field methods in cross-cultural research* (pp. 137–164). Beverly Hills, CA: Sage.

Brislin, R. (Ed.). (1990). *Applied cross-cultural psychology.* Newbury Park, CA: Sage.

Brislin, R. (1993). *Understanding culture's influence on behavior.* Fort Worth, TX: Harcourt Brace.

Brislin, R. W., & Keating, C. F. (1976). Cultural differences in perception of the three-dimensional Ponzo illusion. *Journal of Cross-Cultural Psychology, 7,* 397–411.

Brislin, R., Landis, D., & Brandt, M. (1983). Conceptualizations of intercultural behavior and training. In D. Landis & R. Brislin (Eds.), *Handbook of intercultural training* (Vol. 1, pp. 1–35). New York: Pergamon Press.

Brislin, R. W., Lonner, W. J., & Thorndike, R. M. (1973). *Cross-cultural research methods.* New York: Wiley.

Bronfenbrenner, U. (1970). *Two worlds of childhood: U.S. and U.S.S.R.* New York: Russell Sage Foundation.

Bronfenbrenner, U. (1979). *The ecology of human development: Experiments by nature and design.* Cambridge, MA: Harvard University Press.

Bronfenbrenner, U. (1986). Ecology of the family as a context for human development: Research perspectives. *Developmental Psychology, 22,* 723–742.

Bronfenbrenner, U. (1989). Ecological systems theory. In R. Vasta (Ed.), *Six theories of child development* (Vol. 6, pp. 187–250). Greenwich, CT: JAI Press.

Bronfenbrenner, U. (1993). The ecology of cognitive development: Research models and fugitive findings. In R. H. Wozniak & K. W. Fischer (Eds.), *Development in context: Acting and thinking in specific environments* (pp. 3–44). Hillsdale, NJ: Erlbaum.

Broude, G. J. (1981). The cultural management of sexuality. In R. H. Munroe, R. L. Munroe, & B. B. Whiting (Eds.), *Handbook of cross-cultural human development* (pp. 633–673). New York: Garland.

Brown, G. W., Birley, J.L.T., & Wing, J. K. (1972). Influence of family life on the course of schizophrenic disorder: A replication. *British Journal of Psychiatry, 121,* 241–258.

Brown, J. (1982). Cross-cultural perspectives on middle-aged women. *Current Anthoropology, 23,* 143–156.

Brown, R. (1965). *Social psychology*. New York: Free Press.

Brucks, U. (1994). Psychosoziale und gesundheitliche Probleme der Migration [Psychosocial and health problems of migration]. In A. J. Cropley, H. Ruddat, D. Dehn, & S. Lucassen (Eds.), *Probleme der Zuwanderung* [Problems of immigration] (pp. 53–71). Göttingen: Verlag für Angewandte Psychologie.

Brugger, C. (1931). Versuch einer Geisteskrankenzählung in Thüringen [An attempt to count the mentally ill in Thuringia]. *Zeitschrift für die Gesamte Neurologie und Psychiatrie, 133*, 352–390.

Buck, R. (1984). *The communication of emotion*. New York: Guilford Press.

Burbank, V. K. (1988). *Aboriginal adolescence: Maidenhood in an Australian community*. New Brunswick, NJ: Rutgers University Press.

Burke, A. G. (1977). Family stress and the precipitation of psychiatric disorder: A comparative study among immigrant West Indian and native British patients in Birmingham. *International Journal of Social Psychiatry, 23*, 35–40.

Burling, R. (1964). Componential analysis: God's truth or hocus pocus? *American Anthropologist, 66*, 20–28.

Buss, A. H., & Plomin, R. (1984). *Temperament: Early developing personality traits*. Hillsdale, NJ: Erlbaum.

Butler, R. (1982). Toward a psychiatry of the late life cycle. In S. Zarith (Ed.), *Readings in aging and death*. New York: Harper & Row.

Butzin, C. A., & Anderson, N. H. (1973). Functional measurement of children's judgments. *Child Development, 44*, 529–537.

Campbell, D. T. (1961). The mutual methodological relevance of anthropology and psychology. In F.L.K. Hsu (Ed.), *Psychological anthropology* (pp. 333–352). Homewood, IL: Dorsey.

Campbell, D. T. (1964). Distinguishing differences in perception from failures of communication in cross-cultural studies. In F. Northop & H. Livingston (Eds.), *Cross-cultural understanding: Epistemology in anthropology*. New York: Harper & Row.

Campbell, D. T. (1975). On the conflicts between biological and social evolution and between psychology and moral tradition. *American Psychologist, 30*, 1103–1126.

Campbell, D. T., & Naroll, R. (1972). The mutual methodological relevance of anthropology and psychology. In F.L.K. Hsu (Ed.), *Psychological anthropology* (rev. ed.). Cambridge, MA: Schenkman.

Camus, A. (1955). *The myth of Sisyphus*. London: Hamish Hamilton.

Caprara, G. V., Barbaranelli, C., & Livi, S. (1994). Mapping personality dimensions in the Big Five Model. *European Review of Applied Psychology, 44* (1), 9–15.

Carey, W. B. (1970). A simplified method for measuring infant temperament. *Journal of Pediatrics, 77*, 188–194.

Carment, D. W. (1974). Internal versus external locus of control in India and Canada. *International Journal of Psychology, 9*, 45–50.

Carothers, J. (1948). A study of mental derangement in Africans and an attempt to explain its peculiarities more especially in relation to the African attitude to life. *Psychiatry, 11*, 47–86.

Carraher, T. N., Schliemann, A. D., & Carraher, D. W. (1988). Mathematical concepts in everyday life. In G. B. Saxe & M. Gearhart (Eds.), *Children's math-*

ematics: New directions in child development (pp. 71–87). San Francisco, CA: Jossey-Bass.

Carroll, J. B. (1956). *Language, thought and reality: Selected writings of Benjamin Lee Whorf.* Cambridge, MA: MIT Press.

Carson, R. C. (1989). Personality. In M. R. Rosenzweig & L. W. Porter (Eds.), *Annual review of psychology* (Vol. 40, pp. 227–248). Palo Alto, CA: Annual Reviews.

Carstensen, L. L. (1987). Age-related changes in social activity. In L. L. Carstensen (Ed.), *Handbook of clinical gerontology* (pp. 222–237). New York: Pergamon Press.

Carucci, L. M. (1985). Conceptions of maturing and dying in the "middle of heaven." In D. A. Counts & D. R. Counts (Eds.), *Aging and its transformations: Moving toward death in Pacific societies* (pp. 107–129). Lanham, MD: University Press of America.

Cashmore, J. A., & Goodnow, J. J. (1986). Influences on Australian parents' values: Ethnicity versus socioeconomic status. *Journal of Cross-Cultural Psychology, 17,* 441–454.

Cattell, M. G. (1989). Knowledge and social change in Samia, Kenya. *Journal of Cross-Cultural Gerontology, 4,* 225–244.

Caudill, W., & Plath, D. W. (1966). Who sleeps with whom? Parent-child involvement in urban Japanese families. *Psychiatry, 29,* 344–366.

Cawte, J. E. (1964). Australian ethnopsychiatry in the field: A sampling in North-Kimberly. *Medical Journal of Australia, 1,* 467–472.

Chagnon, N. A. (1983). *Yanomamo: The fierce people* (3rd ed.). New York: CBS College Publishing.

Chamberlain, P., & Patterson, G. R. (1995). Discipline and child compliance in parenting. In M. Bornstein (Ed.), *Handbook of parenting* (Vol. 4, pp. 205–225). Hillsdale, NJ: Erlbaum.

Chang, S. C. (1988). The nature of self: A transcultural view. Part I: Theoretical aspects. *Transcultural Psychiatric Research Review, 25* (3), 169–204.

Channabasavanna, S. M., & Bhatti, R. S. (1982). A study on interactional patterns and family typologies in families of mental patients. In A. Kiev & A. V. Rao (Eds.), *Readings in transcultural psychiatry* (pp. 149–161). Madras: Higginbothams.

Channabasavanna, S. M., Rao, S. R., Embar, P., & Sharieff, I. A. (1970). A review of the cases attending the anxiety neurosis clinic at the Mental Hospital, Bangalore. *Journal of the Indian Medical Profession, 17,* 7733–7737.

Chen, C., & Uttal, D. H. (1988). Cultural values, parents' beliefs, and children's achievement in the United States and China. *Human Development, 31,* 351–358.

Cheng, C.H.K. (1996). Towards a culturally relevant model of self-concept for the Hong Kong Chinese. In J. Pandey, D. Sinha, & D.P.S. Bhawuk (Eds.), *Asian contributions to cross-cultural psychology* (pp. 235–254). New Delhi: Sage.

Chomsky, N. (1965). *Aspects of the theory of syntax.* Cambridge, MA: MIT Press.

Church, A. (1982). Sojourner adjustment. *Psychological Bulletin, 91,* 540–572.

Clark, M. M. (1972). An anthropological view of retirement. In F. Carp (Ed.), *Retirement* (pp. 117–156). New York: Human Sciences Press.

Cleland, J. (1928). Mental diseases amongst Australian aborigines. *Journal of Tropical Medicine, 31*, 326–330.

Cochrane, R. (1977). Mental illness in immigrants to England and Wales: An analysis of mental hospital admissions, 1971. *Social Psychiatry, 12*, 25–35.

Cochrane, R. (1980). Mental illness in England, in Scotland and Scots living in England. *Social Psychiatry, 15*, 9–15.

Cole, M. (1996). *Cultural psychology.* Cambridge, MA: Harvard University Press.

Cole, M., & Cole, S. R. (1996). *The development of children* (3rd ed.). New York: W. H. Freeman.

Colin, V. L. (1996). *Human attachment.* New York: McGraw-Hill.

Comunian, A. L., & Gielen, U. P. (2000). *International perspectives on Human development.* Lengerich, Germany: Pabst Scientific Publishers.

Condon, J. C., & Yousef, F. (1975). *An introduction to intercultural communication.* New York: Macmillan.

Confucius (1979). *The analects (Lun yü).* Translated by D. C. Lau. London, UK: Penguin.

Conoley, J. C., & Impara, J. C. (Eds.). (1995). *The twelfth mental measurement yearbook.* Lincoln, NE: Buros Institute.

Converse, J. M., & Schuman, H. (1974). *Conversation at random: Survey research as interviewers see it.* New York: Wiley.

Cook, T. D., & Campbell, D. T. (1979). *Quasi-experimentation: Design and analysis issues for field settings.* Chicago: Rand McNally.

Costa, P. T., Jr., & McCrae, R. R. (1985). *The NEO-PI-R: Personality Manual.* Odessa, FL: Psychological Assessment Resources.

Costa, P. T., Jr., & McCrae, R. R. (1988). Personality in adulthood: A six-year longitudinal study of self reports and spouse ratings of the NEO Personality Inventory. *Journal of Personality and Social Psychology, 54*, 853–863.

Costa, P. T., Jr., & McCrae, R. R. (1992). *NEO-PI-R: Revised NEO Personality Inventory (NEO-PI-R).* Odessa, FL: Psychological Assessment Resources.

Counts, D. A., & Counts, D. R. (1985). I'm not dead yet. Aging and death: Process and experience in Kalia. In D. A. Counts & D. R. Counts (Eds.), *Aging and its transformations: Moving toward death in Pacific societies* (pp. 131–155). Lanham, MD: University Press of America.

Cowgill, D. O. (1986). *Aging around the world.* Belmont, CA: Wadsworth.

Cowgill, D. O., & Holmes, L. D. (1972). *Aging and modernization.* New York: Appleton-Century Crofts.

Cropley, A. J., Ruddat, H., Dehn, D., & Lucassen, S. (1994). (Eds.). *Probleme der Zuwanderung* [Problems of immigration]. Göttingen: Verlag für Angewandte Psychologie.

Cummings, E., & Henry, W. E. (1961). *Growing old: The process of disengagement.* New York: Basic Books.

Cushner, K. (1990). Cross-cultural psychology and the formal classroom. In R. W. Brislin (Ed.), *Applied cross-cultural psychology* (pp. 98–120). Newbury Park, CA: Sage.

Cushner, K., & Brislin, R. (1996). *Intercultural interactions: A practical guide* (2nd ed.). Thousand Oaks, CA: Sage.

Dacey, J. S. (1989). Peaks of creativity growth across the life-span. *Journal of Creative Behavior, 23* (4), 224–247.

Daedalus (1975). *Wisdom, revelation, and doubt: Perspectives on the First Millennium B.C.* (Vol. *104* [2]).

Dana, R. H. (Ed.). (1982). *Human services for cultural minorities.* Baltimore, MD: University Park Press.

D'Andrade, R. (1990). Some propositions about the relations between culture and human cognition. In J. W. Stigler, R. A. Shweder, & G. Herdt (Eds.), *Cultural psychology* (pp. 65–129). New York: Cambridge University Press.

Darwin, C. (1872). *The expression of the emotions in man and animals.* London: John Murray.

Dasen, P. R. (1994). Culture and cognitive development from a Piagetian perspective. In W. J. Lonner & R. Malpass (Eds.), *Psychology and culture* (pp. 145–149). Boston, MA: Allyn & Bacon.

Davidson, A. R., Jaccard, J. J., Triandis, H. C., Morales, M. L., & Díaz-Guerrero, R. (1976). Cross-cultural model testing: Toward a solution of the etic-emic dilemma. *International Journal of Psychology, 11,* 1–13.

Davies, P. (1990). *God and the new physics.* London: Penguin Books.

de Beauvoir, S. (1972). *Coming of age.* New York: Putnam.

DeHoyos, A., & DeHoyos, G. (1965). Symptomatology differentials between Negro and White schizophrenics. *International Journal of Social Psychiatry, 11,* 245–255.

Delaney, C. H. (1995). Rites of passage in adolescence. *Adolescence, 30,* 891–897.

Denmark, F. L. (1994). Epilogue. In L. L. Adler & U. P. Gielen (Eds.), *Cross-cultural topics in psychology.* Westport, CT: Praeger.

Denmark, F. L., Schwartz, L., & Smith, K. M. (1991). Women in the United States of America and Canada. In L. L. Adler (Ed.), *Women in cross-cultural perspective* (pp. 1–18). Westport, CT: Praeger.

Dentan, R. K. (1968). *The Semai: A nonviolent people of Malaya.* New York: Holt, Rinehart & Winston.

Depner, C., & Ingersoll-Dayton, B. (1985). Conjugal social support: Patterns in later life. *Journal of Gerontology, 40,* 761–766.

Deregowski, J. B. (1980). Perception. In H. C. Triandis & W. Lambert (Eds.), *Handbook of cross-cultural psychology* (3rd ed.). Boston, MA: Allyn & Bacon.

Desjarlais, R., Eisenberg, L., Good, B., & Kleinman, A. (1995). *World mental health. Problems and priorities in low-income countries.* New York: Oxford University Press.

DeVries, M. W. (1994). Kids in context: Temperament in cross-cultural perspective. In W. B. Carey & S. C. Devitt (Eds.), *Prevention and early intervention: Individual differences as risk factors for the mental health of children.* New York: Brunner/Mazel.

DeVries, M. W., & Sameroff, A. J. (1984). Culture and temperament: Influences on temperament in three East African societies. *American Journal of Orthopsychiatry, 54,* 83–96.

Dharmakeerti, U. S. (1982). Review of *"Yoga and cardiovascular management." Yoga, 20* (6), 15–16.

Díaz-Guerrero, R. (1967). Sociocultural premises, attitudes, and cross-cultural research. *International Journal of Psychology, 2,* 79–88.

Díaz-Guerrero, R. (1970). *Estudios de psicología del mexicano* [Studies about the psychology of the Mexican]. (2nd ed.). Mexico: Trillas.

Díaz-Guerrero, R. (1971). La enseñanza de la investigación en psicología en Iberoamérica: Un paradigma. *Revista Latinoamericana de Psicología, 3* (1), 5–36.

Díaz-Guerrero, R. (1972). Una escala factorial de premisas histórico-socioculturales de la familia mexicana. *Revista Interamericana de Psicología, 6* (3–4), 235–244.

Díaz-Guerrero, R. (1977). Culture and personality revisited. In L. L. Adler (Ed.), *Issues in cross-cultural research. Annals of The New York Academy of Sciences, 285,* 119–130. New York: New York Academy of Sciences.

Díaz-Guerrero, R. (1977). A Mexican psychology. *American Psychologist, 32* (11), 934–944.

Díaz-Guerrero, R. (1979). Origines de la personnalité humaine et des systemes sociaux [Origins of the human personality and of human systems]. *Revue de Psychologie Appliquée, 29,* 139–152.

Díaz-Guerrero, R. (1982). The psychology of the historic-sociocultural premises, I. *Spanish Language Psychology, 2,* 383–410.

Díaz-Guerrero, R. (1984). Tristeza y psicopatología en México. *Salud Mental, 7* (2), 3–9.

Díaz-Guerrero, R. (1985). Holtzman Inkblot Technique (HIT) differences across Mexican, Mexican-American and Anglo-American cultures. In E. E. Roskam (Ed.), *Measurement and personality assessment* (pp. 247–259). Amsterdam: Elsevier.

Díaz-Guerrero, R. (1986). Historio-sociocultura y personalidad: Definición y características de los factores de la familia mexicana. *Revista de Psicología Social y Personalidad, 2* (1), 15–42.

Díaz-Guerrero, R. (1987). Historic-sociocultural premises and ethnic socialization. In J. S. Phinney & M. J. Rotheram (Eds.), *Children's ethnic socialization, pluralism and development* (pp. 239–250). Newbury Park, CA: Sage.

Díaz-Guerrero, R. (1989). Una etnopsicología mexicana. *Ciencia y Desarrollo, 15* (86), 69–85.

Díaz-Guerrero, R. (1990). La teoría del ecosistema humano. In J. Cueli & L. Reidl (Eds.), *Teorías de la personalidad* (pp. 578–591). México, D. F.: Trillas.

Díaz-Guerrero, R. (1993). Mexican ethnopsychology. In U. Kim & J. W. Berry (Eds.), *Indigenous psychology* (pp. 44–55). Newbury Park, CA: Sage.

Díaz-Guerrero, R. (1995). Origins and development of Mexican ethnopsychology. *World Psychology, 1,* 49–67.

Díaz-Guerrero, R., & Díaz-Loving, R. (1990). Interpretation in cross-cultural personality assessment. In C. R. Reynolds & R. W. Kamphaus (Eds.), *Handbook of psychological and educational assessment of children: Personality, behavior and context* (Vol. 2, pp. 491–523). New York: Guilford.

Díaz-Guerrero, R., & Iscoe, I. (1984). El impacto de la cultura iberoamericana tradicional y del estrés económico sobre la salud mental y física: Instrumentación y potencial para la investigación transcultural. *Revista Latinoamericana de Psicología, 16* (2), 167–211.

Díaz-Guerrero, R., & Rodriguez de Díaz, H. L. (1993). Mexico. In L. L. Adler (Ed.), *International handbook on gender roles* (pp. 199–217). Westport, CT: Greenwood Press.

Dien, D. S. (1982). A Chinese perspective on Kohlberg's theory of moral development. *Developmental Review, 2*, 331–341.

Digman, J. M. (1990). Personality structure: Emergence of the five-factor model.
Annual Review of Psychology, 41, 417–440.

Digman, J. M., & Inouye, J. (1986). Further specification of the five robust factors
of personality. *Journal of Personality and Social Psychology, 50*, 116–123.

Digman, J. M., & Takemoto-Chok, N. K. (1981). Factors in the natural language
of personality: Re-analysis and comparison of six major studies. *Multivariate
Behavioral Research, 16*, 149–170.

DiNicola, V. F. (1990). Anorexia multiforme: Self-starvation in historical and cultural
context: Part 2, Anorexia nervosa as a culture-reactive syndrome. *Transcultural Psychiatric Research Review, 27*, 245–286.

Diop, M. (1967). La dépression chez le noir africain. *Psychopathologie africaine, 3*,
183–195.

Dixon, L., & Lehman, A. (1996). Family interventions for schizophrenia. *Schizophrenia Bulletin, 21*, 631–643.

Dohrenwend, B. P., & Dohrenwend, B. S. (1969). *Social status and psychological
disorder.* New York: Wiley.

Dohrenwend, B. S., & Dohrenwend, B. P. (Eds.). (1974). *Stressful life events: Their
nature and effects.* New York: Wiley.

Doi, T. (1973). *The anatomy of dependence.* New York: Kodansha International.

Donner, W. W. (1987). Compassion, kinship and fosterage: Context for the care of
childless elderly in a Polynesian community. *Journal of Cross-Cultural Gerontology, 2* (1), 43–60.

Doob, L. W. (1965). Exploring eidetic imagery among the Kamba of Central Kenya.
Journal of Social Psychology, 67, 3–22.

Doob, L. W. (1980). The inconclusive struggles of cross-cultural psychology. *Journal
of Cross-Cultural Psychology, 11*, 59–73.

Draguns, J. G. (1990). Normal and abnormal behavior in cross-cultural perspective:
Toward specifying the nature of their relationship. In J. J. Berman (Ed.), *Ne-
braska symposium on motivation, 1989* (pp. 236–277). Lincoln: University of
Nebraska Press.

Draguns, J. G. (1995). Cultural influences upon psychopathology: Clinical and practical implications. *Journal of Social Distress and the Homeless, 4*, 79–103.

Draguns, J. G. (1996a). Multicultural and cross-cultural assessment of psychological
disorder: Dilemmas and decisions. In G. R. Sodowsky & J. Impara (Eds.),
*Multicultural assessment in counseling and clinical psychology (Buros-Nebraska
Symposium on Measurement and Testing*, Volume 9) (pp. 37–76). Lincoln,
NE: Buros Institute of Mental Measurements.

Draguns, J. G. (1996b). Humanly universal and culturally distinctive: Charting the
course of cultural counseling. In P. B. Pedersen, J. G. Draguns, W. J. Lonner,
& J. E. Trimble (Eds.), *Counseling across cultures* (4th ed., pp. 1–20). Thousand Oaks, CA: Sage.

Draguns, J. G. (1997). Abnormal behavior patterns across cultures: Implications for
counselling and psychotherapy. *International Journal of Intercultural Relations, 21*, 213–248.

Draper, P., & Cashdan, E. (1988). Technological change and child behavior among
the !Kung. *Ethnology, 27*, 339–365.

Dube, K. C. (1970). A study of prevalence and biosocial variables in mental illness in a rural and an urban community in Uttar Pradesh, India. *Acta Psychiatrica Scandinavia, 46*, 327–359.

Dunlap, D. A. (1990). Rural psychiatric rehabilitation and the interface of community development and rehabilitation services. *Psychosocial Rehabilitation Journal, 14*, 67–89.

Durkheim, E. (1897). *Le suicide: Etude de sociologie* [Suicide: A sociological study]. Paris: Felix Alcan.

Durkheim, E. (1912/1915). *The elementary forms of religious life*. London: Allen & Unwin.

Durkheim, E. (1951). *Suicide* (J. A. Spaulding & G. Simpson, trans.). Glencoe, IL: Free Press.

Ebigbo, P. (1982). Development of a culture specific screening scale of somatic complaints indicating psychiatric disturbance. *Culture, Medicine and Psychiatry, 6*, 29–43.

Ebin, V. (1979). *The body decorated*. London: Thames & Hudson.

Ebrahim, S. (1992). Social and medical problems of elderly migrants. *International Migration, 30*, 179–197.

Eckensberger, L. H. (1993). Moralische Urteile als handlungsleitende Regelsysteme im Spiegel der kulturvergleichenden Forschung. In A. Thomas (Ed.), *Einführung in die kulturvergleichende Psychologie* (pp. 259–295). Göttingen: Hogrefe. (in German)

Eckensberger, L. H., & Zimba, R. (1997). The development of moral judgment. In W. Berry, P. R. Dasen, & T. S. Saraswathi (Eds.), *Handbook of cross-cultural psychology*. Vol. 2. *Basic processes and human development* (pp. 299–338). Needham Heights, MA: Allyn & Bacon.

Eckland, B. K. (1968). Theories of mate selection. *Eugenics Quarterly, 15*, 17–23.

Edwards, C. P. (1981). The comparative study of the development of moral judgement and reasoning. In R. H. Munroe, R. L. Munroe, & B. B. Whiting (Eds.), *Handbook of cross-cultural human development* (pp. 501–528). New York: Garland.

Edwards, C. P. (1986). Cross-cultural research on Kohlberg's stages. The basis for consensus. In S. Modgil & C. Mogdil (Eds.), *Lawrence Kohlberg: Consensus and controversy* (pp. 419–430). London: Falmer Press.

Edwards, C. P. (1996). Parenting toddlers. In M. H. Bornstein (Ed.), *Handbook of parenting* (Vol. 1, pp. 41–63). Hillsdale, NJ: Erlbaum.

Efron, D. (1972). *Gesture, race and culture*. Netherlands: Mouton.

Egeland, J. A., Hofstetter, A. M., & Eshleman, S. K. (1983). Amish Study III. The impact of cultural factors on diagnosis of bipolar illness. *American Journal of Psychiatry, 140*, 67–71.

Eibl-Eibesfeldt, I. (1989). *Human ethology*. New York: Aldine de Gruyter.

Ekman, P. (1972). Universals and cultural differences in facial expressions of emotion. In J. Cole (Ed.), *Nebraska symposium on motivation*, 1971. Lincoln: University of Nebraska Press.

Ekman, P. (1980). *The face of man: Expressions of universal emotion in a New Guinea village*. New York: Garland Press.

Ekman, P., & Friesen, W. (1969). The repertoire of nonverbal behavior: Categories, origins, usage, and coding. *Semiotica, 1*, 49–98.

Ekman, P., & Friesen, W. (1971). Constants across cultures in the face and emotion. *Journal of Personality and Social Psychology, 17,* 124–129.

Ekman, P., & Friesen, W. (1978). *Facial action coding system.* Palo Alto, CA: Consulting Psychologists Press.

Ekman, P., & Friesen, W. (1986). A new pan-cultural expression of emotion. *Motivation and Emotion, 10,* 159–168.

Ekman, P., Friesen, W. V., & Ellsworth, P. (1972). *Emotion in the human face: Guidelines for research and integration of findings.* New York: Pergamon Press.

Ekman, P., Friesen, W., O'Sullivan, M., Chan, A., Diacoyanni-Tarlatzis, I., Heider, K., Krause, R., LeCompte, W. A., Pitcairn, T., Ricci-Bitti, P. E., Scherer, K., Tomita, M., & Tzavaras, A. (1987). Universals and cultural differences in the judgments of facial expressions of emotion. *Journal of Personality and Social Psychology, 53,* 712–717.

Ekman, P., Sorenson, E. R., & Friesen, W. (1969). Pan-cultural elements in facial displays of emotion. *Science, 164,* 86–94.

Elder, G. H., Pavalko, E. K., & Clipp, E. C. (1994). *Working with archival data.* Newbury Park, CA: Sage.

Elkind, D. (1984). *All grown up & no place to go.* Reading, MA: Addison-Wesley.

El-Shikh, S. A. (1985). A study of moral thinking in Egyptian adolescents and adults. In F. A. Abou-Hatab (Ed.), *The yearbook of psychology* (Vol. 4, pp. 123–169). Cairo: The Anglo-Egyptian Bookshop. (in Arabic)

Ember, C. R., & Ember, M. (1988). *Guide to cross-cultural research using the HRAF archive.* New Haven, CT: HRAF Press.

Ember, C. R., & Ember, M. (1993). *Cultural anthropology* (7th ed.). Englewood Cliffs, NJ: Prentice Hall.

Endler, N. S., & Parker, J. D. (1990). The multidimensional assessment of coping: A critical evaluation. *Journal of Personality and Social Psychology, 58,* 844–854.

Engle, P. L., Zeitlin, M., Medrano, Y., & Garcia, L. M. (1996). Growth consequences of low-income Nicaraguan mothers' theories about feeding 1-year-olds. In S. Harkness & C. M. Super (Eds.), *Parents' cultural belief systems* (pp. 428–446). New York: Guilford Press.

Enriquez, V. G. (1993). Developing a Filipino psychology. In U. Kim & J. W. Berry (Eds.), *Indigenous psychologies: Research and experience in cultural context* (pp. 152–169). Newbury Park, CA: Sage.

Erikson, E. H. (1963). *Childhood and society* (2nd ed.). New York: Norton.

Estroff, S. (1989). Self, identity, and subjective experiences of schizophrenia: In search of the subject. *Schizophrenia Bulletin, 15,* 189–196.

Evans, G. W., Palsane, M. N., Lepore, S. J., & Martin, J. (1989). Residential density and psychological health: The mediating effects of social support. *Journal of Personality and Social Psychology, 57,* 994–99.

Evans-Pritchard, E. (1937). *Witchcraft, oracles, and magic among the Azande.* Oxford: Clarendon Press.

Eversley, D., & Bonnerjea, L. (1982). Social change and indicators of diversity. In R. N. Rapaport, M. P. Fogarty, & R. Rapaport (Eds.), *Families in Britain* (pp. 75–94). London: Routledge & Kegan Paul.

Eysenck, H. J. (1967). *The biological basis of personality.* Springfield, IL: C. C. Thomas.

Eysenck, H. J. (1994). *The causal role of stress in the aetiology of cancer and coronary heart disease.* Paper read at the 23rd International Congress of Applied Psychology, July 17–22, 1994, Madrid, Spain.

Eysenck, H. J. (1995). Cross-cultural psychology and the unification of psychology. *World Psychology, 1,* 11–30.

Eysenck, H. J., & Eysenck, M. W. (1985). *Personality and individual differences: A natural science approach.* New York: Plenum Press.

Fabrega, H. (1989). The self and schizophrenia: A cultural perspective. *Schizophrenia Bulletin, 15,* 277–290.

Fariante, C. M., Salis, P., Dazzan, P., Carta, M. G., & Carpiniello, B. (1996). Outcome of patients after reform in Italy (letter). *Psychiatric Services, 47,* 266–267.

Favier, J. (Ed.). (1984). *Histoire de France* [History of France]. Paris: Fayard.

Feldman, R. S. (1997). *Essentials of psychology* (3rd ed.). New York: McGraw-Hill.

Fernando, S. (1988). *Race and culture in psychiatry.* London: Croom Helm.

Ferrante, J. (1992). *Sociology: A global perspective.* Belmont, CA: Wadsworth.

Festinger, L., Schachter, S., & Riecken, H. (1958). *When prophecy fails.* Minneapolis: University of Minnesota Press.

Field, D., & Minkler, M. (1988). Continuity and change in social support between young-old, old-old, and very old adults. *Journal of Gerontology, 43,* 100–106.

Fischer, M. (1991). Women in the Arctic (Alaska): A culture in transition. In L. L. Adler (Ed.), *Women in cross-cultural perspective* (pp. 20–25). Westport, CT: Praeger.

Fishbein, M., & Raven, B. (1962). The AB scale: An operational definition of belief and attitude. *Human Relations, 15,* 35–44.

Flew, A. (1989). *An introduction to Western philosophy* (rev. ed.). London: Thames & Hudson.

Flores-Galaz, M., Díaz-Loving, R., & Rivera Aragón, S. (1987). Mera: Una medida de rasgos asertivos para la cultura mexicana. *Revista Mexicana de Psicología, 4* (1), 29–35.

Foundations Center (2000). *Guide to funding for international and foreign programs* (5th ed.). New York: Author.

Fowler, F. J. (1993). *Survey research methods* (2nd ed.). Newbury Park, CA: Sage.

Fowler, R. D. (1997, April 11). *International activities of the American Psychological Association.* In U. P. Gielen (Chair), Symposium on International Psychology, Annual meeting of the Eastern Psychological Association, Washington, DC.

Frackowiak, J., & Jasinska-Kania, A. (1991). *Moral development and the life course: The Polish case.* Unpublished paper, Warsaw University.

Frazer, J. G. (1911). *The golden bough: A study in magic and religion* (3rd ed.). London: Macmillan.

Frazier, C., & Douyon, C. (1989). Social support in the elderly: A cross-cultural comparison. In L. L. Adler (Ed.), *Cross-cultural research in human development: Life-span perspectives* (pp. 216–222). New York: Praeger.

Frederickson, B. L., & Carstensen, L. L. (1990). Choosing social partners: How old age and anticipated endings make people more selective. *Psychology and Aging, 5* (3), 335–347.

Freedman, J. L. (1975). *Crowding and behavior.* San Francisco, CA: W. H. Freeman.

Friesen, W. (1972). *Cultural differences in facial expressions in a social situation: An experimental test of the concept of display rules.* Unpublished doctoral dissertation, University of California, San Francisco.

Fromm, E. (1977). *The anatomy of human destructiveness.* Harmondsworth, GB: Penguin.

Fry, C. L. (1980). *Aging in culture and society: Comparative viewpoints and strategies.* New York: J. F. Bergin.

Fry, C. L. (1990). Cross-cultural comparisons of aging. In K. Ferraro (Ed.), *Perspectives and issues.* New York: Springer.

Fry, D. P. (1992). Respect for the rights of others is peace: Learning aggression versus non-aggression among the Zapotec. *American Anthropologist, 94* (3), 621–639.

Fukada, N. (1991). Women in Japan. In L. L. Adler (Ed.), *Women in cross-cultural perspective* (pp. 205–219). Westport, CT: Praeger.

Funt, A. (1971). What do you say to a naked lady? In A. Rosenthal (Ed.), *The new documentary in action* (pp. 251–253). Berkeley: University of California Press.

Furnham, A., & Bochner, S. (1986, repr. 1989). *Culture shock: Psychological reactions to unfamiliar environments.* London: Methuen.

Furnham, A., & Shiekh, S. (1993). Gender, generation, and social support correlates of mental health in Asian immigrants. *International Journal of Social Psychiatry, 39,* 22–33.

Gardiner, H. W. (1994). Child development. In L. L. Adler & U. P. Gielen (Eds.), *Cross-cultural topics in psychology* (1st ed., pp. 61–72). New York: Praeger.

Gardiner, H. W. (1996). *Cross-cultural content in contemporary developmental textbooks.* Paper presented at the 12th Congress of the International Association for Cross-Cultural Psychology, Montreal, Canada.

Gardiner, H. W., & Gardiner, O. S. (1991). Women in Thailand. In L. L. Adler (Ed.), *Women in cross-cultural perspective.* Westport, CT: Praeger.

Gardiner, H. W., Mutter, J. D., & Kosmitzki, C. (1998). *Lives across cultures: Cross-cultural human development.* Boston, MA: Allyn & Bacon.

Gardiner, H. W., Singh, U. P., & D'Orazio, D. E. (1974). The liberated woman in three cultures: Marital preferences in Thailand, India, and the United States. *Human Organizations, 33,* 413–415.

Garfinkel, H. (1967). *Studies in ethnomethodology.* Cambridge, MA: Polity Press.

Gaw, A. C. (Ed.). (1993). *Culture, ethnicity, and mental illness.* Washington, DC: American Psychiatric Press.

Georgas, J., & Papastylinanou, D. (1994). The effect of time on stereotypes: Acculturation of children of returning immigrants to Greece. In A. M. Bouvy, F.J.R. van de Vijver, P. Boski, & P. Schmitz (Eds.), *Journeys into cross-cultural psychology* (pp. 158–166). Amsterdam: Swets & Zeitlinger.

Georgas, J., & Papastylinanou, D. (1994). Acculturation and ethnic identity: The reimmigration of ethnic Greeks to Greece. In H. Grad, A. Blanco, & J. Georgas (Eds.), *Key issues in cross-cultural psychology* (pp. 114–127). Lisse: Swets & Zeitlinger.

George, P. (1986). *L'immigration en France* [Immigration in France]. Paris: Armand Colin.

German, J. (1972). Aspects of clinical psychiatry in sub-Saharan Africa. *British Journal of Psychiatry, 121,* 461–479.

Gibbons, J. L., Hamby, B. A., & Dennis, W. D. (1997). Researching gender-role

ideologies internationally and cross-culturally. *Psychology of Women Quarterly,*
21 (1), 151–170.

Gielen, U. P. (1986). Moral reasoning in radical and non-radical German students.
Behavior Science Research, 20 (1–4), 71–109.

Gielen, U. P. (1990). Some recent work on moral values, reasoning, and education
in Chinese societies. *Moral Education Forum, 15* (2), 3–22.

Gielen, U. P. (1991). Research on moral reasoning. In L. Kuhmerker with U. P.
Gielen & R. L. Hayes, *The Kohlberg legacy for the helping professions* (pp. 39–
60). Birmingham, AL: R.E.P. Books.

Gielen, U. P. (1993). Traditional Tibetan societies. In L. L. Adler (Ed.), *International handbook on gender roles* (pp. 413–437). Westport, CT: Greenwood
Press.

Gielen, U. P. (1994). *Peace and violence: A comparison of Buddhist Ladakh and the
United States.* Paper presented at the 23rd Annual Meeting of the Society for
Cross-Cultural Research, Santa Fe, NM.

Gielen, U. P. (1995). Epilogue: Traditional Buddhist Ladakh-A society at peace. In
L. L. Adler & F. L. Denmark (Eds.), *Violence and the prevention of violence*
(pp. 191–203). Westport, CT: Praeger.

Gielen, U. P. (1995). Editorial. *World Psychology, 2* (1), v–vii.

Gielen, U. P. (1996). Moral reasoning in cross-cultural perspective: A review of Kohlbergian research. *World Psychology, 2* (3–4), 313–333.

Gielen, U. P. (1997). A death on the roof of the world: The perspective of Tibetan
Buddhism. In C. M. Parkes, P. Laungani, & B. Young (Eds.), *Death and
bereavement across cultures* (pp. 73–97). London: Routledge.

Gielen, U. P., Ahmed, R. A., & Avellani, J. (1992). The development of moral reasoning and perceptions of parental behavior in students from Kuwait. *Moral
Education Forum, 17* (3), 20–37.

Gielen, U. P., & Chirico-Rosenberg, D. (1993). Traditional Buddhist Ladakh and
the ethos of peace. *International Journal of Group Tensions, 23* (1), 5–23.

Gielen, U. P., Cruickshank, H., Johnston, A., Swanzey, B., & Avellani, J. (1986).
The development of moral reasoning in Belize, Trinidad-Tobago and the
USA. *Behavior Science Research, 20* (1–4), 178–207.

Gielen, U. P., Fish, J., & Draguns, J. G. (in prep.). *Handbook of culture, therapy,
and healing.* Boston, MA: Allyn & Bacon.

Gielen, U. P., Markoulis, D., & Avellani, J. (1992). Development of moral reasoning
and perceptions of parental behavior in Greek students. In A. L. Comunian
& U. P. Gielen (Eds.), *Advancing psychology and its applications: International perspectives* (pp. 107–124). Milan: FrancoAngeli.

Gielen, U. P., Miao, E., & Avellani, J. (1990). Perceived parental behavior and the
development of moral reasoning in students from Taiwan. In *Proceedings of
CCU-ICP-International Conference: Moral values and moral reasoning in
Chinese societies* (pp. 464–506). Taipei: Chinese Culture University.

Gilligan, C. (1982). *In a different voice: Psychology theory and women's development.*
Cambridge, MA: Harvard University Press.

Gladstone, W. E. (1858). *Studies on Homer and the Homeric age* (Vol. 3). Oxford:
Oxford University Press.

Gladwin, T., & Sarason, S. B. (1953). *Truk: Man in paradise.* Chicago: University
of Chicago Press.

302   References

Glascock, A. P. (1990). By any other name it is still killing: A comparison of the
    treatment of the elderly in America and other societies. In J. Sokolovsky (Ed.),
    The cultural context of aging: World wide perspectives (pp. 43–56). Westport,
    CT: Bergin & Garvey.
Glascock, A. P., Feinman, S. L. (1981). Social asset or social burden: Treatment of
    the elderly in non-industrial societies. In C. L. Fry (Ed.), *Dimensions: Aging,
    culture, and health.* New York: Praeger.
Glass, D. C., Reim, B., & Singer, J. E. (1971). Behavioral consequences of adapta-
    tion to an environmental stressor. *Journal of Personality and Social Psychology,
    7,* 244–257.
Goethals, G. W. (1971). Factors affecting permissive and nonpermissive rules regard-
    ing premarital sex. In J. M. Henslin (Ed.), *Sociology of sex: A book of readings*
    (pp. 9–26). New York: Appleton-Croft.
Goldberg, L. R. (1981). Language and individual differences: The search for uni-
    versals in personality lexicons. In L. Wheeler (Ed.), *Review of personality in
    social psychology* (Vol. 2, pp. 141–165). Beverly Hills, CA: Sage.
Goldberg, L. R. (1982). From ace to zombie: Some explorations in the language of
    personality. In C. D. Spielberger & J. N. Butcher (Eds.), *Advances in person-
    ality assessment* (Vol. 1, pp. 203–234). Hillsdale, NJ: Erlbaum.
Goldberg, L. R. (1992). The development of markers for the big-five factor structure.
    Psychological Assessment, 4 (1), 26–42.
Gorer, G. (1965). *Death, grief, and mourning in contemporary Britain.* London:
    Cresset Press.
Gorer, G. (1967). The pornography of death. In G. Gorer (Ed.), *Death, grief, and
    mourning* (pp. 169–175). New York: Doubleday.
Gove, W., Hughes, M., & Style, C. (1983). Does marriage have positive effects on
    the psychological well-being of the individual? *Journal of Health and Social
    Behavior, 24* 122–131.
Graubert, J. G., & Adler, L. L. (1982). Attitude toward stigma-related and stigma-
    free stimuli: A cross-national perspective. In L. L. Adler (Ed.), *Cross-cultural
    research at issue* (pp. 335–347). New York: Academic Press.
Graves, T. (1967). Psychological acculturation in a tri-ethnic community. *South-
    Western Journal of Anthropology, 23,* 337–350.
Greenberg, C. I., & Firestone, J. J. (1977). Compensatory response to crowding:
    Effects of personal space and privacy reduction. *Journal of Personality and
    Social Psychology, 35,* 637–644.
Greenberg, J. (1978, July 29). Adulthood comes of age. *Science News,* 74–79.
Greenfield, P. M. (1997). Culture as process: Empirical methods for cultural psy-
    chology. In J. W. Berry, Y. H. Poortinga, & J. Pandey (Eds.), *Handbook of
    cross-cultural psychology* (2nd ed., pp. 301–346). Needham Heights, MA:
    Allyn & Bacon.
Greenfield, P. M., & Cocking, R. R. (1994). *Cross-cultural roots of minority child
    development.* Hillsdale, NJ: Erlbaum.
Greenley, J. (Ed.). (1995). *Research in community and mental health.* Vol. 8. *The
    family and mental illness.* Greenwich, CT: JAI Press.
Griffin, J. (1984). Emotional support providers and psychological distress among
    Anglo- and Mexican-Americans. *Community Mental Health Journal, 20,* 182–
    201.

Gross, J. (1992, June 28). Clinics help Asian immigrants feel at home. *New York Times, 141* (49, 011), p. 10.

Grossarth-Maticek, R., & Eysenck, H. J. (1990). Personality, stress, and disease: Description and validity of a new inventory. *Psychological Reports, 66*, 355–373.

Grzymala-Moszczynska, H. (1991). Women in Poland. In L. L. Adler (Ed.), *Women in cross-cultural perspective* (pp. 54–66). Westport, CT: Praeger.

Gudykunst, W. B., & Kim, Y. Y. (1992). *Communicating with strangers* (2nd ed.). New York: Random House.

Guemple, L. (1974). The dilemma of the aging Eskimo. In C. Beattie & S. Crysdale (Eds.), *Sociology Canada readings* (pp. 203–214). Toronto: Butterworth.

Gulerce, A. (1996). A family structure assessment device for Turkey. In J. Pandey, D. Sinha, & D.P.S. Bhawuk (Eds.), *Asian contributions to cross-cultural psychology* (pp. 108–118). New Delhi: Sage.

Gupta, Y. (1977). The educational and vocational aspirations of Asian immigrant and English school-leavers: A comparative study. *British Journal of Sociology, 28*, 199–225.

Gurland, B., & Zubin, J. (1982). The United States–United Kingdom Cross-National Project: Issues in cross-cultural psychogeriatric research. In L. L. Adler (Ed.), *Cross-cultural research at issue* (pp. 323–334). New York: Academic Press.

Guthrie, G. M., & Bennett, A. B., Jr. (1971). Cultural differences in implicit personality theory. *International Journal of Psychology, 6*, 305–312.

Guthrie, G. M., Jackson, D. N., Astilla, E., & Elwood, B. (1983). Personality measurement: Do the scales have similar meaning in another culture? In S. H. Irvin & J. W. Berry (Eds.), *Human assessment and cultural factors.* New York: Plenum.

Guthrie, G. M., & Lonner, W. J. (1986). Assessment of personality and psychopathology. In W. J. Lonner & J. W. Berry (Eds.), *Field methods in cross-cultural research.* Beverly Hills, CA: Sage.

Gutmann, D. (1987). *Reclaimed powers: Toward a new psychology of men and women in later life.* New York: Basic Books.

Guzewicz, T. D., & Takooshian, H. (1992). Attitudes toward the homeless: A U.S.–Japan comparison. *Journal of Intergroup Relations, 19*, 24–31.

Hall, E. T. (1959). *The silent language.* Garden City, NY: Doubleday.

Hall, E. T. (1966). *The hidden dimension.* Garden City, NY: Doubleday.

Hambleton, R. K. (1994). Guidelines for adapting educational and psychological tests: A progress report. *European Journal of Psychological Assessment, 10*, 229–244.

Hambleton, R. K., Merenda, P. F., & Speilberger, C. D. (in press). *Adapting educational and psychological tests for cross-cultural assessment.* Mawhah, NJ: Erlbaum.

Harding, C. M. (1988). Course types in schizophrenia: An analysis of European and American studies. *Schizophrenia Bulletin, 14*, 633–643.

Harkness, S., & Super, C. M. (1995) Culture and parenting. In M. Bornstein (Ed.), *Handbook of parenting* (Vol. 2, pp. 211–234). Hillsdale, NJ: Erlbaum.

Harkness, S. & Super, C. M. (Eds.). (1996). *Parent's cultural belief systems: Their origins, expressions, and consequences.* New York: Guilford Press.

Harrell, S. (1981). Growing old in rural Taiwan. In P. Amoss & S. Harrell (Eds.),

Other ways of growing old: Anthropological perspectives (pp. 193–210). Stanford, CA: Stanford University Press.

Hatch, E. (1983). *Culture and morality: The relativity of values in anthropology.* New York: Columbia University Press.

Hau, K. T. (1983). *A cross-cultural study of a moral judgment test (The DIT).* Unpublished master's thesis, Chinese University, Hong Kong.

Havighurst, R. (1952). *Developmental tasks and education.* New York: McKay.

Heath, D. B. (1986). Drinking and drunkenness in transcultural perspective. Parts I and II. *Transcultural Psychiatric Research Review, 23,* 7–42, 103–126.

Heisenberg, W. (1930). *The physical principles of the quantum theory.* Berkeley: University of California Press.

Helzer, J. E. & Canino, G. J. (1992). Comparative analysis of alcoholism in ten cultural regions. In J. E. Helzer & G. J. Canino (Eds.), *Alcoholism in North America, Europe, and Asia* (pp. 289–308). New York: Oxford University Press.

Hemsi, L. K. (1967). Psychiatric morbidity of West Indian immigrants. *Social Psychiatry, 2,* 95–100.

Hendry, J. (1993). Becoming Japanese: The arenas and agents of socialization. In R. H. Wozniak (Ed.), *Worlds of childhood reader.* New York: HarperCollins.

Henry, G. T. (1990). *Practical sampling.* Newbury Park, CA: Sage.

Herbart, J. F. (1816). *Lehrbuch zur Psychologie* [Textbook of psychology]. (Translated by Margaret K. Smith. New York: Appleton & Co., 1897).

Herskovits, M. J. (1948). *Man and his works: The science of cultural anthropology.* New York: Knopf.

Higbee, K., Lott, W., & Graves, J. (1976). Experimentation and college students in social psychological research. *Personality and Social Psychology Bulletin, 2,* 239–241.

Hinde, R. A. (1972). *Non-verbal communication.* Cambridge, MA: Cambridge University Press.

Ho, D.Y.F. (1988). Asian psychology: A dialogue on indigenization and beyond. In A. C. Paranjpe, D.Y.F. Ho, & R. W. Rieber (Eds.), *Asian contributions to psychology* (pp. 53–77). New York: Praeger.

Ho, D.Y.F. (1995). Internalized culture, culturocentrism, and transcendence. *The Counselling Psychologist, 23,* 4–24.

Ho, D.Y.F. (1996). Filial piety and its psychological consequences. In M. H. Bond (Ed.), *The handbook of Chinese psychology* (pp. 155–165). Hong Kong: Oxford University Press.

Hockett, C. F. (1960). The origin of speech. *Scientific American,* September.

Hockey, J. (1993). The acceptable face of human grieving? The clergy's role in managing emotional expression during funerals. In D. Clark (Ed.), *The sociology of death* (pp. 129–148). Oxford: Blackwell.

Hofstede, G. (1980). *Culture's consequences: International differences in work-related values.* Beverly Hills, CA: Sage.

Hofstede, G. (1983). Dimensions of national cultures in fifty countries and three regions. In J. Deregowski, S. Dziurawiec, & R. A. Anais (Eds.), *Expiscations in cross-cultural psychology* (pp. 335–355). Lisse: Swets & Zeitlinger.

Hofstede, G. (1991). *Cultures and organizations: Software of the mind.* London: McGraw-Hill.

Hogan, R. T. (1983). A socioanalytic theory of personality. In M. Page (Ed.), *1982 Nebraska Symposium on Motivation* (pp. 55–89). Lincoln: University of Nebraska Press.

Hollos, M., & Leis, P. E. (1989). *Becoming Nigerian in Ijo society*. New Brunswick, NJ: Rutgers University Press.

Holmes, E. R., & Holmes, L. D. (1995). *Other cultures, elder years*. Thousand Oaks, CA: Sage.

Holmes, L. D., & Thomson, J. W. (1986). *Jazz great getting better with age*. New York: Holmes & Meier.

Holtzman, W. H., Díaz-Guerrero, R., & Swartz, J. D. (1975). *Personality development in two cultures*. Austin and London: University of Texas Press.

Horton, D. (1943). The functions of alcohol in primitive societies: A cross-cultural study. *Quarterly Journal Studies of Alcohol, 4*, 199–320.

House, J. (1987). Social support and social structure. *Sociological Forum, 2*, 135–146.

Hsu, F.L.K. (1971). Filial piety in Japan and China: Borrowing, variation and significance. *Journal of Comparative Family Studies*, Spring, 67–74.

Hsu, F.L.K. (1972). American core values and national character. In F.L.K. Hsu (Ed.), *Psychological anthropology* (pp. 241–266). Cambridge, MA: Schenkman.

Hudson, R. A. (1980). *Sociolinguistics*. Cambridge, MA: Cambridge University Press.

Hudson, W. (1960). Pictorial depth perception in sub-cultural groups in Africa. *Journal of Social Psychology, 52*, 183–208.

Hui, C. H., & Triandis, H. C. (1986). Individualism-collectivism: A study of cross-cultural researchers. *Journal of Cross-Cultural Psychology, 17*, 222–248.

Hume, D. (1894). *Essays literary, moral and political*. London: Routledge.

Hunter, J. E., & Schmidt, F. L. (1990). *Methods of meta-analysis: Correcting error and bias in research findings*. Newbury Park, CA: Sage.

Huntingsford, G.W.B. (1960). Nandi age sets. In S. Ottenberg & P. Ottenberg (Eds.), *Cultures and societies of Africa* (pp. 214–226). New York: Random House.

Hurgh, W. M., & Kim, K. C. (1990). Adaptation stages and mental health of Korean male immigrants in the United States. *International Migration Review, 24*, 456–479.

Hwang, K. K. (1979). Coping with residential crowding in a Chinese urban society: The interplay of high-density dwelling and interpersonal values. *Acta Psychologica Taiwanica, 21*, 117–133.

Hyde, J. S. (1985). *Half the human experience: The psychology of women*. Lexington, MA: Ramson University.

Hymes, D. (1962). The ethnography of speaking. *Anthropology and human behavior*. Washington, DC: Anthropological Society of Washington.

Hymes, D. (1965). *Language in culture and society: A reader*. New York: Harper & Row.

Hymes, D. (1972). Models of the interaction of language and social life. *Directions in sociolinguistics: The ethnography of communication*. Oxford and New York: Basil Blackwell.

Ikels, C. (1980). The coming of age in Chinese society: Traditional patterns and contemporary Hong Kong. In C. L. Fry (Ed.), *Aging in culture and society* (pp. 80–100). New York: J. F. Bergin.

Izard, C. E. (1971). *The face of emotion.* New York: Appleton-Century-Crofts.

Izraeli, D. N., & Safir, M. P. (1993). Israel. In L. L. Adler (Ed.), *International hand-book of gender roles* (pp. 144–158). Westport, CT: Greenwood Press.

Jablensky, A., Sartorius, N., Ernberg, A. M., Korten, A., Cooper, J. E., Day, R., & Bertelson, A. (1991). Schizophrenia: Manifestation, incidence, and cause in different cultures: A World Health Organization ten-country study. *Psychological Medicine*, Monograph Supplement 20, whole issue.

Jablensky, A., Sartorius, N., Ernberg, A. M., Korten, A., Cooper, J. E., Day, R., & Bertelson, A. (1992). *Schizophrenia: Manifestation, incidence, and cause in different cultures: A World Health Organization ten-country study.* Cambridge, MA: Cambridge University Press.

Jablensky, A., Sartorius, N., Gulbinat, W., & Ernberg, G. (1981). Characteristics of depressive patients contacting psychiatric services in four cultures. *Acta Psychiatrica Scandinavica, 63*, 367–383.

Jacobi, J. (1973). *The psychology of C. G. Jung.* New Haven, CT: Yale University Press.

Jacobs, J. (1974). *Fun city.* New York: Holt, Rinehart & Winston.

Jahoda, G. (1977). Cross-cultural study of factors influencing orientation errors in reproduction of Kohs-type figures. *British Journal of Psychology, 69*, 45–57.

Jahoda, G. (1977). Psychology and anthropology: Possible common ground in cross-cultural research. In L. L. Adler (Ed.), *Issues in cross-cultural research. Annals of the New York Academy of Sciences, 285*, 13–18. New York: New York Academy of Sciences.

Jahoda, G. (1982). *Psychology and anthropology: A psychological perspective.* London: Academic Press.

Jahoda, G. (1986). A cross-cultural perspective on developmental psychology. *International Journal of Behavioral Development, 9*, 417–437.

Jahoda, G. (1993). *Crossroads between culture and mind.* Cambridge, MA: Harvard University Press.

Jain, U. (1987). *Psychological consequences of crowding.* New Delhi: Sage.

Jakobson, R. O. (1968). *Child language, aphasia and phonological universals.* The Hague: Mouton.

James, W. (1968). The self. In G. Gordon & K. J. Gergen (Eds.), *The self in social interaction.* Vol. 1. New York: John Wiley.

Jaspers, K. (1949). *Vom Ursprung und Ziel der Geschichte* [About the origin and goal of history]. Munich: Piper. Translated by Michael Bullock as: *The origin and goal of history* (1953; New Haven, CT: Yale University Press).

Jayasuriya, L., Sang, D., & Fielding, A. (1992). *Ethnicity, immigration and mental illness: A critical review of Australian research.* Canberra: Bureau of Immigration Research.

Jenkins, J. H., & Karno, M. (1992). The meaning of expressed emotion: Theoretical issues raised by cross-cultural research. *American Journal of Psychiatry, 149*, 9–21.

Jilek, W. G. (1993). Traditional medicine relevant to psychiatry. In N. Sartorius, G. de Girolamo, G. Andrews, G. A. German, & L. Eisenberg (Eds.), *Treatment of mental disorders: A review of effectiveness* (pp. 341–383). Published on behalf of the World Health Organization. Washington, DC: American Psychiatric Press.

Jilek-Aal, L. (1988). Suicidal behavior among youth: A cross-cultural comparison. *Transcultural Psychiatric Research Review, 25*, 87–106.

Jing, Q., & Wan, C. (1997). Socialization of Chinese children. In H.S.R. Kao & D. Sinha (Eds.), *Asian perspectives on psychology* (pp. 25–39). New Delhi: Sage.

Johnson, D. (1995). Families and psychiatric rehabilitation. *International Journal of Mental Health, 24* (1), 47–58.

Jones, K., & Poletti, A. (1985). The Italian transformation of the asylum: A commentary and review. *International Journal of Mental Health, 210*, Spring–Summer.

Jordan, C., Lewellen, A., & Vandiver, V. (1995). Psychoeducation for minority families: A social work perspective. *International Journal of Mental Health, 23* (4), 27–43.

Judd, C. M., Smith, E., & Kidder, L. H. (1991). *Research methods in social relations* (6th ed.). New York: Harcourt Brace Jovanovich.

Kagan, J. (1994). *Galen's prophecy: Temperament in human nature.* New York: Basic Books.

Kagitçibasi, Ç. (1996). *Family and human development across cultures.* Mahwah, NJ: Erlbaum.

Kagitçibasi, Ç. (1997). Individualism and collectivism. In J. W. Berry, M. H. Segall, & Ç. Kagitçibasi (Eds.), *Handbook of cross-cultural psychology,* Vol. 3, *Social behavior and applications* (2nd ed.) (pp. 1–49). Boston: Allyn & Bacon.

Kahn, J. V. (1982). Moral reasoning in Irish children and adolescents as measured by the Defining Issues Test. *The Irish Journal of Psychology, 2*, 96–108.

Kakar, S. (1981). *The inner world—A psychoanalytic study of children and society in India.* Delhi: Oxford University Press.

Kakar, S. (1982). *Shamans, mystics and doctors.* London: Mandala Books, Unwin Paperbacks.

Kaplan, R. M. (1990). Behavior as the central outcome in healthcare. *American Psychologist, 45* (11), 1211–1220.

Katz, A. M., & Katz, V. T. (Eds.). (1983). *Foundations of nonverbal communication.* Southern Illinois University Press.

Keith, J., Fry, C., & Ikels, C. (1990). Community as a context for successful aging. In J. Sokolovsky (Ed.), *The cultural context of aging: Worldwide perspectives.* New York: Bergin & Garvey.

Keith, J., Fry, C., Glascock, A. P., Ikels, C., Dickerson-Putnam, J., Harpending, H. C., & Draper, P. (1994). *The aging experience: Diversity and commonality across cultures.* Thousand Oaks, CA: Sage.

Kelly, G. A. (1955). *The psychology of personal contructs* (Vols. 1–2). New York: Norton.

Kelso, B. J. (September/October 1994). Movement to combat female mutilation. *African Report*, 60–61.

Keniston, K. (1965). Social change and youth in America. In E. H. Erikson (Ed.), *The challenge of youth.* Garden City, NY: Doubleday/Anchor.

Kerlinger, F. N. (1986). *Foundations of behavioral research* (3rd ed.). New York: Holt Rinehart & Winston.

Kett, J. (1977). *Rites of passage: Adolescence in America, 1790 to the present.* New York: Basic Books.

Keyser, D. J., & Sweetland, R. C. (1991). *Tests* (2nd ed.). Kansas City, MO: Test Corporation of America.

Khandelwal, S. K., & Saxena, S. (1990). Anorexia nervosa in people of Asian extraction. *British Journal of Psychiatry, 157,* 784.

Khubalkar, R., Gupta, O. P., & Jain, A. P. (1986). Dhat syndrome in rural India: Some observations. *Proceedings of the Annual Conference of the Indian Association of Clinical Psychology.* Saugar University.

Kiesling, R. (1981). Underdiagnosis of manic-depressive illness in a hospital unit. *American Journal of Psychiatry, 138,* 672–673.

Kilbride, P. L., & Leibowitz, H. W. (1977). The Ponzo illusion among the Baganda of Uganda. In L. L. Adler (Ed.), *Issues in cross-cultural research* (pp. 408–417). *Annals of the New York Academy of Sciences, 285.* New York: New York Academy of Sciences.

Kilbride, P. L., & Leibowitz, H. W. (1982). The Ponzo Illusion among the Baganda of Uganda: Implications for ecological and perceptual theory. In L. L. Adler (Ed.), *Cross-cultural research at issue.* New York: Academic Press.

Kim, U. (1988). *Acculturation of Korean immigrants to Canada.* Unpublished doctoral dissertation, Queen's University, Canada.

Kim, U. (1997). Asian collectivism: An indigenous perspective. In H.S.R. Kao & D. Sinha (Eds.), *Asian perspectives on psychology* (pp. 147–163). New Delhi: Sage.

Kim, U., & Berry, J. W. (1993). *Indigenous psychologies.* Newbury Park, CA: Sage.

Kim, U., Triandis, H. C., & Yoon, G. (Eds.). (1992). *Individualism and collectivism: Theoretical and methodological issues.* Newbury Park, CA: Sage.

Kimura, B. (1995). *Zwischen Mensch und Mensch—Strukturen japanischer Subjektivität* [Between man and man—structures of Japanese subjectivity] (translated and edited by Weinmayr). Darmstadt, Germany: Wissenschaftliche Buchgesellschaft.

King, L. M. (1978). Social and cultural influences upon psychopathology. *Annual Review of Psychology, 29,* 405–434.

Kinsella, K. (1988). *Aging in the Third World* (U.S. Bureau of the Census, International Population Reports, Series P-95, No. 79). Washington, DC: U.S. Government Printing Office.

Kinzie, J. D. (1986). The establishment of outpatient mental health services for Southeast Asian refugees. In C. L. Williams & J. Westermeyer (Eds.), *Refugee mental health in resettlement countries* (pp. 217–231). Washington, DC: Hemisphere.

Kirmayer, L. (1984). Culture, affect, and somatization. Parts 1 and 2. *Transcultural Psychiatric Research Review, 21,* 159–188, 237–262.

Kirmayer, L. J. (1991). The place of culture in psychiatric nosology: *Taijin Kyofushu* and DSM-IIIR. *Journal of Nervous and Mental Disease, 179,* 19–28.

Kleinman, A. (1977). Depression, somatization, and the "new transcultural psychiatry." *Social Science and Medicine, 11,* 3–9.

Kleinman, A. (1982). Neurasthenia and depression: A study of somatization and culture in China. *Culture, Medicine, and Psychiatry, 6,* 117–190.

Kleinman, A. (1986). *Social origins of distress and disease.* New Haven, CT: Yale University Press.

Kleinman, A. (1991, July). *The psychiatry of culture and the culture of psychiatry.* Harvard Mental Health Letter.

Klineberg, O. (1940). *Social psychology*. New York: Holt, Rinehart & Winston.

Klineberg, O. (1980). Historical perspectives: Cross-cultural psychology before 1960. In H. C. Triandis & W. W. Lambert (Eds.). *Handbook of cross-cultural psychology: Perspectives* (Vol. 1, pp. 31–67). Boston: Allyn & Bacon.

Kluckhohn, C., & Murray, H. A. (Eds.). (1953). *Personality in nature, society, and culture*. New York: Knopf.

Knapp, T. J. (1985). Who's who in American introductory psychology textbooks: A citation study. *Teaching of Psychology, 12*, 15–17.

Kogan, N. (1973). Creativity and cognitive style: A life-span perspective. In P. B. Baltes & K. W. Schaie (Eds.), *Lifespan developmental psychology: Personality and socialization* (pp. 145–178). New York: Academic Press.

Kohlberg, L. (1969). Stage and sequence: The cognitive-developmental approach. In D. A. Groslin (Ed.), *Handbook of socialization theory and research* (pp. 347–480). Chicago: Rand McNally.

Kohlberg, L. (1984). *The psychology of moral development*. San Francisco: Harper & Row.

Koller, J. M. (1982). *The Indian way: Asian perspectives*. London: Collier Macmillan.

Korn, S., & Gannon, S. (1983). Temperament, culture variation, and behavior disorders in preschool children. *Child Psychiatry and Human Development, 13*, 203–212.

Kosmitzki, C. (1996). The reaffirmation of cultural identity in cross-cultural encounters. *Personality and Social Psychology Bulletin, 22* (3), 238–248.

Koss-Chioino, J. (1992). *Women as healers, women as patients: Mental health care and traditional healing in Puerto Rico*. Boulder, CO: Westview Press.

Kozulin, A. (1990). *Vygotsky's psychology: A biography of ideas*. New York: Harvester Wheatsheaf.

Krause, N., Jay, G., & Liang, J. (1991). Financial strain and psychological well-being among the American and Japanese elderly. *Psychology and Aging, 6*, 170–181.

Kuhmerker, L., with U. P. Gielen & R. L. Hayes (1991). *The Kohlberg legacy for the helping professions*. Birmingham, AL: Religious Education Press Books.

Kumar, U. (1991). Life stages in the development of the Hindu woman in India. In L. L. Adler (Ed.), *Women in cross-cultural perspective* (pp. 143–158). Westport, CT: Praeger.

Kumar-Reddy, B. S., & Ramamurty, P. V. (1990). Stress and coping strategies of the rural aged. *Journal of Personality and Clinical Studies, 6* (2), 171–175.

Labouvie-Vief, G. (1985). Intelligence and cognition. In J. E. Birren & K. W. Schaie (Eds.), *Handbook of the psychology of aging* (2nd ed., pp. 500–530). New York: Van Nostrand Reinhold.

Lambert, W. (1987). The fate of old country values in a new land: A cross-national study of child rearing. *Canadian Journal of Psychology, 28*, 9–20.

Lambo, T. A. (1978). Psychotherapy in Africa. *Human Nature, 1*, 32–39.

Landis, D., & Bhagat, R. (Eds.). (1996). *Handbook of intercultural training* (2nd ed.). Thousand Oaks, CA: Sage.

Langer, E. (1975). *The psychology of control*. Beverly Hills, CA: Sage.

Lannoy, R. (1976). *The speaking tree*. Delhi: Oxford University Press.

Laungani, P. (1989). Cultural influences on mental illness. *Political & Economic Weekly*, Bombay, October 28, 2427–2430.

Laungani, P. (1990). Turning eastward—An Asian view on child abuse. *Health & Hygiene, 11* (1), 26–29.

Laungani, P. (1990a). *Family life and child abuse: Learning from Asian culture.* Paper read at the 3rd International Child Health Congress, March 19–22, 1990, Kensington Town Hall, London.

Laungani, P. (1991). *Preventing child abuse and promoting child health across cultures.* Paper presented at the United Nations Conference on Action for Public Health, in Sundsvall, Sweden, June 9–15.

Laungani, P. (1991a). *The nature and experience of learning. Cross-cultural perspectives.* Paper read at the Conference on Experiential Learning. University of Surrey, Guildford, July 16–18.

Laungani, P. (1991b). *Stress across cultures: A theoretical analysis.* Paper read at the Conference of The Society of Public Health on Stress and the Health Services at The Royal Society of Medicine, Wimpole Street, London, July 25.

Laungani, P. (1992). Assessing child abuse through interviews of children and parents of children at risk. *Children and Society, 6* (1), 3–11.

Laungani, P. (1993). Cultural differences in stress and its management. *Stress Medicine, 9* (1), 37–43.

Laungani, P. (1994). Cultural differences in stress: India and England. *Counselling Psychology Review, 9* (4), 25–37.

Laungani, P. (1995). Stress in Eastern and Western cultures. In J. Brebner, E. Greenglass, P. Laungani, & A. O'Roark (Eds.), *Stress and emotion, 15* (pp. 265–280). Washington, DC: Taylor & Francis.

Laungani, P. (1996). Research in cross-cultural settings: Ethical considerations. In E. Miao (Ed.), *Cross-cultural encounters. Proceedings of the 53rd Annual Convention of the International Council of Psychologists* (pp. 107–136). Taipei: General Innovation Service (GIS).

Laungani, P. (1997). Death in a Hindu family. In C. M. Parkes, P. Laungani, & B. Young (Eds.), *Death and bereavement across cultures* (pp. 52–72). London: Routledge.

Laungani, P. (1997). Patterns of bereavement in Indian and English society. In J. D. Morgan (Ed.), *Readings in thanatology* (pp. 67–76). Amityville, NY: Baywood.

Laungani, P. (1997a). Cross-cultural investigations of stress, anger, and coronary heart disease. In *Rage and Stress: Proceedings of the National 1996 Conference of the International Stress Management Association* (pp. 16–50). London: ISMA Publications.

Laungani, P. (1998). Cultural influences on identity and behaviour: India and Britain. In Y.-T. Lee, C. R. McCauley, & J. Draguns (Eds.), *Through the looking glass: Personality in culture.* Mahwah, NJ: Erlbaum.

Laungani, P. (1999). *India and England: A psycho-cultural analysis.* Reading, UK: Harwood.

Landrine, H. (1992). Clinical implications of cultural differences: The referential versus the indexical self. *Clinical Psychology Review, 12,* 401–415.

La Rosa, J. (1986). *Escalas de locus de control y autoconcepto: Construcción y validación.* Unpublished doctoral dissertation. National University of Mexico, Mexico City.

La Rosa, J., & Díaz-Loving, R. (1988). Diferencial semántico del autoconcepto en estudiantes. *Revista de Psicología Social y Personalidad, 4*, 39–58.

Laws, R. (1886). *Women's work in heathen lands*. Paisley: Parlane.

Lawton, M. P., & Albert, S. M. (1990). *Affective self-management across the lifespan*. Atlanta, GA: American Psychological Association.

Lazarus, R. S. (1993). From psychological stress to the emotions: A history of changing outlooks. *Annual Review of Psychology, 44*, 1–21.

Lazarus, R. S., & Folkman, S. (1984). *Stress, appraisal and coping*. New York: Springer.

Le Bon, G. (1895). *The crowd*. London: Benn.

Lee, R.P.L. (1981). Stress in urban Hong Kong. In T. P. Khoo (Ed.), *Aspects of mental health care: Hong Kong 1981* (pp. 108–117). Hong Kong: Mental Health Association of Hong Kong.

Lee, S., Chiu, H.F.K., & Chen, C. N. (1989). Anorexia nervosa in Hong Kong?: Why not more in Chinese? *British Journal of Psychiatry, 154*, 683–688.

Lee, S., & Hsu, L.K.G. (1995). Eating disorders in Hong Kong. In T. Y. Lin, W. S. Tseng & E. K. Yeh (Eds.) *Chinese socialites and mental health* (pp. 197–208). Hong Kong: Oxford University Press.

Leff, J. (1981). *Psychiatry around the globe: A transcultural view*. New York: Marcel Dekker.

Leff, J., Sartorius, N., Jablensky, A., Korten, A., & Ernberg, G. (1992). The international pilot study of schizophrenia: Five-year follow-up findings. *Psychological Medicine, 22*, 131–145.

Leff, J., & Vaughn, C. (1985). *Expressed emotion in families*. New York: Guilford.

Lefley, H. P. (1985). Families of the mentally ill in cross-cultural perspective. *Psychosocial Rehabilitation Journal, 8* (4), 57–75.

Lefley, H. P. (1990a). Culture and chronic mental illness. *Hospital & Community Psychiatry, 41*, 277–286.

Lefley, H. P. (1990b). Rehabilitation in mental illness: Insights from other cultures. *Psychosocial Rehabilitation Journal, 14*, 5–11.

Lefley, H. P. (1991). Dealing with cross-cultural issues in clinical practice. In P. A. Keller & S. R. Heyman (Eds.), *Innovations in clinical practice: A sourcebook* (Vol. 10, pp. 99–115). Sarasota, FL: Prof. Resource Exchange.

Lefley, H. P. (1992). Expressed emotion: Conceptual, clinical, and social policy issues. *Hospital & Community Psychiatry, 43*, 591–598.

Lefley, H. P. (1996). *Family caregiving in mental illness*. Thousand Oaks, CA: Sage.

Lefley, H. P. (1997). Advocacy, self-help, and consumer-operated services. In A. Tasman, J. Kay, & J. A. Lieberman (Eds.), *Psychiatry* (Vol. 2, pp. 1770–1780). Philadelphia, PA: Saunders.

Lefley, H. P., & Bestman, E. W. (1991). Public-academic linkages for culturally sensitive community mental health. *Community Mental Health Journal, 27*, 473–488.

Lefley, H. P., Sandoval, M., & Charles, C. (1997). Traditional healing systems in a multi-cultural setting. In S. Okpaku (Ed.), *Clinical methods in transcultural psychiatry*. Washington, DC: American Psychiatric Press.

Legault, F., & Strayer, F. F. (1990). The emergence of sex-segregation in preschool peer groups. In F. F. Strayer (Ed.), *Social interaction and behavioral devel-*

opment during early childhood. Montreal: La Maison D'Ethologie de Montreal.

Lehman, H. C. (1953). *Age and achievement.* Princeton, NJ: Princeton University Press.

Lei, T. (1994). Being and becoming moral in a Chinese culture: Unique or universal? *Cross-Cultural Research, 28* (1), 58–91.

Leighton, A., Lambo, T., Hughes, C., Leighton, D., Murphy, J., & Macklin, D. (1963). *Psychiatric disorder among the Yoruba.* Ithaca, NY: Cornell University Press.

Lepowsky, M. (1985). Gender, aging, and dying in an egalitarian society. In D. A. Counts & D. R. Counts (Eds.), *Aging and its transformations: Moving toward death in Pacific societies* (pp. 157–178). Lanham, MD: University Press of America.

Levine, E. (1997). Jewish views and customs on death. In C. M. Parkes, P. Laungani, & B. Young (Eds.), *Death and bereavement across cultures* (pp. 98–130). London: Routledge.

Levine, R. (1989, October). The pace of life. *Psychology Today,* 42–46.

LeVine, R. A. (1978). Comparative notes on the life course. In T. K. Hareven (Ed.), *Transitions: The family and the life course in historical perspective.* New York: Academic.

Lewittes, H. (1982). Women's development in adulthood and old age: A review and critique. *International Journal of Mental Health: Women and Mental Illness, 11,* 115–134.

Lewittes, H., & Mukherji, R. (1989). Friends of older black and white women: In L. L. Adler (Ed.), *Cross-cultural research in human development: Life-span perspectives* (pp. 193–204). New York: Praeger.

Lieberman, J. A., & Rush, A. J. (1996). Redefining the role of psychiatry in medicine. *American Journal of Psychiatry, 153,* 1388–1397.

Likert, R. (1932). A technique for the measurement of attitudes. *Archives of Psychology, 140.*

Lin, K-M., & Kleinman, A. M. (1988). Psychopathology and clinical course of schizophrenia: A cross-cultural perspective. *Schizophrenia Bulletin, 14,* 555–567.

Lind, G. (1986). Cultural differences in moral judgement competence? A study of West and East European university students. *Behavior Science Research, 20* (1–4), 208–225.

Lindsey, R. (1975, October 26). Economy mars belief in the American dream. *New York Times,* Sec. 1, pp. 1, 48.

Linton, R. (1956). *Culture and mental disorders.* Springfield, IL: Charles C. Thomas.

Little, K. B. (1965). Personal space. *Journal of Experimental Social Psychology, 1,* 237–247.

Loeb, E. M. (1962). In feudal Africa. *International Journal of American Linguistics, 28* (3, Pt.2), p. 137.

Longabaugh, R. (1980). The systematic observation of behavior in naturalistic settings. In H. C. Triandis & J. W. Berry (Eds.), *Handbook of cross-cultural psychology,* Vol. 2, *Methodology* (pp. 57–126). Boston, MA: Allyn & Bacon.

Lonner, W. J. (1980). A decade of cross-cultural psychology: JCCP 1970–1979. *Journal of Cross-Cultural Psychology, 11,* 7–34.

Lonner, W. J., & Berry, J. W. (Eds.). (1986). *Field methods in cross-cultural research.* Beverley Hills, CA: Sage.

Loughery, J. (Ed.). (1995). *Into the widening world.* New York: Persea Books.

Lounsbury, F. (1964). A formal account of the Crow and Omaha-Type kinship terminologies. In W. H. Goodenough (Ed.), *Explorations in cultural anthropology.* New York: McGraw-Hill.

Lowenstein, L. F., & Lowenstein, K. (1991). Women in Great Britain. In L. L. Adler (Ed.), *Women in cross-cultural perspective* (pp. 39–52). Westport, CT: Praeger.

Lozier, J., & Althouse, R. (1975). Retirement to the porch in rural Appalachia. *International Journal of Aging and Human Development, 6,* 7–16.

Lukes, S. (1973). *Individualism.* Oxford: Basil Blackwell.

Luo, Y., & Chen, M. (1996). Managerial implications of *guanxi*-based business strategies. *Journal of International Management, 2,* 293–316.

Lynn, R. (1971). *Personality and national character.* Oxford: Pergamon Press.

Lynn, R. (1975). National differences in anxiety, 1935–1965. In I. G. Sarason & C. D. Spielberger (Eds.), *Stress and anxiety* Vol. 2. Washington, DC: Hemisphere.

Lynn, R., & Hampson, S. L. (1975). National differences in extraversion and neuroticism. *British Journal of Social and Clinical Psychology, 14,* 223–240.

Lynn, R., & Hampson, S. L. (1977). Fluctuations in national level of neuroticism and extraversion, 1935–1970. *British Journal of Social and Clinical Psychology, 16,* 131–137.

Maas, J., & Toivanen, K. (1978). Candid Camera and the behavioral sciences. *Teaching of Psychology, 5,* 226–228.

MacAndrew, C., & Edgerton, R. B. (1969). *Drunken comportment: A social explanation.* Chicago: Aldine.

Maccoby, E. E. (1992). The role of parents in the socialization of children: An historical overview. *Developmental Psychology, 28,* 1006–1017.

Maddox, G. L. (1963). Activity and morale. A longitudinal study of selected elderly subjects. *Social Forces, 42,* 195–204.

Maduro, R. (1974). Artistic creativity and aging in India. *International Journal of Aging and Human Development, 5,* 303–329.

Magnus, H. (1880). *Untersuchungen über den Farbensinn der Naturvölker* [Investigations about the color-sense of the nature peoples] (Ser. 2, No. 7). Jena: Fraher.

Mail, P. D., & McDonald, D. P. (1980). *Tulapai to Tokay: A bibliography of alcohol use and abuse among Native Americans of North America.* New Haven, CT: HRAF Press.

Maloney, C. (Ed.). (1976). *The evil eye.* New York: Columbia University Press.

Malpass, R. S., & Poortinga, Y. H. (1988). Strategies for design and analysis. In W. J. Lonner & J. W. Berry (Eds.), *Field methods in cross-cultural research.* Beverly Hills, CA: Sage.

Malzberg, B., & Lee, E. (1956). *Migration and mental disease.* New York: Social Science Research Council.

Mandelbaum, D. G. (1972). *Society in India.* Vol. 2. Berkeley: University of California Press.

Mandler, G. (1967). Organization and memory. In K. W. Spence & J. T. Spence

(Eds.), *Psychology of learning and motivation* (pp. 327–372). New York: Academic Press.

Marano, L. (1982). Windigo psychosis: The anatomy of an emicetic confusion. In R. C. Simons & C. C. Hughes (Eds.), *The culture-bound syndromes: Folk illnesses of psychiatric and anthropological interest* (pp. 411–448). Boston: Reidel.

Marcia, J. E. (1980). Identity in adolescence. In J. Adelson (Ed.), *Handbook of adolescent psychology* (pp. 150–187). New York: Wiley.

Markoulis, D. C., & Dikaiou, M. (1993). Greece. In L. L. Adler (Ed.), *International handbook on gender roles* (pp. 85–97). Westport, CT: Greenwood Press.

Markoulis, D. C., & Valanides, N. (1997). Antecedent variables for sociomoral reasoning development. Evidence from two cultural settings. *International Journal of Psychology, 32* (5), 301–313.

Markus, H. R., & Kitayama, S. (1991). Culture and the self: Implications for cognition, emotion, and motivation. *Psychological Review, 98* (2), 224–253.

Marsella, A. J. (1979). Cross-cultural studies of mental disorders. In A. J. Marsella, R. G. Tharp, & T. J. Ciborowski (Eds.), *Perspectives on cross-cultural psychology*. New York: Academic Press.

Maslow, A. (1970). *Motivation and personality* (2nd ed.). New York: Harper & Row.

Maslow, A. (1971). *The farther reaches of human nature*. New York: McGraw-Hill.

Matsumoto, D. (1989). Cultural influences on the perception of emotion. *Journal of Cross-Cultural Psychology, 20*, 92–105.

Matsumoto, D. (1990). Cultural similarities and differences in display rules. *Motivation and Emotion, 14*, 195–214.

Matsumoto, D. (1991). Cultural influences on facial expressions of emotion. *Southern Communication Journal, 56*, 128–137.

Matsumoto, D. (1992). American-Japanese cultural differences in the recognition of universal facial expressions. *Journal of Cross-Cultural Psychology, 23*, 72–84.

Matsumoto, D. (1993). Ethnic differences in affect intensity, emotion judgments, display rule attitudes, and self-reported emotional expression in an American sample. *Motivation and Emotion, 17*, 107–123.

Matsumoto, D. (1994). *Cultural influences on research methods and statistics*. Pacific Grove, CA: Brooks/Cole.

Matsumoto, D. (1996). *Culture and psychology*. CA: Brooks/Cole.

Matsumoto, D., & Ekman, P. (1988). *Japanese and Caucasian Facial Expressions of Emotion (JACFEE)* [Slides]. San Francisco: Human Interaction Laboratory, University of California, San Francisco.

Matsumoto, D., & Ekman, P. (1989). American-Japanese cultural differences in intensity ratings of facial expressions of emotion. *Motivation and Emotion, 13*, 143–157.

Matsumoto, D., & Hearn, V. (1991). *Culture and emotion: Display rule differences between the United States, Poland, and Hungary*. Unpublished manuscript.

Matsumoto, D., Kasri, F., Kudoh, T., & Kooken, K. (1996). *American-Japanese cultural differences in judgments of expression intensity and subjective experience*. Unpublished manuscript.

Matsumoto, D., & Kudoh, T. (1993). American-Japanese cultural differences in attributions of personality based on smiles. *Journal of Nonverbal Behavior, 17*, 231–243.

Matsumoto, D., Kudoh, T., Scherer, K., & Wallbott, H. (1988). Emotion antecedents and reactions in the US and Japan. *Journal of Cross-Cultural Psychology*, *19*, 267–286.

Mauro, R., Sato, K., & Tucker, J. (1992). The role of appraisal in human emotions: A cross-cultural study. *Journal of Personality and Social Psychology, 62*, 301–317.

Maxwell, E. K., & Maxwell, R. J. (1992). Insults to the body civil: Mistreatment of elderly in two Plains Indian tribes. *Journal of Cross-Cultural Gerontology, 7*, 3–23.

Maxwell, R. J., & Silverman, P. (1970). Information and esteem: Cultural considerations in the treatment of the aged. *International Journal of Aging and Human Development, 1*, 361–392.

McClelland, D. C. (1961). *The achieving society.* Princeton, NJ: Van Nostrand.

McClelland, D. C., Sturr, J. F., Knapp, R. H., & Wendt, H. W. (1958). Obligations to self and society in the United States and Germany. *Journal of Abnormal and Social Psychology, 56*, 245–255.

McClelland, D. C., & Winter, D. G. (1969). *Motivating academic achievement.* New York: Free Press.

McCrae, R. R., & Costa, P. T. (1985). Updating Norman's "Adequate Taxonomy": Intelligence and personality dimensions in natural language and in questionnaires. *Journal of Personality and Social Psychology, 49* (3), 710–721.

McCrae, R. R., & Costa, P. T. (1986). Clinical assessment can benefit from recent advances in personality psychology. *American Psychologist, 41* (9), 1001–1003.

McCrae, R. R., & Costa, P. T. (1987). Validation of the five factor model of personality across instruments and raters. *Journal of Personality and Social Psychology, 1*, 81–90.

McCrae, R. R., & Costa, P. T. (1997). Personality trait structure as a human universal. *American Psychologist, 52*, 509–516.

McDougall, W. (1903). Cutaneous sensations. In *Reports of the Cambridge Anthropological Expedition to Torres Strait, 2*, 189–195.

McDougall, W. (1908). *Introduction to social psychology.* London: Methuen.

McKellin, W. H. (1985). Passing away and loss of life: Aging and death among the Managalase of Papua New Guinea. In D. A. Counts & D. R. Counts (Eds.), *Aging and its transformations: Moving toward death in Pacific societies* (pp. 181–201). Lanham, MD: University Press of America.

McKenna, J. J. (1993). Cosleeping. In M. A. Carskadon (Ed.), *Encyclopedia of sleep and dreaming.* New York: Macmillan.

Mead, M. (1970). *Culture and commitment.* New York: American Museum of Natural History.

Meijer, L., Super, C. M., & Harkness, S. (1997). *Culture, temperament, and parents' perceptions of children's "difficult" behavior in the Netherlands and the U.S.* Paper presented at the 26th Annual Meeting of the Society for Cross-Cultural Research, San Antonio, TX.

Mencius (1970). *Mencius.* (Translated by D. C. Lau). London, UK: Penguin.

Mendis, N. (1990). A model for the care of people with psychosocial disabilities in Sri Lanka. *Psychosocial Rehabilitation Journal, 14*, 45–52.

Merenda, P. F. (1995). International movements in psychology: The major international associations of psychology. *World Psychology, 1*, 27–48.

Merenda, R., & Mattioni, M. (1993). Italy. In L. L. Adler (Ed.), *International hand-book of gender roles* (pp. 159–173). Westport, CT: Greenwood Press.

Mezzich, J. E., Kleinman, A., Fabrega, H., & Parron, D. L. (1996). *Culture and psychiatric diagnosis: A DSM-IV perspective.* Washington, DC: American Psychiatric Press.

Michael, D. N. (1953). A cross-cultural investigation of closure. *Journal of Abnormal and Social Psychology, 48,* 225–230.

Mignolli, G., Laccincani, C., & Platt, S. (1991). Psychopathology and social performance in a cohort of patients with schizophrenic psychoses: A seven-year follow-up study. *Psychological Medicine,* (Monograph Supplement), *19,* 17–26.

Milgram, S. (1961). Nationality and conformity. *Scientific American, 205,* 45–51.

Milgram, S. (1980, May 3). *Social psychology in the eighties.* Keynote address to the New York Area Social Psychologists, Fordham University, New York City.

Milgram, S., & Sabini, J., (1979, Sept.). Candid Camera as social science. *Society, 16,* 72–75.

Milgram, S., Sabini, J., & Silver, M. (Eds.). (1992). *The individual in a social world: Essays and experiments* (2nd ed.). New York: McGraw-Hill.

Miller, G. E. (1956). The magical number 7, plus-or-minus 2: Some limits on our capacity for processing information. *Psychological Review, 63,* 81–97.

Miller, N. E. (1969). Learning of visceral and glandular responses. *Science, 163,* (3866), 434–435.

Mills, R. T., & Krantz, D. S. (1979). Information, choice, and reactions to stress: A field experiment in a blood bank with laboratory analogue. *Journal of Personality and Social Psychology, 37,* 608–620.

Minai, N. (1981). *Women in Islam: Tradition and transition in the Middle East.* London: John Murray.

Mischel, W. (1973). Toward a cognitive social learning reconceptualization of personality. *Psychological Review, 80,* 252–283.

Mitchell, R. E. (1971). Some social implications of high-density housing. *American Sociological Review, 36,* 18–29.

Moghaddam, F. M., Ditto, B., & Taylor, D. (1990). Attitudes and attributions related to symptomatology in Indian immigrant women. *Journal of Cross-Cultural Psychology, 21,* 335–350.

Moghaddam, F. M., Taylor, D. M., & Wright, S. C. (1993). *Social psychology in cross-cultural perspective.* New York: W. H. Freeman.

Montagu, A.M.F.(1971). *Touching.* New York: Columbia University Press.

Moon, Y. L. (1986). A review of cross-cultural studies on moral judgment development using the Defining Issues Test. *Behavior Science Research, 20* (1–4), 147–177.

Morelli, G. A., Rogoff, B., Oppenheim, D., & Goldsmith, D. (1992). Cultural variation in infants' sleeping arrangements: Questions of independence. *Developmental Psychology, 28,* 604–613.

Morris, C. (1938). *Foundation of the theory of sign.* Chicago: University of Chicago Press.

Morris, D. (1967). *The naked ape.* London: Jonathan Cape.

Morris, D. (1979). *Gestures.* New York: Stein & Day.

Mukerjee, M. (1997, February). Trends in animal research. *Scientific American*, 86–93.

Mulder, M. (1976). Reduction of power differences in practice: The power distance reduction theory and its applications. In G. Hofstede & M. S. Kassem (Eds.), *European contributions to organization theory*. Assen, Netherlands: Van Gorcum.

Mulder, M. (1977). *The daily power game*. Leyden: Martinus.

Mullet, E., & Neto, F. (1991). Intention to migrate, job opportunities and aspirations for better pay: An information integration approach. *International Journal of Psychology, 26,* 95–113.

Mundy-Castle, A. C., & Bundy, R. (1988). Moral values in Nigeria. *Journal of African Psychology, 1,* 25–40.

Munroe, R. H., & Munroe, R. L. (1971). Household density and infant care in East African Society. *Journal of Social Psychology, 83,* 3–13.

Murdock, G. P. (1945). The common denominator or culture. In R. Linton (Ed.), *The science of man in world crisis*. New York: Columbia University Press.

Murdock, G. P. (1964). Cultural correlates of the regulations of premarital sex behavior. In R. A. Manners (Ed.), *Process and pattern in culture*. Chicago: Aldine.

Murdock, G. P. (1967). Ethnographic atlas. *Ethnology, 6,* 109–236.

Murdock, G. P. (1971). *Outline of cultural material* (4th ed.). New Haven, CT: HRAF Press.

Murdock, G. P. (1975). *Outline of world cultures* (5th ed.). New Haven, CT: HRAF Press.

Murphy, H.B.M. (1965). Migration and the major mental disorders. In M. Kantor (Ed.), *Mobility and mental health* (pp. 221–249). Springfield, IL: Thomas.

Murphy, H.B.M. (1982). *Comparative psychiatry*. Berlin: Springer-Verlag.

Murphy, H.B.M., & Raman, A. C. (1971). The chronicity of schizophrenia in indigenous tropical peoples. *British Journal of Psychiatry, 118,* 489–497.

Murphy, H.B.M., Wittkower, E. W., & Chance, N. A. (1967). Cross-cultural inquiry into the symptomatology of depression: A preliminary report. *International Journal of Psychiatry, 3,* 6–15.

Muse, C. J. (1991). Women in Western Samoa. In L. L. Adler (Ed.), *Women in cross-cultural perspective* (pp. 221–240). New York: Praeger.

Musgrave, W., & Sison, A. (1910). Mali-mali: A mimic psychosis in the Philippine Islands. *Philippine Journal of Sciences, 5,* 335.

Myerhoff, B. G. (1978). *Number our days*. New York: Dutton.

Myers, C. S. (1903). Smell. In *Reports of the Cambridge Anthropoligical Expedition to Torres Strait, 2,* 169–185.

Myers, D. G. (1996). *Social psychology* (5th ed.). New York: McGraw-Hill.

Nagar, D., Pandey, J., & Paulus, P. B. (1988). The effects of residential crowding experience on reactivity to laboratory crowding and noise. *Journal of Applied Social Psychology, 18* (16), 1423–1442.

Nagaswami, V. (1990). Integration of psychosocial rehabilitation in national health care programmes. *Psychosocial Rehabilitation Journal, 14,* 53–65.

Naidoo, J. C. (1992). The mental health of visible ethnic minorities in Canada. Special Issue: Immigrant mental health. *Psychology and Developing Societies, 4,* 165–186.

Naroll, R. (1970). The culture-bearing unit in cross-cultural surveys. In R. Naroll & R. Cohen (Eds.), *A handbook of method in cultural anthropology* (pp. 721–765). New York: Natural History Press. (Reprinted New York: Columbia University Press, 1973.)

Naroll, R. (1971a). *Conceptualizing the problem, as seen by an anthropologist.* Paper presented at the American Political Science Association Annual Meeting, Chicago.

Naroll, R. (1971b). The double language boundary in cross-cultural surveys. *Behavioral Science Notes, 6*, 95–102.

Nathan, T. (1994). *L'influence qui quérit* [The influence that heals]. Paris: Odile Jacob.

National Center for Health Statistics (1992). *Vital statistics of the United States 1989, Life Tables* (Vol. 1, Sec. 6). Washington, DC: Public Health Service.

National Institute of Mental Health. (1990). *Clinical training in serious mental illness.* Edited by H. P. Lefley. DHHS Pub. No. (ADM) No. 90-1679. Washington, DC: Superintendent of Documents, U.S. Government Printing Office.

Neki, J. S. (1979). Psychotherapy in India: Traditions and trends. In M. Kapur, V. N. Murthy, K. Satyavathi, & R. L. Kapur (Eds.), *Psychotherapeutic processes* (pp. 113–134). Bangalore: National Institute of Mental Health and Neurosciences.

Nespor, K. (1982). Yogic practices in world medical literature. *Yoga, 20* (1), 29–35.

Neto, F. (1986a). Adaptação psico-social e regresso ao pais natal dos migrantes portugueses em Franca [Psychosocial adaptation and return to the native country of Portuguese migrants in France]. *Psicologia, 5*, 71–86.

Neto, F. (1986b). Aspectos da problematica da segunda geração portuguesa em Franca [Aspects of second generation problems of Portuguese in France]. *Povos e cultura, 1*, 167–186.

Neto, F. (1988). Migration plans and their determinants among Portuguese adolescents. In J. Berry & R. Annis (Eds.), *Ethnic psychology: Research and practice with immigrants, refugees, native peoples, ethnic groups, and sojourners* (pp. 308–314). Amsterdam: Swets & Zeitlinger.

Neto, F. (1989). Representation sociale de la migration portugaise. Le regard des jeunes [Social representation of Portuguese migration: Viewpoint of youths]. In J. Retschitzky, M. Bossel-Lagos, & P. Dasen (Eds.), *La recherche interculturelle* (Vol. 1, pp. 86–99). Paris: L'Harmattan.

Neto, F. (1993). *Psicologia da migração portuguesa* [Psychology of the Portuguese migration]. Lisboa: Universidade Aberta.

Neugarten, B., & Neugarten, D. (1986). Age in the aging society. *Journal of the American Academy of Arts and Sciences, 115*, 31–49.

Nicholson, J. R., & Seddon, G. M. (1977). The influence of secondary depth cues on the understanding by Nigerian schoolboys of spatial relationships in pictures. *British Journal of Psychology, 68*, 327–333.

Nicolopoulou, A. (1993). Play, cognitive development, and the social world: Piaget, Vygotsky, and beyond. *Human Development, 36*, 1–23.

Norman, W. T. (1963). Toward an adequate taxonomy of personality attributes. *Journal of Abnormal and Social Psychology, 66*, 574–583.

Nunes, T., Schliemann, A. D., & Carraher, D. W. (1993). *Street mathematics and school mathematics.* Cambridge: Cambridge University Press.

Nuscheler, F. (1995). *Internationale Migration. Flucht und Asyl [International migration. Escape and asylum].* Opladen: Leske & Budrich.

Oberg, K. (1960). Culture shock: Adjustment to new cultural environments. *Practical Anthropology, 7,* 177–182.

Odejide, A. O. (1979) Cross-cultural psychiatry: A myth or reality? *Comprehensive Psychiatry, 20,* 103–108.

Oerter, R., Oerter, R., Agostiani, H., Kim, H., & Wibowo, S. (1996). The concept of human nature in East Asia. *Culture and Psychology, 2,* 9–51.

O'Flaherty, W. D. (1976). *The origins of evil in Hindu mythology.* Berkeley: University of California Press.

Okafor, N.A.O. (1991). Some traditional aspects of Nigerian women. In L. L. Adler (Ed.), *Women in cross-cultural perspective* (pp. 135–141). Westport, CT: Praeger.

Oliver, R.A.C. (1932). The musical talent of natives of East Africa. *British Journal of Psychology, 22,* 333–343.

Oliver, R.A.C. (1934). Mental tests in the study of the African. *Africa, 7,* 40–46.

Orasanu, J., Slater, M. K., & Adler, L. L. (Eds.). (1979). *Language, sex, and gender: Does la différence make a difference?* New York: New York Academy of Sciences, Annals, #237.

Oriol, M. (1981). *Bilan des études sur les aspects culturels et humains des migrations internationales en Europe Occidentale: 1918–1979* [Survey of studies of cultural and human aspects of international migration in Europe: 1918–1979]. Strasbourg: ESF.

Oser, F., & Gmünder, P. (1991). *Religious judgment: A developmental approach* (translation by N. F. Hahn). Birmingham, AL: Religious Education Press.

Osgood, C. E., May, M. H., & Miron, M. S. (1975). *Cross-cultural universals of affective meaning.* Urbana: University of Illinois Press.

Osgood, C. E., Suci, G. J., & Tannenbaum, P. H. (1957). *The measurement of meaning.* Urbana: University of Illinois Press.

Pande, S. (1968). The mystique of "Western" psychotherapy: An Eastern interpretation. *The Journal of Nervous and Mental Disease, 146,* 425–432.

Pandey, R. S., Srinivas, K. N., & Muralidhar, D. (1980). Sociocultural beliefs and treatment acceptance. *Indian Journal of Psychiatry, 22,* 161–166.

Paris, J. (1991). Personality disorders, parasuicide, and culture. *Transcultural Psychiatric Research Review, 28,* 25–39.

Paris, S. G., & Cross, D. R. (1988). The zone of proximal development: Virtues and pitfalls of a metaphorical representation of children's learning. *Genetic Epistemologist, 26,* 27–37.

Park, J. Y., & Johnson, R. C. (1984). Moral development in rural and urban Korea. *Journal of Cross-Cultural Psychology, 15,* 35–46.

Peltzer, K. (1995). *Psychology and health in African cultures.* Frankfurt/Main: IKO-Verlag für Interkulturelle Kommunikation.

Pepitone, A. (1976). Toward a normative and comparative biocultural social psychology. *Journal of Personality and Social Psychology, 4,* 641–653.

Pepitone, A. (1981). Lessons from the history of social psychology. *American Psychologist, 9,* 972–985.

Pepitone, A. (1986). Culture and the cognitive paradigm in social psychology. *Australian Journal of Psychology, 3*, 245–256.

Pepitone, A., & Triandis, H. (1987). On universality of social psychological theories. *Journal of Cross-Cultural Psychology, 4*, 471–498.

Peplau, L. A., & Taylor, S. E. (Eds.). (1997). *Sociocultural perspectives in social psychology.* Upper Saddle River, NJ: Prentice Hall.

Pestonjee, D. M. (1992). *Stress and coping: The Indian experience.* New Delhi: Sage.

Pettigrew, T. (1997). Generalized intergroup contact effects on prejudice. *Personality and Social Psychology Bulletin, 23*, 173–185.

Petty, R., Wegener, D., & Fabrigar, L. (1997). Attitudes and attitude change. *Annual Review of Psychology, 48*, 609–647.

Pfeiffer, W. M. (1994). *Transkulturelle Psychiatrie* [Transcultural psychiatry] (2nd ed.). Stuttgart: Thieme.

Philip, H., & Kelly, M. (1974). Product and process in cognitive development: Some comparative data on the performance of school age children in different cultures. *British Journal of Educational Psychology, 44*, 248–265.

Pike, K. (1967). *Language in relation to a unified theory of the structure of human behavior.* The Hague: Mouton.

Pillemer, K. A. (1985). The dangers of dependency: New findings on domestic violence against the elderly. *Social Problems, 33*, 146–158.

Pittam, J., Gallois, C., Iwasaki, S., & Kroonenberg, P. (1995). Australian and Japanese concepts of expressive behavior. *Journal of Cross-Cultural Psychology, 26*, 451–473.

Pollitt, E., Gorman, K. S., Engle, P., Martorell, R., & Rivera, J. (1993). Early supplemental feeding and cognition: Effects over two decades. *Monographs of the Society for Research in Child Development, 235, 58*, No. 7.

Popper, K. (1972). *Objective knowledge: An evolutionary approach.* Oxford: Clarendon Press.

Popper, K. (1988). *The open universe: An argument for indeterminism.* London: Hutchinson.

Pratt, M. W., Kerig, P., Cowan, P. A., & Cowan, C. P. (1988). Mothers and fathers teaching 3-year-olds: Authoritative parenting and adult scaffolding of young children's learning. *Developmental Psychology, 24* (6), 832–839.

Prescott, J. W. (1975, April). Body pleasure and the origins of violence. *The Futurist*, 64–74.

Price-Williams, D. R. (1975). *Explorations in cross-cultural psychology.* San Francisco: Chandler & Sharp.

Price-Williams, D. R. (1979). Modes of thought in cross-cultural psychology: An historical overview. In A. J. Marsella, R. G. Tharp, & T. J. Ciborowski (Eds.), *Perspectives on cross-cultural psychology.* New York: Academic Press.

Prince, R. N. (1980). Variations in psychotherapeutic procedures. In H. C. Triandis & J. G. Draguns (Eds.), *Handbook of cross-cultural psychology.* Vol. 6. *Psychopathology* (pp. 291–349). Boston: Allyn & Bacon.

Prince, R. N. (1985). The concept of culture-bound syndromes: Anorexia nervosa and brain fag. *Social Science and Medicine, 21*, 197–203.

Ptak, C., Cooper, J., & Brislin, R. (1995). Cross-cultural training programs: Advice and insights from experienced trainers. *International Journal of Intercultural Relations, 19* (3), 425–453.

Räder, K. K., Krampen, G., & Sultan, A. S. (1990). Kontrollüberzeugungen Depressiver im transkulturellen Vergleich [Depressives' beliefs in internal control: A transcultural comparison]. *Fortschritte der Neurologie und Psychiatrie, 58,* 207–214.

Radford, M.H.B. (1989). *Culture, depression, and decision making behaviour: A study with Japanese and Australian clinical and non-clinical populations.* Unpublished doctoral dissertation, Flinders University of South Australia.

Radhakrishnan, S. (1923/1989). *Indian philosophy.* Vol. 2. Centenary Edition. Delhi: Oxford University Press.

Rathus, S. (1973). A thirty-item schedule for assessing assertive behavior. *Behavior Therapy, 4,* 398–406.

Rao, R.S.K. (1983). The conception of stress in Indian thought: The theoretical aspects of stress in Samkhya and Yoga systems. *NIMHANS Journal, 1,* 115–121.

Rao, V. (1986). Indian and Western psychiatry: A comparison. In J. L. Cox (Ed.), *Transcultural psychiatry* (pp. 291–305). London: Croom Helm.

Report of a World Health Organization (WHO) Meeting on Consumer Involvement in Mental Health Services, Mannheim, Federal Republic of Germany, November 9–12, 1988. (1990). *Psychosocial Rehabilitation Journal, 14,* 13–20.

Rest, J. (1979). *Development in judging moral issues.* Minneapolis: University of Minnesota Press.

Rest J. (1983). Morality. In P. Mussen (Ed.), *Handbook of child psychology.* Vol. 4. *Cognitive development* (pp. 556–629). New York: Wiley.

Rest, J. (1986a). *Manual for the Defining Issues Test: An objective test of moral development* (3rd ed.). Center for the Study of Ethical Development. University of Minnesota, Minneapolis, Minnesota.

Rest, J. (1986b). *Moral development: Advances in research and theory.* New York: Praeger.

Revelle, W. (1995). Personality processes. *Annual Review of Psychology, 46,* 295–328.

Richmond, A. (1993). Reactive migration: Sociological perspectives on refugee movements. *Journal of Refugee Studies, 6,* 7–24.

Riesman, D. (1954). *Individualism reconsidered.* New York: Doubleday Anchor.

Riley, M. W. (1979). Introduction: Life course perspectives. In M. W. Riley (Ed.), *Aging from birth to death: Interdisciplinary perspectives* (pp. 3–13). Boulder, CO: Westview Press.

Ritchie, P.L.J. (1996). *Annual report of the International Union of Psychological Science.* Office of the Secretary-General, Ottawa, Canada.

Rivers, W.H.R. (1901). Vision. In *Physiology and psychology, Part 1. Reports of the Cambridge Anthropological Expedition to Torres Strait.* Cambridge: Cambridge University Press.

Rivers, W.H.R. (1905). Observations on the senses of the Todas. *British Journal of Psychology, 1,* 321–396.

Robertson, I. (1987). *Sociology.* New York: Worth.

Robinson, J. P., Shaver, P. R., & Wrightsman, L. S. (Eds.). (1991). *Measures of personality and social psychological attitudes.* San Diego, CA: Academic Press.

Rodríguez de Díaz, M. L., & Díaz-Guerrero, R. (in press). ¿Son universales los rasgos de la personalidad? *Revista Latinoamericana de Psicología.*

Roetz, H. (1992). *Die chinesische Ethik der Achsenzeit. Eine Rekonstruktion under dem Aspekt des Durchbruchs zu postkonventionellem Denken.* Frankfurt/M: Suhrkamp.

Roetz, H. (1993). *Confucian ethics of the axial age: A reconstruction under the aspect of the breakthrough towards postconventional thinking.* Albany, NY: SUNY Press. [English translation and revision of the original 1992 edition in German.]

Roetz, H. (1996). Kohlberg and Chinese moral philosophy. *World Psychology, 2* (3–4), 335–363.

Rogers, C. (1961). *On becoming a person.* Boston: Houghton Mifflin.

Rogers, C. (1980). *A way of being.* Boston: Houghton Mifflin.

Rogoff, B., & Chavajay, P. (1995). What's become of research on the cultural basis of cognitive development? *American Psychologist, 50,* 859–873.

Rohner, R. P. (1974). Proxemics and stress: An empirical study of the relationship between space and roommate turnover. *Human Relations, 27* (7), 697–702.

Rokeach, M. (1960). *The open and closed mind.* New York: Basic Books.

Rokeach, M. (1973). *The nature of human values.* New York: Macmillan.

Roland, A. (1988). *In search of self in India and Japan.* Princeton, NJ: Princeton University Press.

Roscow, I. (1965). And then we were old. *Transaction, 2* (2), 21–26.

Rosenblatt, P. C. (1997). Grief in small-scale societies. In C. M. Parkes, P. Laungani, & B. Young (Eds.), *Death and bereavement across cultures* (pp. 27–51). London: Routledge.

Rosenzweig, M. R. (1984). U.S. psychology and world psychology. *American Psychologist, 39,* 877–884.

Rosenzweig, M. R. (1992). Psychological science around the world. *American Psychologist, 47,* 718–722.

Ross, E. A. (1908). *Social psychology.* New York: Macmillan.

Rotter, J. B. (1966). Generalized expectancies for internal versus external control of reinforcement. *Psychological Monographs, 80* (Whole No. 609).

Rubinstein, R. L. (1987). Childless elderly: Theoretical perspectives and practical concerns. *Journal of Cross-Cultural Gerontology, 2,* 1–14.

Ruiz, P., & Langrod, J. (1976). The role of folk healers in community mental health services. *Community Mental Health Journal, 12,* 392–398.

Russell, J. G. (1989). Anxiety disorders in Japan: A review of the Japanese literature on *shinkeishitsu* and *taijin kyofusho. Culture, Medicine, and Psychiatry, 13,* 391–403.

Sabatier, C., & Berry, J. W. (1994). Immigration et acculturation [Immigration and Acculturation]. In R. Bourhis & J. P. Leyens (Eds.), *Stereotypes, discrimination et relations intergroupes.* Liege: Mardaga.

Sadoun, R., Lolli, G., & Silverman, M. (1965). *Drinking in French culture.* New Brunswick, NJ: Rutgers Center of Alcohol Studies.

Sachdev, D. (1992). *Effects of psychocultural factors on the socialisation of British born Indian children and indigenous British children living in England.* Unpublished doctoral thesis, South Bank University, London.

Sackett, G. (1966). Monkeys reared in isolation with pictures as visual input: Evidence for an innate releasing mechanism. *Science, 154,* 1468–1473.

Saffiotti, L. (1990). *The selective use of beliefs to interpret major life events.* Unpublished doctoral dissertation, University of Pennsylvania, Philadelphia.

Safir, M. P., & Izraeli, D. N. (1991). Growing up female: A life-span perspective on women in Israel. In L. L. Adler (Ed.), *Women in cross-cultural perspective* (pp. 90–105). Westport, CT: Praeger.

Salisbury, R. (1966). Possession in the New Guinea Highlands: Review of literature. *Transcultural Research.*

Sam, D. L., & Berry, J. W. (1995). Acculturative stress among young immigrants in Norway. *Scandinavian Journal of Psychology, 36,* 10–24.

Samovar, L. A., & Porter, R. E. (Eds.). (1982). *Intercultural communication: A reader* (3rd ed.). Belmore, CA: Wadsworth.

Sampson, E. E. (1977). Psychology and the American ideal. *Journal of Personality and Social Psychology, 15,* 189–194.

Sankar, A. (1981). The conquest of solitude: Singlehood and old age. In C. Fry (Ed.), *Dimensions: Aging, culture and health* (pp. 65–83). South Hadley, MA: J. F. Bergin.

Sapir, E. (1933). The psychological reality of phonemes. In D. Mandelbaum (Ed.), *The selected writings of Edward.* Berkeley: University of California Press.

Sapir, E. (1949). *Culture, language and personality.* Berkeley: University of California Press.

Sapolsky, R. M. (1994). *Why Zebras don't get ulcers.* New York: W. H. Freeman.

Saraswathi, T. S., & Pai, S. (1997). Socialization in the Indian context. In H.S.R. Kao & D. Sinha (Eds.), *Asian perspectives on psychology* (Vol. 19, Cross-Cultural Research and Methodology Series) (pp. 74–92). New Delhi: Sage.

Sarbin, T. R. (1986). Emotion and act: Roles and rhetoric. In R. Harré (Ed.), *The social construction of emotions.* Oxford: Blackwell.

Sartorius, N., de Girolamo, G., Andrews, G., German, G. A., & Eisenberg, L. (Eds.). (1993). *Treatment of mental disorders: A review of effectiveness.* Published on behalf of the World Health Organization. Washington, DC: American Psychiatric Press.

Sartorius, N., & Harding, T. W. (1983). The WHO Collaborative study on strategies for extending mental health care, I: The genesis of the study. *American Journal of Psychiatry, 140,* 1470–1473.

Sartorius, N., Jablensky, A., Ernberg, G., Anker, M., Cooper, J. E., & Day, R. (1986). Early manifestations and first contact incidence of schizophrenia in different cultures: A preliminary report on the initial evaluation phase of the WHO Collaborative Study on Determinants of Outcome of Severe Mental Disorders. *Psychological Medicine, 16,* 909–928.

Sartorius, N., Jablensky, A., Korten, A., & Ernberg, G. (1986). Early manifestation and first contact incidence of schizophrenia. *Psychological Medicine, 16,* 909–928.

Sartorius, N., Jablensky, A., & Shapiro, R. (1977). Two-year follow-up of the patients included in the WHO International Pilot Study of Schizophrenia. *Psychological Medicine, 7,* 529–541.

Sartorius, N., Shapiro, R., & Jablensky, A. (1974). The international pilot study of schizophrenia. *Schizophrenia Bulletin, 11,* 21–34.

Satyavathi, K. (1988). Mental health In J. Pandey (Ed.), *Psychology in India: The state-of-the-art*, Vol. 3: *Organizational behaviour and mental health* (pp. 217–288). New Delhi: Sage.

Saussure, F. de (1959). *Course in general linguistics*. New York: Philosophical Library.

Saville-Troike, M. (1982). *The ethnography of communication*. Oxford, UK: Basil Blackwell.

Scherer, K., Matsumoto, D., Wallbott, H., & Kudoh, T. (1988). Emotional experience in cultural context: A comparison between Europe, Japan, and the USA. In K. Scherer (Ed.), *Facets of emotion: Recent research*. Hillsdale, NJ: Erlbaum.

Scherer, K. R., & Wallbott, H. G. (1994). Evidence for universality and cultural variation of differential emotion response patterning. *Journal of Personality and Social Psychology, 66*, 310–328.

Schimmack, U. (1996). Cultural influences on the recognition of emotion by facial expressions: Individualist or Caucasian cultures? *Journal of Cross-Cultural Psychology, 27*, 37–50.

Schlegel, A. (1972). *Male dominance and female autonomy*. New Haven, CT: Human Relations Area Files.

Schlegel, A., & Barry, H. (1991). *Adolescence: An anthropological inquiry*. New York: Free Press.

Schmitz, P. G. (1987). *Acculturation attitudes and beliefs of immigration*. Paper presented at the First Regional North American Conference of the IACCP, Kingston, Canada.

Schmitz, P. G. (1992a). Personality, stress-reactions, and diseases. *Personality and Individual Differences, 13*, 683–691.

Schmitz, P. G. (1992b). Acculturation styles and health. In S. Iwawaki, Y. Kashima, & K. S. Leung (Eds.), *Innovations in cross-cultural psychology* (pp. 360–370). Amsterdam: Swets & Zeitlinger.

Schmitz, P. G. (1992c). Immigrant mental and physical health. Special Issue: Immigrant mental health. *Psychology and Developing Societies, 4*, 117–132.

Schmitz, P. G. (1993). Personality, stress-reactions, and psychosomatic complaints. In G. van Heck, P. Bonaiuto, & I. Deary (Eds.), *Personality psychology in Europe* (Vol. 4). Amsterdam: Swets & Zeitlinger.

Schmitz, P. G. (1994a). Acculturation and adaptation process among immigrants in Germany. In A. M. Bouvy, F.J.R. van de Vijver, & P. G. Schmitz (Eds.), *Journeys into cross-cultural psychology* (pp. 142–157). Amsterdam: Swets & Zeitlinger.

Schmitz, P. G. (1994b). Personnalité et acculturation [Personality and acculturation]. *Cahiers Internationaux de Psychologie Sociale, 24*, 33–53.

Schmitz, P. G. (1994c). Se puede generalizar el modelo de aculturación de John Berry (Can John Berry's model of acculturation be generalized?) *Revista de Psicología Social y Personalidad, 10*, 17–35.

Schmitz, P. G. (1996). Cultural identity problems and solution strategies. In P. G. Schmitz & F. Neto (Chairs), *Socio-cultural identity and adaptation*. Symposium at the 12th Congress of the International Association for Cross-Cultural Psychology, Montreal, Canada.

Schultz, D. P., & Schultz, S. E. (1994). *Psychology and work today* (6th ed.). New York: Macmillan.

Schulz, C. M. (1980). Age, sex, and death anxiety in a middle-class community. In C. Fry (Ed.), *Aging in culture and society: Comparative viewpoints and strategies* (pp. 239–252). New York: J. F. Bergin.

Schwartz, S. H. (1990). Individualism-collectivism: Critique and proposed refinements. *Journal of Cross-Cultural Psychology, 21* (2), 139–115.

Schwartz, T. (1981). The acquisition of culture. *Ethos, 9,* 4–17.

Sears, D. O. (1986). College sophomores in the laboratory: Influences of a narrow data base on social psychology's view of human nature. *Journal of Personality and Social Psychology, 51,* 515–530.

Sechrest, L. (1970). Experiments in the field. In R. Naroll & R. Cohen (Eds.), *A handbook of method in cultural anthropology* (pp. 196–209). Garden City, NY: Natural History Press.

Sechrest, L. (1975). Another look at unobtrusive measures: An alternative to what? In W. Sinaiko & L. Broedling (Eds.), *Perspectives on attitude assessment: Surveys and their alternatives.* Washington, DC: Smithsonian Institution.

Sechrest, L. (Ed.). (1979). *Unobtrusive measurement today: New directions for methodology of behavioral science.* San Francisco, CA: Jossey-Bass.

Sechrest, L., Fay, T., Zaidi, H., & Florez, L. (1973). Attitudes toward mental disorder among college students in the United States, Pakistan, and the Philippines. *Journal of Cross-Cultural Psychology, 4,* 342–360.

Schwendler, W. (1984). UNESCO's project on the exchange of knowledge for endogenous development. In D. Sinha & W. H. Holtzman (Eds.), *The impact of psychology on Third World development.* Special Issue of the *International Journal of Psychology, 19* (1–2), 3–15.

Segall, M. H. (1979). *Cross-cultural psychology: Human behavior in global perspective.* Monterey, CA: Brooks/Cole.

Segall, M. H. (1984). More than we need to know about culture, but are afraid not to ask. *Journal of Cross-Cultural Psychology, 15,* 153–162.

Segall, M., Dasen, P. R., Berry, J. W., & Poortinga, Y. H. (1990). *Human behavior in global perspective: An introduction to cross-cultural psychology.* New York: Pergamon.

Seligman, M.E.P. (1975). *Helplessness: On depression, development and death.* San Francisco, CA: Freeman.

Selvini-Palazzoli, M. (1985). Anorexia nervosa: A syndrome of the affluent society. *Transcultural Psychiatric Research Review, 22* (3), 199–205.

Serpell, R. (1993). *The significance of schooling: Life-journeys in an African society.* Cambridge, UK: Cambridge University Press.

Sethi, B. B., & Manchanda, R. (1978). Family structure and psychiatric disorders. *Indian Journal of Psychiatry, 20,* 283–288.

Sexton, V. S. (1984, April 14). *Is American psychology xenophobic?* Presidential address to the Eastern Psychological Association, Baltimore.

Sexton, V. S., & Hogan, J. D. (Eds.). (1992). *International psychology: Views from around the world.* Lincoln: University of Nebraska Press.

Sexton, V. S., & Misiak, H. (1984). American psychologists and psychology abroad. *American Psychologist, 39,* 1026–1031.

Shahrani, M. N. (1981). Growing in respect: Aging among the Kirghiz of Afghanistan. In P. Amoss & S. Harrell (Eds.), *Other ways of growing old: Anthropological perspectives* (pp. 175–191). Stanford, CA: Stanford University Press.

Shakespeare, W. (1957). As you like it. In J. Munro (Ed.), *The London Shakespeare.* New York: Simon & Schuster.

Shakoor, M. A. (1992). *Kontrollüberzeugungen Depressiver im transkulturellen Vergleich. Eine Studie über kognitive Orientierungen afghanischer, agyptischer und deutscher Patienten* [Control beliefs of depressives in cross-cultural comparison. A study about cognitive orientations among Afghan, Egyptian, and German patients]. Unpublished doctoral dissertation in Medicine, Georg-August University in Göttingen, Germany.

Shankar, R., & Menon, M. S. (1991). Interventions with families of people with schizophrenia: The issues facing a community-based rehabilitation center in India. *Psychosocial Rehabilitation Journal, 15,* 85–90.

Sharabany, R., & Wiseman, H. (1993). Close relationships in adolescence: The case of the kibbutz. *Journal of Youth and Adolescence, 22,* 671–695.

Sharma, S. (1988). Stress and anxiety. In J. Pandey (Ed.), *Psychology in India: The-state-of-the-art* (Vol. 1, pp. 191–248). New Delhi: Sage.

Sharp, H. S. (1981). Old age among the Chipewyan. In P. Amoss & S. Harrell (Eds.), *Other ways of growing old: Anthropological perspectives* (pp. 99–109). Stanford, CA: Stanford University Press.

Sherif, M., & Sherif, C. W. (1969). *Social psychology.* New York: Harper & Row.

Shouksmith, G. (1992). Psychology in New Zealand. In V. S. Sexton & J. D. Hogan (Eds.), *International psychology: Views from around the world* (pp. 303–313). Lincoln: University of Nebraska Press.

Shrimali, S., & Broota, K. (1987). Effect of surgical stress on belief in God and superstition. *Journal of Personality and Clinical Studies, 2,* 135–138.

Shwalb, B. J., Shwalb, D. W., & Shoji, J. (1994). Structure and dimensions of maternal perceptions of Japanese infant temperament. *Developmental Psychology, 30,* 131–141.

Shweder, R. A., Jensen, L. A., & Goldstein, W. M. (1995). Who sleeps with whom revisited: A method for extracting the moral goods implicit in practice. In J. J. Goodnow, P. J. Miller, & F. Kessel (Eds.), *Cultural practices as contexts for development* (pp. 21–39). San Francisco: Jossey-Bass.

Shweder, R. A., Mahapatra, M., & Miller, J. G. (1990). Culture and moral development. In J. W. Stigler, R. A. Shweder, & G. Herdt (Eds.), *Cultural psychology* (pp. 130–204). Cambridge, U.K.: Cambridge University Press.

Siegel, J. S., & Davidson, M. (1984). *Demographic and socioeconomic aspects of aging in the United States.* Current population reports, Series P-23, No. 138. U.S. Bureau of the Census. Washington, DC: U.S. Government Printing Office.

Silver, S. O., & Pollack, R. H. (1967). Racial differences in pigmentation of the fundus oculi. *Psychonomic Science, 7,* 159–160.

Silverman, P. (1987). *The elderly as modern pioneers.* Bloomington: Indiana University Press.

Silverman, P., & Maxwell, R. (1978). How do I respect thee? Let me count the ways: Deference towards elderly men and women. *Behavior Science Research, 13,* 91–108.

Simmons, L. (1945). *The role of the aged in primitive society.* New Haven, CT: Yale University Press.

Simmons, L. (1960). Aging in preindustrial societies. In C. Tibbitts (Ed.), *Handbook of social gerontology.* Chicago: University of Chicago Press.

Simpson, E. L. (1974). Moral development research: A case study of scientific cultural bias. *Human Development, 17*, 81–106.

Sinari, R. A. (1984). *The structure of Indian thought.* Delhi: Oxford University Press.

Sinha, D., & Holtzman, W. H. (1984). Foreword. In D. Sinha & W. H. Holtzman (Eds.), *The impact of psychology on Third World development.* Special Issue of the *International Journal of Psychology, 19* (1–2), 1.

Sinha, D., & Kao, H.S.R. (1997). The journey to the East: An introduction. In H.S.R. Kao & D. Sinha (Eds.), *Asian perspectives on psychology* (Vol. 19, Cross-Cultural Research and Methodology Series) (pp. 9–22). New Delhi: Sage.

Sinha, D., Mishra, R. C., & Berry, J. W. (1996). Some eco-cultural and acculturational factors in intermodal perception. In J. Pandey, D. Sinha, & D.P.S. Bhawuk (Eds.), *Asian contributions to cross-cultural psychology* (pp. 151–164). New Delhi: Sage.

Singhal, U., & Mrinal, N. R. (1991). Tribal women of India: The Tharu women. In L. L. Adler (Ed.), *Women in cross-cultural perspective* (pp. 160–173). Westport, CT: Praeger.

Small, S. A., Zeldin, R. S., & Savin-Williams, R. C. (1981). *Professional behavior: A case for consistency.* Paper presented at the Annual Meeting of the Western Psychological Association, Los Angeles, CA.

Snarey, J. R. (1985). Cross-cultural universality of social-moral development: A critical review of Kohlbergian research. *Psychological Bulletin, 97*, 202–232.

Snarey, J. R., & Keljo, K. (1991). In a *Gemeinschaft* voice: The cross-cultural expansion of moral development theory. In W. Kurtines & J. Gewirtz (Eds.), *Handbook of moral behavior and development: Theory* (Vol. 1, pp. 395–424). Hillsdale, NJ: Erlbaum.

Snarey, J. R., Reimer, J., & Kohlberg, L. (1985). Development of social-moral reasoning among kibbutz adolescents: A longitudinal cross-cultural study. *Developmental Psychology, 21*, 3–11.

Snyder, C. R. (1958). *Alcohol and the Jews.* Glencoe, IL: Free Press.

Spence, J. T. (1985). Achievement American style: The rewards and costs of individualism. *American Psychologist, 40*, 1285–1295.

Spradly, J. P. (1968). A cognitive analysis of tramp behavior. In *Proceedings of the Eighth International Congress of Anthropological and Ethnological Sciences,* Japan Science Council, Tokyo.

Spradly, J. P. (1970). *You owe yourself a drunk: An ethnography of urban nomads.* Boston, MA: Little, Brown.

Spradly, J. P. (1971). Beating the drunk charge. In J. P. Spradly & D. W. McCurdy (Eds.), *Conformity and conflict: Readings in cultural anthropology* (pp. 351–358). Boston, MA: Little, Brown.

Spradly, J. P. (1979). *The ethnographic interview.* New York: Holt, Rinehart & Winston.

Spradly, J. P. (1980). *Participant observation.* New York: Holt, Rinehart & Winston.

Spradly, J. P., & Mann, B. (1975). *The cocktail waitress: Women's work in a male world.* New York: Wiley.

Srinivasa, D. K., & Trivedi, S. (1982). Knowledge and attitude of mental diseases in a rural community of South India. *Social Science Medicine, 16*, 1635–1639.

Stephan, W. (1985). Intergroup relations. In G. Lindzey & E. Aronson (Eds.),

Handbook of social psychology (3rd ed.) (Vol. 2, pp. 599–658). New York: Random House.

Steward, E. P. (1994). *Beginning writers in the zone of proximal development.* Hillsdale, NJ: Erlbaum.

Stewart, D. W., & Shamdasani, P. N. (1990). *Focus groups: Theory and practice.* Newbury, CA: Sage.

Stiles, D. de Silva, & Gibbons, J. (1996). Girls' relational self in Sri Lanka and the United States. *Journal of Genetic Psychology, 157,* 191–203.

Stivers, R. (1976). *A hair of the dog: Irish drinking and American stereotype.* University Park: Pennsylvania University Press.

Sudanow (1985). *Sudanese Monthly Magazine,* March, p. 7.

Sukemune, S., Shiraishi, T., Shirakawa, Y., & Matsumi, J. T. (1993). Japan. In L. L. Adler (Ed.), *International handbook on gender roles* (pp. 174–186). Westport, CT: Greenwood Press.

Super, C. M., & Harkness, S. (1986). The developmental niche: A conceptualization of the interface of child and culture. *International Journal of Behavioral Development, 9,* 545–570.

Super, C. M., & Harkness, S. (1994). The developmental niche. In W. J. Lonner & R. Malpass (Eds.), *Psychology and culture* (pp. 95–99). Needham Heights, MA: Allyn & Bacon.

Super, C. M., Harkness, S., & Blom, M. (1997). *Cultural differences in Dutch and American infants' sleep patterns: How do they get that way?* Paper presented at the 26th Annual meeting of the Society for Cross-Cultural Research, San Antonio, TX.

Suzuki, P. T. (1981). Psychological problems of Turkish migrants in West Germany. *American Journal of Psychotherapy, 35,* 187–194.

Suzuki, D., & Knudtson, P. (1992). *Wisdom of the elders.* New York: Bantam Books.

Taft, R. (1977). Coping with unfamiliar cultures. In N. Warren (Ed.), *Studies in cross-cultural psychology* (pp. 121–151). London: Academic Press.

Takooshian, H. (1979). *Helping behavior as a social indicator.* Unpublished doctoral dissertation, City University of New York (40/05-B, #7923772).

Takooshian, H. (1985). Non-verbal reasoning. In D. J. Keyser & R. C. Sweetland (Eds.), *Test critiques* (Vol. 4, pp. 463–468). Kansas City, MO: Test Corporation of America.

Tanaka-Matsumi, J. (1979). *Taijin-kyofusho*: Diagnostic and cultural issues in Japanese psychiatry. *Culture, Medicine, and Psychiatry, 3,* 231–245.

Tanaka-Matsumi, J., & Draguns, J. G. (1997). Culture and psychopathology. In J. W. Berry, M. H. Segall, & Ç. Kagitçibasi (Eds.), *Handbook of cross-cultural psychology.* Vol. 3. *Social behavior and applications* (2nd ed.) (pp. 449–491). Boston: Allyn & Bacon.

Tartara, T. (1990). *Summaries of national elder abuse data: An exploratory study of state statistics based on a survey of state adult protective service and aging agencies.* Washington, DC: National Aging Resource Center on Elder Abuse.

Tarde, G. (1903). *The laws of imitation.* New York: Holt.

Thacore, V. R. (1973). *Mental illness in an urban community.* Allahabad: United Publishers.

Thoma, S. (1986). Estimating gender differences in the comprehension and preference of moral issues. *Developmental Review, 6,* 165–180.

Thomae, H. (1988). *Das Individuum und seine Welt. Eine Persönlichkeitstheorie* [The individual and his world: A theory of personality] (2nd ed.). Göttingen: Hogrefe.

Thomas, A., & Chess, S. (1977). *Temperament and development.* New York: Bruner/ Mazel.

Thompson, S. C. (1981). Will it hurt if I can control it? A complex answer to a simple question. *Psychological Bulletin, 90,* 89–101.

Thouless, R. H. (1933). A racial difference in perception. *Journal of Social Psychology, 4,* 330–339.

Tobin, J. J. (1987). The American idealization of old age Japan. *The Gerontologist, 27,* 53–58.

Tomkins, S. S. (1962). *Affect, imagery, and consciousness* (Vol. 1). New York: Springer.

Tomkins, S. S. (1963). *Affect, imagery, and consciousness* (Vol. 2). New York: Springer.

Torrey, B. B., Kinsella, K., & Taeuber, C. M. (1987). *An aging world.* International population reports. Series P-95, No. 78. Bureau of the Census. Washington, DC: U.S. Government Printing Office.

Torry, W. I. (1986). Morality and harm: Hindu peasant adjustment to famine. *Social Science Information, 25* (1), 125–160.

Trefil, J. (1980). *From atoms to quarks: An introduction to the strange world of particle physics.* New York: Charles Scribner.

Trevor-Roper, H. (1967). The European witchcraze of the sixteenth and seventeenth centuries. In *The crisis of the seventeenth century.* New York: Harper & Row.

Triandis, H. C. (1989). The self and social behavior in differing cultural contexts. *Psychological Review, 96,* 506–520.

Triandis, H. C. (1994). *Culture and social behavior.* New York: McGraw-Hill.

Triandis, H. C. (1995). *Individualism and collectivism.* Boulder, CO: Westview.

Triandis, H. C., Bontempo, R., Betancourt, H., Bond, M., Leung, K., Brenes, A., Georgas, J., Hui, H. C., Marin, G., Setiadi, B., Sinha, J.B.P., Verma, J., Spangenberg, J., Touzard, H., & de Montmollin, G. (1986). The measurement of the etic aspects of individualism and collectivism across cultures. *Australian Journal of Psychology, 38,* 257–267.

Triandis, H. C., Lambert, W. W., Berry, J. W., Brislin, R. W., Draguns, J., Lonner, W., & Heron, A. (Eds.). (1980). *Handbook of cross-cultural psychology* (Vols. 1–6). Boston: Allyn & Bacon.

Triandis, H. C., Malpass, R. S., & Davidson, A. (1972). Cross-cultural psychology. *Biennial Review of Anthropology,* 1–84.

Triandis, H. C., Malpass, R. S., & Davidson, A. R. (1973). Psychology and culture. *Annual Review of Psychology, 24,* 355–378.

Tsai, H.-Y. (1995). Sojourner adjustment: The case of foreigners in Japan. *Journal of Cross-Cultural Psychology, 26,* 523–526.

Tseng, W. S., & McDermott, J. F. (1981). *Culture, mind, and therapy.* New York: Brunner/Mazel.

Tseng, W. S., Asasi, M., Jieqiu, L., Wibulswasd, P., Suryani, L. K., Wen, J. K., Brennan, J., & Heiby, E. (1990). Multicultural study of minor psychiatric disorders in Asia: Symptom manifestations. *International Journal of Social Psychiatry, 36,* 252–264.

Turnbull, C. M. (1965). *Wayward servants*. New York: Natural History Press.

Tylor, E. B. (1889). On a method of investigating the development of institutions: Applied to laws of marriage and descent. *Journal of the Anthropological Institute of Great Britain and Ireland, 18,* 245–269.

Tzuriel, D. (1992). The development of ego identity at adolescence among Israeli Jews and Arabs. *Journal of Youth and Adolescence, 21,* 551–571.

Uzgiris, I. C., & Raeff, C. (1995). Play in parent-child interactions. In M. H. Bornstein (Ed.), *Handbook of parenting*. Mahwah, NJ: Erlbaum.

Uzoka, A. F. (1979). The myth of the nuclear family: Historical background and clinical implications. *American Psychologist, 34,* 1095–1106.

Vahia, N. S. (1982). Yoga in psychiatry. In A. Kiev & A. V. Rao (Eds.) *Readings in transcultural psychiatry* (pp. 11–19). Madras: Higginbothams.

Van Brero, P. (1895). Latah. *Journal of Mental Science, 41,* 537–538.

van de Vijver, F.J.R., & Leung, K. (1997a). Methods and data analysis of comparative research. In J. W. Berry, Y. H. Poortinga, & J. Pandey (Eds.), *Handbook of cross-cultural psychology* (2nd ed.) (Vol. 1, pp. 257–300). Needham Heights, MA: Allyn & Bacon.

van de Vijver, F.J.R., & Leung, K. (1997b). *Methods and data analysis for cross-cultural research*. Newbury Park, CA: Sage.

Vasudev, J., & Hummel, R. (1987). Moral stage sequence and principled reasoning in an Indian sample. *Human Development, 30* 105–118.

Vaughn, C. & Leff, J. (1976). The influence of family and social factors on the course of psychiatric illness: A comparison of schizophrenic and depressed neurotic patients. *British Journal of Psychiatry, 129,* 125–137.

Vine, I. (1982). Crowding and stress: A personal space approach. *Psychological Review, 2* (1), 1–18.

Vine, I. (1986). Moral maturity in socio-cultural perspective: Are Kohlberg's stages universal? In S. Modgil & C. Modgil (Eds.), *Lawrence Kohlberg: Consensus and controversy* (pp. 431–450). London: Falmer Press.

von-Fürer-Haimendorf, C. (1974). The sense of sin in cross-cultural perspective. *Man, 9,* 539–556.

Vygotsky, L. S. (1978). *Mind in society: The development of higher psychological processes*. Cambridge, MA. Harvard University Press.

Vygotsky, L. S. (1934/1986). *Thought and language* (translated and revised by A. Kozulin). Cambridge, MA: MIT Press.

Walker, L. J. (1991). Sex differences in moral reasoning. In W. M. Kurtines & J. L. Gewirtz (Eds.), *Handbook of moral behavior and development* (Vol. 2, pp. 333–364). Hillsdale, NJ: Erlbaum.

Wallace, A.F.C. (1965). The problem of the psychological validity of componential analysis. *American Anthropologist, 67* (#5, Part 2), 229–248.

Wallbott, H. G., & Scherer, K. R. (1986). How universal and specific is emotional experience? Evidence from 27 countries on five continents. *Social Science Information, 25,* 763–795.

Walter, T. (1997). Secularization. In C. M. Parkes, P. Laungani, & B. Young (Eds.), *Death and bereavement across cultures* (pp. 166–187). London: Routledge.

Ward, C. A. (1996). Acculturation. In D. Landis & R. Bhagat (Eds.), *Handbook of Intercultural Training* (2nd ed.). Newbury, CA: Sage.

Ward, C. A., & Kennedy, A. (1992). Locus of control, mood disturbance and social difficulty during cross-cultural transitions. *International Journal of Intercultural Relations, 16,* 175–194.

Ward, C. A., & Kennedy, A. (1996). Crossing cultures: The relationship between psychological and socio-cultural dimensions of cross-cultural adjustment. In J. Pandey, D. Sinha, & D.P.S. Bhawuk (Eds.), *Asian contributions to cross-cultural psychology* (pp. 289–306). New Delhi: Sage.

Ward, C. A., & Searle, W. (1991). The impact of value discrepancies and cultural identity on psychological and sociocultural adjustment of sojourners. *International Journal of Intercultural Relations, 15,* 209–225.

Warner, R. (1994). *Recovery from schizophrenia: Psychiatry and political economy* (2nd ed.). London: Routledge.

Wassmannn, J., & Dasen, P. R. (1994). Yupno number system and counting. *Journal of Cross-Cultural Psychology, 25* (1), 78–94.

Waterman, A. A. (1981). Individualism and interdependence. *American Psychologist, 36,* 762–773.

Watson, J. L. (Ed.). (1977). *Between two cultures: Migrants and minorities in Britain.* Oxford: Blackwell.

Watson, W. (1983). *A study of factors affecting the development of moral judgement.* Unpublished manuscript, Monash Chirering, Victoria, Australia.

Webb, S. D. (1978). Privacy and psychosomatic stress: An empirical analysis. *Social Behaviour and Personality, 6* (2), 227–234.

Weber, M. (1963). *The sociology of religion* (4th ed.). London. Allen & Unwin.

Wechsler, D. (1958). *The measurement and appraisal of adult intelligence.* Baltimore, MD: Williams & Wilkins.

Weinreich, U. (1954). *Languages in contact.* New York: Linguistic Circle of New York.

Weissman, M. M., Bland, R. C., Canino, G. J., Faravelli, C., Greenwald, S., Hwu, H. G., Joyce, P. R., Karam, E. G., Lee, C. K., Lellouch, J., Lépine, J. P., Newman, S. C., Rubio-Stipec, M., Wells, J. E., Wickmaratne, P. J., Wittchen, H. U., & Yeh, E. K. (1996). Cross-national epidemiology of major depression and bipolar disorder. *Journal of American Medical Association, 276,* 293–299.

Wertsch, J. V., & Tulviste, P. (1994). Lev Semyonovich Vygotsky and contemporary developmental psychology. In R. D. Parke, P. A. Ornstein, J. J. Rieser, & C. Zahn-Waxler (Eds.), *A century of developmental psychology.* Washington, DC: American Psychological Association.

Westermeyer, J. (1986). Migration and psychopathology. In C. L. Williams & J. Westermeyer (Eds.), *Refugee mental health in resettlement countries.* Washington, DC: Hemisphere.

Westermeyer, J. (1989). Psychiatric epidemiology across cultures: Current issues and trends. *Transcultural Psychiatric Research Review, 26,* 5–25.

Whiting, B. B. (1963). *Six cultures: Studies of child rearing.* Cambridge, MA: Harvard University Press.

Whiting, B. B., & Edwards, C. P. (1988). *Children of different worlds: The formation of social behavior.* Cambridge, MA: Harvard University Press.

Whiting, B. B., & Whiting, J.W.M. (1975). *Children of six cultures: A psycho-cultural analysis.* Cambridge, MA: Harvard University Press.

Whiting, J.W.M., & Child, I. L. (1953). *Child training and personality.* New Haven, CT: Yale University Press.

Whiting, J.W.M., & Whiting, B.B. (1978). A strategy for psychocultural research. In G. D. Spindler (Ed.), *The making of psychological anthropology*. Berkeley: University of California Press.

Wig, N. N., Menon, D. K., Bedi, H., Ghosh, A., Kuipers, L., Leff, J., Karten, A., Day, R., Sartorius, N., Ernberg, G., & Jablensky, A. (1987). Expressed emotion and schizophrenia in Northern India, I: Cross-cultural transfer of ratings of relatives' expressed emotion. *British Journal of Psychiatry, 151*, 156–160.

Williams, J. E., & Best, D. L. (1990a). *Measuring sex stereotypes: A multination study*. Newbury Park, CA: Sage.

Williams, J. E., & Best, D. L. (1990b). *Sex and psyche: Gender and self viewed cross-culturally*. Newbury Park, CA: Sage.

Wiseman, H., & Lieblich, A. (1992). Individuation in a collective community. *Adolescent Psychiatry, 18*, 156–179.

Witkin, H. A. (1965). Psychological differentiation and forms of pathology. *Journal of Abnormal Psychology, 70*, 317–336.

Witkin, H. A. (1975). Psychological differentiation in cross-cultural perspective. *Journal of Cross-Cultural Psychology, 6*, 4–87.

Wolf, A. W., Lozoff, B., Latz, S., & Pauladetto, R. (1996). Parental theories in the management of sleep routines in Japan, Italy and the United States. In S. Harkness & C. M. Super (Eds.), *Parents' cultural belief systems*. New York: Guilford.

World Health Organization. (1973). *Report of the International Pilot Study of Schizophrenia*. Geneva: Author.

World Health Organization. (1979). *Schizophrenia: An international follow-up study*. New York: Wiley.

World Health Organization. (1983). *Depressive disorders in different cultures: Report of the WHO collaborative study of standardized assessment of depressive disorders*. Geneva: Author.

World Health Organization Report. (1978). *The promotion and development of traditional medicine*. WHO Technical Report Series No. 622 (Geneva, WHO).

Wright, J. W. (1998). *The universal almanac, 1998*. Kansas City, MO: Andrews & McMeel.

Wundt, W. (1910–1920). *Völkerpsychologie: Eine Untersuchung der Entwicklungsgesetze von Sprache, Mythos, und Sitte* [Folk psychology: An investigation of the developmental laws of language, myth, and custom] (Vols. 1–10). Leipzig: Engelmann.

Wylie, L. (1974). *Village in the Vaucluse* (3rd ed.). Cambridge, MA: Harvard University Press.

Yang, K. S. (1997). Theories and research in Chinese personality: An indigenous approach. In H.S.R. Kao & D. Sinha (Eds.), *Asian perspectives on psychology* (pp. 236–264). New Delhi: Sage.

Yap, P. M. (1951). Mental disease peculiar to certain cultures: A survey of comparative psychiatry. *Journal of Mental Science, 97*, 313–327.

Yap, P. M. (1965). Phenomenology of affective disorder in Chinese and other cultures. In A. deReuck & R. Porter (Eds.), *Transcultural psychiatry*. Boston: Little, Brown.

Yegorov, V. F. (1992). And how is it over there, across the ocean? *Schizophrenia Bulletin, 18*, 7–14.

Yu, L. C. (1989). Cross-cultural perspective of the changing role of the care provider for the aged in a Chinese context. In L. L. Adler (Ed.), *Cross-cultural research in human development: Life-span perspectives* (pp. 205–215). New York: Praeger.

Yu, L. C., & Carpenter, L. (1991). Women in China. In L. L. Adler (Ed.), *Women in cross-cultural perspective* (pp. 189–203). Westport, CT: Praeger.

Yucun, S., Changhui, C., Weixi, Z., Tingming, X., & Yunhua, T. (1990). An example of a community based mental health/home-care programme: Haidian District in the suburbs of Beijing, China. *Psychosocial Rehabilitation Journal, 14*, 29–34.

Zatrick, D. F., & Lu, F. G. (1991). The ethnic/minority focus unit as a training site in transcultural psychiatry. *Academic Psychiatry, 15*, 218–225.

Zeldine, G., Ahvi, R., Leuckx, R., Boussat, M., Saibou, A., Hanck, C., Collignon, R., Tourame, G., & Collomb, H. (1975). A propos de l'utilisation d'une échelle d'évaluation en psychiatric transculturelle. *L'Encéphale, 1*, 133–145.

Zheng, X., & Berry, J. W. (1991). Psychological adaptation of Chinese sojourners in Canada. *International Journal of Psychology, 26*, 451–470.

Zimmer, H. (1951/1989). *Philosophies of India.* Bollingen Series XXVI. Princeton, NJ: Princeton University Press.

Zuckerman, M. (1979). *Sensation seeking: Beyond the optimal level of arousal.* Hillsdale, NJ: Erlbaum.

Zuckerman, M. (1994). *Behavioral expressions and biosocial bases of sensation seeking.* New York: Cambridge University Press.

Index

Page numbers appearing in italics denote pages containing tables.

variation in, 73; infancy and, 74–75; Japanese mothers vs. American mothers and, 73–74; language and, 53–55; moral reasoning measurement and, 88–89; scaffolding and, 74; talking to learn and, 74; Vygotsky's sociocultural theory of development and, 72–73; zone of proximal development (ZPD) and, 72

Cognitivism: expressions of feelings and emotions and, 156; relationship-centered society and, 155–157; self-control and, 156; shared commonalities and, 156; time and, 156; work and activity centered society and, 155–157

Colombian schizophrenia, 248–250

Communalism: cast and, 154; community and, 153; *extended family networks* and, 153; familial and communal norms and, 154; Indian society and, 153; lack of choice/independence and, 154, 155; noise and overcrowding and, 154

Communication, 47–48; acceptable talk and, 58–59; actions, 52; body language, gesture, and posture, 49–50; collectivism socialization and, 215, 222–223, 224–225; distance and space, 51; dress and body alteration, 51–52; *guanxi* and, 215–216; individualistic socialization and, 215, 222–223, 224–225; participants in, 48–49; touching, 51. *See also* Contact; Language

Comparative linguistics, 52–53

Componential analysis of language, 55

Confucius, 95–97, 98–100; golden rule, 88

Consumer movement, 276–278, 279

Contact: affirmative action and, 216, 220, 226; communication and, 213–216; complex concept and, 215–226; concept absence and, 214; contact hypothesis of, 216; critical incidents and, 223–224; cultural assimilator and, 214, 223–224; cultural difference and, 214; cultural relativity and, 219; culture and, 214; desires and,

216; equal status and, 219–220, 226; facilitators of, 220–224; interactions and, 214; intercultural and, 213–227; interventions and, 223; intimacy and, 218–219, 226; miscommunication and, 214–216; opportunities for, 217–218; racists and, 222; shared goals and, 217, 222, 226; stereotypes and, 218, 219

Coping Inventory for Stressful Situations (CISS), 238

Creole language, 55–56

Cross-cultural psychologist. *See* Multinational enterprises (MNE)

Cross-cultural psychology, 69–70, 74; analytic concepts used in, 7–9; applicability of findings of, x–xi; archetypes, 23; beginnings of, 16–17; Carl Jung's influence, 22–23; collective unconscious, 23; comparison as hallmark of, 5; conceptual, methodological issues in, 9–13; cultural similarities vs. differences, ix–x; culture vs. psychological variables of, 6–7, 10–13; definition of, 4–5; deviance research and, 24; emerging discipline of (Germany), 17–18; Franz Boas, U.S. influence of, 21–22; French, British influences on, 18–21; mainstream psychology self-examination by, 3–4; mental disorders and, 24; modern developments in, 27–28; other national influences on, 23; perception research and, 24–25; personality research and, 25–27; psychopathology, 247–248, 260–262; scope of, 5; strengths of, 5–7, 281. *See also* Aging, old age; Cultural social psychology; Emotion; Multinational enterprises (MNE); Personality; Principled moral reasoning; Research methods; Women

Cross-cultural research in context: cultural psychologists and, 30; universal psychologists and, 30

Cross-cultural testing: culture fair, 43; culture specific, 43; personality and, 43

Crowd, The (Le Bon), 19

About the Editors and Contributors

LEONORE LOEB ADLER is professor emerita of psychology in the Department of Psychology and the director of the Institute for Cross-Cultural and Cross-Ethnic Studies, of which she is the founder, at Molloy College. She is also a member of the Advisory Board of the Institute for International and Cross-Cultural Psychology at St. Francis College. She has edited or coedited 15 books, and two additional volumes are projected for the near future. She has published about 70 chapters and journal articles and has presented her research reports and papers at meetings and symposia held in the United States, Canada, Mexico, Europe, and Asia. Dr. Adler has been a consulting reader for *Psychological Reports* and *Perceptual and Motor Skills;* she was the associate editor first and then for many years the managing editor of the *International Journal of Group Tensions,* where she is currently a member of the editorial board. She has contributed a column for the social division of NYSPA to the *New York State Psychologist.* At present, Dr. Adler is a consulting editor for *World Psychology,* the publication of the International Council of Psychologists. Dr. Adler has been honored with the Molloy College President's Medal, along with awards from the Queens County Psychological Association, International Organization for the Study of Group Tensions, the Committee of Women's Issues of the New York Psychological Association, and numerous other organizations. Currently, she is the representative of psychology for the Society for Cross-Cultural Research and a fellow of the advisory committee of psychology at the New York Academy of Sciences. She has been for many years the faculty advisor for the Psi Chi Chapter of the Honor Society of Psychology at Molloy College.

JOHN BEATTY is professor of anthropology at Brooklyn College of the City University of New York. He received his Ph.D. from the City University of New York Graduate Center. Dr. Beatty's publications include books on Mohawk grammar, Kiowa Apache music and dance, and intercultural communication, as well as numerous articles on a wide variety of topics, such as Japan, satanism, criminal justice, art and music. Currently, he is conducting research that deals with cross-cultural studies on the nature of elegance and manners, especially as they relate to the presentation of food.

RICHARD W. BRISLIN is the director of the Ph.D. program in international management and is a professor of management and industrial relations at the College of Business Administration, University of Hawaii. He directs a yearly program for university professors planning to introduce cross-cultural studies into their courses. He is the developer of materials used in cross-cultural training programs (e.g., *Intercultural Interactions: A Practical Guide*, 2nd ed., with Kenneth Cushner, 1996) and is the author of a text in cross-cultural psychology (*Understanding Culture's Influence on Behavior*, 2000). He has coedited two volumes of modules for training and educational programs with Tomoko Yoshida Isogai and Kenneth Cushner: *Improving Intercultural Interactions: Modules for Cross-Cultural Training Programs.* One of Dr. Brislin's books, *The Art of Getting Things Done: A Practical Guide to the Use of Power* (Praeger/Greenwood Press), was a Book of the Month Club Selection in 1992. Dr. Brislin is frequently asked to give workshops for American and Asian managers working on international assignments. In addition, the training materials he has prepared are widely used in various international organizations.

JUSTIN P. CAREY, Distinguished Professor of management and past chair of the department of management at St. John's University, is a former president of the New York State Psychological Association. Since 1981, he has been the executive editor of *Psychology & Marketing* and is now the executive editor emeritus. Dr. Carey has lectured, consulted, and presented his research on six continents. He was the guest of the Polish Academy of Sciences in Warsaw in 1991. In addition, Dr. Carey completed a three-year project using qualitative methodology to study the dynamics of entrepreneurship in Poland, the Czech and Slovak Federated Republic, and Lithuania.

FLORENCE L. DENMARK is a Robert Scott Distinguished Professor, chair of the psychology department at Pace University, and adjunct professor at the graduate school of the City University of New York. She has authored or edited 15 books, almost 100 articles and book chapters, and has given 50 scholarly presentations at universities in the United States of America, Europe, and Israel. Dr. Denmark has been honored on numerous occasions.

She is a member of many scientific associations, including Phi Beta Kappa, Psi Chi, and Alpha Theta. Dr. Denmark has been the recipient of innumerable awards, including several from the American Psychological Association for Distinguished Contributions and Outstanding Achievement in Psychology, and for Service to Women in Psychology. From the New York State Psychological Association she received the Kurt Lewin Award and the Wilhelm Wundt Award, awards for National and International Achievements in Psychology, and the First National Distinguished Service Award from Psi Chi. In addition she has received awards from the Organization for Professional Women, the Association for Women in Science, and the Association for Women in Psychology, among others. Dr. Denmark is currently a Fellow of the New York Academy of Sciences and the American Psychological Association and eight of its Divisions. In addition, she is a member of the Advisory Board of the Institute for Cross-Cultural and Cross-Ethnic Studies, Molloy College.

ROGELIO DÍAZ-GUERRERO, Distinguished Research Professor Emeritus of psychology at the Universidad Nacional Autonoma de México, is a member of the advisory board of the Institute for Cross-Cultural and Cross-Ethnic Studies at Molloy College. He has initiated research on Mexican culture and personality, as well as on cross-cultural research. Besides having written many papers and books in psychology applied to Mexican problems, Dr. Díaz-Guerrero has made extensive contributions to research in the area of culture and personality and cross-cultural psychology. Some highlights include Holtzman, Díaz-Guerrero, and Swartz, *Personality Development in Two Cultures* (1975); Díaz-Guerrero and Díaz-Loving, "Interpretations in Cross-Cultural Personality Assessment" (1990); and Díaz-Guerrero and Szalay, *Understanding Mexicans and Americans* (1991). Dr. Díaz-Guerrero was invested as honorary professor in Santo Domingo.

ROLANDO DÍAZ-LOVING is professor and head of the Psychosocial Research Unit in the Faculty of Psychology of the National Autonomous University of Mexico. His research interests range from applied work in prevention of HIV-AIDS to basic research on couple relations, personality, and culture. Dr. Díaz-Loving has published more than 150 journal articles and chapters on these topics. He is cofounder and past president of the Mexican Association of Social Psychology and has received the Mexican and Interamerican Awards of Psychology.

JURIS G. DRAGUNS, professor emeritus of psychology, completed his primary schooling in Latvia, his native country, graduated from high school in Germany, and embarked on his university studies in the United States of America. He has been on the faculty of Pennsylvania State University for the past 30 years. Dr. Draguns has held visiting professorships at the

Johannes Gutenberg University in Mainz, Germany; the East-West Center in Honolulu, Hawaii; Flinders University of South Australia; the Florida Institute of Technology; the National Taiwan University of Taipei, Taiwan; and the University of Latvia. He is a member of the advisory boards of the Multicultural Research Center in Daugavpils, Latvia, and the Institute for International and Cross-Cultural Psychology at St. Francis College. Dr. Draguns is the author or coauthor of more than 120 publications, many of which deal with psychopathology and personality across cultures.

CYNTHIA L. FRAZIER is a clinical psychologist currently practicing in Raleigh, North Carolina. Recently, she has focused on the treatment of women across the life span. In her work both locally and abroad, Dr. Frazier has been most interested in the influence of culture on behavior and the determination of psychopathology. In addition to her clinical work, she trains professionals in the field of aging; consults with organizations, hospitals, and aging facilities; and conducts cross-cultural research as well. Dr. Frazier has presented her findings internationally and has published several articles in the area of aging, Alzheimer's disease, and culture.

HARRY W. GARDINER is a professor of psychology at the University of Wisconsin, La Crosse, where he teaches courses in cross-cultural psychology, child development, humor in education, and orientation to study abroad. Dr. Gardiner has been secretary-treasurer and is currently the president of the Society for Cross-Cultural Research, editor of the teaching forum in the *Cross-Cultural Bulletin*, and a consulting editor for the *Journal of Cross-Cultural Psychology*. His most recent book, coauthored with J. D. Mutter and C. Kosmitzki (1998), is titled *Lives Across Cultures: Cross-Cultural Human Development*.

UWE P. GIELEN is professor of psychology and director of the Institute for International and Cross-Cultural Psychology at St. Francis College, New York City. He also taught at Shanghai Normal University and Padua University and has lectured in more than twenty-five countries. A fellow of both the American Psychological Association and the American Psychological Society, he is the current chair of the Psychology Section of the New York Academy of Sciences. He has served as president of both the International Council of Psychologists and the Society for Cross-Cultural Research. He is the recipient of the Kurt Lewin Award and the Wilhelm Wundt Award, both from the New York State Psychological Association. He has been editor of *World Psychology* and serves as editor-in-chief of the *International Journal of Group Tensions*. He has served as chair, co-chair, and Steering Committee member of several international psychology conferences that took place in Portugal, Indonesia, Italy, and the U.S.A. His areas of interest include moral development, international and cross-cultural psychology, and

Tibetan Buddhism. He is co-editor/co-author of eight books, including *The Kohlberg Legacy for the Helping Professions* and *Psychology in International Perspective: 50 years of the International Council of Psychologists.*

ANTHONY P. GLASCOCK is professor of anthropology and director of the Center for Applied Neurogerontology at Drexel University, Philadelphia, Pennsylvania. Most recently, Dr. Glascock was distinguished visiting chair of gerontology at St. Thomas University, Fredericton, New Brunswick. In 1997, he was awarded Drexel University's Research Award as the university's outstanding researcher. Currently, Dr. Glascock is on the editorial board of the *Journal for Cross-Cultural Gerontology*; he is a member of the external review panel for the University of Miami Center for applied gerontology; he is a fellow of the Gerontological Society of America; and he is the president of Gerotech, Inc. On four separate occasions, he lived and conducted research in Ireland. Dr. Glascock has published with anthropologists, sociologists, psychologists, and human factor engineers in numerous journals and books. He has also published extensively on a comparison of the treatment of the elderly in the United States of America and other societies with a focus on assisted suicide and death-hastening behavior.

DAVID YAU-FAI HO is presently visiting chair professor at Lingnan University in Hong Kong. He is committed to the enrichment of mainstream psychology derived from the intellectual traditions of Asia. His current interest focuses on explicating methodological relationalism, a general framework for the analysis of thought and action. Dr. Ho was elected president of the International Council of Psychologists (1988–1989). He is the author of numerous contributions in psychology, psychiatry, sociology, and education. He has had multicultural experiences in North America, the Philippines, Taiwan, and mainland China.

JOHN D. HOGAN is professor of psychology at St. John's University in New York. He received his Ph.D. in developmental psychology from Ohio State University in 1970. He is the coeditor of two books: *International Psychology: Views from Around the World* with V. S. Sexton (1992), and *A History of Developmental Psychology in Autobiography* with D. Thompson (1996). In addition, Dr. Hogan has written more than 100 chapters, articles, and book reviews. He is a fellow of the American Psychological Association.

CHIKAKO IMAI received her B.A. in general psychology from San Francisco State University. She is currently enrolled in the marriage, family, and child counseling graduate program at the University of San Francisco, California. Ms. Imai's academic and professional focus is on culture-sensitive counseling style.

KRISTIE KOOKEN is currently finishing her master of arts degree in research psychology at San Francisco State University in California. Her academic and research interests have emphasized culture and emotion, particularly the role of culture in facial expression recognition of emotion.

PITTU LAUNGANI is an associate professor in psychology at South Bank University, London, England. His research interests are in the field of cross-cultural psychology. Over the years, he has published more than 50 research papers in academic journals and contributed several book-chapters on topics related to identity, mental illness, therapy, counseling, stress, death and bereavement, and child abuse, as well as on health and illness—all of them from a cross-cultural perspective. Dr. Laungani has also written and edited four books, the most recent ones including *Death and Bereavement Across Cultures* (1997), *India and England: A Psychocultural Analysis* (1998), and a play titled *The Strange Affiliation of Hamlet, Prince of Denmark* (1997). His play, *Pillars of Society*, had its world premiere in Melbourne, Australia (1998), at the time of the convention of the International Council of Psychologists.

HARRIET P. LEFLEY is professor of psychiatry and behavioral sciences, University of Miami School of Medicine, Miami, Florida. She has been a full-time faculty member since 1973. Her experience also includes that of resident consultant in social research to the government of the Bahamas, director of the University of Miami–Jackson Memorial Medical Center Community Mental Health Center, and principal investigator and director of the NIMH-sponsored Cross-Cultural Training Institute for Mental Health Professionals. Dr. Lefley has editorial or reviewer roles on 19 scientific journals. She has published seven books and authored more than 100 scientific papers, articles, and book chapters on cultural issues in mental health service delivery, community mental health models, and family support systems for persons with mental illness. Dr. Lefley was named a National Switzer Scholar by the National Rehabilitation Association in 1988. In 1992 she received the Steven V. Logan Award as Outstanding Psychologist from the National Alliance for the Mentally Ill, and a Special Achievement Award from the Division of Psychologists in Public Service of the American Psychological Association. In 1995, she received the McNeil Pharmaceutical Award from the American Association of Community Psychiatrists for Outstanding Contributions to Community Mental Health.

DIOMEDES C. MARKOULIS is professor emeritus in the department of psychology and education at the University of Thessaloniki in Greece. Dr. Markoulis is a member of many national and international professional organizations. His fields of interest focus on cognitive and sociocognitive development and sociomoral reasoning processes. Dr. Markoulis is the coauthor of *Prosocial and Antisocial Dimensions of Behavior*. In addition, he also has published many articles in professional journals.

DAVID MATSUMOTO is professor of psychology and director of the culture and emotion research laboratory at San Francisco State University. He earned his B.A. from the University of Michigan, and his M.A. and Ph.D. from the University of California, Berkeley. He has studied emotion, human interaction, and culture for more than 15 years. Dr. Matsumoto is a recognized expert in this field. He is the author of more than 170 works on culture and emotion, including original research articles, paper presentations, books, book chapters, videos, and assessment instruments. He has given invited addresses to professional and scientific groups both in the United States and internationally. Dr. Matsumoto also serves as an intercultural consultant to various domestic and international businesses.

PETER F. MERENDA is professor emeritus of psychology and statistics, University of Rhode Island. A former associate dean of the graduate school and university coordinator of research, he was also Fulbright-Hays Senior Research Scholar in Psychology to Italy. Dr. Merenda is a former president of the International Council of Psychologists, the Division of Psychological Assessment in the International Association of Applied Psychology, the New England Psychological Association, the Rhode Island Psychological Association, the APA Committee on International Relations in Psychology, and the APA Committee on Academic Freedom and Conditions of Employment. He is also a member of the advisory board of the Institute for Cross-Cultural and Cross-Ethnic Studies, Molloy College. In addition, Dr. Merenda is the recipient of the Distinguished Contributions Award (1997) by the New England Psychological Association. He has coauthored a book on multivariate statistics and educational measurement, and he is a coauthor of teacher rating scales for young schoolchildren, personality assessment instruments, and multiple aptitude test batteries.

NIHAR R. MRINAL is a faculty member of the department of psychology at Nagpur University, Nagpur, India. His major areas of interest are research methods, as well as clinical and cross-cultural psychology. Dr. Mrinal is an honorary consultant at the Ketki Research Institute of Medical Sciences, as well as a hypnotherapist. He is a fellow and executive member of the Indian Psychological Association, where he is an elected executive. Dr. Mrinal is also a life member of the Indian Society for Clinical and Experimental Hypnosis. In addition, he is a member of PRACHI: Association of Psychocultural Dimensions; a life member of the Indian Sciences Congress; and a member of the advisory board of the Institute for Cross-Cultural and Cross-Ethnic Studies, Molloy College. Dr. Mrinal has published and presented more than 50 articles and papers in various journals and at many conferences. In addition, he is a consultant to the National Institute of Social Defence, Delhi; the Indian Institute of Youth Welfare, Nagpur; and the Tribal Welfare Organization, Nagpur, India.

UMA SINGHAL MRINAL is the chair of the department of psychology at the Bhagwandin Arya Kanya College, Lakhimpur Kheri, Uttar Pradesh, India. Her areas of interest are cross-cultural, community, and women's psychology. The author of various psychological tests and papers, Dr. Singhal Mrinal also writes articles on a variety of topics in psychology in order to foster public awareness. She is a life member of the Indian Science Congress Association and a member of the Advisory Board of the Institute for Cross-Cultural and Cross-Ethnic Studies, Molloy College. As a community activist, she pays much attention to the Tharu Tribe, which lives on the Indo-Nepal border. In addition, Dr. Singhal Mrinal is the honorary director of the Manasi Institute for Development, Welfare, and Management. Recently, she founded a school for mentally handicapped children in Lakhimpur.

ALBERT PEPITONE is professor emeritus at the University of Pennsylvania. He has been a Fulbright research fellow at the University of Groningen, the Netherlands, and the National Institute of Psychology in Rome, and has been visiting professor at Bologna and Venice Universities. Dr. Pepitone has been the president of several scholarly organizations, such as the Society for Cross-Cultural Research, Personality and Social Psychology (APA, Division 8), the Psychological Study of Social Issues (APA, Division 9), and the Society for the Advancement of Field Theory. He has also been the vice president of the Interamerican Society of Psychology. In addition, he has published numerous theory and research articles, chapters, and a book in cognitive, interpersonal, and group psychology. Dr. Pepitone's current research interests center on nonmaterial belief systems, cultural identities, and mass behavior.

MARIA LUCY RODRÍGUEZ DE DÍAZ is a clinical psychologist in private practice in Cuernavaca, Mexico. She obtained her Ph.D. degree in clinical psychology from the Universidad Iberoamericana in Mexico City. Previously, she had received a degree in education in Bolivia. For seven years she was the director of the Pedro Poveda school system (primary and high school) in Cochabamba, Bolivia, where she introduced personalized education. Dr. Rodríguez de Díaz received psychodynamic training from 1982 to 1987 and worked for the Instituto de Investigatión en Psicología Clinica y Social. For eight years she worked as a psychopedagogical consultant in the Dirección General de Educación Indigena of the Mexican Ministry of Public Education, creating reading and writing textbooks for several Mexican indigenous languages.